A CLASSICAL DICTIONARY

OF THE VULGAR TONGUE
BY CAPTAIN FRANCIS GROSE
EDITED WITH A BIOGRAPHICAL
AND CRITICAL SKETCH AND AN
EXTENSIVE COMMENTARY BY ERIC PARTRIDGE,
M.A., B. LITT. (OXON.)

A maker of dictionaries is an active laborious creature, the navvy of scholarship, carrying his head backward and forward from one learned library to another. : : OSBERT BURDETT There is far more of imagination and enthusiasm in the making of a good dictionary than in the average novel. : :
CORRIE DENISON

DORSET PRESS
NEW YORK

TO
PROFESSOR ERNEST WEEKLEY
AN ETYMOLOGIST WHO
—AS BRILLIANT AS HE IS ENTERTAINING—
INVESTS A REMARKABLE ERUDITION
WITH THE CHARM OF FICTION
A LEXICOGRAPHER WHO
—EASY OF APPROACH—
COMBINES A RARE PERSPICACITY
WITH A WITTY PERSPICUITY
A WRITER WHOSE STYLE
IS URBANE YET INCISIVE
LEISURELY YET ECONOMICAL

This edition published by Dorset Press,
a division of Marboro Books Corp.

1992 Dorset Press

ISBN 0-88029-766-2

Printed and bound in the United States of America

M 9 8 7 6 5 4 3 2 1

CONTENTS

PREFACE

I HAD originally planned to reprint the second edition of Grose's Dictionary, but I have good reason to believe that the third edition incorporates many of Grose's addenda and corrigenda, for the second was published three years before his death: and Grose was not the sort of man to rest upon his laurels. No editor's name appears on the title-page of the third edition, whereas the re-issue of 1811 purported to be by 'A Member of the Whip Club' and was entitled *Lexicon Balatronicum*, and the edition of 1823 was by Pierce Egan. The 1811 adds extremely little, the 1823 a fair amount,—but the additions are typically early-nineteenth century: Grose's *Dictionary* is especially valuable because it does present so wonderful a picture of eighteenth-century colloquialisms, slang, and cant. The few additions of 1811, the numerous ones in 1823 may be regarded, in all fairness, as intrusions. The third edition, 1796, may on the other hand be considered the most important of those which Grose himself revised. The text, then, is that of 1796.

The sketch of Grose's life and work is designed, not to exhaust the subject but merely to 'place' the writer and his Dictionary.

The method adopted in editing the *Dictionary of the Vulgar Tongue* is this. Except to put into their correct positions some few words wrongly placed in Grose and to rearrange the I's and J's and the U's and V's, I have let Grose's text stand precisely as in the original, with the further exception that several obvious printer's-errors have been rectified. My own comments follow straight on, but in parentheses; this simple device not only removes the necessity for either footnotes or end-notes but precludes the use of more than one size of type.

I am neither philologist in general nor etymologist in particular; where I myself hazard an etymology, it is based on semantics, not on phonetics. My only claim to competence rests on a close observation of slang during a period of some sixteen or seventeen years.

I have not tried, for I did not consider it desirable, to annotate or remark on every entry: in my cursory commentary I have picked out such words as were particularly interesting in themselves or raised interesting questions. There will, of course, be many to ask "why was this word passed over?" or "why was that word dealt with?"

I have not presumed to bowdlerise Grose; the coarsest entries, however, stand without comment. On certain vulgarisms I have attempted a brief commentary, for I feel it necessary that something should be said about such words as, though forming part of the language and being neither slang nor cant, are debarred simply because of the language or action to which they refer. In this respect it is worthy of note that the Oxford Dictionary excludes certain words that appear in the English Dialect Dictionary: and *vice versa*. Needless to say, I have followed the example of John Farmer in having this reprint privately subscribed. In fact, the edition is limited to so small a number in order that not even the most censorious may (justifiably) take exception to this reprint of one of the most valuable books in our language.

I have to thank Dr F. E. Budd for reading the proofs. Of written authorities, the most useful have been Farmer & Henley, Hotten, The Oxford Dictionary, The Dialect Dictionary, Dr Onions' Shakespeare Glossary, and the Etymological Dictionary and other works of Professor Ernest Weekley. I wish also to thank my friend Mr. H. P. R. Finberg for the indication of several most useful sources. Such scholarship in a printer is a rare and pleasant quality. The full list of immediate sources used in the course of the 'commentary' is as follows:—

B.   Frank C. Bowen: "Sea Slang," 1930.

B & P. John Brophy & Eric Partridge: "Songs and Slang of the British Soldier, 1914—1918," 1930; second edition revised and enlarged, 1930.

GB.   George Borrow: "Romano Lavo-Lil," 1874.

D.   Daniel Defoe: "Moll Flanders," 1721.

EDD. Joseph Wright: "English Dialect Dictionary," 1898-1905.

F.   J. S. Farmer & W. E. Henley: "Slang and its Analogues," 1890—1904.

F & G. Edward Fraser & John Gibbons: "Soldier and Sailor Words and Phrases," 1925.

G. Francis Grose: "A Provincial Glossary," 1787.

G&K. J. B. Greenough & G. L. Kittredge: "Words and their Ways in English Speech," 1902; edition used, 1920.

H. John Camden Hotten: "The Slang Dictionary," 1859, revised and enlarged 1874; edition used, 1925.

I. Godfrey Irwin: "American Tramp and Underworld Slang," 1931.

O. C. T. Onions: "A Shakespeare Glossary," 1911.

OD. The Oxford Dictionary.

P. Samuel Pegge: "The Supplement to the Provincial Glossary of Francis Grose," 1814.

S. Logan Pearsall Smith: "Words and Idioms," 1925; edition used, that in Constable's Miscellany, 1928.

W. Ernest Weekley: "An Etymological Dictionary of Modern English," 1921.

W: ROW. Ernest Weekley: "The Romance of Words."

W: RON. Ernest Weekley: "The Romance of Names."

W: S. Ernest Weekley: "Surnames."

W: A. Ernest Weekley: "Adjectives and other Words."

W: WAM. Ernest Weekley: "Words Ancient and Modern."

W: MWAM. Ernest Weekley: "More Words Ancient and Modern."

Of these last six works, I have used the latest edition available at the end of 1930.

Where no reference is given, either the comment is so short that to cite a reference would be pedantry or else it springs from that knowledge of English which may be demanded from anyone claiming to have more than a bowing acquaintance with English. If the 'unauthorised' comment is of any length, it may be assumed that all responsibility will be accepted by

London, April 1931. ERIC PARTRIDGE

P.S. By cant is meant the specific slang of gipsies and other vagabonds, of thieves and other malefactors: what is often called thieves' cant.

Vulgarism signifies good English that is not used in polite speech.

C16, C17, etc., or C17-18, 18-19, etc., indicate the period or century.

Florio=Italian-English Dictionary, 1598; 2nd edition, 1611.

Cotgrave=French-English Dictionary, 1611.

Miège=New Dictionary French and English, with another, English and French, 1679; enlarged 1688.

Skinner=Etymologicon Linguae Anglicanae, 1671.

Bailey=English Dictionary, 1721, 1727; enlarged, 1730.

=signifies 'is (are) equivalent to' or 'equivalent to.'

AS=Anglo-Saxon; ME=Middle English; L=Latin, Gr.= Greek, Ger.=German, Fr.=French, It.=Italian, Sp.=Spanish.

PREFACE TO THE SECOND IMPRESSION

In 1931 the Scholartis Press—which I had founded in 1927—published my edition of Grose's *Vulgar Tongue*. The Oxford University Press took over the book early in 1932; it went out of print in either 1947 or 1948. Appearing during the great economic depression, it did not, except for a very few isolated copies, even reach the Unites States, or go much abroad. The book received an excellent press, in the periodicals that matter.

Apart from the correction of some printer's and other slight errors, my edition of Grose's justly famous (but almost unprocurable) book remains as it stood in 1931.

September, 1962.   E. P.

CORRIGENDA & CONSIDERANDA

P.x. *Add:* By "good English" (n., ajd.) is meant English neither loose, low nor pedantic; cant, slang, dialect, etc., are, of course, excluded.

P.68, l.15. Comma after "also," not after "canting."

P.102, l.2. Venery. The editor uses this word always in its archaic sense: matters amatory.

P.113. CURSE OF SCOTLAND:—Heraldically Grose is wrong—or rather the theory he reports is wrong—about the Argyle arms, which do *not* resemble the nine of diamonds.

P.119, l.20. *For* stealthesword *read* steal the sword.

P.113, l.20 schoolboys. So spelt on pp. 156, 157, 351; but on pp. 40, 89, 281 G. hyphenates. Grose is very inconsistent and uncertain with hyphens; see, e.g., his spelling of:—ale(-)house, chamber(-)pot, cock(-)pit, decent(-)looking, fire(-)shovel, horse(-)race, house(-)breaker, mean(-)looking, pawn(-)broker, shop(-)keeper, sponging(-)house, tale(-)bearer, turkey(-)cock, etc., etc.

P.151, l.1. *For* Afool *read* A fool.

P.154, l.28. (TO FRIG) Many, however, have since 1850 heard the word only as variant of "to f—k."

P.182, l.16. For *Hat*is read *Hat* is.

P.205, l.20. lock or door: "or" is probably Grose's misprint for "on" or "for."

P.216. The following entry has been omitted:—LARE-OVERS FOR MEDDLERS. An answer frequently given to children, or young people, as a rebuke for their impertinent curiosity, in inquiring what is contained in a box, bundle, or any other closed conveyance; perhaps from a layover, or turnover, a kind of tart not baked in a pan, but made to contain the fruit by turning one end of the crust over the other. Medlar tarts were probably so made in former times.

P.219. (LIFT) Cf. Australianism *crook* (more generally *bend) the elbow*, to drink too much.

P.235, l.19. *For* 20 *read* 200.

P.255, l.8; 285, l.9. *Mallum;* Melham. This name is spelt

both ways.

P.256. Between the last two sentences in PAY, the following has been omitted: "To pay away; to fight manfully, also to eat voraciously."

P.264, l.18; 310, l.6. receipt; recipe. Grose spells it both ways.

P.267, l.7. (POPE'S NOSE) Cf. *pope's-eye*, piece of fat in middle of leg of mutton.

P.291, l.18. (ROUND SUM) Modern use differs, of course.

P.308, l.27; 394, l.11. Judgment. Editor spells both ways; just as he uses either *s* or *z* in verbs and hyphenates individually.

P.311, l.34; 368, l.14-17. Whisky. Both Grose and editor spell either way.

P.320, l.28; 353, l.25. Presbyterians, presbyterian. Sometimes Grose preferred the capital, as at p. 106, l.33.

P.332, l.5. methodists. But at p.369, l.17, with capital; cf. Grose's inconsistency with "(P) (p)resbyterian."

P.335. (TAILOR) Grose spells either "taylor" (more often) or "tailor."

P.345, l.28. *For* I.e. *read* Grose undoubtedly means. Grose would hardly confuse the two trees; certainly not the two drinks.

P.382, l.21; 396, l.3. For *Eighteenth Century* read *Eighteenth-Century.*

PREFACE TO THE SECOND EDITION

THE favourable reception with which this Book was honoured by the Public, has encouraged the Editor to present a second edition, more correctly arranged, and very considerably enlarged. Some words and explanations in the former edition having been pointed out as rather indecent or indelicate, though to be found in Le Roux, and other Glossaries of the like kind, these have been either omitted, softened, or their explanations taken from books long sanctioned with general approbation, and admitted into the seminaries for the education of youth—such as Bailey's, Miège's, or Philips's Dictionaries; so that it is hoped this work will now be found as little offensive to delicacy as the nature of it would admit.

A list is here added of such books as have been consulted for the additions.

A
CAVEAT

FOR

COMMON CURSETORS,

VULGARLY CALLED
VAGABONES;

SET FORTH BY
THOMAS HARMAN, Esquier,

FOR THE
Utilitie and Proffyt of hys Naturall Countrye.

Newly Augmented and Imprinted, Anno Domini
M.D.LXVII.

Viewed, Examined, and Allowed according unto
the Queen's Majestye's Injunctions.

Imprinted at London, in Flete-street, at the Signe of the Faul-
con, by William Gryffith; and are to be solde at his Shoppe
in Saynt Dunstone's Churche Yarde, in the West.

THE

CANTING ACADEMY;

OR,

VILLANIES DISCOVERED:

WHEREIN ARE SHEWN

The Mysterious and Villanous Practices of that Wicked Crew,
commonly known by the Names of

HECTORS, TRAPANNERS, GILTS, &c.

With several NEW CATCHES and SONGS.

ALSO A

COMPLEAT CANTING DICTIONARY,

BOTH OF

Old Words, and such as are *now most in Use*.

A Book very useful and necessary (to be known, but not practised) for all People.

THE SECOND EDITION.

LONDON;

Printed by F. LEACH, for MAT. DREW; and are to be sold by the
booksellers.

N.B. The Dedication is signed, R. HEAD.

HELL upon EARTH;

OR THE MOST PLEASANT AND DELECTABLE

HISTORY
OF
WHITTINGTON'S COLLEDGE,

OTHERWISE (VULGARLY) CALLED

NEWGATE.

Giving an Account of the HUMOURS of those COLLEGIANS who are strictly examined at the OLD BAILY, and take their highest Degrees near HYDE PARK CORNER.

Being very useful to all Persons, either Gentle or Simple, in shewing them the Manner of the ROBBERIES and CHEATS, committed by Villains on the Nation: whereby they may be the more careful of being wronged by them for the future.

LONDON
PRINTED IN THE YEAR 1703.

THE
SCOUNDREL'S DICTIONARY

OR, AN

EXPLANATION

OF THE

CANT WORDS used by THIEVES, HOUSE-
BREAKERS, STREET ROBBERS, and
PICKPOCKETS about Town.

TO WHICH ARE PREFIXED

Some CURIOUS DISSERTATIONS on the ART

of WHEEDLING,

AND A

Collection of their FLASH SONGS, with a
PROPER GLOSSARY.

The whole printed from a *Copy taken on one of their Gang*, in the
late Scuffle between the Watchmen and a Party of them on
Clerkenwell Green; which Copy is now in the Custody of one
of the Constables of that Parish.

LONDON:
Printed for J. BROWNELL, in Pater-noster-row.
M.DCC.LIV.
[Price Sixpence.]

PREFACE TO THE FIRST EDITION

THE great approbation with which so polite a nation as France has received the Satirical and Burlesque Dictionary of Monsieur Le Roux, testified by the several editions it has gone through, will, it is hoped, apologize for an attempt to compile an English Dictionary on a similar plan; our language being at least as copious as the French, and as capable of the witty equivoque; besides which, the freedom of thought and speech arising from, and privileged by, our constitution, gives a force and poignancy to the expressions of our common people not to be found under arbitrary governments, where the ebullitions of vulgar wit are checked by the fear of the bastinado, or of a lodging during pleasure in some gaol or castle.

The many vulgar allusions and cant expressions that so frequently occur in our common conversation and periodical publications, make a work of this kind extremely useful, if not absolutely necessary, not only to foreigners, but even to natives resident at a distance from the Metropolis, or who do not mix in the busy world: without some such help, they might hunt through all the ordinary Dictionaries, from Alpha to Omega, in search of the words, "black legs, lame duck, a plumb, malingeror, nip cheese, darbies, and the new drop," although these are all terms of well-known import at Newmarket, Exchange-alley, the City, the Parade, Wapping, and Newgate.

The fashionable words, or favourite expressions of the day, also find their way into our political and theatrical compositions: these, as they generally originate from some trifling event, or temporary circumstance, on falling into disuse, or being superseded by new ones, vanish without leaving a trace behind. Such were the late fashionable words, *a bore* and *a twaddle*, among the great vulgar; *maccaroni* and *the barber*, among the small: these, too, are here carefully registered.

The Vulgar Tongue consists of two parts: the first is the Cant Language, called sometimes Pedlars French, or St. Giles's Greek; the second, those burlesque phrases, quaint allusions,

7

and nick-names for persons, things, and places, which, from long uninterrupted usage, are made classical by prescription.

Respecting the first, that is, the canting language, take the account given of its origin, and the catastrophe of its institutor, from Mr Harrison's Description of England, prefixed to Hollingshead's Chronicle; where, treating of beggars, gypsies, &c. he says, "It is not yet fifty years sith this trade began: but how " it hath prospered sithens that time, it is easy to judge; for they " are now supposed, of one sexe and another, to amount unto " above ten thousand persons, as I have harde reported. More- " over in counterfeiting the Egyptian roges, they have devised " a language among themselves, which they name Canting, " but others Pedlars French, a speache compact thirty years " since of English, and a great number of odde words of their " own devising, without all order or reason; and yet such it is, " as none but themselves are able to understand. The first de- " viser thereof was hanged by the neck, as a just reward, no " doubt, for his desartes, and a common end to all of that pro- " fession.

"A gentleman (Mr Thomas Harman) also of late hath taken " great paines to search out the secret practizes of this ungrac- " ious rabble; and, among other things, he setteth down and " describeth twenty-two sorts of them, whose names it shall " not be amisse to remember, whereby each one may gather " what wicked people they are, and what villany remaineth in " them."

For this list see the word Crew.—This was the origin of the cant language; its terms have been collected from the following Treatises:

The Bellman of London, bringing to light the most notorious villanies that are now practised in the kingdom. Profitable for gentlemen, lawyers, merchants, citizens, farmers, masters of households, and all sorts of servants, to marke, and delightfull for men to reade.—Lege, Perlege, Relege.—1608.

8

Thieves falling out, true men come by their goods.—1615.

English Villanies, seven severall times prest to death by the printers; but (still reviving againe) are now the eighth time (as the first) discovered by lanthorne and candle-light: and the help of a new cryer, called O-per-se-O; whose loud voyce proclaims, to all that will hear him, another conspiracy of abuses lately plotting together, to hurt the peace of the kingdom; which the bell-man (because he ther went stumbling i'th'dark) could never see till now; and because a company of rogues, cunning canting gypsies, and all the scumme of our nation, fight under their tattered colours. At the end is a canting dictionary to teach their language, with canting songs. A booke to make gentlemen merry, citizens warie, countrymen carefull; fit for justices to reade over, because it is a pilot by whom they may make strange discoveries.—London, 1638.

Bailey's, and the new Canting Dictionary, have also been consulted, with the History of Bamfield More Carew, the Sessions Papers, and other modern authorities. As many of these terms are still professionally used by our present race of free-booters of different denominations, who seem to have established a systematical manner of carrying on their business, a knowledge of them may therefore be useful to gentlemen in the commission of the peace.

The second part, or burlesque terms, have been drawn from the most classical authorities; such as soldiers on the long march, seamen at the capstern, ladies disposing of their fish, and the colloquies of a Gravescend boat.

Many heroic sentences, expressing and inculcating a contempt of death, have been caught from the mouths of the applauding populace, attending those triumphant processions up Holborn-hill, with which many an unfortunate hero till lately finished his course; and various choice flowers have been collected at executions, as well those authorised by the sentence

9

of the law, and performed under the direction of the sheriff, as those inflicted under the authority and inspection of that impartial and summary tribunal, called the Mob, upon the pickpockets, informers, or other unpopular criminals.

In the course of this work many ludicrous games and customs are explained, which are not to be met with in any other book: the succession of the triumph or ovation of Holborn-hill, with the introduction of the present mode of execution at Newgate, are chronologically ascertained; points of great importance to both the present and future compilers of the Tyburn Chronicle.

To prevent any charge of immorality being brought against this work, the Editor begs leave to observe, that when an indelicate or immodest word has obtruded itself for explanation, he has endeavoured to get rid of it in the most decent manner possible; and none have been admitted but such as either could not be left out without rendering the work incomplete, or in some measure compensate by their wit for the trespass committed on decorum. Indeed, respecting this matter, he can with great truth make the same defence that Falstaff ludicrously urges in behalf of one engaged in rebellion, viz. that he did not seek them, but that, like rebellion in the case instanced, they lay in his way, and he found them.

The Editor likewise begs leave to add, that if he has had the misfortune to run foul of the dignity of any body of men, profession, or trade, it is totally contrary to his intention; and he hopes the interpretations given to any particular terms that may seem to bear hard upon them, will not be considered as his sentiments, but as the sentiments of the persons by whom such terms were first invented, or those by whom they are used.

A CLASSICAL DICTIONARY OF THE VULGAR TONGUE

ABBESS, or LADY ABBESS. A bawd, the mistress of a brothel. [For a most informative passage on this word and on the corresponding *abbot*, see F & H, who note that, in old French cant, a brothel was *l'abbaye des s'offre à tous*.]

ABEL-WACKETS. Blows given on the palm of the hand with a twisted handkerchief, instead of a ferula; a jocular punishment among seamen, who sometimes play at cards for wackets, the loser suffering as many strokes as he has lost games. [Properly *able-whackets*. "In the old days of sail, a very popular forecastle game." B.—The word was obsolete by 1883 according to W. Clark Russell's *Sailors' Language* of that date; that it had only just become obsolete would appear from Smyth's *Sailor's Word Book*, 1867. F.]

ABIGAIL. A lady's waiting-maid. [Not from Abigail Hill, i.e. Mrs Masham, lady-in-waiting to Queen Anne, as suggested, but from the character in Beaumont and Fletcher's very popular play *The Scornful Lady;* the dramatists may have thought of the Biblical Abigail, who often applied to herself the phrase 'thine handmaid.' OD.]

ABRAM. Naked. *Cant.* [Back-formation from *Abram-man.* As in the other entries, *Abram* has a variant *Abraham*.]

ABRAM COVE. A cant word among thieves, signifying a naked or poor man: also a lusty, strong rogue.

ABRAM MEN. Pretended mad men. [Much has been written about *Abram, Abraham*, but little certainty attained. There is probably an allusion to the Biblical Abraham connected with Lazarus. Now obsolete, the term *Abram Men* dates back to the 16th century. F.—The Abraham Ward in Bedlam (Bethlehem Hospital) contained those lunatics who were, on certain days, allowed to go a-begging. *Cant.* H.—Also, in 18th and 19th centuries, "beggars who pretended that they were old naval ratings, cast on the streets when their services were finished with." B.]

TO SHAM ABRAM. To pretend sickness. [In 1700-1870, approximately, the phrase was common among sailors to signify: to malinger. B.—Also *Abram-sham.* H.]

ACADEMY, or PUSHING SCHOOL. A brothel.—The Floating Academy; the lighters on board of which those persons are confined, who by a late regulation are condemned to hard labour instead of transportation.—Campbell's Academy; the same, from a gentleman of that name, who had the contract for finding and victualling the hulks or lighters.

ACCOUNTS. To cast up one's accounts; to vomit.

ACORN. You will ride a horse foaled by an acorn; i.e. the gallows, called also the Wooden and Three-legged Mare. You will be hanged.—See THREE-LEGGED MARE. [This phrase was in the 19th century used (as F tells us) by Bulwer Lytton and Harrison Ainsworth, who, like Disraeli, used cant very freely in several somewhat mannered novels of the underworld. Like Scott before them, these three actual or would-be exquisites rifled Grose's Dictionary at every turn: apparently in Pierce Egan's edition, which, enjoying some popularity, may have been the prompter of Lytton, Ainsworth and Disraeli.]

ACT OF PARLIAMENT. A military term for small beer, five pints of which, by an act of parliament, a landlord was formerly obliged to give to each soldier gratis.

ACTEON. A cuckold, from the horns planted on the head of Acteon by Diana.

ADAM'S ALE. Water. [Apparently first used by Prynne in 1643; Scotticè, *Adam's Wine.* F;H.—Both phrases seem to have been, at first, dialect slang, the former becoming general English slang *ca.* 1700 (the shady Tom Brown used the never-common abbreviation, *Adam,* about 1704), the latter general Scottish slang rather later. EDD; OD.]

ADAM TILER. A pickpocket's associate, who receives the stolen goods, and runs off with them. *Cant.* [*Adam:* an accomplice. *Tiler:* a watchman.F.]

ADAMS. The most ancient, honourable, and venerable society of the name of Adams, A.D. 1750, held their meetings at the Royal Swan, Kingsland Road, kept by George Adams.

ADDLE PATE. An inconsiderate foolish fellow. [Like the next, not slang, but dialect till *ca.* 1800, when they acquired the status of good English. F. Of *addle pate* the dialectal variants in C18-19 were *addle-cap, -head, -headed, -pated,* the first being the rarest. EDD.]

ADDLE PLOT. A spoil-sport, a mar-all.

ADMIRAL OF THE BLUE, who carries his flag on the mainmast. A landlord or publican wearing a blue apron, as was formerly the custom among gentlemen of that vocation. [Cf. *admiral of the red,* C19 slang for a wine-bibber. F.]

ADMIRAL OF THE NARROW SEAS. One who from drunkenness vomits into the lap of the person sitting opposite to him. *Sea phrase.*

ADRIFT. Loose, turned adrift, discharged. *Sea phrase.* [Now good English in the first and the second sense: cf. *aground.*—In C20 sailorese, the adjective denotes "anything that is not to be found when wanted, from a seaman who fails to answer his name at a muster to a boot which has got mislaid." B.]

AFFIDAVIT MEN. Knights of the post, or false witnesses, said to attend Westminster Hall, and other courts of justice, ready to swear any thing for hire; distinguished by having straw stuck in the heels of their shoes. [*Affidavit* is Late Latin: he has testified. Compare the following Latin verbs that, because of their frequency in documents or in colloquial legal phrase, have become English nouns: exit, exeat, caveat, cognovit, fiat, tenet, veto. W: ROW.]

AFTER-CLAP. A demand after the first given in has been discharged; a charge for pretended omissions; in short, any thing disagreeable happening after all consequences of the cause have been thought at an end. [Apparently first used by Occleve, about 1420. OD.—In West Somersetshire dialect=*arrière-pensée.* In Cornish: superfluous finery. EDD.]

AGAINST THE GRAIN. Unwilling. It went much against the grain with him, i.e. it was much against his inclination, or against his pluck. [Dryden, 1673.F.]

AGOG, ALL-A-GOG. Anxious, eager, impatient; from the Italian *agogare*, to desire eagerly. [In a C12 French poem occurs the phrase, *tout vient à gogue;* cf. Cotgrave: "*Estre en ses gogues*, to be frolick, lusty, lively, wanton, gamesome." In C18-19 dialect *agog* meant on the move, going. EDD.]

AGROUND. Stuck fast, stopped, at a loss, ruined; like a boat or vessel aground.

AIR AND EXERCISE. He has had air and exercise, i.e. he has been whipped at the cart's tail, or, as it is generally, though more vulgarly, expressed, at the cart's a-se. [Now, or at any rate it did until recently, the phrase means (among criminals): penal servitude.F.]

AKERMAN'S HOTEL. Newgate. In 1787, a person of that name was the gaoler, or keeper.

ALDERMAN. A roasted turkey garnished with sausages; the latter are supposed to represent the gold chain worn by those magistrates.[Originally, and long as a variant: an alderman in chains.]

ALDGATE. A draught on the pump at Aldgate; a bad bill of exchange, drawn on persons who have no effects of the drawer.

ALE DRAPER. An alehouse keeper. [A man is so described in a Lincolnshire parish register in 1477: from jocular, the term had —in that locality at least—become serious. OD.—As dialect, it was confined to Yorkshire and Lincolnshire and appears to have fallen into disuse *ca.* 1800.EDD.]

ALL-A-MORT. Struck dumb, confounded. [From French *à la mort* and used by Shakespeare in the forms *all-amort* and *amort* and in the senses: sick to death, dispirited, dejected. O.]

ALE POST. A may-pole.

ALL HOLIDAY. It is all holiday at Peckham, or it is all holiday with him; a saying signifying that it is all over with the business or person spoken of or alluded to.

ALL HOLLOW. He was beat all hollow, i.e. he had no chance of conquering: it was all hollow, or a hollow thing; it was a decided thing from the beginning. See HOLLOW.

ALL NATIONS. A composition of all the different spirits sold in a dram-shop, collected in a vessel, into which the drainings of the bottles and quartern pots are emptied. [In C19 slang: a parti-coloured garment. F.]

ALLS. The five alls is a country sign, representing five human figures, each having a motto under him. The first is a king in his regalia; his motto, I govern all: the second, a bishop in pontificals; motto, I pray for all: third, a lawyer in his gown; motto, I plead for all: fourth, a soldier in his regimentals, fully accoutred; motto, I fight for all: fifth, a poor countryman with his scythe and rake; motto, I pay for all.

ALSATIA THE HIGHER. White Friars, once a place privi-ledged from arrests for debt, as was also the Mint, but suppressed on account of the notorious abuses committed there. [The district of Alsatia is excellently described in M. Melville Balfour's histor-ical novel, *The Long Robe*, 1930.—Swift has *Alsatia phrase* to de-note a slang or a cant term. F. Besides Shadwell's *Squire of Alsatia*, consult E. Beresford Chancellor's *Annals of Fleet Street*, Macau-lay's *History* at i, iii, and especially Scott's *Fortunes of Nigel*.]

ALSATIA THE LOWER. The Mint in Southwark.

ALSATIANS. The inhabitants of White Friars or the Mint.

ALTAMEL. A verbal or lump account, without particulars, such as is commonly produced at bawdy-houses, spunging-houses, &c. *Vide* DUTCH RECKONING. [OD spells *altumal* from *al-tum* (the deep sea) + *al*. Modern Dutch is *allemaal*, which tallies with Grose's explanation. W.]

ALTITUDES. The man is in his altitudes, i.e. he is drunk. [Dates back to early C17 and was used by Beaumont-Fletcher, Dryden, Vanbrugh. F.]

AMBASSADOR. A trick to duck some ignorant fellow or lands-man, frequently played on board ships in the warm latitudes. It is thus managed: A large tub is filled with water, and two stools placed on each side of it. Over the whole is thrown a tarpawlin, or old sail: this is kept tight by two persons, who are to represent the king and queen of a foreign country, and are seated on the stools. The person intended to be ducked plays the Ambassador, and after repeating a ridiculous speech dictated to him, is led in

15

great form up to the throne, and seated between the king and queen, who rising suddenly as soon as he is seated, he falls backwards in the tub of water.

AMBIDEXTER. A lawyer who takes fees from both plaintiff and defendant, or that goes snacks with both parties in gaming. [This figurative use is the earliest and goes back to 1532.OD.]

AMEN. He said Yes and Amen to every thing; he agreed to every thing.

AMEN CURLER. A parish clerk. [A C17-18 variant: amen clerk. EDD.—In late C19 Army slang the chaplain's clerk was called amen wallah, a term that, in 1914-1918, was extended to mean the chaplain himself, more frequently and pleasantly described—and nearly always addressed—as padre.]

AMES ACE. Within ames ace; nearly, very near. [From ambsace, the double ace, the lowest throw at dice, much more widely, after about 1800, known as the deuce.]

AMINIDAB. A jeering name for a Quaker.

TO AMUSE. To fling dust or snuff in the eyes of the person intended to be robbed; also to invent some plausible tale, to delude shopkeepers and others, thereby to put them off their guard. *Cant.*

AMUSERS. Rogues who carried snuff or dust in their pockets, which they threw into the eyes of any person they intended to rob; and running away, their accomplices (pretending to assist and pity the half-blinded person) took that opportunity of plundering him.

ANABAPTIST. A pickpocket caught in the fact, and punished with the discipline of the pump or horse-pond.

ANCHOR. Bring your a-e to an anchor, i.e. sit down. To let go an anchor to the windward of the law; to keep within the letter of the law. *Sea wit.*

ANGLERS. Pilferers, or petty thieves, who, with a stick having a hook at the end, steal goods out of shop windows, grates, &c.; also those who draw in or entice unwary persons to prick at the belt, or such like devices.

ANGLING FOR FARTHINGS. Begging out of a prison window with a cap, or box, let down at the end of a long string.

ANKLE. A girl who is got with child is said to have sprained her ankle. [Cf. the French phrase, *Elle a mal aux genoux.*]

ANODYNE NECKLACE. A halter. [Necklace=halter as early as 1639, anodyne necklace=halter as early as 1766 (Goldsmith). F.]

ANTHONY or TANTONY PIG. The favourite or smallest pig in the litter.—To follow like a tantony pig, i.e. St Anthony's pig; to follow close at one's heels. St Anthony the hermit was a swineherd, and is always represented with a swine's bell and a pig. Some derive this saying from a privilege enjoyed by the friars of certain convents in England and France (sons of St Anthony), whose swine were permitted to feed in the streets. These swine would follow any one having greens or other provisions, till they obtained some of them; and it was in those days considered an act of charity and religion to feed them. [Grose in his Provincial Glossary says that the word is Kentish; an early possessor of my copy, evidently a very able scholar, notes that the form *T'antony* obtained in Berkshire; Joseph Wright records that Salmon in his *History of Hertfordshire* (1728), writes, "We call a poor starved creature a Tantony pig;" the Oxford Dictionary notes that sometimes just *Anthony* was used; Professor Weekley, antedating the earliest Oxford reference by a hundred years, finds the term to have been first used by Stow in his *Survey of London*. Apperson, *English Proverbs*, 1930, quotes "nantyng gryce," *ca.* 1460.]

TO KNOCK ANTHONY. Said of an in-kneed person, or one whose knees knock together; to cuff Jonas. See JONAS.

APE LEADER. An old maid: their punishment after death, for neglecting to increase and multiply, will be, it is said, leading apes in hell.

APOSTLES. To manœuvre the apostles, i.e. rob Peter to pay Paul; that is, to borrow money of one man to pay another.

APOTHECARY. To talk like an apothecary; to use hard, or gallipot words; from the assumed gravity and affectation of knowledge generally put on by the gentlemen of that profession, who are commonly as superficial in their learnings as they are pedantic in their language.

APOTHECARY'S BILL. A long bill.

APOTHECARY'S, or LAW LATIN. Barbarous Latin, vulgarly called Dog Latin, in Ireland Bog Latin.

APPLE CART. Down with his apple-cart; knock or throw him down.[As employed by Grose, the term=the human body. In the phrase *upset the apple-cart*, there is apparently a merging of two senses: body, and the dialectal one=plan: this phrase, once dialect and/or slang, has since about 1870 become a colloquialism, and in 1931 it is knocking at the door labelled 'good spoken English,' thanks partly to Shaw's brilliant play, *The Apple Cart*. Note, however, that this phrase is in Andrews' mid-C19 *Latin-English Dictionary* for Plautus's *plaustrum percellere*(W).]

APPLE DUMPLIN SHOP. A woman's bosom.

APPLE-PYE-BED. A bed made apple-pye fashion, like what is called a turnover apple-pye, where the sheets are so doubled as to prevent any one from getting at his length between them; a common trick played by frolicsome country lasses on their sweethearts, male relations, or visitors. [A possible but less likely etymology is *à plis*. F.—W. is wrong about the earliest record of the phrase.—Contrast *apple-pie order*, perfect order, as in Scott in 1813.F.]

APRIL FOOL. Any one imposed on, or sent on a bootless errand, on the first of April; on which day it is the custom among the lower people, children, and servants, by dropping empty papers, carefully doubled up, sending persons on absurd messages, and such like contrivances, to impose on every one they can, and then to salute them with the title of April Fool. This is also practised in Scotland under the title of Hunting the Gowke. [The custom originated in England in the C17; the French equivalent is *poisson d'avril*. W.—In France, if one goes to a dance on the night of April 1st, one receives a little fish made of chocolate.—The C19 dialectal variants were *April-gawby,-gob,-gobby,-gowk* (the general Scottish term), and *-noddy*.EDD.]

APRON STRING HOLD. An estate held by a man during his wife's life. [More often and originally *Tenure*, which began as a legal phrase. W.—Cf. the dialectal *apron-trade*=women.]

AQUA PUMPAGINIS. Pump water. *Apothecaries Latin*.

ARBOR VITÆ. A man's penis.

ARCH DUKE. A comical or eccentric fellow. [Possibly suggested by the Duke in *Measure for Measure:* certainly eccentric enough to serve as an archetype.]

ARCH ROGUE, or DIMBER DAMBER UPRIGHT MAN. The chief of a gang of thieves or gypsies. [The *arch*=chief, principal, is hyphenatedly used by Shakespeare with *enemy, mock, villain.* O.]

ARCH DELL, or ARCH DOXY, signifies the same in rank among the female canters or gypsies.

ARD. Hot. *Cant.* [Presumably from French *ardent.* There is in English cant a large Romance, and a considerable Teutonic (German, Dutch) element, nor is the debt to the Ancient Classics negligible. (I hope to work out these themes before long.)]

ARISTIPPUS. A diet drink, or decoction of sarsaparilla, china, &c. sold at certain coffee-houses, and drunk as tea. [*China*=cinchona bark.]

ARK. A boat or wherry. Let us take an ark and winns; let us take a sculler. *Cant.* [In Northumberland it used to mean a large chest, from Latin *arca*, G.—Cf. Noah's Ark.W.]

ARK RUFFIANS. Rogues who, in conjunction with watermen, robbed, and sometimes murdered, on the water, by picking a quarrel with the passengers in a boat, boarding it, plundering, stripping, and throwing them overboard, &c. A species of badger. *Cant.* [Perhaps there is also an allusion to *arch*=chief.]

ARMOUR. In his armour, pot valiant: to fight in armour; to make use of Mrs Philip's ware. See C—D—M. [Cf. Dutch courage.]

ARRAH NOW. An unmeaning expletive, frequently used by the vulgar Irish.

ARS MUSICA. A bum-fiddle. ["The *podex* when used as a noisy vent. A play on words." F.]

ARSE. To hang an arse; to hang back, to be afraid to advance. He would lend his a-se, and sh-te through his ribs; a saying of any one who lends his money inconsiderately; He would lose his a-se if it was loose; said of a careless person. A-se about; turn round. [A vulgarism, not slang nor colloquialism. Until *ca.* 1700, it was quite respectable English. Frederic Manning was considered extremely audacious (January 1930) to use the word in his supreme war-novel *Her Privates We*.—The word ("obsolete in polite use" says the OD in 1888) had long served in dialect for the bottom or hinder part of anything as in *sack-arse*. EDD.—As a C19 slang verb it meant transitively: to kick; intransitively: to depart, move away. In 1914-1918 soldiers used the verb transitively to mean: to kick out, to dismiss, e.g. "He was arsed out of his job," and intransitively as in "to arse about," to fool about, to waste time; some people think this phrase is merely *ass about*, to play the donkey, the fool, as in many instances—but not in the soldiers'—it certainly is.]

ARSY VARSEY. To fall arsy varsey, i.e. head over heels. [A more logical transcription would be *arsey varsey* or, better still, *arsy varsy*, or, best of all, *arsy-versy*.—The latter part derives from Latin *versus*, turned; for reduplication of sound, cf. higgledy-piggledy. F.—Especially Derbyshire. G.—But in general C19 dialect the phrase meant also: deceit, flattery; and as adjective: fanciful, disobedient. EDD.— In normal English of C17, the adjective signified contrary, perverse, preposterous. OD.]

ARTHUR; KING ARTHUR. A game used at sea, when near the line, or in a hot latitude. It is performed thus: A man who is to represent king Arthur, ridiculously dressed, having a large wig made out of oakum, or of some old swabs, is seated on the side, or over a large vessel of water. Every person in his turn is to be ceremoniously introduced to him, and to pour a bucket of water over him, crying, Hail, king Arthur! If during this ceremony the person introduced laughs or smiles (to which his majesty endeavours to excite him, by all sorts of ridiculous gesticulations), he changes place with, and then becomes, king Arthur, till relieved by some brother tar, who has as little command over his muscles as himself.

ARTICLES. Breeches; coat, waistcoat, and articles.

ASK, or AX MY A -- E. A common reply to any question; still deemed wit at sea, and formerly at court, under the denomination of selling bargains. See BARGAIN.

ASSIG. An assignation.

ATHANASIAN WENCH, or QUICUNQUE VULT. A forward girl, ready to oblige every man that shall ask her.

AUNT. Mine aunt; a bawd or procuress; a title of eminence for the senior dells, who serve for instructresses, midwives, &c. for the dells. *Cant.* See DELLS. [In Shakespeare: a loose woman. O.— In dialect, though rarely: a prostitute. EDD.]

AUTEM. A church. [*Cant.* Every *autem* compound is cant, whether or not the second element is a cant word.]

AUTEM BAWLER. A parson. *Cant.*

AUTEM CACKLERS. Dissenters of every denomination. *Cant.*

AUTEM PRICKEARS. The same.

AUTEM CACKLE TUB. A conventicle or meeting-house for dissenters. *Cant.*

AUTEM DIPPERS. Anabaptists. *Cant.*

AUTEM DIVERS. Pickpockets who practise in churches; also churchwardens and overseers of the poor. *Cant.*

AUTEM GOGLERS. Pretended French prophets. *Cant.* [Explained in Duncombe's *Sinks of London Laid Open*, 1848, as conjurers, fortune-tellers. F.]

AUTEM MORT. A married woman; also a female beggar with several children hired or borrowed to excite charity. *Cant.* [Cf. autem cove: a married man.]

AUTEM QUAVERS. Quakers.

AUTEM QUAVER TUB. A Quaker's meeting-house. *Cant.*

AVOIR DU POIS LAY. Stealing brass weights off the counters of shops. *Cant.*

BABBLE. Confused, unintelligible talk, such as was used at the building the tower of Babel. [The word belongs to the related group "*babble*, infantile utterance, *bauble*, a child's plaything, and *baboon*, a grimacing and gibbering animal." The speech-element of this group (Babel is popularly connected) is common to many European languages. W:A.]

BABES IN THE WOOD. Criminals in the stocks, or pillory.

BACK BITER. One who slanders another behind his back, i.e. in his absence. His bosom friends are become his back biters, said of a lousy man.

BACKED. Dead. He wishes to have the senior, or old squaretoes, backed: he longs to have his father on six men's shoulders; that is, carrying to the grave.

BACK UP. His back is up, i.e. he is offended or angry; an expression or idea taken from a cat; that animal, when angry, always raising its back. An allusion also sometimes used to jeer a crooked man; as, So, Sir, I see somebody has offended you, for your back is up. [Used by Vanbrugh and Cibber in *TheProvoked Husband*.F.]

BACON. He has saved his bacon; he has escaped. He has a good voice to beg bacon; a saying in ridicule of a bad voice. [The former phrase dates back to 1691. Bacon here=hide, body. F.]

BACON FACED. Full faced. [Traceable to Otway, 1684.F.]

BACON FED. Fat, greasy.

BACK GAMMON PLAYER. A sodomite.

BACK DOOR (USHER, or GENTLEMAN OF THE). The same.

BAD BARGAIN. One of his majesty's bad bargains; a worthless soldier, a malingeror. See MALINGEROR.

BADGE. A term used for one burned in the hand. He has got his badge, and piked; he was burned in the hand, and is at liberty. *Cant.*

BADGE COVES. Parish pensioners. *Cant.*

BADGERS. A crew of desperate villains who robbed near rivers, into which they threw the bodies of those they murdered. *Cant.* [For these malefactors, see Harrison Ainsworth's *Jack Sheppard.* F.—Northern dialect for a huckster.G.—The huckster sense probably derives from C15-17 *badger*, a legal term for a dealer in corn. EDD.]

TO BADGER. To confound, perplex, or teize. [From the sport of badger-baiting, whence also *badger-drawing*, a special kind of baiting. W:A. More generally, to treat like a badger which is accustomed to being hunted: see Wood's once famous *Anecdotes of Animal Life*, 1855. EDD.—The verb was first used by the dramatist O'Keeffe in 1794. OD.As a sea-term it meant originally "to confuse by contradictory orders; now generally used in the shore sense of worrying in any way." B.]

22

BAG. He gave them the bag, i.e. left them. [In C19 dialect, to give the bag to=to discharge, to dismiss; to take, get the bag=to be dismissed. EDD.—Grose's phrase and sense occur in Greene, 1592. F.]

BAG OF NAILS. He squints like a bag of nails, i.e. his eyes are directed as many ways as the points of a bag of nails. The old BAG OF NAILS at Pimlico; originally the BACCHANALS.

BAGGAGE. Heavy baggage; women and children. Also a familiar epithet for a woman; as, cunning baggage, wanton baggage, &c. [As an adjective=worthless, it was used by Gabriel Harvey in 1593. F.—As a wanton, it became established in C17: "a baggage or souldiers punk, *scortum castrense*," Robertson, 1693; see also Cotgrave, whose definition tends to show that *baggage* is connected with the French *bagasse*, a trull, prostitute, wanton, flirt. EDD.]

BAKER-KNEE'D. One whose knees knock together in walking, as if kneading dough. [The earlier form seems to have been *baker-legged*, which appears in Dekker in 1607. F.—As Cotgrave, 1611, bears out.]

BAKER'S DOZEN. Fourteen; that number of rolls being alowed to the purchasers of a dozen. [More usually 13, as in Florio, 2nd edition 1611 (the first being 1598), and in Cleveland, 1651. EDD.]

BALDERDASH. Adulterated wine. [An early sense was that of frothy talk, nonsense, and the modern nuance derives from a fusion of the two earlier meanings. OD.—In C18, the word meant also obscene talk and, in the Devonshire dialect, impudent or abusive language. EDD.]

BALLOCKS. The testicles of a man or beast; also a vulgar nick name for a parson. [In C19 dialect *ballocky, bollocky*=left handed, clumsy. EDD.—This may partly account for the mythical Ballocky (pronounced Bollicky) Bill the Sailor, of whom one heard much in the War army.]

BALLUM RANCUM. A hop or dance, where the women are all prostitutes. N.B. The company dance in their birth-day suits.

BALSAM. Money. [A neat derivative from the original meaning: a healing soothing agent or agency.]

BAM. A jocular imposition, the same as a humbug. See HUM-
BUG. [The noun first appeared, in the 5th edition (1748) of T.
Dyche's *Dictionary*, and the verb (q.v.) in the 2nd edition, 1754, of
H. Martin's Dictionary. F.—Both derive from *bamboozle*, which,
used in 1703 by Cibber, was in 1710 condemned by Swift; Swift
at the same time censured—as the inventions of certain 'pretty
fellows'—*banter, country put*, and *kidney*. G & K.]

TO BAM. To impose on any one by a falsity; also to jeer or make
fun of any one.

TO BAMBOOZLE. To make a fool of any one, to humbug or
impose on him.

BANAGHAN. He beats Banaghan; an Irish saying of one who
tells wonderful stories. Perhaps Banaghan was a minstrel famous
for dealing in the marvellous.

BANBURY STORY OF A COCK AND A BULL. A roundabout, nonsensical story. [In C19 dialect the phrase was
Banbury (or, *Bamberry*) *tale*, due probably to the famous nursery-
rhyme, "Ride a-cock horse to Banbury Cross." EDD.—It looks
as if Banbury in the old days was notorious for silly talk.]

BANDBOX. Mine a-se on a bandbox; an answer to the offer of
any thing inadequate to the purpose for which it is proffered, like
offering a bandbox for a seat.

BANDOG. A bailiff or his follower; also a very fierce mastiff:
likewise, a bandbox. *Cant*. [Literally band-dog, *canis catenatus* as
Robertson in 1693 had it, or *canis vinctus* as Skinner in 1671 preferred. A fanciful and erroneous derivation is bane-dog, a troublesome dog. EDD.]

BANDORE. A window's mourning peak; also a musical instrument. [As a musical instrument it is Spanish *bandurria* (Minshu,
1623) from Italian *pandora* (Florio), and is the same word as *ban-
jo*. EDD.]

TO BANG. To beat. [Bang appears in Henry Carey's *Sally in our
Alley;* it had been in print almost two centuries earlier. F.]

BANGING. Great; a fine banging boy. [From the obviously expletive sense of the present participle become adjective. EDD.]

BANG STRAW. A nick name for a thresher, but applied to all
the servants of a farmer. [A provincialism.]

BANKRUPT CART. A one-horse chaise, said to be so called by a Lord Chief Justice, from their being so frequently used on Sunday jaunts by extravagant shopkeepers and tradesmen.

BANKS'S HORSE. A horse famous for playing tricks, the property of one Banks. It is mentioned in Sir Walter Raleigh's Hist. of the World, p.178; also by Sir Kenelm Digby and Ben Jonson. [This famous horse, named Morocco and kept by one Banks, is mentioned in *Love's Labour's Lost*. O.]

BANTLING. A young child. [Used by Drayton in 1593. OD.— Originally and properly it meant "a child begotten on a bench and not in the marriage-bed" (Grimm). EDD.]

BANYAN DAY. A sea term for those days on which no meat is allowed to the sailors: the term is borrowed from the Banyans in the East Indies, a cast that eat nothing that had life. [First used in print, by Purchas indirectly in 1609; by Smollett directly in 1748. W. and OD. The term early made its way into dialect, a Yorkshire variant being little-fare day. EDD.]

BAPTIZED, or CHRISTENED. Rum, brandy, or any other spirits, that have been lowered with water. [Used in Healey's *Theophrastus* in 1636. F.]

BARBER. That's the barber; a ridiculous and unmeaning phrase, in the mouths of the common people about the year 1760, signifying their approbation of any action, measure, or thing.

BARBER'S CHAIR. She is as common as a barber's chair, in which a whole parish sit to be trimmed; said of a prostitute. [The metaphor occurs in Burton's *Anatomy*, 1621.F.]

BARBER'S SIGN. A standing pole and two wash-balls. [Barbers having been also surgeons and treaters of venereal disease. EDD.]

BARGAIN. To sell a bargain; a species of wit, much in vogue about the latter end of the reign of Queen Anne, and frequently alluded to by Dean Swift, who says the maids of honour often amused themselves with it. It consisted in the seller naming his or her hinder parts, in answer to the question. What? which the buyer was artfully led to ask. As a specimen, take the following instance: A lady would come into a room full of company, apparently in a fright, crying out, It is white, and follows me! On any

25

of the company asking, What? she sold him the bargain, by saying, Mine a--e. ['To sell (a person) a bargain' is used by Shakespeare as meaning to make a fool of him. O.]

BARKER. The shopman of a bow-wow shop, or dealer in second-hand clothes, particularly about Monmouth-street, who walks before his master's door, and deafens every passenger with his cries of—Clothes, coats, or gowns—what d'ye want, gemmen?—what d'ye buy? See BOW-WOW SHOP.

BARKING IRONS. Pistols, from their explosion resembling the bow-wow or barking of a dog. *Irish.* [Grose's definition—as many of his others do—comes straight from Bampfylde-Moore Carew's *Life.*—The term occurs in Parker's *Life's Painter*, 1789, and the C19-20 variant is *barker*. F.—*Barker* is not an Irishism and it figures notably in Scott's *Guy Mannering* in the phrase 'barkers and slashers,' pistols and swords. EDD.—The term *barker* was frequently used by soldiers in 1914-18. F & G.]

BARKSHIRE. A member or candidate for Barkshire; said of one troubled with a cough, vulgarly styled barking.

BARN. A parson's barn; never so full but there is still room for more. Bit by a barn mouse; tipsey, probably from an allusion to barley.

BARNABY. An old dance to a quick movement. See Cotton, in his Virgil Travesti; where, speaking of Eolus, he has these lines:

> Bounce cry the port-holes, out they fly,
> And make the world dance Barnaby.

['To dance Barnaby' came in the C19 to mean to move in a lively manner. F.—There are several anonymous C17 books describing one Barnaby's jests and dances.]

BARNACLE. A good job, or snack easily got: also shell fish growing at the bottoms of ships; a bird of the goose kind; an instrument like a pair of pincers, to fix on the noses of vicious horses whilst shoeing; a nick name for spectacles, and also for the gratuity given to grooms by the buyers and sellers of horses. [The plural =spectacles, dates back to 1571. F.—This sense is connected with that of horse-pincers. P.—As=spectacles the word was in common slang and dialectal use from *ca.* 1660.—In the sense of 'goose' it was used by Shakespeare for "a species of goose form-

26

erly supposed to be hatched from the fruit of a tree or from sea-shells growing on it." O.]

BARREL FEVER. He died of the barrel fever; he killed himself by drinking.

BARTHOLOMEW BABY. A person dressed up in a tawdry manner, like the dolls or babies sold at Bartholomew fair. [This sense was in print at least as early as 1681. F.]

BAR WIG. A wig between a Dalmahoy and a double cauliflower or full bottom. See DALMAHOY.

BASKET. An exclamation frequently made use of in cock-pits, at cock-fightings, where persons refusing or unable to pay their losings, are adjudged by that respectable assembly to be put into a basket suspended over the pit, there to remain during that day's diversion: on the least demur to pay a bet, Basket is vociferated *in terrorem*. He grins like a basket of chips; a saying of one who is on the broad grin.

BASKET-MAKING. The good old trade of basket-making; copulation, or making feet for children's stockings.

BASTARD. The child of an unmarried woman. [Grose's inclusion of this good-English word would tend to show that it had already acquired a bad odour, probably from its use in curses. During the War it was very frequent among British troops of all countries and most counties. As both noun and adjective it connoted either opprobrium ("You dirty bastard!", "the bastard thing") or affection ("You old bastard! it's good *or* great to see you again"); or as a noun it meant simply 'chap,' 'fellow,' 'man,' as when, learning of an acquaintance's death, the troops might be heard to exclaim: "Poor old bastard!"]

BASTARDLY GULLION. A bastard's bastard.

TO BASTE. To beat. I'll give him his basting; I'll beat him heartily. [Dates from C16.F.—In general dialectal and fairly frequent colloquial use in both England and Scotland from about 1700. EDD.]

BASTING. A beating.

BASTONADING. Beating any one with a stick; from baton, a stick, formerly spelt baston.[Shakespeare has it in form bastinado. O.—From Spanish *bastonada*, beating, from *baston*, a cudgel. "The limitation of meaning to beating the soles of the feet is comparatively modern." W.]

BATCH. We had a pretty batch of it last night; we had a hearty dose of liquor. Batch originally means the whole quantity of bread baked at one time in an oven. [Also, in Grose's own day, it meant a number or quantity of things, a party of persons (as in Burns' *Holy Fair*). EDD.—Northern (mainly) and analogous to a *clatch* of poultry. P.]

BATCHELOR'S FARE. Bread and cheese and kisses. [See Swift: *Polite Conversation*, no. 1. F.]

BATCHELOR'S SON. A bastard.

BATTLE-ROYAL. A battle or bout at cudgels or fisty-cuffs, wherein more than two persons are engaged: perhaps from its resemblance, in that particular, to more serious engagements fought to settle royal disputes. [A general engagement between two teams of fighting-cocks. Earlier in the Middle Ages, the term described a battle with a King in command on both sides. W:A. Bailey in 1721 defines it as a fight between three, five, or seven cocks of which the one left standing is acclaimed the winner. EDD.]

BATTNER. An ox: beef being apt to batten or fatten those that eat it. The cove has hushed the battner; i.e. has killed the ox.

BAUDRANS. A cat. *Scotch*. [More usually *baudrons;* used also in the North Country. EDD.]

BAWBEE. A halfpenny. *Scotch*.

BAWBELS, or BAWBLES. Trinkets; a man's testicles.

BAWD. A female procuress.

BAWDY BASKET. The twenty-third rank of canters, who carry pins, tape, ballads, and obscene books to sell, but live mostly by stealing. *Cant*. [Described fully in Harman's *Caveat*, 1567. F.]

BAWDY-HOUSE BOTTLE. A very small bottle; short measure being among the many means used by the keepers of those houses to gain what they call an honest livelihood: indeed this is one of the least reprehensible; the less they give a man of their infernal beverages for his money, the kinder they behave to him.

BAY WINDOWS. Old projecting windows. [Good English.]

BAYARD OF TEN TOES. To ride bayard of ten toes, is to

walk on foot. Bayard was a horse famous in old romances. [Breton's employment of the word in *Good and Bad* tends to show that it was a common expression before 1606. F.]

BEAK. A justice of peace, or magistrate. [In sense of policeman and in form *beck* the word was used in C16. As=magistrate it became established about 1700. F.—Sir John Fielding was known as 'The Blind Beak' *ca.* 1750.—"Quite modern in sense of assistant master." W.—The word as=a magistrate is of frequent dialectal use. The tendency of *beck-beak* has been slowly and consistently towards respectability. EDD.—The commonest use of the word since *ca.* 1860 has been in the phrase: 'up before the beak.' The early form *beck* may be connected with, even an anglicisation of, French *bec*, a beak: this theory would account for the dropping of *beck* for *beak*.—In North America it was frequently used before 1914 to mean either a judge or a justice of the peace but it is not often heard to-day. I.]

BEAR. One who contracts to deliver a certain quantity or sum of stock in the public funds, on a future day, and at a stated price; or, in other words, sells what he has not got, like the huntsman in the fable, who sold the bear's skin before the bear was killed. As the bear sells the stock he is not possessed of, so the bull purchases what he has not money to pay for; but in case of any alteration in the price agreed on, either party pays or receives the difference. *Exchange Alley.*

BEAR-GARDEN JAW or DISCOURSE. Rude, vulgar language such as was used at the bear-gardens.

BEAR LEADER. A travelling tutor. [In a letter by Horace Walpole in 1749; apparently first in print in 1756. OD.]

BEARD SPLITTER. A man much given to wenching. [In modern American Slang of trampdom and the underworld, there is the analogous *beard-jammer.* I.]

BEARINGS. I'll bring him to his bearings; I'll bring him to reason. *Sea term.*

BEAST. To drink like a beast, i.e. only when thirsty.

BEAST WITH TWO BACKS. A man and woman in the act of copulation. *Shakespeare in Othello.*

BEATER CASES. Boots. *Cant.* [Nearly obsolete by 1860, by which date the term in vogue was *trotter-cases*. H.]

BEAU-NASTY. A slovenly fop; one finely dressed, but dirty.

BEAU TRAP. A loose stone in a pavement, under which water lodges, and, on being trod upon, squirts it up, to the great damage of white stockings; also a sharper neatly dressed, lying in wait for raw country squires, or ignorant fops.

BECALMED. A piece of sea wit, sported in hot weather. I am becalmed, the sail sticks to the mast; that is, my shirt sticks to my back.

BECK. A beadle. See HERMANBECK. [Read: 'See Harman-beck.']

BED. Put to bed with a mattock, and tucked up with a spade; said of one that is dead and buried. You will go up a ladder to bed, i.e. you will be hanged. In many country places, persons hanged are made to mount up a ladder, which is afterwards turned round or taken away; whence the term, 'Turned off.' [The C19 slang phrase (one still hears it occasionally) was "to put to bed with a pickaxe and shovel." F.—In C19-20 dialect we find: "To be put to bed with a shovel." EDD.]

BEDAWBED ALL OVER WITH LACE. Vulgar saying of any one dressed in clothes richly laced.

BEDFORDSHIRE. I am for Bedfordshire, i.e. for going to bed. [Found earliest in a poem by Charles Cotton, C17. OD.]

BEDIZENED. Dressed out, over-dressed, or awkwardly ornamented.

BEEF. To cry beef; to give the alarm. They have cried beef on us. *Cant.*—To be in a man's beef; to wound him with a sword. To be in a woman's beef; to have carnal knowledge of her. Say you bought your beef of me; a jocular request from a butcher to a fat man, implying that he credits the butcher who serves him. [*To cry beef* had the variant *to give (hot) beef*. C19 thieves' slang-phrase *to make beef* meant to decamp. In Bampfylde-Moore Carew's *Life* (edition of 1791) occurs the sentence: "They whiddle beef and we must brush," they cry *thief* and we must get away: Wright therefrom argues that beef is "riming slang for 'Stop thief!'" but so far as we know, rhyming slang did not exist at that date. EDD.

Farmer calls it a 'rhyming synonym,' a rather different mat-ter.—Rhyming synonyms were probably the result sometimes of accident, sometimes of fear, sometimes of both: they might easily develop into, or suggest the possibility and potentialities of, rhyming slang. As for the little-explored territory of this slang, the fringe has been reached in H, B & P, while in F & G there are numerous examples of 1914-1918 soldiers' rhyming slang; for a brief and elementary essay on the subject, see *Every-man*, March, 1931. I hope to deal adequately with the subject when leisure offers.—Derivative senses of *to cry beef* are seen in the United States naval slang *to beef*, to complain. B.—In the U.S., too, in tramp and underworld slang, the verb *beef* means: to com-plain, to inform, to turn State's Evidence, while the noun signi-fies either a complaint made against a criminal or an informa-tion laid against a criminal or a suspect. I.]

BEEF EATER. A yeoman of the guards, instituted by Henry VII. Their office was to stand near the bouffet, or cupboard, thence called Bouffetiers, since corrupted to Beef Eaters. Others suppose they obtained this name from the size of their persons, and the easiness of their duty, as having scarce more to do than to eat the king's beef. [The latter of Grose's explanations is correct in that here is a man fortunately able to count on his daily beef, i.e. his daily food. The Bouffetiers are imaginary, and the success of this myth was promoted by Mrs Markham's inclusion of the story in her once-household *History of England*. W:ROW and much more fully in W:MWAM.]

BEETLE-BROWED. One having thick projecting eyebrows. [Apparently first used by Langland and quite common in late Middle English; *beetle brows* occurs in Spenser, while Purchas in 1607 applies it to an African fish. See a most suggestive article in W:MWAM.]

BEETLE-HEADED. Dull, stupid. [Shakespeare has it in the same sense.O.]

BEGGAR MAKER. A publican, or ale-house keeper.

BEGGARS BULLETS. Stones. The beggars bullets began to fly, i.e. they began to throw stones. [In the form *beggar's bolts*, it dates back to C16.F.]

31

BEILBY'S BALL. He will dance at Beilby's ball, where the sheriff pays the music; he will be hanged. Who Mr Beilby was, or why that ceremony was so called, remains with the quadrature of the circle, the discovery of the philosopher's stone, and divers other desiderata yet undiscovered.

BELCH. All sorts of beer; that liquor being apt to cause eructation. [In print in 1698 (Ward's *London Spy*), but probably existent long before that date: cf. Sir Toby Belch in *Twelfth Night*. F.—In C19 North Lincolnshire, worthless or smutty talk. EDD.]

BELL, BOOK, AND CANDLE. They cursed him with bell, book, and candle; an allusion to the popish form of excommunicating and anathematizing persons who had offended the church. [Used by Shakespeare. O.]

TO BEAR THE BELL. To excel or surpass all competitors, to be the principal in a body or society; an allusion to the fore horse or leader of a team, whose harness is commonly ornamented with a bell or bells. Some suppose it a term borrowed from an ancient tournament, where the victorious knights bore away the *belle* or *fair lady*. Others derive it from a horse-race, or other rural contentions, where bells were frequently given as prizes.

BELLOWS. The lungs. [An early example occurs in James Miller's play, *Humours of Oxford*, 2nd edition 1730. Etymologically the word is related to *belly*. OD.]

BELLOWER. The town crier.

BELLY. His eye was bigger than his belly; a saying of a person at a table, who takes more on his plate than he can eat.

BELLYFULL. A hearty beating, sufficient to make a man yield or give out. A woman with child is also said to have got her belly full.

BELLY CHEAT. An apron. [Dekker, 1609. F.—*cheat*, earlier *chete*,=a thing.]

BELLY PLEA. The plea of pregnancy, generally adduced by female felons capitally convicted, which they take care to provide for, previous to their trials; every gaol having, as the Beggar's Opera informs us, one or more child getters, who qualify the ladies for that expedient to procure a respite. [Compare: "My mother pleaded her belly, and being found quick with child, she was respited for about seven months."D.]

BELLY TIMBER. Food of all sorts. [Occurs in Cotton in 1678, in 1637 in Massinger, and in a translation of Terence in 1614. F.—Common in dialect. EDD.—Persisted into C19 slang and only obsolescent to-day.]

BELL SWAGGER. A noisy bullying fellow.

BELL WETHER. The chief or leader of a mob: an idea taken from a flock of sheep, where the wether has a bell about his neck.

BEN. A fool. *Cant*.

BENE. Good.—BENAR. Better. *Cant*. [Also *benat*, best. All three belong to the oldest English cant: that which sprang up *ca.* 1500 or a little later. F.]

BENE BOWSE. Good beer, or other strong liquor. *Cant*. [Dates back to C16. F.]

BENE COVE. A good fellow. *Cant*. [In 1860 the thieves' term was *ben cull*. H.]

BENE DARKMANS. Good night. *Cant*.

BENE FEAKERS. Counterfeiters of bills. *Cant*.

BENE FEAKERS OF GYBES. Counterfeiters of passes. *Cant*.

BENESHIPLY. Worshipfully. *Cant*.

BENISH. Foolish.

BENISON. The beggar's benison; May your ***** and purse never fail you.

BERMUDAS. A cant name for certain places in London, privileged against arrests, like the Mint in Southwark. *Ben Jonson*.

BESS, or BETTY. A small instrument used by house-breakers to force open doors. Bring bess and glym; bring the instrument to force the door, and the dark lantern. Small flasks like those for Florence wine, are also called betties. [See Head in *The English Rogue*, 1671. F.—The instrument is now of the male sex: *Jemmy* (American underworld *jimmy*); cf. the German *Dietrich*, *Peterchen*, *Klaus*, and the Italian *grimaldello*. W:ROW.]

BESS. See BROWN BESS.

BETHLEHEMITES. Christmas carol singers. *Cant*.

BEST. To the best in Christendom, i.e. the best****in Christendom; a health formerly much in vogue.

BET. A wager.—TO BET. To lay a wager.

BETTY MARTIN. That's my eye, Betty Martin; an answer to

33

any one that attempts to impose or humbug. [*All my Eye* is perhaps the earliest form (Goldsmith has it in 1768), although it is clear that Grose's version was already familiar in 1785. On the face of it, the longer forms are probably the later; among these is that now prevalent: That's (all) my eye and Betty Martin. We can discount as too ingenious—and inaccurate—the view propounded by Hotten:—"*All my eye.* Condensation of 'All my eye and Betty Martin,' a vulgar phrase constructed from the commencement of a Roman Catholic prayer to St Martin '*O, mihi, beate Martine,* which in common with many another fell into discredit and ridicule after the Reformation." The latest authoritative pronouncement is that "The origin of the phrase is unknown and the identity of the lady is as vague as that of Tommy in like hell and Tommy." W. Cf. the French *mon œil!* F.]

BETWATTLED. Surprised, confounded, out of one's senses; also bewrayed.

BEVER. An afternoon's luncheon; also a fine hat; bevers fur making the best hats. [Grose obviously lumps together two words usually spelt differently nowadays; though a frequent variant of the snack is *beaver;* much less frequent are *bevir, bœvir. Bever* is the Anglo-French infinitive of the Latin *bibere,* to drink, influenced by the Old French *beivre,* to drink but also and especially a drinking. A light refreshment (often beer and bread-and-cheese) taken between meals, e.g. at 10 (or 11) and 4 o'clock. A bever-cake is one made to eat, at 4 p.m., with ale; bever-time is an interval for refreshment. Mainly South Country. The bever taken in the morning was in some parts of England known as *elevens*; the Suffolk term is *doggy;* the North Country prefers, or rather did prefer until *ca.* 1910, *biting-on.* EDD.—In the latter half of the C19, the term bever, at Eton, Westminster, and Winchester schools, denoted a snack or other between-meals repast, especially in the afternoon. F.—The word has come, in several dialects, to signify a light lunch (beer; bread-and-cheese) taken at noon.]

BEVERAGE. Garnish money, or money for drink, demanded of any one having a new suit of clothes. [In C19, it broadened to: A tip. F.]

34

BIBLE. A boatswain's great axe. *Sea term.* [Defined by Admiral Smyth in the *Sailor's Word Book* (1867) as a hand-axe; it also was a small holy-stone, according to the novelist W. Clark Russell's *Sailors' Language*, 1883. F.]

BIBLE OATH. Supposed by the vulgar to be more binding than an oath taken on the Testament only, as being the bigger book, and generally containing both the Old & New Testament.

BIDDY, or CHICK-A-BIDDY. A chicken, and figuratively a young wench. [Cf. the modern *Irish biddy*, an Irish girl, often specifically an Irish servant girl, though here from *Bridget.*]

BIDET, commonly pronounced BIDDY. A kind of tub, contrived for ladies to wash themselves, for which purpose they bestride it like a little French poney, or post-horse, called in France bidets.

BIENLY. Excellently. She wheedled so bienly: she coaxed or flattered so cleverly. *French.*

BILBOA. A sword. Bilboa in Spain was once famous for well-tempered blades: these are quoted by Falstaff, where he describes the manner in which he lay in the buck-basket. Bilboes; the stocks. *Cant.* [Correctly *Bilbao;* in Shakespeare as *bilbo*.O. —The form *Bilboa* as applied to the place was general in England until the C19, and according to Moll's *Geography*, 1701, these swords were (at that date 'are') famous all over Europe. OD.—The word was on the border line between good spoken English and colloquialism.]

TO BILK. To cheat. Let us bilk the rattling cove; let us cheat the hackney coachman of his fare. *Cant.*—Bilking a coachman, a box-keeper, and a poor whore, were formerly, among men of the town, thought gallant actions. [Perhaps a doublet of *balk.* In Wycherley, 1677. In C19 used as a noun, though less frequently, in both slang and dialect. F; EDD. In Hotten's day the noun (=a cheat, swindler) was confined to the streets.]

BILL OF SALE. A widow's weeds. See HOUSE TO LET.

BILLINGSGATE LANGUAGE. Foul language, or abuse. Billingsgate is the market where the fish-women assemble to purchase fish; and where, in their dealings and disputes, they are somewhat apt to leave decency and good manners a little

35

on the left hand. [References about as early as C17. F. "Famous for rhetoric" is Weekley's dry comment.]

BING. To go. *Cant.*—Bing avast; get you gone. Binged avast in a darkmans; stole away in the night. Bing we to Rumeville; shall we go to London? [In Harman's *Caveat*, 1567. OD.]

BINGO. Brandy or other spirituous liquor. *Cant.* [Perhaps on the analogy of the earlier stingo (C17-19) from *binge*, literally to soak, to steep (cf. 'a good binging shower,' Northants), and derivatively to drink heavily. In dialect the noun meant a drinking bout, a sense that passed into Oxford University slang, whence it filtered into general slang. (A development of EDD and OD* evidence.) In 1914-1918 the word *binge* (= drinking bout or expedition) became very popular, while *bingo* survived in the musical comedy, *The Bing Boys*. B & P.

*It is only fair to the OD to state that Sir James Murray considered *bingo* to be a composite of *B* (=brandy) + *stingo*. My theory is perhaps assisted by the fact that the nautical phrase, to *binge a cask*, means "to get the remaining liquor from the wood by rinsing it with water." (This practice, which yields a very potent drink and is 'carefully guarded against in the Navy,' is known also as *bulling a cask*. B.)]

BINGO BOY. A dram drinker. *Cant.*

BINGO MORT. A female dram drinker. *Cant.*

BINNACLE WORD. A fine or affected word, which sailors jeeringly offer to chalk up on the binnacle.

BIRD AND BABY. The sign of the eagle and child.

BIRD-WITTED. Inconsiderate, thoughtless, easily imposed on. [Used by Bacon in 1605. OD.]

BIRDS OF A FEATHER. Rogues of the same gang.

BIRTH DAY SUIT. He was in his birth-day suit, that is, stark naked. [The phrase appears in Smollett's *Humphry Clinker*, 1771.]

BISHOP. A mixture of wine and water, into which is put a roasted orange. Also one of the largest of Mrs Philip's purses, used to contain the others. [This sweet drink is mentioned in Tusser's *Husbandry*. EDD.—The word appears in Ward's *English Spy*, 1703. F.]

BISHOPED, or TO BISHOP. A term among horse-dealers, for burning the mark into a horse's tooth, after he has lost it by age; by bishoping, a horse is made to appear younger than he is. It is a common saying of milk that is burnt to, that the bishop has set his foot in it. Formerly, when a bishop passed through a village, all the inhabitants ran out of their houses to solicit his blessing, even leaving their milk &c. on the fire, to take its chance; which, when burnt to, was said to be bishoped. [As a horse-dealing term, bishop is, I believe, first defined in R. Bradley's Family Dictionary, 1727 (F). See also Knowlson's *Cattle Doctor*, 1843. In dialect the phrase about burnt milk was frequent; the more allusive 'the bishop's foot,' fairly common. EDD.]

BIT. Money. He grappled the cull's bit; he seized the man's money. A bit is also the smallest current coin in Jamaica, equal to about sixpence sterling. [Sometimes spelt *bite*, the word dates back to early C16.F. In C19 Scottish, a bit=3d, as in Barrie: *A Window in Thrums*, 1889. EDD.]

BITCH. A she dog, or doggess: the most offensive appellation that can be given to an English woman, even more provoking than that of whore, as may be gathered from the regular Billingsgate or St Giles's answer—"I may be a whore, but can't be a bitch." [In C19 dialect the term could be used quite inoffensively of a woman or a little girl. EDD.]

TO BITCH. To yield, or give up an attempt through fear. To stand bitch; to make tea, or do the honours of the tea-table, performing a female part: bitch there standing for woman, species for genus. [Later than Grose, the verb also meant to go whoring, transitively to spoil, to ruin, the latter being still in use. As early as the C16 there was a noun *bitchery*=harlotry, lewdness.F. In dialect the 'to ruin' sense has long obtained. *Bitch tea* became Cambridge University-slang *ca.* 1800 (EDD) and endured as such till the end of the century (see Charles Whibley's *Cap and Gown*, 1889), but seems to have died out a year or two before the Great War.]

BITCH BOOBY. A country wench. *Military term.*

BITE. A cheat; also a woman's privities. The cull wapt the

mort's bite; the fellow enjoyed the wench heartily. *Cant.* [As=
a cheat, the word, according to Swift, originated with a nobleman in his day. H.—In the second sense, cf. the French slang
bite.]

TO BITE. To over-reach, or impose; also to steal. *Cant.*—
Biting was once esteemed a kind of wit, similar to the humbug.
An instance of it is given in the Spectator: A man under sentence of death having sold his body to a surgeon rather below
the market price, on receiving the money, cried, A bite! I am
to be hanged in chains.—To bite the roger; to steal a portmanteau. To bite the wiper; to steal a handkerchief. To bite on the
bridle; to be pinched or reduced to difficulties. Hark ye, friend,
whether do they bite in the collar or the cod-piece. *Water wit
to anglers.*

BITER. A wench whose **** is ready to bite her a-se; a lascivious, rampant wench. [Perhaps connected with the North
Country verb *bite*=to smart, to sting. EDD.— *Biter* more generally meant a hoaxer or a trickster, this sense surviving in the
proverbial phrase 'the biter bit.' F.]

BLAB. A tell-tale, or one incapable of keeping a secret. [Cf.
"He that is a blab is a scab" (Ray's Proverbs, 1678) and the
dialectal compounds *blab-chops,-mouth,-tit,-tongue:* a tell-tale;
and the dialectal adjectives *blab-mouthed* and-*tongued.* The verb,
defined by Skinner in 1671 as *garrire, effutire,* was in general use
in C18; note also the Irish and North-Country frequentative
blabber or *blobber,* to talk far too much. EDD.]

BLACK AND WHITE. In writing. I have it in black and
white; I have written evidence. [Ben Jonson, 1596.F.]

BLACK A-SE. A copper or kettle. The pot calls the kettle
black a-se. *Cant.* [The proverbial phrase has, in transit from
cant to colloquialism, dropped the *a-se.* This illustrates a common process in the history of the spoken language, but, for English at least, it has never, so far as I know, been thoroughly or
even adequately treated. The process works in contrary directions, for while it considerably enriches the language quantita-
tively by throwing open, to the general respectable public,
words and phrases previously unknown or debarred, it also

38

devitalizes the original denotation and impoverishes the original connotation. Probably a thesis will be written on the subject some day.]

BLACK ART. The art of picking a lock. *Cant.* [Dates back to C16. OD.]

BLACK BOOK. He is down in the black book, i.e. has a stain in his character. A black book is kept in most regiments, wherein the names of all persons sentenced to punishment are recorded. [Mentioned in C16. W.]

BLACK BOX. A lawyer. *Cant.*

BLACK EYE. We gave the bottle a black eye, i.e. drank it almost up. He cannot say black is the white of my eye: he cannot point out a blot in my character.

BLACK FLY. The greatest drawback on the farmer is the black fly, i.e. the parson who takes tithe of the harvest.

BLACK-GUARD. A shabby, dirty fellow; a term said to be derived from a number of dirty, tattered, and roguish boys, who attended at the Horse Guards, and parade in St James's Park, to black the boots and shoes of the soldiers, or to do any other dirty offices. These, from their constant attendance about the time of guard mounting, were nick-named the black-guards. [Apparently the learned Gifford was the first to explain correctly the origin of the term. H.—The earliest mention was in 1535. "The *black guard* consisted of the lowest menials of a large household, who took charge of pots and pans on journeys, also hangers-on of an army." W.—There is also an excellently suggestive and extensive account in Farmer and Henley.]

BLACK JACK. A jug to drink out of, made of jacked leather.

BLACK JOKE. A popular tune to a song, having for the burden, "Her black joke and belly so white:" figuratively the black joke signifies the monosyllable. See MONOSYLLABLE.

BLACK INDIES. Newcastle upon Tyne, whose rich coal-mines prove an Indies to the proprietors.

BLACK LEGS. A gambler or sharper on the turf or in the cock-pit: so called, perhaps, from their appearing generally in boots; or else from game cocks, whose legs are always black.

[First recorded example in print, B. Parsons: *Newmarket*, 1771. OD.—"Perhaps descriptive of the *rook*," thus wittily W.— Usually, by about 1860, shortened to *leg*. H.]

BLACK MONDAY. The first Monday after the school-boys holidays, or breaking up, when they are to go to school, and produce or repeat the tasks set them. [Occurs in *Tom Jones*.F. —"Monday morning in the 17th century Navy, when the ships' boys received their accumulated week's whipping." B.]

BLACK MUNS. Hoods and scarves of alamode lutestring.

BLACK PSALM. To sing the black psalm; to cry: a saying used to children.

BLACK SPY. The Devil.

BLACK STRAP. Bene Carlo wine; also port. A task of labour imposed on soldiers at Gibraltar, as a punishment for small offences. [As simply *strap*, the term occurs in Dekker's *Bellman of London*, 1608. F.—It is used in America, and occasionally in British sailing ships, to mean molasses. B.—Port wine, especially if thick and sweet.H.]

BLANK. To look blank; to appear disappointed or confounded. [In C19 dialect the word was used as verb, noun and adjective, all with the idea of disappointment very prominent. EDD.]

BLARNEY. He has licked the Blarney stone; he deals in the wonderful, or tips us the traveller. The blarney stone is a triangular stone on the very top of an ancient castle of that name, in the county of Cork in Ireland, extremely difficult of access; so that to have ascended to it, was considered as a proof of perseverance, courage, and agility, whereof many are supposed to claim the honour who never achieved the adventure: and to tip the blarney, is figuratively used for telling a marvellous story, or falsity; and also sometimes to express flattery. *Irish*.

A BLASTED FELLOW or BRIMSTONE. An abandoned rogue or prostitute. *Cant*.

TO BLAST. To curse. [The OD. gives *The Gentleman's Magazine*, 1762, as the earliest example, but F cites Chapman's *Revenge for Honour*. Originally Army slang. H.]

BLATER. A Calf. *Cant*. [Probably *bleater* corrupted. F.]

BLEACHED MORT. A fair-complexioned wench.

40

BLEATERS. Those cheated by Jack in a box. *Cant.* — See JACK IN A BOX.

BLEATING CHEAT. A sheep. *Cant.* [Old cant *cheat, cheate, chete,* the thing robbed, hence a thing, was often used to form the name of an animal: a grunting cheat was a pig; a cackling cheat, a fowl; and so forth.F,OD.]

BLEATING RIG. Sheep stealing. *Cant.* [Variant *b. prig.* A *bleating cull* was a sheep-stealer. F.]

BLEEDING CULLY. One who parts easily with his money, or bleeds freely. [The verb *bleed,* to lose or to part with money, appears in Dryden in 1668; the transitive seems to have been first used by Thackeray in 1849. OD; F.]

BLEEDING NEW. A metaphor borrowed from fish, which will not bleed when stale.

BLESSING. A small quantity over and above the measure, usually given by hucksters dealing in peas, beans, and other vegetables. [The word survives in Staffordshire and Shropshire. EDD.]

BLEW JOHN. Ash or after-wort. [*Afterwort,* the second run of beer, is recorded for 1795. OD.—*Ash* I conjecture to be an error for *Wash,* which, as the OD. shows, occurs with *afterworts* in 1683 in this precise technical sense. *Blew* is properly *Blue.*]

BLIND. A feint, pretence, or shift. [In Dryden's *Wild Gallant,* 1663. F.—In C19, it passed into general colloquial use.EDD.]

BLIND CHEEKS. The breech. Buss blind cheeks; kiss mine a-se.

BLIND EXCUSE. A poor or insufficient excuse. A blind ale-house, lane, or alley; an obscure, or little-known or frequented ale-house, lane, or alley.

BLIND HARPERS. Beggars counterfeiting blindness, playing on fiddles, &c.

BLINDMAN'S BUFF. A play used by children, where one being blinded by a handkerchief bound over his eyes, attempts to seize any one of the company, who all endeavour to avoid him; the person caught must be blinded in his stead.

BLINDMAN'S HOLIDAY. Night, darkness. [Used by Nash in 1599. During the C19 it came to mean the morning or the

41

evening, but especially the evening, twilight: a sense foreshadowed by Swift. F.—Dusk, work attempted in the dusk. The phrase is in Florio. EDD.]

BLOCK HOUSES. Prisons, houses of correction, &c. [The word became common *ca.* 1500, or slightly earlier than the German equivalent *Blockhaus*. OD.]

BLOOD. A riotous disorderly fellow. [In 1860, "a fast or high-mettled man. Nearly obsolete, but much used in George the Fourth's time." H.—Here we have what the Oxford Dictionary considers the origin of that adjective whose publicity man has been the public itself ever since George Bernard Shaw foisted it on us in *Pygmalion*. Professor Weekley (in WAM and A) denies this and cites an adverbial use in Marston, 1606; "merely an intensive of the same type as *awfully*, *thundering*, etc. . . and the word was not originally offensive" (Etymological Dictionary). It is, however, to be noted that Shakespeare used the noun to denote 'a man of fire, spirit, mettle' (O), which links up with Grose's sense. It is true that, colloquially and expletively, the adverb *bloody* (earlier *bloodily*) precedes the adjective, but even in Marston's phrase, "a man cruelly eloquent and bluddily learned," it is noticeable that *cruelly*, which later came to mean merely 'very,' retains something of the sense of 'cruelly,' 'severely,' 'distressingly,' and that *bluddily* may well mean 'spiritedly,' 'somewhat heatedly.' The root-idea of blood as something vivid and/or distressing is never quite absent in the adjective, and it is, it seems to me, certain that adverbs lose their original signification more rapidly than adjectives. In 1914-1918, when language was sadistically or cynically or desperately debased by the soldiers, one could, with a fine disregard for discrimination (see B & P), say that "snow was bloody, khaki was bloody, the sky was bloody, green envelopes were bloody," W.V. Tilsley, *Other Ranks*, 1931.— Here may be quoted two opinions of some importance. In 1929 Dean Inge remarked that in the speech of the British workman, *bloody* served merely to indicate that a noun might be expected, and in 1926 C. E. Montague, referring to about the year 1910, made one of the characters in *Rough Justice* say:

42

"All the little different emphasising particles in Greek mean what an English workman means by bloody," a very acute criticism indeed. The word is in dialect used with a superb ignoring of the hypersensitive, just as, in Devonshire, *bugger* is quite mild. This latter word is treated fully in both EDD and OD, yet they exclude two definitely language-words (that for *coire, coitus*, and that for the *pudendum muliebre*) that are essentially less offensive; Wright inconsistently included other slang words for the pudend. Well, well!]

BLOOD FOR BLOOD. A term used by tradesmen for bartering the different commodities in which they deal. Thus a hatter furnishing a hosier with a hat, and taking payment in stockings, is said to deal blood for blood.

BLOODY BACK. A jeering appellation for a soldier, alluding to his scarlet coat.

BLOSS or BLOWEN. The pretended wife of a bully, or shoplifter. *Cant.* [Probably an abbreviation of *blossom* (though perhaps not uninfluenced by *blowse*), it was applied generically to a woman, whether girl, wife, or mistress. F.— In dialect an endearment, a buxom lass. EDD.]

TO BLOT THE SKRIP AND JARK IT. To stand engaged or bound for any one. *Cant.* [Literally the phrase=to write on the scrip (i.e. paper) and seal it. *Jark*=a seal; *jarkman*, a licensed beggar. F.]

BLOW. He has bit the blow, i.e. he has stolen the goods. *Cant.*

BLOWER OR BLOWEN. A mistress or whore of a gentleman of the scamp. [*Scamp* here=highway; the woman is therefore a highwayman's mistress.—Cant of gipsy origin, "signifying a sister in debauchery...the Beluñi of the Spanish Gypsies." *Blowen* occurs in Byron's *Don Juan* in the sense of mistress. More properly spelt *bloen*, with variant *blowing*.GB.]

TO BLOW THE GROUNSILS. To lie with a woman on the floor. *Cant.* [Properly groundsels. F.]

TO BLOW THE GAB. To confess, or impeach a confederate. *Cant.* [A transferred sense of *blow*: to breathe out, to give forth by breathing. The earliest form of the phrase is simply *blow* and was so used in the Elizabethan play *Appius and Virgin-*

43

ia. F.—Later, *blow the gaff*, probably owing to *penny gaff*, a low class entertainment; cf. *give away the show*. W.—In dialect, *blow* =to divulge, to betray. EDD.]

BLOW-UP. A discovery, or the confusion occasioned by one. [In this phrase, *blow*=to suspect, inform against, as one sees from the use of the p.pcpl. passive, *blown* in early C18, as in Defoe's *Colonel Jack*. As verb *blow-up*=scold, make a noise, and began as cant; it became slang and by 1860 was an ordinary colloquialism: "a recognised and respectable phrase," H.— From *ca.* 1880, *to blow up* has meant to reprimand very severely.]

A BLOWSE, or BLOWSABELLA. A woman whose hair is dishevelled, and hanging about her face; a slattern. [Shakespeare has it for 'a ruddy-faced fat wench.' O.—By 1860 the word has taken the form *blowsey*. H.]

BLUBBER. The mouth.—I have stopped the cull's blubber; I have stopped the fellow's mouth; meant either by gagging or murdering him. [*Cant.*]

TO BLUBBER. To cry. [As early as 1400; Smollett, who has done so much to invigorate our language, gave it the stamp of his authority in *Roderick Random*, 1748. F.—North Country has variant *blub*.]

TO SPORT BLUBBER. Said of a large coarse woman, who exposes her bosom.

BLUBBER CHEEKS. Large flaccid cheeks, hanging like the fat or blubber of a whale.

BLUE. To look blue; to be confounded, terrified, or disappointed. Blue as a razor; perhaps, blue as azure.

BLUE BOAR. A venereal bubo. [Possibly from the famous Blue Boar Tavern, which, at the corner of Oxford Street and Tottenham Court Road, was right in the 'Latin Quarter' of *ca.* 1750-1850 and therefore, presumably, of no immaculate reputation. (E. Beresford Chancellor, *London's Old Latin Quarter*, 1930.)]

BLUE DEVILS. Low spirits. [By 1860, this phrase, as a colloquialism, meant (as it still often means) the forms and figures seen by habitual drunkards in delirium tremens. H.—As slang, it meant the police till *ca.* 1900 or a little later. F.]

44

BLUE FLAG. He has hoisted the blue flag; he has commenced publican, or taken a public house, an allusion to the blue apron worn by publicans. See ADMIRAL OF THE BLUE.

BLUE AND ORANGE. This society, styling themselves Loyal and Friendly, met, 1742, at Kouli Khan's head, Leicester-fields.

BLUE PIGEONS. Thieves who steal lead off houses and churches. *Cant.* [Originally a cant term for roofing-lead. F.]

BLUE PLUMB. A bullet.—Surfeited with a blue plumb; wounded with a bullet. A sortment of George R—'s blue plumbs; a volley of ball, shot from soldiers' firelocks. [C19 synonyms were *blue pill* (English) and *blue whistler* (American). F.]

BLUE SKIN. A person begotten on a black woman by a white man. One of the blue squadron; any one having a cross of the black breed, or, as it is termed, a lick of the tar brush.

BLUE TAPE, or SKY BLUE. Gin. [By 1860, *blue ruin*. H.]

BLUFF. Fierce, surly. He looked as bluff as bull beef. [In Johnson's and Grose's day, it signified imperious, domineering, blustering. This sense prevailed till 1808, when, in *Marmion*, Scott drew so vivid a picture of 'bluff King Hal' that the present sense almost immediately superseded Johnson's. W:A.— The modern sense has long been current in dialect. EDD.]

BLUFFER. An inn-keeper. *Cant.* [May be connected with dialectal *bluff*=to blindfold (see EDD), and the modern colloquial verb, to deceive by ostentation, and the corresponding noun, an imposition or a 'cheery' deception, probably derive from that dialectal verb. The origin is usually given as United States, but is it? So many English dialectal words emigrate to the U.S. and return to England dressed as Americans, as e.g. *hick*.]

BLUNDERBUSS. A short gun, with a wide bore, for carrying slugs; also a stupid, blundering fellow.

BLUNT. Money. *Cant.* [H learnedly supports the derivation from French *blond*. F & H note three suggested origins: Hotten's; the blunt rim; John Blunt, the chairman of the South Sea Bubble, this last being improbable. G's entry antedates the OD record by sixteen years.]

TO BLUSTER. To talk big, to hector or bully.

BOARDING SCHOOL. Bridewell, Newgate, or any other prison, or house of correction.

BOB. A shoplifter's assistant, or one that receives and carries off stolen goods. All is bob; all is safe. *Cant.*

BOBBED. Cheated, tricked, disappointed. [In Shakespeare, as in Bailey, the verb signifies to cheat.F.]

BOBBISH. Smart, clever, spruce. [Occurs in one of Scott's letters in 1819. F.—In dialect=blithe, cheerful, lively, often 'pretty bobbish.' EDD.]

BOB-STAY. A rope which holds the bowsprit to the stem or cutwater. Figuratively, the frenum of a man's yard.

BOB TAIL. A lewd woman, or one that plays with her tail; also an impotent man, or an eunuch. Tag, rag, and bobtail; a mob of all sorts of low people. To shift one's bob; to move off, or go away. To bear a bob; to join in chorus with any singers. Also a term used by the sellers of game, for a partridge.

BODIES. The foot guards, or king's body guards.

BODY SNATCHERS. Bum bailiffs. [In modern good English, exhumers of corpses for purposes of dissection.—In nautical slang, any member of the ship's police-force.B.]

BODY OF DIVINITY BOUND IN BLACK CALF. A parson.

BOG HOUSE. The necessary house. ["*Bog*, or *bog-house*, a privy, is distinguished from a water-closet. Originally printers' slang, but now very common, and not applied to any particular form of *cabinet d'aisance*. 'To bog' is to ease oneself by evacuation." F.—In modern university slang, especially at Oxford, the term is *the bogs*. The locus classicus on this unpleasing subject is Harington's *Metamorphosis of Ajax*.]

BOG LANDER. An Irishman; Ireland being famous for its large bogs, which furnish the chief fuel in many parts of that kingdom. [The name of an Irishman in Ward's *London Spy*, *ca.* 1700.F.]

BOG TROTTER. The same. [In Miège, who says: 'satirical.' Camden had, long before, used the term of the dwellers or frequenters of the 'debateable land' in the borders of England and Scotland. H.]

BOG LATIN. Barbarous Latin. *Irish.*—See DOG LATIN and APOTHECARIES LATIN.

BOGY. Ask bogy, i.e. ask mine a-se. *Sea wit.*

BOH. Said to be the name of a Danish general, who so terrified his opponent Foh, that he caused him to bewray himself. Whence, when we smell a stink, it is customary to exclaim, Foh! i.e. I smell general Foh. He cannot say Boh to a goose; i.e. he is a cowardly or sheepish fellow.

BOLD. Bold as a miller's shirt, which every day takes a rogue by the collar.

BOLT. A blunt arrow. [Out of place in this dictionary.]

BOLT UPRIGHT. As erect, or strait up, as an arrow set on its end.[Chaucer has the phrase twice; the dialectal equivalent is 'as straight as a bolt.' EDD.]

TO BOLT. To run suddenly out of one's house, or hiding-place, through fear; a term borrowed from a rabbit-warren, where the rabbits are made to bolt, by sending ferrets into their burrows; we set the house on fire, and made him bolt. To bolt, also means to swallow meat without chewing: the farmers' servants in Kent are famous for bolting large quantities of pickled pork. [As=to escape, to run away (quickly), the word appears first in print in 1611.OD.]

BOLTER OF WHITE FRIARS, or THE MINT. One that peeps out, but dares not venture abroad for fear of arrests.

BOLUS. A nick name for an apothecary. [Literally: a big pill.]

BONE BOX. The mouth. Shut your bone-box; shut your mouth.

BONE PICKER. A footman.

BONED. Seized, apprehended, taken up by a constable. *Cant.* [In 1914-1918, among the troops, to be boned=to be arrested by the Military Police ('the Red Caps'); while to bone=to purloin, to steal, 'to make', 'to win.'—Dyche in the 5th edition of his Dictionary, 1748, gives this latter sense, also 'to cheat,' 'to rob.'F]

BONE SETTER. A hard trotting horse.

BOOBY, or DOG BOOBY. An aukward lout, clodhopper, or country fellow. See CLODHOPPER and LOUT.—A bitch booby; a country wench.

BOOBY HUTCH. A one-horse chaise, noddy, buggy, or leathern bottle. [In dialect, any clumsy carriage; also a simpleton. EDD.]

BOOK-KEEPER. One who never returns borrowed books. Out of one's books; out of one's favour.

BOOSE, or BOUSE. Drink. [The oldest forms are *bouse* and *boose* and *bouze*; *booze* (the modern spelling) had appeared by 1714. As=a drinking bout, it is first seen in Ainsworth's *Rookwood*, 1834. As a verb it goes back to 1300. The noun began as cant.F.—Very common in dialect and slang.EDD.]

BOOSEY. Drunk. [Earlier spellings (as in Skelton, Greene, Ben Jonson, Dryden): *bowsie, bouzy, bowsy, boozy*. F.]

BOOT CATCHER. The servant at an inn whose business it is to clean the boots of the guests.

BOOTS. The youngest officer in a regimental mess, whose duty it is to skink, that is, to stir the fire, snuff the candles, and ring the bell. See SKINK.—To ride in any one's old boots; to marry or keep his cast-off mistress.

BOOTY. To play booty; cheating play, where the player purposely avoids winning. [The phrase is traceable to Awdelay's *The Fraternitye of Vagabondes*, 1561. OD.]

BO-PEEP. One who sometimes hides himself, and sometimes appears publicly abroad, is said to play at bo-peep. Also one who lies perdue, or on the watch.

BORACHIO. A skin for holding wine, commonly a goat's; also a nick name for a drunkard.

BORDE. A shilling. A half borde; sixpence. [Used by Thomas Harman in his invaluable *Caveat or Warening for Common Cursetors;* the four editions 1566, 1567, 1567, 1573. "What Grose's *Dictionary* was to the authors of the earlier part of the (19th) century, Harman's was to the Deckers, and Bromes, and Heads of the seventeenth." H.]

BORDELLO. A bawdy-house. [The word, with variant *bordel,*

was fairly common in the C16-18, when, however, the stock name was *the stews*. This last dates from the C14 and, like *bagnio* later, shows a perversion of the original sense—a special kind of public bath. OD.—For a striking account of such establishments, see ch. viii of E. Beresford Chancellor's *Pleasure Haunts of London*, 1925.]

BORE. A tedious, troublesome man or woman, one who bores the ears of his hearers with an uninteresting tale; a term much in fashion about the years 1780 and 1781. [The *Gradus ad Cantabrigiam* suggests an origin in Greek *baros*, a burden. H.— But undoubtedly a development from Anglo-Saxon *borian*, to pierce; the sense of wearying became established *ca.* 1750.W.]

BORN UNDER A THREEPENNY HALFPENNY PLANET, NEVER TO BE WORTH A GROAT. Said of any person remarkably unsuccessful in his attempts or profession.

BOTCH. A nick name for a taylor.

BOTHERED, or BOTH-EARED. Talked to at both ears by different persons at the same time, confounded, confused. *Irish phrase.* [From an Irish verb and first used by Anglo-Irish writers such as Swift and Sheridan. W.]

BOTHERAMS. A convivial society.

BOTTLE-HEADED. Void of wit.

BOTTOM. A polite term for the posteriors. Also, in the sporting sense, strength and spirits to support fatigue: as a bottomed horse. Among bruisers it is used to express a hardy fellow who will bear a good beating. The bottom of a woman's tu quoque; the crown of her head. [As=posterior, the word passed out of literary usage *ca.* 1860 (Carlyle had it in 1837 in *The French Revolution*); as=capital, resources, it dates back at least as far as 1662 (Fuller's Worthies); as=stamina and/or grit it was 'dignified' by Captain Godfrey in *The Science of Defence*, 1747.F.]

BOTTOMLESS PIT. The monosyllable.

BOUGHS. He is up in the boughs; he is in a passion.

TO BOUNCE. To brag or hector; also to tell an improbable story. [As=to tell a lie, suitably sponsored by Foote's play *The Liar*, 1762; as=to bully, no less suitably in Fletcher's *Night Walker*, 1626; and as a noun=a brag or a falsehood, most suitably of all in Steele's *Lover*, 1714, F.—Originally cant. H.—In 1888, the verb meant to scold roundly. OD.]

BOUNCER. A large man or woman; also a great lie. [In C18, also=an habitual liar, a bully. F.]

BOUNCING CHEAT. A bottle; from the explosion in drawing the cork. *Cant.*

BOUNG. A purse. *Cant.* [A frequent spelling was *bung.* Very old cant, origin unknown, but its resemblance to old English *pung*, a purse, probably gives the clue. OD.—*Bung* (cf. next entry) also, in C16-17, meant a pickpocket (itself of C16 origin). F.]

BOUNG NIPPER. A cut-purse. *Cant.*—Formerly purses were worn at the girdle, from whence they were cut.

BOWSING KEN. An ale-house or gin-shop.

BOWSPRIT. The nose, from its being the most projecting part of the human face, as the bowsprit is of a ship.

BOW-WOW. The childish name for a dog; also a jeering appellation for a man born at Boston in America. [As=dog, 'dignified' by Cooper in his poem *The Beau's Reply.* F.]

BOW-WOW MUTTON. Dog's flesh.

BOW-WOW SHOP. A salesman's shop in Monmouth-street; so called because the servant barks and the master bites. See BARKER.

BOWYER. One that draws a long bow, a dealer in the marvellous, a teller of improbable stories, a liar: perhaps from the wonderful shots frequently boasted of by archers.

TO BOX THE COMPASS. To say or repeat the mariner's compass, not only backwards or forwards, but also to be able to answer any and all questions respecting its divisions. *Sea term.* [The phrase appears in Smollet's *Peregrine Pickle*, 1751. F.]

TO BOX THE JESUIT, and GET COCK ROACHES. A sea term for masturbation; a crime, it is said, much practised by the reverend fathers of that society.

BRACE. The brace tavern; a room in the S.E. corner of the King's Bench, where, for the convenience of prisoners residing thereabouts, beer purchased at the tap-house was retailed at a halfpenny per pot advance. It was kept by two brothers of the name of Partridge, and thence called the *Brace.*

BRACKET-FACED. Ugly, hard-featured.

BRAGGET. Mead and ale sweetened with honey. [In dialect =honey and ale fermented together; also new ale sugar-spiced. *Bragget-Sunday*, on which, until perhaps 1890, bragget was ceremoniously drunk, was the fourth Sunday in Lent. EDD.]

BRAGGADOCIO. A vain-glorious fellow, a boaster. [Like its sympathetic *blatant*, invented by Spenser. W:A.]

BRAINS. If you had as much brains as guts, what a clever fellow you would be! a saying to a stupid fat fellow. To have some guts in his brains; to know something.

BRAN-FACED. Freckled. He was christened by a baker, he carries the bran in his face. [Cf. the dialectal *bran-in-the-face*= freckles. EDD.]

BRANDY-FACED. Red-faced, as if from drinking brandy. [From the earlier *brandy-face*, a drunkard, a term occurring in 1687 in Charles Cotton. F.]

BRANDY. Brandy is Latin for a goose; a memento to prevent the animal from rising in the stomach by a glass of the good creature.

["What is Latin for a goose?" *Anser*.

    Answer: *brandy*, brandy following goose as quickly as answer follows question. A later variant is *Brandy is Latin for fish*, tentatively explained in Mayhew's *London Labour and London Poor*, 1851. F.]

BRAT. A child or infant. [Pejorative.]

BRAY. A vicar of Bray; one who frequently changes his principles, always siding with the strongest party: an allusion to a vicar of Bray, in Berkshire, commemorated in a well-known ballad for the pliability of his conscience. [Two miles from Taplow is this village, which has been described by Frank Binder, in *A Journey in England*, 1931, as "one of the lingering yesterdays of Southern England. It offers nothing to the eye of the approaching traveller save plain fields, ambling paths, and a vacant river. But Bray has traditions, and though by vicarious fame it is known for pendulum opinions, fluctuating faiths, and elastic loyalties, it has been left up to our own day unaffected by fashion and unruffled by the rush of reformations and of years. .... The ancient vicar was not without excuse, and no one need wonder why he lived on in the fullness of his beliefs and died finally in the emptiness of his days." He lived in the reigns of Henry VIII, Edward VI, Mary, Elizabeth: papist, protestant, papist, protestant: accused of fickleness, he replied, "No, I am steadfast; however other people change, I remain Vicar of Bray."]

BRAZEN-FACED. Bold-faced, shameless, impudent.

BREAD AND BUTTER FASHION. One slice upon the other. John and his maid were caught lying bread and butter fashion.—To quarrel with one's bread and butter; to act contrary to one's interest. To know on which side one's bread is buttered; to know one's interest, or what is best for one. It is no bread and butter of mine; I have no business with it; or rather, I won't intermeddle, because I shall get nothing by it.

BREAD AND BUTTER WAREHOUSE. Ranelagh. ["An allusion to the scenes of infamy and debauchery which once characterised the place."F.—Vauxhall, having begun its career as the resort of fashion in 1728 and in its improved state in 1732, lasted till 1841: Ranelagh, opening in April 1742 and closing in July 1803, outshone Vauxhall until *ca.* 1775 and again from *ca.* 1790 to 1798. For an amusing satire, see Joseph Warton's *Ranelagh House*, 1747. A lucid description of both places is to be found in Chancellor's *Pleasure Haunts of London* and in his *XVIIIth Century in London.*]

BREAD. Employment. Out of bread; out of employment. In bad bread; in a disagreeable scrape, or situation.

BREAD BASKET. The stomach; a term used by boxers. I took him a punch in his bread basket; i.e. I gave him a blow in the stomach. [Occurs in Foote's entertaining *Englishman in Paris*, 1753. F.—Variants in the old boxing days, says H in 1860, were *dumpling-depot, victualling-office,* while blows to this part were called *porridge-disturbers.*]

BREAKING SHINS. Borrowing money; perhaps from the figurative operation being, like the real one, extremely disagreeable to the patient.

BREAK-TEETH WORDS. Hard words, difficult to pronounce.

BREAST FLEET. He or she belongs to the breast fleet; i.e. is a Roman Catholic; an appellation derived from their custom of beating their breasts in the confession of their sins.

BREECHES. To wear the breeches; a woman who governs her husband is said to wear the breeches. [As early as 1553. OD. —In French, 1450.F.—Shakespeare has it.O.]

BREECHES BIBLE. An edition of the bible printed in 1598. wherein it is said that Adam and Eve sewed fig-leaves together. and made themselves breeches.

BREEZE. To raise a breeze; to kick up a dust or breed a disturbance. [As=quarrel, disturbance, it is common in dialect. The obvious explanation is that breeze=wind; just possibly, however, the sense comes from the dialectal *breeze* or *breese*, a gadfly. EDD.]

BREWES, or **BROWES.** The fat scum from the pot in which salted beef is boiled.

BRIDGE. To make a bridge of any one's nose; to push the bottle past him, so as to deprive him of his turn of filling his glass; to pass one over.

BRIM. (Abbreviation of Brimstone.) An abandoned woman; perhaps originally only a passionate or irascible woman, compared to brimstone for its inflammability. [May be influenced by the dialectal verb brim, which, as applied to swine,=to be in heat, to copulate. (EDD).]

BRISKET BEATER. A Roman catholic. See **BREAST FLEET** and **CRAW THUMPER.**

BRISTOL MILK. A Spanish wine called sherry, much drunk at that place, particularly in the morning. [Originated in C17, the phrase occurs in Fuller's *Worthies*, 1662, and attains the stability of a museum piece in Macaulay's *History of England*.F.]

BROGANIER. One who has a strong Irish pronunciation or accent.

BROGUE. A particular kind of shoe without a heel, worn in Ireland, and figuratively used to signify the Irish accent.

BROTHER OF THE BLADE. A soldier.

BROTHER OF THE BUSKIN. A player.

BROTHER OF THE BUNG. A brewer.

BROTHER OF THE COIF. A serjeant at law.

BROTHER OF THE GUSSET. A pimp.

BROTHER OF THE QUILL. An author.

BROTHER OF THE STRING. A fiddler.

BROTHER OF THE WHIP. A coachman.

BROTHER STARLING. One who lies with the same woman, that is, builds in the same nest.

BROUGHTONIAN. A boxer: a disciple of Broughton, who was a beef-eater, and once the best boxer of his day. [In December 1734 Broughton took over Figg's Theatre, which, better known as the Boarded House, stood at the East corner of Euston Road and Tottenham Court Road; he there had much success with the boxing matches that he promoted. In 1747, though he had retired from the Ring some years earlier, he there fought and was beaten by John Slack, and soon after this he retired into private life. His bust was set up in the famous Cock and Pye tavern in Rathbone Place. Chancellor's *London's Old Latin Quarter*.]

BROWN BESS. A soldier's firelock. To hug brown Bess; to carry a firelock, or serve as a private soldier. [G's is the earliest mention, though *brown musquet* occurs in 1708. *Bess* may be Dutch *bus*, the barrel of a gun; *bus* survives in *arquebuse* and in *blunderbuss*. F. — "More probably a personal name." W. The gun had a brown stock.—An old variant was *black Bess*. H.]

BROWN GEORGE. An ammunition loaf. [As ammunition loaf, the term occurs in Urquhart's *Rabelais* in 1653, in Dryden's *Persius* in 1693. F.— "The old Navy name for bread supplied by contract. Also called Munition Bread (presumably the origin of G's definition). In the Merchant Service it was a particularly hard and coarse ship's biscuit." B.—Cf. the entry at *Tommy*, and see my essay, "Some Soldiers' Slang with a Past," in *The Quarterly Review*, April 1931. —As=a brown wig, it became popular *ca.* 1780, George III wearing such a wig. As=a jug (usually of brown earthenware), it belongs to C19.F.—All three senses exist in dialect, with variant form *Geordie*, and there, the bread was made of barley and rye and leavened with a piece of left-over soft dough. EDD.]

BROWN MADAM, or MISS BROWN. The monosyllable.

BROWN STUDY. Said of one absent, in a reverie, or thoughtful.

BRUISER. A boxer, one skilled in the art of boxing; also an inferior workman among chasers. [*Bruiser* and *Bruising* (boxing) both achieved print *ca.* 1750. OD.]

BRUISING, or rather BREWISING, THE BED. Bewraying the bed; from BREWES [*q.v.*]

TO BRUSH. To run away. Let us buy a brush and lope; let us go away or off. To have a brush with a woman; to lie with her. To have a brush with a man; to fight with him. [The verb arose in C17; cf. "With that he rose up and brushed off."D.— As=a hasty departure, in *Tom Jones;* as=a hasty decamper, in Dyche's *Dictionary*, 5th ed., 1748.F.—In Shakespeare, *brush* =a hostile encounter (O), while dialect shows that the three noun-meanings quoted by G are developments of the old dialectal *brush*, a struggle, a tussle.EDD.]

BRUSHER. A bumper, a full glass. See BUMPER.

BUB. Strong beer. [In Head's *English Rogue*, 1671. The word is either onomatopoeic or a derivative of Latin *bibere*, to drink. Used as a verb in C17, when also, as in C18, there existed *bubbing*, tippling. OD; F.—These two words are cant.]

BUBBER. A drinking bowl; also a great drinker; a thief that steals plate from public houses. *Cant.*

THE BUBBLE. The party cheated, perhaps from his being like an air bubble, filled with words, which are only wind, instead of real property. [Shakespeare, 1598; Shadwell, 1688; Swift (1711): "We are thus became the dupes and bubbles of Europe." One of the latest instances: T. Barrington's most interesting book, *The New London Spy*, 1805.F.]

TO BUBBLE. To cheat. [As early as Etherege's *Comical Revenge*, 1664, and as late as McCarthy's *Own Times*, 1880.F.]

TO BAR THE BUBBLE. To except against the general rule, that he who lays the odds must always be adjudged the loser; this is restricted to betts laid for liquor.

BUBBLY JOCK. A turkey-cock. *Scotch.* ["Probably in allusion to the cry of the bird," it meant also, in C19, a stupid bragger, a prig, a cad. F.—Found also in Northumberland and Cumberland before it was adopted into general slang and, *ca.* 1840, shortened frequently to *bubbly.* EDD.—The entry in G (the first edition has it) antedates that in OD by 29 years.]

BUBBLE & SQUEAK. Beef and cabbage fried together. It is so called from its bubbling up and squeaking whilst over the fire.

BUBE. The venereal disease.

BUCK. A blind horse; also a gay debauchee. [In the latter sense a development from *buck,* the male of the fallow deer. At first it denoted "a forward daring person of either sex" (*New Canting Dictionary,* 1725); then a man of spirit or one of gay conduct, as in Fielding's *Amelia;* then a gay debauchee; then, in early C19, as a fop. F.]

TO RUN A BUCK. To poll a bad vote at an election. *Irish term.*

BUCK BAIL. Bail given by a sharper for one of the gang.

A BUCK OF THE FIRST HEAD. One who in debauchery surpasses the rest of his companions, a blood or choice spirit. There are in London divers lodges or societies of Bucks, formed in imitation of the Free Masons: one was held at the Rose, in Monkwell-street, about the year 1750. The president is styled the Grand Buck.—A buck sometimes signifies a cuckold.

BUCK'S FACE. A cuckold.

BUCK FITCH. A lecherous old fellow. [*Fitch,* here, presumably means polecat, but the origin of the term is obscure.]

BUCKEEN. A bully. *Irish.* [Properly a young man belonging to the poorer Irish aristocracy. F.—Properly the word=a young dandy, derivatively from that of a well-to-do farmer; the *een* is the Irish diminutive suffix as in *squireen.* EDD.]

BUCKET. To kick the bucket; to die. [Peter Pindar, *Tristia,* 1796, has "Pitt has kicked the bucket." F.]

BUCKINGER'S BOOT. The monosyllable. Matthew Buckinger was born without hands and legs; notwithstanding which he drew coats of arms very neatly, and could write the Lord's Prayer within the compass of a shilling: he was married to a tall handsome woman, and traversed the country, shewing himself for money.

BUDGE, or SNEAKING BUDGE. One that slips into houses in the dark, to steal cloaks or other clothes. Also lambs' fur, formerly used for doctors' robes, whence they were called budge doctors. Standing budge; a thief's scout or spy. [*Budge* defined by Head in 1671 as a stealer of cloaks; *sneaking budge* occurs in Fielding. F.—Related perhaps is Southern dialectal adjective *budge*, grave, solemn. EDD.]

TO BUDGE. To move, or quit one's station. Don't budge from hence; i.e. don't move from hence, stay here.[Cf. Shakespeare's *budger*, one who flinches. O.—An old cant phrase was *budge-a-beak*, originally to run away from a policeman, i.e. from justice, then simply to run away. F.

BUDGET. A wallet. To open the budget; a term used to signify the notification of the taxes required by the minister for the expences of the ensuing year; as, To-morrow the minister will go to the house, and open the budget.

BUFE. A dog. Bufe's nob; a dog's head. *Cant.* [In Harman. From the sound of the bark. OD.]

BUFE NABBER. A dog stealer. *Cant.*

BUFF. All in buff; stript to the skin, stark naked. [In allusion to the colour. Originally *buffalo;* Cotgrave defines French *buffle* as "the buffe, buffle, bugle, or wild oxe." W.]

BUFF. To stand buff; to stand the brunt. [The phrase was used by Butler, 1680.F.—From the dialectal and old English *buff*, a blow, which seems to come from Low German. EDD.—Cf. *buffet, buffeting* (e.g. of the waves).]

BUFFER. One that steals and kills horses and dogs for their skins; also an inn-keeper: in Ireland it signifies a boxer. [The old cant *buffer*=dog is a false scent. To W's terse summary:— "In ME. stammerer, in Scottish foolish fellow, in obsolete slang suborned witness," one may add that *ca.* 1750 *buffer*=a mean fellow and that, like *codger* and *geezer*, it is very frequently associated with old age. As=a boxer, presumably from *buff*, a blow.]

BUFFLE-HEADED. Confused, stupid. [Pepys, 1663, and as late as Baring Gould, 1883. The noun *buffle-head* originated in early C17 and amplifies *buffle*, *bufle*, a fool (Fr. *buffle*), which occurs as early as 1580.F.—Wright suggested derivation from Dutch *buffel*, blockhead.]

BUG. A nick name given by the Irish to Englishmen; bugs having, as it is said, been introduced into Ireland by the English.

TO BUG. A cant word among journeymen hatters, signifying the exchanging some of the dearest materials of which a hat is made for others of less value. Hats are composed of the furs and wools of divers animals, among which is a small portion of bevers' fur. Bugging, is stealing the bever, and substituting in lieu thereof, an equal weight of some cheaper ingredient.— Bailiffs who take money to postpone or refrain the serving of a writ, are said to bug the writ.

BUG-HUNTER. An upholsterer. [In C19 slang, a robber of the drunk. EDD.]

BUGABOO, A scare-babe, or bully-beggar. [Cf. the Shakespearean *bug*, hobgoblin, bogey, imaginary object of terror. O.]

BUGAROCH. Comely, handsome. *Irish.*

BUGGY. A one-horse chaise.

BUGHER. A little yelping dog. [Cf. *buffer* and *bufe*, both=a dog.OD.]

BULK AND FILE. Two pickpockets; the bulk jostles the party to be robbed, and the file does the business. [*Cant.* Recorded in Head's *Canting Academy*, 1674. F.]

BULKER. One who lodges all night on a bulk or projection before old-fashioned shop-windows. [The word early got the meaning of a low, homeless prostitute (Shadwell, 1691); the 1790 edition of Bailey comments thus: "One who would lie down on a bulk to anyone." F.]

BULL. An Exchange Alley term for one who buys stock on speculation for time, i.e. agrees with the seller, called a Bear, to take a certain sum of stock at a future day, at a stated price:

58

if at that day stock fetches more than the price agreed on, he receives the difference; if it falls, or is cheaper, he either pays it, or becomes a lame duck, and waddles out of the Alley. See LAME DUCK and BEAR. [Used by Cibber in *The Refusal*. F.]

BULL. A blunder; from one Obadiah Bull, a blundering lawyer of London, who lived in the reign of Henry VII; by a bull, is now always meant a blunder made by an Irishman. A bull was also the name of false hair formerly much worn by women. To look like bull beef, or as bluff as bull beef; to look fierce or surly. Town bull, a great whore-master. [Milton, 1642, has *bull*, blunder. F.—Earlier=jest and not at first associated with Ireland. Obadiah Bull is an invention. W.]

BULL BEGGAR, or BULLY BEGGAR. An imaginary being with which children are threatened by servants and nurses, like raw head and bloody bones. [Early forms of bugbear (1581). *Bull-beggar* is recorded for 1584, *bully beggar* for C18; earliest of all, apparently, is *bull-bear*, 1561. OD.]

BULL CALF. A great hulkey or clumsy fellow. See HULKEY. [In C16-17, the term was abusive for a big, blustering fellow. O.]

BULL CHIN. A fat chubby child.

BULL DOGS. Pistols. [Farquhar's *Constant Couple*, 1699. F.]

BULL'S EYE. A crown piece.

BULL'S FEATHER. A horn: he wears the bull's feather; he is a cuckold. [Cf. the C17 song thus entitled and the French phrase, *planter des plumes de bœuf*. F.]

TO BULLOCK. To hector, bounce, or bully. [Recorded for 1716. F.—Cf. the Kentish *bullying*=strutting. P.—In dialect, too, *bullocky*=swaggering. EDD.]

BULLY. A cowardly fellow, who gives himself airs of great bravery. A bully huff cap; a hector. See HECTOR.

BULLY BACK. A bully to a bawdy-house; one who is kept in pay, to oblige the frequenters of the house to submit to the impositions of the mother abbess, or bawd; and who also sometimes pretends to be the husband of one of the ladies, and under that pretence extorts money from greenhorns, or ignorant

59

young men, whom he finds with her. See GREENHORN. [Employed by Amherst in 1726.F.]

BULLY COCK. One who foments quarrels in order to rob the persons quarrelling.

BULLY RUFFIANS. Highwaymen who attack passengers with oaths and imprecations.

BULLY TRAP. A brave man, with a mild or effeminate appearance, by whom bullies are frequently taken in.

BUM. The breech, or backside. [As early as 1387: Trevisa, spelling it *bom*. Also: Shakespeare, 1592; Dekker, 1600; Jonson, 1614; Swift, 1729; Shenstone, 1742; Wolcot (Peter Pindar), 1782. OD; F.—In C20 rather a schoolboy's than a man's word. It is also short (as in *Hudibras*, 1663) for *bum-bailiff*, and means, further, to arrest. EDD.]

BUM BAILIFF. A sheriff's officer, who arrests debtors; so called perhaps from following his prey, and being at their bums, or, as the vulgar phrase is, hard at their a-ses. Blackstone says, it is a corruption of bound bailiff, from their being obliged to give bond for their good behaviour. [Is in Shakespeare *bum bailey*. F.]

BUM BRUSHER. A schoolmaster. [Occurs in the versatile and shady T. Brown in 1704.F.]

BUM BOAT. A boat attending ships to retail greens, drams, &c. commonly rowed by a woman; a kind of floating chandler's shop. [At first, C17, sailor's slang for scavenger boat.W.]

BUM FODDER. Soft paper for the necessary house or torchecul. [Urquhart, 1653.F.—In 1914-1918 much used by officers in abbreviation *bumf*, which was a pre-War public school term.]

BUMFIDDLE. The backside, the breech. See ARS MUSICA.

BUMBO. Brandy, water, and sugar; also the negro name for the private parts of a woman. [Smollett, 1748, describes the drink as composed of rum, sugar, water and nutmeg.F.—For rum, gin was occasionally substituted. EDD.]

BUMKIN. A raw country fellow. [A common C18 spelling. First recorded, there spelt *bunkin*, in Levins, *Manipulus Vocabulorum*, 1570. OD.—Probably a diminutive of Dutch *boom*, a tree, log. W.]

BUMMED. Arrested.

BUMPER. A full glass; in all likelihood from its convexity or bump at the top: some derive it from a full glass formerly drunk to the health of the pope—*au bon père*.

BUMPING. A ceremony performed on boys perambulating the bounds of the parish on Whit-monday; when they have their posteriors bumped against the stones marking the boundaries, in order to fix them in their memory.

BUN. A common name for a rabbit, also for the monosyllable. To touch bun for luck; a practice observed among sailors going on a cruize. [For a rabbit used only in vocative, whence *bunny*. EDD.]

BUNDLING. A man and woman sleeping in the same bed, he with his small cloths, and she with her petticoats on; an expedient practised in America on a scarcity of beds, where, on such an occasion, husbands and parents frequently permitted travellers to bundle with their wives and daughters. [In America the practice, strangely enough, prevailed only in New England, but it existed also in Wales till *ca.* 1870. In Cumberland and Westmorland, however, the word was applied to another practice: that of a betrothed couple going to bed together in their clothes (see John Brand's *Popular Antiquities*, but the practice persisted long after Brand's day). EDD.—Washington Irving comments on the custom of bundling, American style, in his *Knickerbocker History of New York*, 1809. For notable accounts see W.H. Dixon's *Spiritual Wives*, 1866, and H. R. Styles' *Bundling, its Origin, Progress, and Decline.* F.—Consult also the authoritative histories of *a*) marriage, *b*) morals.]

BUNG UPWARDS. Said of a person lying on his face.

BUNG YOUR EYE. Drink a dram; strictly speaking, to drink till one's eye is bunged up or closed.

BUNT. An apron.

TO BUNT. To run against or jostle. [A colloquial extension of the good-English sense: to push, butt, or strike with the head, horns, or feet. EDD.]

BUNTER. A low dirty prostitute, half whore and half beggar. [Contemptuous too for any low woman. In Ward's *Hudibras*

Redivivus we find the phrase: "Punks, strollers, market dames, and bunters." T. Dyche in his *Dictionary*, edition of 1748, defines however as: "one who goes about the streets to gather rags, bones, etc." and Mayhew in *London Labour and London Poor* bears this out. F.—Probably such prostitutes, in hard times, had recourse to the rag-and-bone trade: and *vice versa*.]

BUNTLINGS. Petticoats. *Cant.*

BURN CRUST. A jocular name for a baker.

BURN THE KEN. Strollers living in an alehouse without paying their quarters, are said to burn the ken. *Cant.* [In thieves' cant, burn=thieve, and ken=inn, tavern, or generically a place. F.]

BURNING THE PARADE. Warning more men for a guard than were necessary, and excusing the supernumeraries for money. This was a practice formerly winked at in most garrisons, and was a very considerable perquisite to the adjutants and serjeant majors; the pretence for it was, to purchase coal and candle for the guard, whence it was called burning the parade.

BURNING SHAME. A lighted candle stuck into the parts of a woman, certainly not intended by nature for a candlestick.

BURNER. He is no burner of navigable rivers; i.e. he is no conjurer, or man of extraordinary abilities; or rather, he is but a simple fellow. See THAMES.

BURNT. Poxed or clapped. He was sent out a sacrifice, and came home a burnt offering; a saying of seamen who have caught the venereal disease abroad. He has burnt his fingers; he has suffered by meddling. [Shakespeare in *King Lear* has the pun: "No heretics burn'd but wenches' suitors." F.]

BURR. A hanger on, or dependant: an allusion to the field burrs, which are not easily got rid of. Also the Northumbrian pronunciation: the people of that country, but chiefly about Newcastle and Morpeth, are said to have a burr in their throats, particularly called the Newcastle burr.

BUSHEL BUBBY. A full-breasted woman.

BUSK. A piece of whalebone or ivory, formerly worn by women, to stiffen the fore part of their stays: hence the toast—

Both ends of the busk. [Whence, possibly, the C19 slang verb *busk*, to sell obscene songs. H.]

BUSS BEGGAR. An old superannuated fumbler, whom none but beggars will suffer to kiss them.

BUS-NAPPER. A constable. *Cant.*

BUS-NAPPER'S KENCHIN. A watchman. *Cant.*

BUSY. As busy as the devil in a high wind; as busy as a hen with one chick.

BUTCHER. A jocular exclamation used at sea, or by soldiers on a march, when one of their comrades falls down; and means —Butcher! butcher! where are you? here is a calf that has the staggers, and wants bleeding.

BUTCHER'S DOG. To be like a butcher's dog, i.e. lie by the beef without touching it; a simile often applicable to married men.

BUTCHER'S MEAT. Meat taken up on trust, which continues the butcher's till paid for.

BUTCHER'S HORSE. That must have been a butcher's horse, by his carrying a calf so well; a vulgar joke on an awkward rider.

BUTT. A dependant, poor relation, or simpleton, on whom all kinds of practical jokes are played off: and who serves as a butt for all the shafts of wit and ridicule.

BUTTER. A butter; an inch of butter, that commodity being sold at Cambridge by the yard, in rolls of about an inch diameter. The word is used plurally, as—Send me a roll and two butters.

BUTTER BOX. A Dutchman, from the great quantity of butter eaten by the people of that country. [Variant *butter-bag.* For the former, Dekker's *Gentle Craft*, 1600; for the latter, Howell's *Familiar Letters*, 1650. F.]

TO BUTTER A BET. To double or treble it.

BUTTERED BUN. One lying with a woman that has just lain with another man, is said to have a buttered bun. [Used absolutely, *buttered bun*=a mistress, or a prostitute: see W. Cullen's *Flock of Court Misses*, 1679. F.]

BUTTER TEETH. Large broad fore teeth. [In dialect, the upper front teeth; derivatively, broad yellow teeth. EDD.]

BUTTER AND EGGS TROT. A kind of short jogg trot, such as is used by women going to market, with butter and eggs. —She looks as if butter would not melt in her mouth, yet I warrant you cheese would not choak her; a saying of a demure looking woman, of suspected character. Don't make butter dear; a gird at the patient angler. [*Butter and eggs*, meaning such a trot, survived till late in C19. The earliest example of *to look . . . one's mouth* is in 1530, while the first of G's fuller saying is in Swift. F.—Cheese was a synonym of *mettle, spunk*.]

BUTTOCK. A whore. *Cant*. [Head's *Canting Academy*, 1674; Shadwell's *Squire of Alsatia*, 1688. F.—In the old days, the fine exacted by the ecclesiastical courts for fornication was ridiculed in the name *buttock-mail*, the *mail* being the same as in *blackmail*. EDD.]

BUTTOCK BROKER. A bawd, or match-maker. *Cant*.

BUTTOCK BALL. The amorous congress. *Cant*. [Cf. *buttock banquetting*, harlotry. The term was also applied to a dance attended by prostitutes; cf. the phrase *ballum rancum, buff ball*. In 1880, Greenwood in *Strange Company* has this description: "The most favourite entertainment at this place is known as buff-ball, in which both sexes—innocent of clothes—madly join, stimulated with raw whiskey, and the music of a fiddle and a tin whistle." F.]

BUTTOCK AND FILE. A common whore and a pickpocket. *Cant*. [Used both of a woman combining these activities and of a prostitute and her pickpocket companion. Cf. *bulk and file, q.v.* F.]

BUTTOCK AND TWANG, or A DOWN BUTTOCK AND SHAM FILE. A common whore, but no pickpocket. [Also cant.]

BUTTON. A bad shilling, among coiners. His a-se makes buttons; he is ready to bewray himself through fear. *Cant*. [A derivative sense was that of a decoy. F.]

BUZMAN. A pickpocket. *Cant*. [Perhaps connected with *buz* (*z*), to move hurriedly. EDD.—C19 variants were *buz-bloke* and *buzzer*. H.—For a pertinent comment see H. Mayhew's *Great World of London*, 1856. F.—Mayhew's books, by the way, are invaluable for their pictures of London life in mid-C19, and one of them is being edited by the present writer and a friend.]

BUZZA. To buzza one, is to challenge him to pour out all the wine in the bottle into his glass, undertaking to drink it, should it prove more than the glass will hold: it is commonly said to one who hesitates to empty a bottle that is nearly out. Some derive it from *bouze all*, i.e. drink it all.

BUZZARD. A simple fellow. A blind buzzard; a purblind man or woman. ["The derived figurative sense of 'simpleton' is supposed by some to be represented in Shakespeare, *The Taming of the Shrew*, II, i, 207." O. But as O remarks, the word may there mean a buzzing insect.—In C19 dialect, a coward, especially one afraid in the dark. EDD.]

BYE BLOW. A bastard. [As in Barnfield's *Affectionate Shepherd*, 1594. Common C17 variants were *by-chop* (Ben Jonson, 1632) and *by-slip* (Hacket's *Life of Williams*, 1692).OD; F.— Dialectal variants were *bye-begit*, *bye-child*, *bye-come*, *bye-leap*, *bye-wipe*, in which *by-* is often used, as in *by-chap*, an illegitimate son. EDD.]

CABALLARIANS. The very honourable order of Caballarians was held at the Magpye Tavern, without Bishopsgate.

CABBAGE. Cloth, stuff, or silk, purloined by taylors from their employers, which they deposit in a place called *hell*, or their *eye:* from the first, when taxed with their knavery, they equivocally swear, that if they have taken any, they wish they may find it in *hell;* or, alluding to the second, protest, that what they have over and above is not more than they could put in their *eye.*—When the scrotum is relaxed or whiffled, it is said they will not cabbage.

CACAFEUGO. A sh-te-fire, a furious braggadocio or bully huff. [Properly *cacafuego*. In the earliest example (perhaps a reminiscence of the fact that in 1577 Drake captured a Spanish galleon of that name), Fletcher's *Fair Maid*, 1625, it appears as *cacafugo*. OD.]

CACKLE. To blab, or discover secrets. The cull is leaky, and cackles; the rogue tells all. *Cant.*—See LEAKY. [In C19 theatrical slang, a *cackling cove* was an actor. H.]

CACKLERS KEN. A hen roost. *Cant.* [*Cacklers* is given by Head; Bailey sets aside the suggestion of cant and defines it as "a humorous word for capons or fowl." F.]

CACKLING CHEATS. Fowls. *Cant.* [In C20 American tramp and underworld slang, both *cackleberry* and *cackler*=an egg.I.]

CACKLING FARTS. Eggs. *Cant.*

CAFFAN. Cheese. *Cant.* [This should be either *cassan* or *cassam*. H.—Harman has *cassan*, and other variants were *casum* and *casson*. OD; F. Ultimately from L. *caseus*, cheese.—In Romany, *cas*, "used by the hikers or tramps, as well as by the Gypsies." G.B.]

CAGG. To cagg; a military term used by the private soldiers, signifying a solemn vow or resolution not to get drunk for a certain time; or, as the term is, till their cagg is out; which vow is commonly observed with the strictest exactness. Ex. I have cagg'd myself for six months. Excuse me this time, and I will cagg myself for a year. This term is also used in the same sense among the common people of Scotland, where it is performed with divers ceremonies. [*Cag* is almost certainly a development from the old and widely-known dialectal verb *cag*, to annoy, vex, grieve. (EDD.)—"A sea argument—often described as dogmatic assertion followed by flat contradiction and personal abuse."B.]

CAGG MAGGS. Old Lincolnshire geese, which having been plucked ten or twelve years, are sent up to London to feast the cockneys. [Usually *cag-mags*. The practice was mentioned by Pennant in his *Tour in Scotland*, 1774. In C19 the word came to mean refuse or rubbish or odds and ends. *Cag-mag* also signified a plain or dirty woman.F.—Hotten's suggestion that *cag-mag* was originally university slang for a bad cook, Gr. *kakos mageiros*, may be dismissed as ingenious.—In dialect (where

66

spelt also *keg-meg*) the term had five chief meanings, the one leading to the rest: tough old goose; tough inferior meat; bad, unwholesome food; refuse, anything worthless; a term of opprobrium applied to persons. As a dialectal adjective: coarse, inferior, mongrel, spurious. EDD.]

CAKE, or CAKEY. A foolish fellow.

CALF-SKIN FIDDLE. A drum.—To smack calf's-skin; to kiss the book in taking an oath. It is held by the St Giles's casuist that by kissing one's thumb instead of smacking calf's skin, the guilt of taking a false oath is avoided.

CALIBOGUS. Rum and spruce beer, an American beverage.

CALLE. A cloak or gown. *Cant.*

CALVES. His calves are gone to grass; a saying of a man with slender legs without calves. Veal will be cheap, calves fall; said of a man whose calves fall away.

CALVES HEAD CLUB. A club instituted by the Independents and Presbyterians, to commemorate the decapitation of King Charles I. Their chief fare was calves heads; and they drank their wine and ale out of calves sculls. [There is an interesting chapter on this actually harmless club in *The Club Life of London*, 2 vols., 1866, by John Timbs, who states that it had ceased to exist by or before 1735.]

CAMBRIDGE FORTUNE. A wind-mill and a water-mill, used to signify a woman without any but personal endowments.

CAMBRIDGE OAK. A willow. [Willows abounding in that county; cf. *Cambridgeshire nightingale*=frog. F.]

CAMERADE. A chamber fellow; a Spanish military term. Soldiers were in that country divided into chambers, five men making a chamber, whence it was generally used to signify companion. [The word links up with Ger. *Kamerad*, the entreaty for mercy employed by German prisoners in 1914-1918. Cf. too the use of Fr. *chambrée*.]

CAMESA. A shirt or shift. *Cant, Spanish*. [From Sp. *camisa* or It. *camicia*, as we see by the C17 forms: *camesa, camisa, camise, camiscia, kemesa*. F.]

CAMP CANDLESTICK. A bottle, or soldier's bayonet.

CAMPBELL'S ACADEMY. The hulks or lighters, on board

of which felons are condemned to hard labour. Mr Campbell was the first director of them. See ACADEMY and FLOATING ACADEMY. [See G. Parker's very readable *View of Society*, 1781.]

CANARY BIRD. A jail bird, a person used to be kept in a cage; also, in the canting sense, guineas.

CANDLESTICKS. Bad, small, or untunable bells. Hark! how the candlesticks rattle.

CANDY. Drunk. *Irish*. [Not in EDD.]

CANE. To lay Cane upon Abel; to beat any one with a cane or stick.

CANK. Dumb. [Obsolete before 1897. But in dialect *cank* survives as to cackle (of geese), hence to talk rapidly, to gabble, gossip, chatter. EDD.]

CANNIKEN. A small can; also in the canting, sense, the plague.

CANT. An hypocrite, a double-tongued palavering fellow. See PALLAVER. [From Old Northern French *cant=chant=* singing; "hence the whining speech of beggars; in C17-18 the secret jargon of the criminal and vagabond classes. Modern sense (humbug) springs from hostile application of the term to phraseology of certain sects and groups," doubtless from the offence given by their tendency to whine. "*Canting arms* (heraldry) are punning or allusive; cf. Fr. *armes parlantes*." Harman's *Caveat*, 1567, has *canting* in the sense of thieves' slang. This admirable summary, lifted from Professor Weekley's *Dictionary*, serves as the best jumping-off place. *Canting*, as applied to the whining enunciation, existed long before the time of Andrew Cant and his son Oliver: see Pennant, *Tour in Scotland*, I, 122. *Canting Crew* originated about 1650, *canters* about 1600; *canting* for the use of a special phraseology is first recorded in Ben Jonson, 1625; *cant* =thieves' jargon, in Phillips, 1706; *cant* as a special phraseology, 1684; as a verb, *cant*, to speak with a whine, appears (of beggars) in Harman's *Caveat*, and as to speak in the jargon peculiar to malefactors and vagabonds, in Dekker, 1609. Note that *Thieves' Latin* is the jargon of thieves, *Pedlar's French* the jargon or cant not only of thieves but of other criminals and vagabonds as well, and *St Giles' Greek* the

68

C18 term for slang as distinguished from cant; *Thieves' Latin* originating about 1800, sometimes known as *Thieves' Slang*. But in the C18, the *French* and *Greek* combinations were used so loosely as to be interchangeable; *Pedlar's French*, recorded by Harman, is much the earlier, the other originating about 1700. Moreover in C18, *the slang* was sometimes employed to mean cant; so did *canting lingo*, and in Grose himself we find *Flash Lingo* defined as "the canting or slang language." *Flash Language* occurs in 1746, and ten years later we have simply *flash; flash* was originally an adjective=relative to criminals, vagabonds and prostitutes, as in the title, *The Regulator of Thieves, etc., with an Account of Flash Words*, by Charles Hitchin(g), 1718. (In C19, *flash* came to mean the idiom of the man-about-town.) There were certain words peculiar to thieves' jargon and to vagabonds' and beggars' cant, many to 'Gipsy,' but the generality of words formed a corpus of 'secret language' familiar to all the criminal and vagabond classes. It has never been determined what, precisely, were the contributions (quantitative or qualitative) of the various groups to the common store of jargon or cant, but I venture to think that the descending order of importance is criminals; vagabonds and beggars; gipsies; prostitutes; itinerant vendors and craftsmen (especially tinkers) other than gipsies. The Irish tinkers, by the way, have long had a cant of their own, *Shelta*, just as the Gipsies had a language of their own (*Romany*). While most of the vocabulary of cant seethed to the top from the turmoiling populace, some came from French, Italian, Spanish, from Dutch and German, and from *lingua franca*, that makeshift Italian which, mongrelised still further by elements from other Mediterranean languages and from Oriental languages, was, and to some extent still is, spoken in the Levant. There were also the learned influences of Greek and Latin, engrafted on the plebeian stock by certain of the Elizabethan, Jacobean and Caroline writers and wits.— The dated details are based on W, OD, and F; for the generalisations I must take all responsibility.]

CANT. To cant; to toss or throw: as, Cant a slug into your bread room; drink a dram. *Sea wit.*

CANTICLE. A parish clerk.

CANTING. Preaching with a whining, affected tone, perhaps a corruption of chaunting; some derive it from Andrew Cant, a famous Scotch preacher, who used that whining manner of expression. Also a kind of gibberish used by thieves and gypsies called likewise pedlars French, the slang, &c. &c.

CANTERS, or THE CANTING CREW. Thieves, beggars, and gypsies, or any others using the canting lingo. See LINGO.

CANTERBURY STORY. A long roundabout tale. [Cf. *Canterbury gallop* (the pace of pilgrims riding to the shrine of St Thomas), whence *canter*. John Dennis, of Pope: "Boileau's Pegasus has all his paces. The pegasus of Pope is always on the Canterbury." W:ROW.—In Sussex in C19 a Canterbury denoted a gossip or a busybody. EDD.]

TO CAP. To take one's oath. I will cap downright; I will swear home. *Cant*.

TO CAP. To take off one's hat or cap. To cap the quadrangle; a lesson of humility, or rather servility, taught undergraduates at the university, where they are obliged to cross the area of the college cap in hand, in reverence to the Fellows who sometimes walk there. The same ceremony is observed on coming on the quarter deck of ships of war, although no officer should be on it. ["How they would cap me were I in velvet," 1593; in 1803, in that curious work the *Gradus ad Cantabrigiam*, "Other bores are to attend a sermon at St Mary's on Sunday....to cap a fellow." F.]

CAP ACQUAINTANCE. Persons slightly acquainted, or only so far as mutually to salute with the hat on meeting. A woman who endeavours to attract the notice of any particular man, is said to set her cap at him. [The latter phrase occurs in Graves's *Spiritual Quixote*, 1773. F.]

CAPER MERCHANT. A dancing master, or hop merchant; marchand des capriolles. *French term*.—To cut capers; to leap or jump in dancing. See HOP MERCHANT. [*Caper* is ultimately Latin for a goat and is connected with *caprice*, which probably meant, originally, the skipping movement of a goat. G & K.]

CAPPING VERSES. Repeating Latin verses in turn, beginning with the letter with which the last speaker left off.

CAPON. A castrated cock, also an eunuch.

CAPRICORNIFIED. Cuckolded, hornified.

CAPSIZE. To overturn or reverse. He took his broth till he capsized; he drank till he fell out of his chair. *Sea term.*

CAPTAIN. Led captain; an humble dependant in a great family, who, for a precarious subsistence, and distant hopes of preferment, suffers every kind of indignity, and is the butt of every species of joke or ill-humour. The small provision made for officers of the army and navy, in time of peace, obliges many in both services to occupy this wretched station. The idea of the appellation is taken from a led horse, many of which for magnificence, appear in the retinues of great personages on solemn occasions, such as processions, &c.

THE CAPTAIN IS COME, or AT HOME. The catamenia are come down.

CAPTAIN COPPERTHORNE'S CREW. All officers; a saying of a company where every one strives to rule.

CAPTAIN HACKUM. A blustering bully.

CAPTAIN LIEUTENANT. Meat between veal and beef, the flesh of an old calf; a military simile, drawn from the officer of that denomination, who has only the pay of a lieutenant, with the rank of captain: and so is not entirely one or the other, but between both.

CAPTAIN PODD. A celebrated master of a puppet-shew, in Ben Jonson's time, whose name became a common one to signify any of that fraternity.

CAPTAIN QUEERNABS. A shabby ill-dressed fellow.

CAPTAIN SHARP. A cheating bully, or one in a set of gamblers, whose office it is to bully any pigeon, who, suspecting roguery, refuses to pay what he has lost. *Cant.*

CAPTAIN TOM. The leader of a mob; also the mob itself.

CARAVAN. A large sum of money; also, a person cheated of such sum. *Cant.* [The former in B.E's. *Dictionary of the Canting Crew, ca.* 1690; the latter in Etherege's *Man of Mode,* 1676. F.]

CARBUNCLE FACE. A red face, full of pimples.

71

CARDINAL. A cloak in fashion about the year 1760. The cardinal is come; see THE CAPTAIN, &c.

TO CAROUSE. To drink freely or deep: from the German word expressing *all out*. [I.e. *garaus* (*trinken*), to drink bumpers. Sometimes spelt *garous* and even *garaus* in C17 English. W:ROW.—Earliest forms: *to drink* or *quaff carouse*, 1586, 1567; as noun indicative of the action or procedure, 1559; as bumper, 1594 and soon obsolete; the sense of carousal, drinking bout, did not come in till 1690, though the verb in its various senses appeared *ca*. 1580. OD.]

CARRIERS. A set of rogues who are employed to look out and watch upon the roads, at inns, &c. in order to carry information to their respective gangs, of a booty in prospect. [Verbatim from *The New Dictionary of the Canting Crew*, 1725. As messenger in Shakespeare. O.]

CARRION HUNTER. An undertaker; called also a cold cook, and death hunter. See COLD COOK & DEATH HUNTER.

CARROTS. Red hair. [Originated in C17. F.]

CARROTTY-PATED. Ginger-hackled, red-haired. See GINGER-HACKLED.

CARRY WITCHET. A sort of conundrum, puzzlewit, or riddle.

CART. To put the cart before the horse; to mention the last part of a story first. To be flogged at the cart's a-se or tail; persons guilty of petty larceny are frequently sentenced to be tied to the tail of a cart, and whipped by the common executioner, for a certain distance: the degree of severity in the execution is left to the discretion of the executioner, who, it is said, has cats of nine tails of all prices.

CARTING. The punishment formerly inflicted on bawds, who were placed in a tumbrel or cart, and led through a town, that their persons might be known.

CARVEL'S RING. The private parts of a woman. Hans Carvel, a jealous old doctor, being in bed with his wife, dreamed that the Devil gave him a ring, which, so long as he had it on his finger, would prevent his being made a cuckold: waking, he found he had got his finger the Lord knows where.

TO CASCADE. To vomit. [Smollett's *Humphry Clinker*, 1771. A vulgarism. OD.]

CASE. A house; perhaps from the Italian *casa*. In the canting lingo it meant store or ware house, as well as dwelling house. Tout that case; mark or observe that house. It is all bob, now let's dub the gigg of the case; now the coast is clear, let us break open the door of the house. [As house in Marvell, 1678. English variants: *casa, caser, carser, carsey*. F.]

A CASE VROW. A prostitute attached to a particular bawdy house. [From *case* in sense of prostitute+Dutch for woman. F.]

CASH, or CAFFAN. Cheese. *Cant.* —See CAFFAN.

CASTER. A cloak. *Cant.* [In Harman's *Caveat*. F.]

CASTING UP ONE'S ACCOUNTS. Vomiting. [Dekker, 1607. F.]

CAT. A common prostitute. An old cat; a cross old woman. [As whore in a poem of 1401. OD.—A much later and derivative sense is 'a lady's muff,' and in 1857 we find an English periodical audaciously defining *to steal a muff* as 'to free a cat,' which emerges into lucidity in F's definition of cat as *pudendum muliebre*, Fr. *le chat*, vulgarly *pussy*.]

TO CAT, or SHOOT THE CAT. To vomit from drunkenness. [Earliest form, *to jerk the cat*, 1609, while *to whip the cat*, a vulgarism still current, occurs as early as 1630. F.]

CAT AND BAGPIPEAN SOCIETY. A society which met at their office in the great western road; in their summons, published in the daily papers, it was added, that the kittens might come with the old cats without being scratched.

CAT CALL. A kind of whistle, chiefly used at theatres, to interrupt the actors, and damn a new piece. It derives its name from one of its sounds, which greatly resembles the modulations of an intriguing boar cat.

CAT-HARPING FASHION. Drinking cross-ways, and not, as usual, over the left thumb. *Sea term.*

CAT IN PAN. To turn cat in pan, to change sides or parties; supposed originally to have been to turn *cate* or *cake* in pan. [C16. F.]

CAT'S FOOT. To live under the cat's foot; to be under the

dominion of a wife, hen-pecked. To live like dog and cat; spoken of married persons who live unhappily together. As many lives as a cat; cats, according to vulgar naturalists, have nine lives, that is, one less than woman. No more chance than a cat in hell without claws; said of one who enters into a dispute or quarrel with one greatly above his match.

CAT LAP. Tea, called also scandal broth. See SCANDAL BROTH. [Appears in dialect with variants *cat-blash,-wab*= weak, thin drink and, derivatively, silly talk or worthless argument. EDD.]

CAT MATCH. When a rook or cully is engaged amongst bad bowlers.

CAT OF NINE TAILS. A scourge composed of nine strings of whipcord, each string having nine knots.

CAT'S PAW. To be made a cat's paw of: to be made a tool or instrument to accomplish the purpose of another; an allusion to the story of a monkey, who made use of a cat's paw to scratch a roasted chesnut out of the fire. [In M. Hawke's *Killing is Murder*, 1657. OD.]

CAT'S SLEEP. Counterfeit sleep: cats often counterfeiting sleep, to decoy their prey near them, and then suddenly spring on them.

CAT STICKS. Thin legs, compared to sticks with which boys play at cat. See TRAPSTICKS.

CAT WHIPPING, or WHIPPING THE CAT. A trick often practised on ignorant country fellows, vain of their strength, by laying a wager with them that they may be pulled through a pond by a cat. The bet being made, a rope is fixed round the waist of the party to be catted, and the end thrown across the pond, to which the cat is also fastened by a packthread, and three or four sturdy fellows are appointed to lead and whip the cat: these, on a signal given, seize the end of the cord, and pretending to whip the cat, haul the astonished booby through the water.—To whip the cat, is also a term among tailors for working jobs at private houses, as practised in the country. [Ben Jonson, 1614. For its use by tailors, see De Vere, *Americanisms*, 1871, for a long and informative comment. F.]

74

CATAMARAN. An old scraggy woman; from a kind of float made of spars and yards lashed together, for saving shipwrecked persons. [A navigable raft, in short. From two Tamil words. W.]

CATCH CLUB. A member of the catch club; a bum bailiff.

CATCH FART. A footboy; so called from such servants commonly following close behind their master or mistress.

CATCH PENNY. Any temporary contrivance to raise a contribution on the public.

CATCH POLE. A bum bailiff, or sheriff's officer. [As early as 1377. OD.—Neither *pole* nor *poll* is involved: the Picard *cache-pole*, i.e. *chasse-poule*, was an official whose main work was to collect dues or, failing these, poultry. W:ROW.]

CATCHING HARVEST. A dangerous time for a robbery, when many persons are on the road, on account of a horserace, fair, or some other public meeting.

CATER COUSINS. Good friends. He and I are not cater cousins, i.e. we are not even cousins in the fourth degree, or four times removed; that is, we have not the least friendly connexion. [Fr. *quatre*. Used by Shakespeare as good friends; still so used in dialect. O.]

CATERPILLAR. A nick name for a soldier. In the year 1745, a soldier quartered at a house near Derby, was desired by his landlord to call upon him whenever he came that way; for, added he, soldiers are the pillars of the nation. The rebellion being finished, it happened the same regiment was quartered in Derbyshire, when the soldier resolved to accept of his landlord's invitation, and accordingly obtained leave to find a very cold reception; whereupon expostulating with his landlord, he reminded him of his invitation, and the circumstance of his having said, soldiers were the pillars of the nation. If I did, answered the host, I meant *cater*pillars.

CATERWAULING. Going out in the night in search of intrigues, like a cat in the gutters. [Nashe, 1567, has it=to make love, to be lecherous. OD.]

CATHEDRAL. Old-fashioned. An old cathedral bedstead, chair, &c. [Johnson, 1755: "In low phrase, antique, venerable,

75

old." F.—But Johnson often says 'low' when he means not a vulgarism but a mere colloquialism.]

CATTLE. Sad cattle; whores or gypsies. Black cattle; lice. *Cant.*

CAUDGE-PAWED. Left-handed.

CAULIFLOWER. A large white wig, such as is commonly worn by the dignified clergy, and was formerly by physicians. Also the private parts of a woman; the reason for which appellation is given in the following story: A woman, who was giving evidence in a cause wherein it was necessary to express those parts, made use of the term cauliflower; for which the judge on the bench, a peevish old fellow, reproved her, saying she might as well call it artichoke. Not so, my lord, replied she; for an artichoke has a bottom, but a **** and a cauliflower have none.

CAUTIONS. The four cautions:—I. Beware of a woman before.—II. Beware of a horse behind.—III. Beware of a cart side-ways.—IV. Beware of a priest every way.

CAVAULTING SCHOOL. A bawdy-house. [Variant *cavolting*, from Lingua Franca *cavolta*, sexual intercourse. F.]

CAW-HANDED, or CAW-PAWED. Awkward, not dexterous, ready, or nimble. [Dialectal *caw*=a fool: whence *caw-baby*, an awkward or timid boy. EDD.]

CAXON. An old weather-beaten wig.

CELTIBERIANS. A society of the brethren of this most ancient and honourable brotherhood was held at the Swan and Rummer, Fleet-street.

CENT PER CENT. An usurer.

CHAFED. Well beaten; from *chauffé*, warmed.

CHALKERS. Men of wit in Ireland, who in the night amuse themselves with cutting inoffensive passengers across the face with a knife. They are somewhat like those facetious gentlemen some time ago known in England by the title of Sweaters and Mohocks.

CHALKING. The amusement above described.

CHAP. A fellow. An odd chap; a strange fellow. [Short of course for *chapman*, a merchant, probably from Latin *caupo*, a tavern-keeper. W:ROW.—In C19 dialect, *chap* means variously a farm-servant or handyman, a male sweetheart or a

76

husband, a purchaser or a customer. In C18 dialect, a dealer: cf. M.E. *chepynge*, a market (as in Chipping Campden), *chapman*, *chapfare*, trading,—all connected with *chaffare*, to engage in trade, the 'key' being M.E. *chapfare*, the modern-dialect *chapfair*. EDD.—Hence the C19-20 slang use of customer=chap=fellow=man.]

CHAPERON. The cicisbeo, or gentleman usher, to a lady; from the French.

CHAPT. Dry or thirsty. [From *chap*, to crack from want of moisture. F.]

CHARACTERED, or LETTERED. Burnt in the hand. They have palmed the character upon him; they have burned him in the hand. *Cant.*—See LETTERED.

CHARM. A picklock. *Cant.*

CHARREN. The smoke of Charren.—His eyes water from the smoke of Charren; a man of that place coming out of his house weeping, because his wife had beat him, told his neighbours the smoke had made his eyes water.

CHATES. The gallows. *Cant.* [Harman, 1567. OD.]

CHATTER BOX. One whose tongue runs twelve score to the dozen, a chattering man or woman.

CHATTER BROTH. Tea. See CAT LAP and SCANDAL BROTH.

CHATTS. Lice; perhaps an abbreviation of chattels, lice being the chief live stock or chattels of beggars, gypsies, and the rest of the canting crew. *Cant.*—Also, according to the canting academy, the gallows. ["The Norman *catel* passed later into *cattell*, and these forms were in C16 restricted to live stock, *chattell* passing from legal French into general use for the wider sense—article of property." *Chatts* is in B.E.'s cant dictionary, 1690. As=the gallows, a variant of *chates*, itself a variant of *cheates*, *cheats*, *chetes*, things. F.—*Chatts*, lice, and *chatty*, lousy, were much used in 1914-1918. B & P.]

CHAUNTER CULLS. Grub-street writers, who compose songs, carrols, &c. for ballad singers. *Cant.* [*Cull*, a man; *chaunter*, a street singer of ballads. See Parker's invaluable *View of Society*, 1781. F.]

CHEAPSIDE. He came at it by way of Cheapside; he gave little or nothing for it, he bought it cheap.

CHEATS. Sham sleeves to put over a dirty shirt or shift. See SHAMS. [Recorded in 1688. OD.—In C19 dialect a *cheat* is a loose shirt front, a 'dickey.' EDD.]

CHEEK BY JOWL. Side by side, hand to fist. [So in Shakespeare.O.—H includes it as slang, but it was never lower than colloquial in C19, and in C20 it is good, almost 'literary' English.]

CHEEKS. Ask cheeks near cunnyborough; the repartee of a St Giles's fair one, who bids you ask her backside, *Anglicè* her a-se. A like answer is current in France: any one asking the road or distance to Macon, a city near Lyons, would be answered by a French lady of easy virtue, 'Mettez votre nez dans mon cul, & vous serrez dans les Fauxbourgs.' [*Con*=C**t.]

CHEESE TOASTER. A sword. [Jocular in the British Tommies' way. In Thackeray's *Virginians*. F.]

CHELSEA. A village near London, famous for the military hospital. To get Chelsea; to obtain the benefit of that hospital. Dead Chelsea, by G-D! an exclamation uttered by a grenadier at Fontenoy, on having his leg carried away by a cannon-ball.

CHEST OF TOOLS. A shoe-black's brush and wig, &c. *Irish*.

CHERRY-COLOURED CAT. A black cat, there being black cherries as well as red.

CHERUBIMS. Peevish children, because cherubims and seraphims continually do cry.

CHESHIRE CAT. He grins like a Cheshire cat; said of any one who shews his teeth and gums in laughing.[Earliest record 1782. OD. Origin unknown.]

CHICK-A-BIDDY. A chicken, so called to and by little children. [The endearment arose in dialect and then passed into slang, then into colloquial speech. EDD.—Almost every animal-'personality,' whether favourable or pejorative, originated in the country, as was only natural.]

CHICKEN-BREASTED. Said of a woman with scarce any breasts.

CHICKEN BUTCHER. A poulterer.

CHICKEN-HAMMED. Persons whose legs and thighs are bent or arched outwards.

CHICKEN-HEARTED. Fearful, cowardly.

CHICKEN NABOB. One returned from the East Indies with but a moderate fortune of fifty or sixty thousand pounds, a diminutive nabob; a term borrowed from the chicken turtle.

CHILD. To eat a child; to partake of a treat given to the parish officers, in part of commutation for a bastard child: the common price was formerly ten pounds and a greasy chin. See GREASY CHIN.

CHIMNEY CHOPS. An abusive appellation for a negro.

CHINK. Money. [In plural often used by Elizabethans for money. O.—In Tusser, 1557, as *chinkes*. OD.]

CHIP. A child. A chip of the old block: a child who either in person or sentiments resembles its father or mother. [From *ca*. 1626. OD.]

CHIPS. A nick name for a carpenter. [Common among soldiers in 1914-1918.]

CHIRPING MERRY. Exhilarated with liquor. Chirping glass; a cheerful glass, that makes the company chirp like birds in spring.

CHIT. An infant or baby. [Dialectally applied to various things of small size. EDD.]

CHITTERLINS. The bowels. There is a rumpus among my chitterlins; i.e. I have the colic. [Properly *chitterlings*, a pig's entrails.]

CHITTY-FACED. Baby-faced; said of one who has a childish look.

CHIVE, or CHIFE. A knife, file, or saw. To chive the darbies, to file off the irons or fetters. To chive the boungs of the frows; to cut off women's pockets. [In Romany, *chive* has the specific sense, to stab, from *chiv*, *chiva* (*chive*), *chuva*, to cast, fling, throw, also to place, put. G.B.—The sailors' slang for a knife is *chivey*. B.—Cf. *chiving lay*.]

CHIVEY. I gave him a good chivey; I gave him a hearty scolding. [Possibly, says H, from the game of *chevy-chase*, in which the word *chevy* is shouted.—Dialect prefers *chevy*, as both

79

noun and verb (pursue, chase about, worry, tease). EDD.—
Modern pronunciation: *chivvy*.—Properly, from the hunting-cry in the Ballad of Chevy Chase. W.]

CHIVING LAY. Cutting the braces of coaches behind, on which the coachman quitting the box, an accomplice robs the boot; also, formerly, cutting the back of the coach to steal the fine large wigs then worn. [*Boot*=receptacle for luggage.]

CHOAK. Choak away, the church yard's near; a jocular saying to a person taken with a violent fit of coughing, or who has swallowed any thing, as it is called, the wrong way. Choak chicken, more are hatching; a like consolation.

CHOAK PEAR. Figuratively, an unanswerable objection; also a machine formerly used in Holland by robbers; it was of iron, shaped like a pear; this they forced into the mouths of persons from whom they intended to extort money; and, on turning a key, certain interior springs thrust forth a number of points, in all directions, which so enlarged it, that it could not be taken out of the mouth: and the iron, being case-hardened, could not be filed: the only methods of getting rid of it, were either by cutting the mouth, or advertising a reward for the key. These pears were also called pears of agony. [Originally a very hard winter pear. EDD.]

CHOAKING PYE, or COLD PYE. A punishment inflicted on any person sleeping in company: it consists in wrapping up cotton in a case or tube of paper, setting it on fire, and directing the smoak up the nostrils of the sleeper. See HOWELL'S COTGRAVE. [Howell's ed. of Cotgrave's *Dictionary*, 1650.]

CHOCOLATE. To give chocolate without sugar; to reprove. *Military term.*

CHOICE SPIRIT. A thoughtless, laughing, singing, drunken fellow.

CHOP. A blow. *Boxing term.*

TO CHOP AND CHANGE. To exchange backwards and forwards. To chop, in the canting sense, means making dispatch, or hurrying over any business: ex. The *autem bawler* will soon quit the *hums*, for he *chops up* the *whiners*; the parson will soon quit the pulpit, for he hurries over the prayers. See AUT-

EM BAWLER, HUMS, and WHINERS. [*Chop*=to barter. A very old phrase.F.]

CHOP CHURCHES. Simoniacal dealers in livings, or other ecclesiastical preferments.

CHOPPING. Lusty. A chopping boy or girl: a lusty child. [Dialectally only of a boy. EDD.]

CHOPS. The mouth. I gave him a wherrit, or a souse, across the chops; I gave him a blow over the mouth. See WHERRIT. [Also, lips, jaw. C16 origin. OD.]

CHOSEN PELLS. Highwaymen who rob in pairs, in the streets and squares of London: to prevent being followed by the sound of their horses shoes on the stones, they shoe them with leather. [I.e. *Pals*, a cant word of gipsy origin and denoting 'a brother in villainy.' G.B.]

CHOUDER. A sea dish, composed of fresh fish, salt pork, herb and sea-biscuits, laid in different layers, and stewed together. [Usually *chowder*, a stew containing fish or clams. Now used in North America and probably from Fr. *chaudière*, a cauldron.W]

TO CHOUSE. To cheat or trick; he choused me out of it. Chouse is also the term for a game like chuck-farthing. [Became common in C17, when also *chiaus;* Turkish *chaush* = a messenger.W.]

CHRIST-CROSS ROW. The alphabet in a horn-book: called Christ-cross Row, from having, as an Irishman observed, Christ's cross *prefixed* before and *after* the twenty-four letters. [The cross (Christ's cross) came normally only at the beginning of the alphabet. *Christ-cross*, a slovenly pronunciation, led to the further corruptions *Chris-cross, criss-cross.* In the old horn-books the consonants formed the upright, the vowels the cross-piece.EDD.]

CHRISTENING. Erasing the name of the true maker from a stolen watch, and engraving a fictitious one in its place. [A cant variant: *to church.* F.]

CHRISTIAN PONEY. A chairman. [Old Irish slang.F.]

CHRISTIAN COMPLIMENTS. A cough, kibed heels, and a snotty nose.

CHUB. He is a young chub, or a mere chub; i.e. a foolish fellow easily imposed on: an allusion to a fish of that name, easily taken.

CHUBBY. Round-faced, plump.

CHUCK. My chuck; a term of endearment. [Connected with *chick*: cf. dialectal *chuck-a-biddy*, *chucken* (Scottish). EDD.]

TO CHUCK. To shew a propensity for a man. The mort chucks; the wench wants to be doing.

CHUCK FARTHING. A parish clerk. [The game so called occurs in *The London Spy*, 1703.F.]

CHUCKLE-HEADED. Stupid, thick-headed.

CHUFFY. Round-faced, chubby. [More usually *chuff* and rather dialect than colloquialism.]

CHUM. A chamber-fellow, particularly at the universities and in prison. [Creech dedicated his *Theocritus*, 1684, to his "chum Mr Hody of Wadham College;" B.E., 1690, defines thus: "a chamber fellow, or constant companion." In C19 the word came to mean not a chamber-fellow at all, but an intimate or a very frequent companion. OD,W. In C19 Essex dialect=a helpmate, especially a wife, a man saying naturally "Me and my oad chum." EDD. In 1914-1918, "more popular, at least with non-Cockney troops, than either *mate* or *pal*." B & P.— Probably a slurred abbreviation of *chamber* (*-fellow*). W.]

CHUMMAGE. Money paid by the richer sort of prisoners in the Fleet and King's Bench, to the poorer, for their share of a room. When prisons are very full, which is too often the case, particularly on the eve of an insolvent act, two or three persons are obliged to sleep in a room. A prisoner who can pay for being alone, chuses two poor chums, who for a stipulated price, called chummage, give up their share of the room, and sleep on the stairs, or, as the term is, ruff it. [The word had another sense, as in Howard's *State of Prisons in England and Wales*, 1777: "A cruel custom obtains in most of our gaols, which is that of the prisoners demanding of a new comer *garnish*, *footing*, or (as it is called in some London gaols) *chummage*." (In 1859, G. A. Sala refers to the term as applied to universities. OD.—) Yet a third prison-custom, *chumming-up*, is described by H: "When a fresh man was admitted (to a debt-prison), rough music was made with pokers, tongs, sticks and saucepans. For this ovation the initiated prisoner had to pay, or 'fork over' (nowadays *fork out*) half a crown—or submit to the loss of coat and waistcoat."]

CHUNK. Among printers, a journeyman who refuses to work for legal wages; the same as a flint among taylors. See FLINT.

CHURCH WARDEN. A Sussex name for a shag, or cormorant, probably from its voracity. [Also in Hampshire.EDD.]

CHURCH WORK. Said of any work that advances slowly.

CHURCHYARD COUGH. A cough that is likely to terminate in death.

CHURK. The udder. [Only in Gloucestershire dialect: since *ca.* 1800, at any rate. EDD.]

CHURL. Originally, a labourer or husbandman; figuratively a rude, surly, boorish fellow. To put a churl upon a gentleman; to drink malt liquor immediately after having drunk wine. [In Shakespeare in these senses.O.]

CINDER GARBLER. A servant maid, from her business of sifting the ashes from the cinders. *Custom-house wit.*

CIRCUMBENDIBUS. A roundabout way, or story. He took such a circumbendibus: he took such a circuit. [Dryden, 1681. OD.]

CIT. A citizen of London. [Abbreviation that left only the first syllable was common in C17; cf. *mob, pun.* W:ROW.]

CITY COLLEGE. Newgate.

CIVILITY MONEY. A reward claimed by bailiffs, for executing their office with civility.

CIVIL RECEPTION. A house of civil reception; a bawdy-house, or nanny-house. See NANNY HOUSE.

CLACK. A tongue, chiefly applied to women; a simile drawn from the clack of a water-mill. [As early as 1440 for idle talk, gossip. OD.—Dialectal variant: *clacker.* EDD.—In 1914-1918 the soldiers used *clack* to mean gossip, a rumour, *clacker* to denote a chatterer, a spreader of rumours, a loose talker. F & G.]

CLACK-LOFT. A pulpit, so called by orator Henley.

CLAMMED. Starved. [From the very general dialect verb *clam*, to starve (transitive and intr.). EDD.]

83

CLAN. A family's tribe or brotherhood: a word much used in Scotland. The head of the clan; the chief: an allusion to a story of a Scotchman, who, when a very large louse crept down his arm, put him back again, saying he was the head of the clan, and that, if injured, all the rest would resent it.

CLANK. A silver tankard. *Cant.* [Obviously onomatopoeic. In C19 dialect, as verb=to strike with noise, as noun=a sounding blow, a noise. EDD.]

CLANK NAPPER. A silver tankard stealer. See RUM BUBBER. [*Nabber, napper*=thief.]

CLANKER. A great lie.

CLAP. A venereal taint. He went out by Had'em, and came round by Clapham home; i.e. he went out a wenching, and got a clap. [From C16 onwards. Now a vulgar, but until *ca.* 1830 a polite, word for gonorrhœa. Early as a verb, even in such a figurative, anti-Puritan sense as "Atropos clapt him, a pox on the drab" (1658). F.]

CLAP ON THE SHOULDER. An arrest for debt; whence a bum bailiff is called a shoulder-clapper. [The earlier form of *shoulder-clapper* was *clap-shoulder*, as in Taylor the Water-Poet, 1630. F.]

CLAPPER. The tongue of a bell, and figuratively of a man or woman.

CLAPPER CLAW. To scold, to abuse, or claw off with the tongue. [Derivatively from the Shakespearean sense, to maul, thrash, drub. O.]

CLAPPERDOGEON. A beggar-born. *Cant.* [More correctly *clapperdudgeon*. Found in Harman, Ben Jonson, Ned Ward, Sala. F.]

CLARET. French red wine; figuratively blood. I tapped his claret; I broke his head, and made the blood run. Claret-faced; red-faced. [Dekker, 1604, "my head runs claret lustily." OD. —"(French 'vin clairet') light-red wine. The name 'claret' was originally opposed to 'white' and to 'red,' but in time became transferred to red wines (now, those from Bordeaux)". O.— Onions' Shakespearean glossary is a model of what that sort of dictionary should be.]

84

CLAWED OFF. Severely beaten or whipped; also smartly poxed or clapped. [In Shakespeare *to claw* meant to seize, grip.O.]

CLEAR. Very drunk. *The cull is clear, let's bite him;* the fellow is very drunk, let's cheat him. *Cant.* [In Shadwell, who had a very fair knowledge of 'Alsatia' and similar quarters.]

CLEAVER. One that will cleave; used of a forward or wanton woman.

CLERKED. Soothed, funned, imposed on. *The cull will not be clerked;* i.e. the fellow will not be imposed on by fair words. [The word significantly reflects the attitude of the illiterate, who, if they do not admire, distrust intensely the educated person.]

CLEYMES. Artificial sores, made by beggars to excite charity.

CLICK. A blow. *A click in the muns;* a blow or knock in the face. *Cant.*

TO CLICK. To snatch. *To click a nab;* to snatch a hat. *Cant.* [To catch, snatch away. Northern dialect. G.—Whence, by natural transition, the modern slang use: to make heterosexual friends unintroduced; cf. *pick up.*]

CLICKER. A salesman's servant; also, one who proportions out the different shares of the booty among thieves. [In B.E.'s Dictionary, Ward, Dyche.F.—H: "A female touter at a bonnet shop."]

CLICKET. Copulation of foxes; and thence used, in a canting sense, for that of men and women: as, *The cull and the mort are at clicket in the dyke;* the man and woman are copulating in the ditch. [Lancashire. The verb=to be in heat.EDD.]

CLICKMAN TOAD. A watch; also an appellation for a West-countryman, said to have arisen from the following story: —A West-country man, who had never seen a watch, found one on a heath near Pool, which, by the motion of the hand, and the noise of the wheels, he concluded to be a living creature of the toad kind; and, from its clicking, he named it a clickman toad.

CLIMB. *To climb the three trees with a ladder;* to ascend the gallows.

CLINCH. A pun or quibble. To clinch, or to clinch the nail; to confirm an improbable story by another: as, A man swore he drove a tenpenny nail through the moon; a bystander said it was true, for he was on the other side and clinched it.

CLINK. A place in the Borough of Southwark, formerly privileged from arrests; and inhabited by lawless vagabonds of every denomination, called, from the place of their residence, clinkers. Also a gaol, from the clinking of the prisoners' chains or fetters: he is gone to clink. [The 'place' was in G's day, as it had long been, the noted gaol: *The Clink*. Originally a sanctuary district: 'the liberty of the Clink' was, then, the sanctuary afforded by that district. By a play on *liberty*, *clink* came to mean *the Clink gaol;* thence, *the Clink* became any gaol. EDD.— Always slang; from *ca.* 1880, frequent in the Army. While *clink* is probably connected with *clinch*, to clutch, etc., whence *clinch* also = a gaol, it is probable that the onomatopoeic associations may have helped to popularise *clink* as gaol. F,OD, W.]

CLINKERS. A kind of small Dutch bricks; also irons worn by prisoners; a crafty fellow.

TO CLIP. To hug or embrace: to clip and cling. To clip the coin; to diminish the current coin. To clip the king's English: to be unable to speak plain through drunkenness.

CLOAK TWITCHERS. Rogues who lurk about the entrance into dark alleys, and bye-lanes, to snatch cloaks from the shoulders of passengers.

CLOD HOPPER. A country farmer, or ploughman.

CLOD PATE. A dull, heavy booby.

CLOD POLE. The same. [In Shakespeare: *clodpole* or *clotpoll*. O.]

CLOSE. As close as God's curse to a whore's a-se; close as shirt and shitten a-se.

CLOSE-FISTED. Covetous or stingy.

CLOSH. A general name given by the mobility to Dutch seamen, being a corruption of *Claus*, the abbreviation of Nicholas, a name very common among the men of that nation. [For *Claus* read *Klaas;* for *Nicholas, Nicolaas.* EDD.]

CLOTH MARKET. He is just come from the cloth market, i.e. from between the sheets, he is just risen from bed. [Swift, 1738. OD.]

CLOUD. Tobacco. Under a cloud; in adversity.

CLOUT. A blow. I'll give you a clout on your jolly nob; I'll give you a blow on the head. It also means a handkerchief. *Cant.*

CLOUTED SHOON. Shoes tipped with iron. [Cf. G in his much less interesting but valuable *Provincial Glossary:* "*Clout.* To piece or mend with cloth or iron. N."—The term occurs in Shakespeare.O.]

CLOUTING LAY. Picking pockets of handkerchiefs.

CLOVEN, CLEAVE, or CLEFT. A term used for a woman who passes for a maid, but is not one. [*Cleft* also as noun: *pudendum muliebre.* F.]

CLOVEN FOOT. To spy the cloven foot in any business: to discover some roguery or something bad in it: a saying that alludes to a piece of vulgar superstition, which is, that, let the Devil transform himself into what shape he will, he cannot hide his cloven foot.

CLOVER. To be, or live, in clover; to live luxuriously. Clover is the most desirable food for cattle.

CLOWES. Rogues.

CLOY. To steal. To cloy the clout; to steal the handkerchief. To cloy the lour; to steal money. *Cant.* [Variant *cly.* F.]

CLOYES. Thieves, robbers, &c.

CLUB. A meeting or association, where each man is to spend an equal and stated sum, called his club. [For London clubs in G's day, see E. Beresford Chancellor's valuable book: *The XVIIIth Century in London*, 1920, excellently illustrated.]

CLUB LAW. Argumentum bacculinum, in which an oaken stick is a better plea than an act of parliament. [Note that "*Prentices and clubs* was the rallying cry of London apprentices." O.]

CLUMP. A lump. Clumpish; lumpish, stupid.

CLUNCH. An awkward clownish fellow. [Like *clump, clunch* originally meant a lump, a mass. EDD.]

TO CLUTCH THE FIST. To clench or shut the hand. Clutch-fisted; covetous, stingy. See CLOSE-FISTED.

CLUTCHES. Hands, gripe, power.

CLUTTER. A stir, noise, or racket; what a confounded clutter here is! [Note the Northern *clut*, to strike a blow, and *cluttert*, in heaps. G.—"There is always a great running and clutter just as the King passes." D.—In C19 dialect, *clutter* retains the sense in Grose, but also that of a heap, disorder, confusion, and, as a verb, to heap up without order. EDD.—What *racket* is to sound and *confusion* or *disorder* to arrangement, so is *clutter* to both. Nowadays the verb is usually *clutter up*, to litter, while the noun =a confused mass, or a hubbub, and both verb and noun are 'good English' with a faint and pleasant reminiscence of colloquialism.]

CLY. Money; also a pocket. He has filed the cly; he has picked a pocket. *Cant.* [*Filing a cly* occurs in that wonderful record of robust roguery: Charles Johnson's *Highwaymen and Pirates*, 1742. F.]

CLY THE JERK. To be whipped. *Cant.* [Harman, who spells it *gerke*. F.]

CLYSTER PIPE. A nick name for an apothecary. [*Clyster*, an injection for costiveness. F.]

COACH WHEEL. A half crown piece is a fore coach wheel, and a crown piece a hind coach wheel; the fore wheels of a coach being less than the hind ones.

TO COAX. To fondle, or wheedle. To coax a pair of stockings; to pull down the part soiled into the shoes, so as to give a dirty pair of stockings the appearance of clean ones. Coaxing is also used, instead of darning, to hide the holes about the ancles. [Stigmatised by Johnson as a 'low word.']

COB. A Spanish dollar. ["(Nautical.) Money. Especially . . . . a Spanish coin formerly current in Ireland, worth about 4s. 8d. Also name still given (1896) at Gibraltar to a Spanish dollar." F.]

COB, or **COBBING.** A punishment used by the seamen for petty offences, or irregularities, among themselves; it consists in bastonadoing the offender on the posteriors with a cobbing stick, or pipe staff; the number usually inflicted is a dozer. At the first stroke the executioner repeats the word *watch*, on which all persons present are to take off their hats, on pain of like punishment: the last stroke is always given as hard as possible, and is called *the purse*. Ashore, among soldiers, where this punishment is sometimes adopted, *watch* and *the purse* are not included in the number, but given over and above, or, in the vulgar phrase, free gratis for nothing. This piece of discipline is also inflicted in Ireland, by the school-boys, on persons coming into the school without taking off their hats; it is there called school butter.

COBBLE. A kind of boat.

TO COBBLE. To mend, or patch; likewise to do a thing in a bungling manner. [Properly, to repair roughly or to patch up temporarily. EDD.]

COBBLE COLTER. A turkey. [This strange term occurs in Disraeli's strangest novel, *Venetia*. F.]

COBBLER. A mender of shoes, an improver of the understandings of his customers; a translator.

COBBLER'S PUNCH. Treacle, vinegar, gin, and water. [Dialectally, warm ale thickened, sweetened, and mixed with spirits. EDD.]

COCK, or CHIEF COCK OF THE WALK. The leading man in any society or body; the best boxer in a village or district. [So used in *The Spectator*, 1711. OD.]

COCK ALE. A provocative drink. [The *membrum virile* sense of *cock* figures in Shakespeare's *Henry V*, 1600; in Beaumont & Fletcher's bawdy *Custom of the Country* rather later; in the 1737 translation of Rabelais, in Longman's edition of R. in 1807 and in Bohn's in 1849. The term *cock-ale* is in the play, *Woman Turned Bully*, 1675. F.—Sir James Murray on *cock* (1893): "The current name among the people, but, *pudoris causa*, not permissible in polite speech or literature;" in origin, he says, it is "perhaps intimately connected with sense 12," i.e. "a spout or short pipe....;a tap." OD.]

COCK ALLEY, or COCK LANE. The private parts of a woman.

COCK AND A BULL STORY. A roundabout story, with-

89

out head or tail, i.e. beginning or ending. [In John Day, 1603; Sterne, 1759. Compare the French *coq-à-l'âne*. F, OD.]

COCK-A-WHOOP. Elevated, in high spirits, transported with joy. [More generally *hoop*, from *coq à houppe*, a crested cock, so that the phrase also=swaggering. F.—The OD calls F's etymology (from Phillips) 'folk etymology' and rejects other theories in one of those concise essays-in-little which are one of the glories of that great Dictionary.—It is interesting to see that Shakespeare used *set cock-a-hoop* as 'to cast off all restraint,' and, before Shakespeare, the phrase meant "to drink without stint, to make good cheer recklessly." O, whose work in the OD from *See* onwards merits the highest praise for its unerring precision and its truly remarkable lucidity.]

COCK BAWD. A male keeper of a bawdy-house.

COCKER. One fond of the diversion of cock-fighting.

COCK HOIST. A cross buttock.

COCKISH. Wanton, forward. A cockish wench; a forward coming girl.

COCKLES. To cry cockles: to be hanged: perhaps from the noise made whilst strangling. *Cant.*—This will rejoice the cockles of one's heart; a saying in praise of wine, ale, or spirituous liquors. [The colloquial phrase was first recorded in 1669. OD. —There are several 'people's games' of cockles; the scabrous one is mentioned in G.F. Northall's *English Folk Rhymes* (1892), a veritable storehouse of folk-lore compiled by a very able folklorist and glossarist.]

COCKNEY. A nick name given to the citizens of London, or persons born within the sound of Bow bell, derived from the following story: A citizen of London being in the country, and hearing a horse neigh, exclaimed, Lord! how that horse laughs! A by-stander telling him that noise was called *neighing*, the next morning ,when the cock crowed, the citizen, to show he had not forgot what was told him, cried out, Do you hear how the *cock neighs?* The king of the Cockneys is mentioned among the regulations for the sports and shows formerly held in the Middle Temple on Childermas Day, where he had his officers, a marshal, constable, butler, &c. See Dugdale's Origines Juridiciales, p. 247.—Ray says, the interpretation of the word Cockney, is, a young person coaxed or coquered, made wanton; or a nestle cock, delicately bred and brought up, so as, when arrived at man's estate, to be unable to bear the least hardship. Whatever may be the origin of this appellation, we learn from the following verses, attributed to Hugh Bigot, Earl of Norfolk, that it was in use in the time of king Henry II.

> Was I in my castle at Bungay,
> Fast by the river Waveney,
> I would not care for the king of Cockney.

i.e. the king of London. [The horse story comes from Minsheu. On this difficult word see especially Halliwell (the pioneer here as in so many directions), the OD, Dr Scott on the OD, and Weekley.—Ray the antiquarian was on the right track, for the word was applied to a milksop by Chaucer, and in C16 was commonly used thus by country people of those living in great towns. York, London, Perugia, says Harman, 1567, in the wake of Whitinton, 1521, were nests of Cockneys. Cooper in 1573 glosses *delicias facere* as "to play the wanton, to dally, to play the cockney." In this sense cf. Fr. *acoquiné*, "made tame... growne as lazy.... as a beggar," Cotgrave. By about 1600 the word began to be freely applied to Londoners, Minsheu in 1617 defining *Cockney* as "one born within the sound of Bow Bells," and Rowlands in 1600 had written: "I scorne to let a Bow-bell Cockney put me down." OD, F, W.—In C19 Leicestershire dialect the word still meant dainty, delicate. EDD.— The full history of *Cockney* has still to be written: we can but hope that either Professor Weekley or Dr Onions will write it. Meanwhile I trepidantly suggest that in the verses cited by Grose, *Cockney* may possibly mean *Cockaigne*, "an imaginary land of idleness and luxury" and that it has not yet been disproved that *Cockney* as=London may be due to a confusion, or else to a mingling, of the two ideas: "soft, dainty, urban" and "Cockaigne." (Why, by the way, is 'Cockney' not more generally recognised as a dialect, for it is neither received standard English nor slang?)]

COCK PIMP. The supposed husband of a bawd.

COCK ROBIN. A soft, easy fellow.

COCKSHUT TIME. The evening, when fowls go to roost. [In Shakespeare=the evening twilight: a) the time when woodcocks were caught in nets as they 'shot' through the glades; b) that at which poultry are shut up. O.]

COCK-SURE. Certain: a metaphor borrowed from the cock of a firelock, as being much more certain to fire than the match. [F suggests *cocky-sure* abbreviated; W: *God sure* euphemised; OD resorts to the certainty of a tap. Yet perhaps Grose is right, for it is significant that not a single example of any shade of the word as given in the OD dates before 1520. Gunpowder was invented about 1320, cannon were in fairly general use by 1350; the smaller firearms were first employed in England during the Wars of the Roses although they did not supersede the longbow until about 1540. (Oman on the Art of War in *Medieval England*, 1924.)]

COCK'S TOOTH. I live at the sign of the cock's tooth and head-ach; an answer to an impertinent person, who asks where one lives.

COCK YOUR EYE. Shut one eye: thus translated into apothecaries Latin—*Gallus tuus ego*.

COD. A cod of money; a good sum of money. [By itself meant a purse, A.S. *cod*, a small bag. F.]

CODDERS. Persons employed by the gardeners to gather peas. [Usually Welsh women; used in London. A Southern word. G.]

CODGER. An old codger; an old fellow. [Earliest as *old codger* (Colman, Smollett, 1760; Murphy, 1765). A variant of and sense-divergence from *cadger*. F, OD,W.—In C19 dialect, a slovenly worker. EDD.]

COD PIECE. The fore flap of a man's breeches. Do they bite, master? where, in the cod piece or collar?—a jocular attack on a patient angler by watermen, &c. ["Made indelicately conspicuous in Shakespeare's time." O.]

CODS. The scrotum. Also a nick name for a curate: a rude fellow meeting a curate, mistook him for the rector, and accosted him with the vulgar appellation of Bol—ks the rector. No, Sir, answered he; only Cods the curate, at your service. [Precisely, *cod*=scrotum, *cods*=testicles.F.]

COD'S HEAD. A stupid fellow. [A C17 word.]

CODS HEADS. A society who met in London.

COFFEE HOUSE. A necessary house. To make a coffee-house of a woman's **** ; to go in and out and spend nothing. [From the popularity of the C17-18 coffee-house proper, for which see Chancellor's *XVIIIth Century in London.*]

COG. The money, or whatsoever the sweeteners drop to draw in a bubble.

TO COG. To cheat with dice; also to coax or wheedle. To cog a die; to conceal or secure a die. To cog a dinner; to wheedle one out of a dinner. [In Shakespeare, to cheat.O.]

COGUE. A dram of any spirituous liquor. [A sailors' term is "*cogueing the nose*, having a good strong drink, hot."B.—In Kentish dialect, *cog*. EDD.]

COKER. A lie.

COKES. The fool in the play of Bartholomew Fair: perhaps a contraction of the word *coxcomb*. [A C16-17 word. Perhaps related to Cockney. OD.]

COLCANNON. Potatoes and cabbage pounded together in a mortar, and then stewed with butter: an Irish dish. [The *col*= Irish *cál*, cabbage. EDD.]

COLD. You will catch cold at that; a vulgar threat or advice to desist from an attempt. He caught cold by lying in bed bare-foot; a saying of any one extremely tender or careful of himself.

COLD BURNING. A punishment inflicted by private soldiers, on their comrades for trifling offences, or breach of their mess laws; it is administered in the following manner: The prisoner is set against the wall, with the arm which is to be burned tied as high above his head as possible. The executioner then ascends a stool, and having a bottle of cold water, pours it slowly down the sleeve of the delinquent, patting him, and leading the water gently down his body, till it runs out at his breeches knees: this is repeated to the other arm, if he is sentenced to be burned in both.

93

COLD COOK. An undertaker of funerals, or carrion hunter. See CARRION HUNTER.

COLD IRON. A sword, or any other weapon for cutting or stabbing. I gave him two inches of cold iron into his beef.

COLD MEAT. A dead wife is the best cold meat in a man's house. [This sense probably led to *cold meat*=a corpse, whence *c.m. box*=a coffin. H.—These in turn yielded the 1914-1918 'neologism,' *cold-meat ticket*, an identity disc. B & P.]

COLD PIG. To give cold pig is a punishment inflicted on sluggards who lie too long in bed: it consists in pulling off all the bed clothes from them, and throwing cold water upon them.

COLD PUDDING. This is said to settle one's love. [In C19 dialect, an antidote against love-sickness. EDD.]

COLE. Money. Post the cole; pay down the money. [Variant *coal*. In Head's *English Rogue* and Barham's *Ingoldsby Legends*. F.—Barham used much cant and more slang.]

COLIANDER, or CORIANDER SEEDS. Money. [These seeds were covered with sugar and eaten as sweetmeats. EDD.]

COLLAR DAY. Execution day.

COLLECTOR. A highwayman.

COLLEGE. Newgate, or any other prison. New College; the Royal Exchange. King's College; the King's Bench prison. [Originated in C17. OD.]

COLLEGIATES. Prisoners of the one, and shopkeepers of the other of those places.

TO COLLOGUE. To wheedle or coax. [So used from Nashe, 1596, to George Eliot, 1861. F, OD. In dialect (e.g. in Burns), *collogue*=to conspire, to be in league with. EDD.]

COLQUARRON. A man's neck. His colquarron is just about to be twisted; he is just going to be hanged. *Cant.*

COLT. One who lets horses to highwaymen; also a boy newly initiated into roguery; a grand or petty juryman on his first assize. *Cant.* [In Shakespeare: a young, inexperienced fellow, and, as a verb, to befool. O.—In dialect, an apprentice, a newcomer to a job, hence *colting*, the 'fine' paid on entering a new employment, the same as Grose's *coltage* but more widely employed. EDD.]

COLTAGE. A fine or beverage paid by colts on their first entering into their offices.

COLT BOWL. Laid short of the jack by a colt bowler, i.e. a person raw or unexperienced in the art of bowling.

COLT'S TOOTH. An old fellow who marries, or keeps a young girl, is said to have a colt's tooth in his head.

COLT VEAL. Coarse red veal, more like the flesh of a colt than that of a calf.

COLUMBRARIANS. The brethren of this honourable society assembled, A.D. 1743, at the Bull-Inn, Bishopsgate-street.

COMB. To comb one's head: to clapperclaw, or scold any one; a woman who lectures her husband, is said to comb his head. She combed his head with a joint stool; she threw a stool at him. [So used by Shakespeare.F.—So too in dialect, with the slight variations, *comb the hair*, to scold; *comb the hair* (or *head*) *with a three-legged stool*, to beat, knock about. EDD.]

COME. To come; to lend. Has he come it; has he lent it? To come over any one; to cheat or over-reach him. Coming wench; a forward wench, also a breeding woman. [In Shakespeare *come off*=to pay, disburse, and with the coming wench cf. *coming-on*=complaisant.O.]

COMING! SO IS CHRISTMAS. Said of a person who has long been called, and at length answers, Coming!

COMFORTABLE IMPORTANCE. A wife. [Occasionally *Comfortable Impudence*, which, however, was more properly applied to a mistress in a wife's position.F.]

COMMISSION. A shirt. *Cant.* [Harman, 1567. Anglicised corruption of *camicia:* see *camesa* and *mish*, supra and subter.]

COMMODE. A woman's head-dress.

COMMODITY. A woman's commodity; the private parts of a modest woman, and the public parts of a prostitute. [Shakespeare used it thus, a figurative development from *commodity*, wares, merchandise: "Tickling commodity; commodity—the bias of the world." O.]

COMMONS. The house of commons; the necessary house.

COMPANY. To see company; to enter into a course of prostitution.

COMPLIMENTS. See CHRISTMAS.

COMUS'S COURT. A social meeting formerly held at the Half Moon tavern, Cheapside.

CONFECT. Counterfeited.

CONGER. To conger; the agreement of a set or knot of booksellers of London, that whosoever of them shall buy a good copy, the rest shall take off such a particular number, in quires, at a stated price; also booksellers joining to buy either a considerable or dangerous copy. ['Copy'=a manuscript, an unpublished writing. The booksellers were, of course, booksellerpublishers. Grose's definition comes almost verbatim from B.E.'s canting dictionary.—Bailey, 1731, shows that the association was carried on not merely for the better handling of books but also to squeeze out 'young and single traders.' OD. —A not dissimilar practice is sometimes detectable even today, when it is called 'good business.']

CONGO. Will you lap your congo with me? will you drink tea with me? [Usually *congou*, from a Chinese word. First recorded about 1725.OD.]

CONNY WABBLE. Eggs and brandy beat up together. *Irish*.

CONSCIENCE KEEPER. A superior, who by his influence makes his dependents act as he pleases.

CONTENT. The cull's content; the man is past complaining: a saying of a person murdered for resisting the robbers. *Cant*. [A euphemism not *pudoris* but *periculi causa*.]

CONTENT. A thick liquor, in imitation of chocolate, made of milk and gingerbread.

CONTRA DANCE. A dance where the dancers of the different sexes stand opposite each other, instead of side by side, as in the minuet, rigadoon, louvre, &c. and now corruptly called a country dance. [Not so; contra a supposed anglicising of Fr. contre-danse, but the French is a mere adaptation of the original English *country-dance*. W.]

CONUNDRUMS. Enigmatical conceits. [A term of abuse, 1596; a whim, conceit, 1605; pun, 1645; a riddle, late C18.OD.]

CONVENIENT. A mistress. *Cant*. [Etherege, 1676.F.]

CONY, or TOM CONY. A silly fellow. [Literally a rabbit; cf. the modern slang use of *rabbit*.]

COOK RUFFIAN, who roasted the devil in his feathers. A bad cook.

COOL CRAPE. A shroud.

COOLER. A woman. [C. Johnson, 1742. F.—In 1914-1918, a prison, this sense coming from U.S.A., where first recorded for 1884. (OD.)]

COOL LADY. A female follower of the camp, who sells brandy.

COOL NANTS. Brandy.

COOL TANKARD. Wine and water, with lemon, sugar, and burrage. [Borage is still so used. OD.]

COOPED UP. Imprisoned, confined like a fowl in a coop. [In 1914-1918, *coop* was one of the many slang synonyms used by soldiers for either guard-room or military prison. F & G.]

COQUET. A jilt.

CORINTH. A bawdy-house. *Cant.* [So in Shakespeare.O.]

CORINTHIANS. Frequenters of brothels. Also an impudent, brazen-faced fellow, perhaps from the Corinthian brass. [Shakespeare, 1598, has it for 'gay, spirited fellows.'O.—Milton also uses the word. Corinth, as the temple-city of Aphrodite, was the centre of Greek prostitution, mentioned in one of Horace's Epistles (I, xvii, 36): "Non cuivis homini contingit adire Corinthum." F;H.]

CORK-BRAINED. Light-headed, foolish. [Aberdeenshire for *cork-headed*. EDD.]

CORNED. Drunk. [From *corn*, to be drunk. Scottish. See Jamieson's *Etymological Dictionary of the Scottish Language*, 1808.F.]

CORNELIAN TUB. The sweating tub, formerly used for the cure of the venereal disease.

CORNEY-FACED. A very red pimpled face.

CORNISH HUG. A particular lock in wrestling, peculiar to the people of that country.

CORPORAL. To mount a corporal and four: to be guilty of onanism: the thumb is the corporal, the four fingers the privates.

CORPORATION. A large belly. He has a glorious corporation; he has a very prominent belly.

CORPORATION. The magistrates, &c. of a corporate town, *Corpus sine ratione*. Freeman of a corporation's work; neither strong nor handsome.

COSSET. A foundling. Cosset colt or lamb; a colt or lamb brought up by hand. [Long good English for: to pamper, pet, fondle.—In C18 was, in Norfolk and Suffolk, applied to an animal. G.]

COSTARD. The head. I'll smite your costard; I'll give you a knock on the head. [Jocular since 1530. The *costard*, later *costard apple*, still later *custard apple*, was very large. OD.—In dialect often opprobrious. EDD.—Hence the surnames *Coster*, *Custer*, *Custard*. W:S.]

COSTARD MONGER. A dealer in fruit, particularly apples. [Barclay, 1514, has *costermonger* a year before the earliest record for *costardmonger*. Shakespeare uses it as a term of contempt: "these costermonger times." The abbreviation *coster* apparently first recorded by Mayhew in 1851. OD.—Ca. 1860 the London costermongers numbered more than 30,000, and at one time—though not, one gathers, later than 1850—"cut off from the rest of metropolitan society by their low habits, general improvidence, pugnacity, love of gambling, total want of education, disregard for lawful marriage ceremonies, and their use of a peculiar slang language." H.]

COT, or QUOT. A man who meddles with women's household business, particularly in the kitchen. The punishment commonly inflicted on a quot, is pinning a greasy dishclout to the skirts of his coat. [In Shakespeare as *cot-quean*.O.]

COTTEREL. Sir James Cotter, or Cotterel's sallad: hemp. Sir James Cotterel was condemned for a rape. *Irish.*

COTSWOULD LION. A sheep. Cotswould, in Gloucestershire, is famous for its breed of sheep. [Early C16 in English, C14 in Anglo-Norman. OD.]

TO COUCH A HOGSHEAD. To lie down to sleep. *Cant.* [*Hogshead*=head. Scott has the phrase in *Midlothian*.F.]

COUNTERFEIT CRANK. A general cheat, assuming all sorts of characters; one counterfeiting the falling sickness.

COUNTRY HARRY. A waggoner. *Cant.*

COUNTRY PUT. An ignorant country fellow. [In B.E.'s dictionary. OD.]

COURT CARD. A gay fluttering coxcomb. [Probably from the C18 slang came the Cumberland and North Lincolnshire sense: a person socially important.EDD.]

COURT HOLY WATER. Fair speeches and promises, without performance.

COURT PROMISES. The same.

COURT OF ASSISTANTS. A court often applied to by young women who marry old men.

COURT OF NUL TIEL RECORD. A society held A.D. 1756, at the One Tun, in the Strand.

COVE. A man, a fellow, a rogue. The cove was bit; the rogue was outwitted. The cove has bit the cole; the rogue has got the money. *Cant.* [Variants *covey, cofe, cuffing*, and feminine *covess*. Perhaps from Romany *cova, covo*, that man, and *covi*, that woman. Less likely: from North Country *coof*, a lout or dolt. Early examples, Harman, 1567, *cofe*, simply a person; Dekker, 1609, *cove, cofe, cuffin*, a man, a fellow; Witts, 1654, cove, a person, or man. F.—Origin doubtful says OD; "probably identical with Scottish *cofe*, hawker," thinks W.—In several dialects, an overseer, a master.EDD.]

COVENT, or CONVENT GARDEN, vulgarly called COMMON GARDEN. Anciently, the garden belonging to a dissolved monastery; now famous for being the chief market in London for fruit, flowers, and herbs. The two theatres are situated near it. In its environs are many brothels, and, not long ago, the lodgings of the second order of ladies of easy virtue were either there, or in the purlieus of Drury Lane. [A full and most readable account is given in one of the best of Mr Beresford Chancellor's books on London: *The Annals of Covent Garden* (1930), for which, also, consult the chapter on Drury Lane to get a commentary on G's Drury Lane Vestal.]

99

COVENT GARDEN ABBESS. A bawd.

COVENT GARDEN AGUE. The venereal disease. He broke his shins against Covent Garden rails; he caught the venereal disorder.

COVENT GARDEN NUN. A prostitute.

COVENTRY. To send one to Coventry; a punishment inflicted by officers of the army on such of their brethren as are testy; or have been guilty of improper behaviour, not worthy the cognizance of a court martial. The person sent to Coventry is considered as absent; no one must speak to or answer any question he asks, except relative to duty, under penalty of being also sent to the same place. On a proper submission, the penitent is recalled, and welcomed by the mess, as just returned from a journey to Coventry. [A popular corruption of *quarantine*. S. Favoured by F, who remarks that in 1821 Croker wrote: "I found MacMahon in a kind of Coventry, and was warned not to continue my acquaintance with him." Also explained as from Coventry Gaol, famous in the Civil War; and as from Coventry as a city of exceptional trading privileges: to the former the OD gives cautious allegiance. W, less illuminating than usual, is even more cautious.—It may be noted that in County Antrim one says, or in C19 said: "He's gone to Dingley couch," he has acted discreditably; and in Ulster "to send a man to Dinglety-cootch" signifies to Coventry. *Dingle-i-Coush* was the old name for the remote and inaccessible Dingle in County Kerry. (EDD.)]

COVEY. A collection of whores. What a fine covey here is, if the Devil would but throw his net!

COW. To sleep like a cow, i.e. with a **** at one's a-se; said of a married man; married men being supposed to sleep with their backs towards their wives, according to the following proclamation:

> *All you that in your beds do lie,*
> *Turn to your wives, and occupy:*
> *And when that you have done your best,*
> *Turn a-se to a-se, and take your rest.*

[The first couplet of this stanza had a variant, according to a manuscript note to the British Museum copy of the third edition:

> All people that on earth do dwell
> Turn to your wives and f— them well.]

COW JUICE. Milk.

COW'S BABY. A calf.

COW'S COURANT. Gallop and sh—e.

COW-HANDED. Awkward.

COW-HEARTED. Fearful. [As timid, it appears in several dialects; in West Somersetshire it was in C19 applied to sickly plants.EDD.]

COW-ITCH. The product of a sort of bean, which excites an insufferable itching, used chiefly for playing tricks. [In Northumberland a powder given to cows to *cure* them of the itch. EDD.]

COW'S SPOUSE. A bull.

COW'S THUMB. Done to a cow's thumb; done exactly.

COXCOMB. Anciently, a fool. Fools, in great families, wore a cap with bells, on the top of which was a piece of red cloth, in the shape of a cock's comb. At present, coxcomb signifies a fop, or vain self-conceited fellow. [As fool, frequent in Shakespeare, who uses it also for the cap and as a ludicrous name for the head. O.—For a notable account of this word, see W:MWAM.]

CRAB. To catch a crab; to fall backwards by missing one's stroke in rowing.

CRAB LANTHORN. A peevish fellow.

CRAB LOUSE. A species of louse peculiar to the human body; the male is denominated a cock, the female a hen. [In soldiers' slang, 1914-1918, body lice were called *crabs*, sometimes *coots*, most often *chatts*. B & P.—*Crab* is the general term in American tramp and underworld slang.I.]

CRAB SHELLS. Shoes. *Irish.*

CRABS. A losing throw to the main at hazard.

CRABBED. Sour, ill-tempered, difficult. ["Falcons that clawed and scratched their fellows were said to *crab* each other." W:A.]

CRACK. A whore. [D'Urfey, 1676.OD.—Probably deriving from *crack*, the pudendum muliebre.F.—Terms of venery usually have a long history.]

TO CRACK. To boast or brag; also to break. I cracked his napper; I broke his head. [In Shakespeare, to utter a boast loudly or smartly. O.—"She's nought to crack on, i.e. not good for much. North." P.—In several dialects in C19, as in C17 ordinary English, there was the noun *crack*=boast, boasting, pride.EDD.]

THE CRACK, or ALL THE CRACK. The fashionable theme, the go. The Crack Lay, of late is used, in the cant language, to signify the art and mystery of house-breaking.

CRACKER. Crust, sea biscuit, or ammunition loaf; also the backside. Farting crackers; breeches.

CRACKISH. Whorish.

CRACKMANS. Hedges. The cull thought to have loped by breaking through the crackmans, but we fetched him back by a nope on the costard, which stopped his jaw; the man thought to have escaped by breaking through the hedge, but we brought him back by a great blow on the head, which laid him speechless. [Same form in singular; variant *cragmans;* first recorded, 1610. F.—Cant, as are all nouns ending in -mans: cf. *darkmans, lightmans, togemans.* This *-mans* is obscure and seems to mean 'state of,' or 'thing,' according as an abstraction or an object is signified.]

CRAG. The neck. [In Scottish and N. Cy dialect, the neck, also the throat. EDD.]

CRAMP RINGS. Bolts, shackles, or fetters. *Cant.* [Dekker, 1609. F.—In N. Cy dialect, rings made out of the handles of decayed coffins and worn as charms against cramp; in older times they were, on Good Friday, consecrated by the Kings of England.EDD.—The cant sense almost certainly is derivative.]

CRAMP WORDS. Sentence of death passed on a criminal by a judge. He has just undergone the cramp word; sentence has just been passed on him. *Cant.* [Dyche, 5th ed., 1748, while recording the cant sense, notes that the ordinary colloquial

meaning is "hard, difficult, unusual or uncommon words."F.
—In dialect, any long, technical, or rare word.EDD.]

CRANK. Gin and water; also, brisk, pert.

CRANK. The falling sickness. *Cant.* [So used by Harman, who,
stating its cant origin, applies it to a rogue counterfeiting the
falling sickness, *counterfeit crank* (q.v.) being the full description.
H.—*Cranky,* sickly, existed in dialect by 1787; as out of order,
ca. 1860; capricious, cross, *ca.*1820; eccentric, crotchety, *ca.*
1850; crooked, *ca.* 1830.OD.]

CRAP, or CROP. Money. [Northern dialect.G.—Recorded
by Dyche, 1748,F.]

CRAPPED. Hanged. *Cant.* [More usually *cropped;* conversely
croppen ken (see *croppen*) is generally *crapping ken.* H.—Both
Bulwer Lytton and Harrison Ainsworth used *crap* as=the gal-
lows.F.—A *crapper* is a dialectal variant of *cropper,* one who har-
vests by cutting the plant: this buttresses the contention that
crapped=harvested, cut down.W:S.]

TO CRASH. To kill. Crash that cull; kill that fellow. *Cant.*
[An urban, criminal development of the Scottish and N. Cy
dialectal term for 'to smash.' EDD.]

CRASHING CHEATS. Teeth.

CRAW THUMPERS. Roman catholics, so called from their
beating their breasts in the confession of their sins. See BRIS-
KET BEATER, and BREAST FLEET. [Wolcot (Peter Pin-
dar), 1785.OD.]

CREAM-POT LOVE. Such as young fellows pretend to
dairymaids, to get cream and other good things from them.

TO CREEME. To slip or slide any thing into the hands of
another. *Cant.* [In Lancashire and Cheshire dialects as *creem,*
to give or take privately, slyly; also to hide, conceal.EDD.—
Ray records it in 1674. Origin doubtful.OD.]

CREEPERS. Gentlemen's companions, lice. [That sort of
euphemism which may be termed apologetic.]

CREW. A knot or gang; also a boat or ship's company. The
canting crew are thus divided into twenty-three orders, which
see under the different words:

MEN

1	Rufflers	9	Jarkmen, or Patricoes
2	Upright Men	10	Fresh Water Mariners, or
3	Hookers or Anglers		Whip Jackets
4	Rogues	11	Drummerers
5	Wild Rogues	12	Drunken Tinkers
6	Priggers of Prancers	13	Swadders, or Pedlars
7	Palliardes	14	Abrams.
8	Fraters		

WOMEN

1	Demanders for Glim-	5	Walking Morts
	mer or Fire	6	Doxies
2	Bawdy Baskets	7	Delles
3	Morts	8	Kinching Morts
4	Autem Morts	9	Kinching Coes.

[Short for *accrewe* (C16), from Fr. *accroître*, to accrue.W.]

TO CRIB. To purloin, or appropriate to one's own use, part of any thing intrusted to one's care. [Dyche, 1748.OD.]

TO FIGHT A CRIB. To make a sham fight. *Bear Garden term.*

CRIBBAGE-FACED. Marked with the small pox, the pits bearing a kind of resemblance to the holes in a cribbage-board. [As in dialect, which has also the meanings: thin or wrinkled or crabbed of face.EDD.]

CRIBBEYS, or CRIBBY ISLANDS. Blind alleys, courts, or byeways; perhaps from the houses built there being cribbed out of the common way or passage; and islands, from the similarity of sound to the Caribbee Islands. [Cf. *Bermudas.*—In the western quarter of the Covent Garden area, the congeries of alleys and courts was in C16-17 known as *The Bermudas* and in the C18 as *The Caribbee Islands*, soon corrupted—probably deliberately—to *The Cribbee Islands* as they were still known *ca.* 1820. Porridge Island (q.v.) was part of this quarter. Beresford Chancellor, *Covent Garden.*]

CRIM. CON. MONEY. Damages directed by a jury to be paid by a convicted adulterer to the injured husband, for criminal conversation with his wife. [The abbreviation for *criminal conversation* appears first in one of Foote's plays, 1770. OD.]

CRIMP. A broker or factor, as a coal crimp, who disposes of the cargoes of the Newcastle coal ships; also persons employed to trapan or kidnap recruits for the East Indian and African companies. To crimp, or play crimp: to play foul or booty; also a cruel manner of cutting up fish alive, practised by the London fishmongers, in order to make it eat firm; cod, and other crimped fish, being a favourite dish among voluptuaries and epicures.

CRINKUM CRANKUM. A woman's commodity. See *Spectator*. [Properly a winding way. In C19 dialect, any mechanical toy or device; in plural, curiosities, knick-knacks. Connected with dialectal *crinkle*, to wind tortuously, and *crinkle-crankle* (adjective and adverb), zigzag, sinuous(ly), winding in and out. EDD.]

CRINKUMS. The foul or venereal disease.

CRIPPLE. Sixpence, that piece being commonly much bent and distorted.

CRISPIN. A shoemaker: from a romance, wherein a prince of that name is said to have exercised the art and mystery of a shoemaker, thence called the gentle craft: or rather from the saints Crispinus and Crispianus, who, according to the legend, were brethren born at Rome, from whence they travelled, to Soissons in France, about the year 303, to propagate the Christian religion; but because they would not be chargeable to others for their maintenance, they exercised the trade of shoemakers: the governor of the town discovering them to be Christians, ordered them to be beheaded, about the year 303; from which time they have been the tutelar saints of the shoemakers.

CRISPIN'S HOLIDAY. Every Monday throughout the year, but most particularly the 25th of October, being the anniversary of Crispinus and Crispianus.

CRISPIN'S LANCE. An awl. [Properly *St Crispin's lance*.F.]

CROAKER. One who is always foretelling some accident or misfortune: an allusion to the croaking of a raven; supposed ominous.

CROAKUMSHIRE. Northumberland, from the particular croaking in the pronunciation of the people of that county, especially about Newcastle and Morpeth, where they are said to be born with a burr in their throats, which prevents their pronouncing the letter *r*.

CROCKERS. Forestallers, called also Kidders and Tranters.

CROCODILE'S TEARS. The tears of a hypocrite. Crocodiles are fabulously reported to shed tears over their prey before they devour it. [Early *crocodile tears*. The fable is first recorded *ca.* 1400 in Mandeville.OD.]

CROCUS, or CROCUS METALLORUM. A nick name for a surgeon of the army and navy. [Another variant is *croakus*, which suggests derivation from *croak*, to die.F.—Cf. the cant *crocussing*, quackery, and *crokus chovy*, a chemist's shop. EDD.]

CROKER. A groat or fourpence.

CRONE. An old ewe whose teeth are worn out: figuratively, a toothless old beldam.

CRONY. An intimate companion, a comrade: also a confederate in a robbery.

CROOK. Sixpence. [Dialectal variant, *crookie*.]

CROOK BACK. Sixpence: for the reason of this name, see CRIPPLE.

CROOK YOUR ELBOW. To crook one's elbow, and wish it may never come straight, if the fact then affirmed is not true —according to the casuists of Bow-street and St Giles's, adds great weight and efficacy to an oath.

CROOK SHANKS. A nick name for a man with bandy legs. He buys his boots in Crooked Lane, and his stockings in Bandy-legged Walk; his legs grew in the night, therefore could not see to grow straight: jeering sayings of men with crooked legs. [*Crookshanks* (*Cruickshanks*) is a genuine sobriquet; cf. *Shanks* and *Sheepshanks* as surnames.W:S.]

CROP. A nick name for a Presbyterian; from their cropping their hair, which they trimmed close to a bowl-dish, placed as a guide on their heads; whence they were likewise called roundheads. See ROUNDHEADS...

CROP. Money. See CRAP. *Cant*.

CROP THE CONJUROR. Jeering appellation of one with short hair.

CROPPING DRUMS. Drummers of the foot guards, or Chelsea hospital, who find out weddings, and beat a point of war to serenade the new-married couple, and thereby obtain money.

CROPPEN. The tail. The croppen of the rotan; the tail of the cart. Croppen ken; the necessary house. *Cant.*

CROPSICK. Sickness in the stomach, arising from drunkenness.

CROSS. To come home by weeping cross; to repent at the conclusion.

CROSS BITE. One who combines with a sharper to draw in a friend; also to counteract or disappoint. *Cant.*—This is peculiarly used to signify entrapping a man so as to obtain *crim. con.* money, in which the wife, real or supposed, conspires with the husband. [Various senses, C16. OD.]

CROSS BUTTOCK. A particular lock or fall in the Broughtonian art, which, as Mr Fielding observes, conveyed more pleasant sensations to the spectators than the patient. [Recorded for 1742; *buttock-cross* at least fifty years earlier. F.]

CROSS PATCH. A peevish boy or girl, or rather an unsocial ill-tempered man or woman. [Occurs in the old nursery-rhyme:
Cross-Patch,
Draw the latch,
Sit by the fire and spin. F.]

TO CROW. To brag, boast, or triumph. To crow over any one; to keep him in subjection: an image drawn from a cock, who crows over a vanquished enemy. To pluck a crow; to reprove any one for a fault committed, to settle a dispute. To strut like a crow in a gutter; to walk proudly, or with an air of consequence. [*To pluck a crow* is in Shakespeare and Nashe. F.]

CROWD. A fiddle: probably from *crooth*, the Welch name for that instrument. [The more accurate spelling of the Welsh original is *crwth;* in Old Cornish, *crowd*. EDD.—In C18 an Exmoor word. G.]

CROWDERO. A fiddler. [Usually *crowder*.]

CROWDY. Oatmeal and water, or milk: a mess much eaten

in the north. [As a nautical term, "meal and milk mixed cold. Also oatmeal and hot water eaten with treacle." B.]

CROW FAIR. A visitation of the clergy. See REVIEW OF THE BLACK CUIRASSIERS.

CROWN OFFICE. The head.

CRUISERS. Beggars, or highway spies, who traverse the road, to give intelligence of a booty; also, rogues ready to snap up any booty that may offer, like privateers or pirates on a cruise.

CRUMMY. Fat, fleshy. A fine crummy dame; a fat woman. He has picked up his crumbs finely of late; he has grown very fat, or rich, of late. [From provincial *crum* or *crom*, to stuff. F.— Soldiers' slang, 1914-1918, for lousy. F&G. For a paragraph on slang words for lice, see my essay in *A Martial Medley*, 1931. The word had, in London slang, got this meaning before 1860. H.]

CRUMP. One who helps solicitors to affidavit men, or false witnesses.—'I wish you had, Mrs Crump;' a Gloucestershire saying, in answer to a wish for any thing; implying, you must not expect any assistance from the speaker. It is said to have originated from the following incident: One Mrs Crump, the wife of a substantial farmer, dining with the old Lady Coventry, who was extremely deaf, said to one of the footmen, waiting at table, 'I wish I had a draught of small beer,' her modesty not permitting her to desire so fine a gentleman to bring it; the fellow, conscious that his mistress could not hear either the request or answer, replied, without moving, 'I wish you had, Mrs Crump.' These wishes being again repeated by both parties, Mrs Crump got up from the table to fetch it herself; and being asked by my lady where she was going, related what had passed. The story being told abroad, the expression became proverbial.

CRUMP-BACKED. Hump-backed.

CRUSTY BEAU. One that uses paint and cosmetics, to obtain a fine complexion.

CRUSTY FELLOW. A surly fellow. [Crusty is so used by Lyly and Shakespeare. OD.]

CUB. An unlicked cub; an unformed, ill-educated young man, a young nobleman or gentleman on his travels: an allusion to the story of the bear, said to bring its cub into form by licking. Also, a new gamester. [In Shakespeare.F.]

CUCKOLD. The husband of an incontinent wife: cuckolds, however, are Christians, as we learn by the following story: An old woman hearing a man call his dog Cuckold, reproved him sharply, saying, 'Sirrah, are you not ashamed to call a dog by a Christian's name?' To cuckold the parson; to bed with one's wife before she has been churched.

CUCUMBERS. Taylors, who are jocularly said to subsist, during the summer, chiefly on cucumbers. [In tailors' parlance, *cucumber-time* is the dull season. Possibly from Ger. *die saure Gurken zeit*, the time of pickled gherkins. During the late C18 and the C19, many London tailors were Germans.F.]

CUFF. An old cuff; an old man. To cuff Jonas; said of one who is knock-kneed, or who beats his sides to keep himself warm in frosty weather; called also Beating the Booby. [Cotton, *Scarronides*, 1678. F. And sixty years earlier. OD. The word has died out, even in dialect. EDD.]

CUFFIN. A man. [Harman, 1567. The origin of the former.F.]

CULL. A man, honest or otherwise. A bob cull; a goodnatured, quiet fellow. *Cant.* [A man, companion, partner. Specifically a fool, or a dupe. Perhaps abbreviated from *cully*, itself perhaps from *cullion*, Fr. *couillon*. *Cully* in C17, almost always a dupe or fool, and Head, 1671, defines *culle* as 'a sap-headed fellow.' Congreve, 1693: "Man was by nature woman's cully made." Dyche, 1748, of *cull* says: "A cant word for a man, either good or bad, but usually means one that a wench has picked up for some naughty purpose." *Cull* occurs in Lytton and Ainsworth in the 18-30's.F, OD.—While in cant *cull* is neutral, in dialect it is always pejorative (simpleton, fool); *cully* in both is a fool. Perhaps a variant of the Elizabethan *gull*, dupe, fool: cf. the analogy of Grose's *cullability* with the early C19 colloquial, the post-1850 good-English, *gullibility*. EDD, OD.]

CULLABILITY. A disposition liable to be cheated, an unsuspecting nature, open to imposition.

CULLY. A fop or fool; also, a dupe to women; from the Italian word *coglione*, a blockhead.

CULP. A kick or blow; from the words *mea culpa*, being that part of the popish liturgy at which the people beat their breasts; or, as the vulgar term it, thump their craws. [In East Anglian, Norfolk and Suffolk dialects, a hard and heavy blow; in the first, the proverbial phase, 'a kick for a culp'='a Roland for an Oliver.' EDD.]

CUNDUM. The dried gut of a sheep, worn by men in the act of coition, to prevent venereal infection; said to have been invented by one colonel Cundum. These machines were long prepared and sold by a matron of the name of Phillips, at the Green Canister, in Half-moon-street, in the Strand. That good lady having acquired a fortune, retired from business: but learning that the town was not well served by her successors, she, out of a patriotic zeal for the public welfare, returned to her occupation; of which she gave notice by divers hand-bills, in circulation in the year 1776. Also, a false scabbard over a sword, and the oil-skin case for holding the colours of a regiment. [From a colonel in the Guards, *temp.* Charles II. Rochester, Roscommon and Dorset collaborated in a *Panegyric upon Cundum.* F.]

CUNNINGHAM. A punning appellation for a simple fellow.

CUNNING MAN. A cheat, who pretends by his skill in astrology to assist persons in recovering stolen goods; and also to tell them their fortunes, and when, how often, and to whom they shall be married; likewise answers all lawful questions, both by sea and land. This profession is frequently occupied by ladies. [In dialect, a wizard; there too a *cunning woman* is a witch. EDD.]

CUNNING SHAVER. A sharp fellow, one that trims close, i.e. cheats ingeniously.

CUNNY-THUMBED. To double one's fist, with the thumb inwards, like a woman.

C**T. The *konnos* of the Greek, and the *cunnus* of the Latin dictionaries; a nasty name for a nasty thing: *un con* (Miège). [Omitted by the OD and the EDD, yet both include words that mean precisely the same thing. While granting that it is a very ugly term, the writer feels that to ignore a very frequently used word—one used indeed by a large proportion, though not the majority, of the white population of the British Empire—is to ignore a basic part of the English language. No decent man employs, or wishes to employ, this word, but that hardly furnishes a sufficient reason for its existence being thus arbitrarily 'forgotten.' It is not slang, nor is it cant: it definitely is a 'language' word, of Classical origin and belonging to the class of vulgarisms. The etymology is obscure. The Greek *konmos*, a trinket, the beard, the fashion of wearing the hair with a tuft, is not necessarily the sense-original of the Latin *cunnus*: *kusos* and *kusthos* (related to Sanskrit *cushi*, a ditch) supply that. *Cunnus*, the pudendum muliebre, was by metonymy applied to a prostitute (cf. the dual usage of *crack*), as in the genial Horace. Cicero, in his work on oratory, says that *cunnus* is to be avoided as obscene. It passed into French as *con*, though the medieval French writers used *coing*, cf. modern Fr. slang, *petit coin*. *Con* is still used in France—but not in polite society; two irate taxi-drivers may be heard apostrophising each other as *espèce de con*. Among the soldiers in 1914-1918 the word was perhaps heard most often in some such phrase as "you silly *or* you great c—," though its literal application was frequent. Many avoided it; the others, if displeased with rifle or knapsack or indeed almost any object, occasion or person, would describe it as 'a c—.' They also employed it as an adjective formed by the adding of *ing*. Of this word along with *f—k* and *b—r*, John Brophy (in B & P) has written: "all three words are ugly, in form and in sound. They are sexual but utterly unvoluptuous. Their use will coarsen and degrade, but it will not soften or seduce.... They are impossible for literature, because, used however carefully and literally, they still carry.... the filthiness of their past. They are unshriven and, seemingly, past redemption." C—t served also, as it had long served, to connote the sexual pleasure produced by a woman in a man, and indeed all that a woman-as-sex signifies to a man, both physically and spiritually: this extension of meaning did not hold of the two colloquial alternatives popular in the Army: *quim* (rejected by the OD) and *twat* (admitted by the OD). Chaucer had spelt it *queynte* or *queinte*, a pronunciation that, as *quaint*, survived in the North Country till 1890 at least. Chaucer may have combined Old French *coing* with M.E. *cunte*, or he may have been influenced by the Old. Fr. adjective *coint*, neat, dainty, pleasant. The normal M.E. form is *cunte*, from Old Norse *kunta* =Old Frisian *kunte*=vulva. (The L. *cunnus* and the old Frisian *kunte* are cognate forms, and while French naturally followed the former, English as naturally followed the latter: certainly no contra-indication is to be found in the remarkable dictionaries of Cotgrave, Miège, and Godefroy.) Banished from all previous editions, but dared in *The Letters of John Keats*, ed. by M. Buxton Forman, March 1931, is the following passage, which in a letter of January 5, 1818, concerns a dance at the Redhalls:

"There was a younger Brother of the Squibs made himself very conspicuous after the Ladies had retired from the supper table by giving Mater Omnium—Mr Redhall said he did not understand any thing but plain english—whereat Rice egged the young fool on to say the word plainly out. After which there was an enquiry about the derivation of the word C—t when while two parsons and Grammarians were sitting together and settling the matter Wm Squibs interrupting them said a very good thing—Gentlemen says he I have always understood it to be a Root and not a Derivitive! (*sic*)." Notable examples occur in Fletcher and Rochester, and some authorities maintain that this is the word that ends *The Sentimental Journey*. (F, the great Greek and Latin dictionaries, Godefroy, Stratmann & Bradley have been drawn-upon.)

CUP OF THE CREATURE. A cup of good liquor.

CUP-SHOT. Drunk. [First in sermon of *ca.* 1593.OD.]

CUPBOARD LOVE. Pretended love to the cook, or any other person, for the sake of a meal. My guts cry cupboard, i.e. I am hungry. [Herrick:

A cupboard love is seldom true
A love sincere is found in few.   F.]

CUPID, BLIND CUPID. A jeering name for an ugly blind man; Cupid, the god of love, being frequently painted blind.

CUR. A cut or curtailed dog. According to the forest laws, a man who had no right to the privilege of the chase, was obliged to cut or law his dog; among other modes of disabling him from disturbing the game, one was by depriving him of his tail; a dog so cut was called a cut or curtailed dog, and, by contraction, a cur. A cur is figuratively used to signify a surly fellow. [I need hardly say that the etymology is erroneous.]

CURBING LAW. The act of hooking goods out of windows; the curber is the thief, the curb the hook. *Cant.* [From old cant *curb*, to steal.]

CURE A-SE. A dyachilon plaster, applied to the parts galled by riding.

CURJEW. The vulgar seaman's pronunciation of the Courageux ship of war.

CURLE. Clippings of money, which curls up in the operation. *Cant.*

CURMUDGEON. A covetous old fellow, derived, according to some, from the French term *cœur méchant*. [Derivation unknown. G's suggestion comes from Dr Johnson: "an ingenious specimen of pre-scientific etymology." OD.—W, however, shows that Johnson may have been right.—In Fifeshire, *curmudge*=a mean fellow, *curmudgeous*, mean. EDD.]

CURRY. To curry favour; to obtain the favour of a person by coaxing or servility. To curry any one's hide; to beat him. [*Curry favour* is a corruption of M.E. *to curry favel*, to curry a horse of a tawny colour. In the C14 poem *Le Roman de Fauvel*, *faveau* or *fauvel* is the name of a horse that, symbolising mundane vanity, is pampered by all classes. Palsgrave, 1530, has *curry-favell*, a flatterer. W:ROW.]

CURSE OF SCOTLAND. The nine of diamonds; diamonds, it is said, imply royalty, being ornaments to the imperial crown; and every ninth king of Scotland has been observed, for many ages, to be a tyrant and a curse to that country. Others say it is from its similarity to the arms of Argyle; the Duke of Argyle having been very instrumental in bringing about the union, which, by some Scotch patriots, has been considered as detrimental to their country. [The card was nicknamed *the Justice-Clerk*, in allusion to the Lord Justice-Clerk Ormistone, who, for his severity in repressing the rebellion of 1715, was called the Curse of Scotland. F.]

CURSITORS. Broken pettyfogging attornies, or Newgate solicitors. *Cant.* [Earlier often *cursetor.* The derivative sense was a low tramp or vagabond. The legal sense, which gave rise to Cursitor Street, running east from Chancery Lane (London), originated not in the fact that these men were messengers but that they made out writs in the ordinary way of routine: *de cursu.* F,W.]

CURTAILS. Thieves who cut off pieces of stuff hanging out of shop windows, the tails of women's gowns, &c.; also thieves wearing short jackets. [A sense-development from *curtail,* a dog with a tail cut short (rarely a bob-tailed horse). A corruption of *curtal,* it comes through French (*courtault* as in Palsgrave, 1530) from Low Latin *curtaldus,* Latin *curtus,* docked, cut short. W:WAM.]

CURTAIN LECTURE. A woman who scolds her husband when in bed, is said to read him a curtain lecture.

CURTEZAN. A prostitute. [C20 spelling, *courtesan.* In Queen Victoria's reign, it came to mean a refined or a high-placed harlot. In our modern sense, a courtesan approximates to the hetaira of Classical Greece: see R.B.Ince, *Lipstick,* Part iii, Aspasia, in *The Window,* October 1930.]

CUSHION. He has deserved the cushion; a saying of one whose wife is brought to bed of a boy; implying, that having done his business effectually, he may now indulge or repose himself.

CUSHION THUMPER, or DUSTER. A parson; many of whom, in the fury of their eloquence, heartily belabour their cushions. [Later, *cushion-smiter.* F.]

CUSTARD CAP. The cap worn by the sword-bearer of the city of London, made hollow at the top like a custard.

CUSTOM-HOUSE GOODS. The stock in trade of a prostitute, because fairly entered.

CUT. Drunk. A little cut over the head; slightly intoxicated. To cut; to leave a person or company. To cut up well; to die rich. [First, recorded in Dyche, 1748. F.]

TO CUT BENE. To speak gently. To cut bene whiddes; to give good words. To cut queer whiddes; to give foul language. To cut a bosh, or a flash; to make a figure. *Cant.*

TO CUTTY-EYE. To look out of the corners of one's eyes, to leer, to look askance. The cull cutty-eyed at us; the fellow looked suspicious at us.

DAB. An adept; a dab at any feat or exercise. Dab, quoth Dawkins, when he hit his wife on the a-se with a pound of butter. [In 1733, Lord Chesterfield: "Known dabs at finding out mysteries;" in 1748, Dyche remarks: "An expert gamester is so called;" in 1759 Goldsmith uses it as=an expert. Modern form, dabster. OD, F.—Also in C18 dialect and familiar literature, e.g. Graham's *Gwordy*, 1778, and Taylor's *Poems*, 1787. EDD.—In American tramp and underworld slang, *darb*, unusually skilled or able. I.—As a light blow, a small quantity, in general provincial use.]

DACE. Two pence. Tip me a dace; lend me two pence. *Cant.* [Fr. *deux*, or *deuce*.F.]

DADDLES. Hands. Tip us your daddle; give me your hand. *Cant.* [Also C18-19 dialect. EDD.]

DADDY. Father.Old daddy; a familiar address to an old man. To beat daddy mammy; the first rudiments of drum beating, being the elements of the roll. [For an extremely interesting note on *dad*, *daddy* (recorded in C15), see W:A.]

DAGGERS. They are at daggers drawing; i.e. at enmity, ready to fight.

DAIRY. A woman's breasts, particularly one that gives suck. She sported her dairy; she pulled out her breast.

DAISY CUTTER. A jockey term for a horse that does not lift up his legs sufficiently, or goes too near the ground, and is therefore apt to stumble. [Now a term in cricket.]

DAISY KICKERS. Hostlers at great inns.

DALMAHOY. A Dalmahoy wig; a particular kind of bushy bob wig, first worn by a chymist of that name, and afterwards adopted by tradesmen, apothecaries, &c.

DAM. A small Indian coin, mentioned in the Gentoo code of laws; hence etymologists may, if they please, derive the common expression, I do not care a dam, i.e. I do not care half a farthing for it. [F. supports G's tentative derivation, which, rejected by the OD, is championed by W.—Not that I consider my opinion worth a dam(n), but G, F, and W seem to me to be right.]

DAMBER. A rascal. See DIMBER.

DAMME BOY. A roaring, mad, blustering fellow, a scourer of the streets, or kicker up of a breeze. [Variant *dammy-boy*. In print by 1654. The C17 rakes carried swearing too far, hence this name for the roisterers of 1650-1800. OD, F.]

DAMNED SOUL. A clerk in a counting-house, whose sole business it is to clear or swear off merchandise at the custom-house; and who, it is said, guards against the crime of perjury, by taking a previous oath, never to swear truly on those occasions.

DAMPER. A luncheon, or snap before dinner; so called from its damping or allaying the appetite; eating and drinking, being as the proverb wisely observes, apt to take away the appetite. [For *snap* we say *snack*. In dialect applied also to an afternoon snack. Cf. *bever, doggy, elevener*. EDD.]

DANCERS. Stairs. [*Cant*. One phrase was: 'track up the dancers,' ascend. F.—*Dancers* is one of those sparkish plurals so common in C17-18 cant. Compare the Oxford University slang, e.g. *divvers*=Divinity examination, *collekkers*= college terminal examination, and *godders and langers*, the collective singing of *God Save the King* and *Auld Lang Syne*. But then the plural in these Oxford words is probably incidental, for *Radder* =the Radcliffe Camera, *Bodder*=the Bodleian Library, and so on.]

DANDY. That's the dandy; i.e. the ton, the clever thing; an expression of similar import to "That's the barber." See BARBER.

DANDY GREY RUSSET. A dirty brown. His coat's dandy grey russet, the colour of the Devil's nutting bag. [In dialect, *dandy-go-russet*, of worn-out or rusty-coloured clothing, also of an ancient wig. EDD.]

DANDY PRAT. An insignificant or trifling fellow. [In *Lingua, or the Five Senses*, 1580. Variant *dandiprat(t)*. From *dandipratt*, a half farthing of Henry VII'S time. F.]

TO DANGLE. To follow a woman without asking the question. Also, to be hanged: I shall see you dangle in the sheriff's picture-frame; I shall see you hanging on the gallows.

DANGLER. One who follows women in general, without any particular attachment.

DAPPER FELLOW. A smart, well-made, little man. [Spenser, in *The Shepherd's Calendar*, has *dapper ditties* and in the gloss explains *dapper* as pretty.—In dialect, *dapper*=sprightly; cf. C19 *dapperwit* (Northants and Warwicks.), a lively, spruce little man, though Dapperwit had also been a character in Wycherley.EDD.]

DARBIES. Fetters. *Cant*. [The statement that handcuffs, when used to tie prisoners together, were called *Darbies and Joans* is misleading, for *darbies* as fetters occurs in 1673, *Darby and Joan* not till 1735. *Darbies* in this sense undoubtedly derives from *Derby's* or *Darby's bands* or *bonds*, a rigid and rigorous legal or near-legal document recorded in C16. H, corrected by OD,W.]

DARBY. Ready Money. *Cant*.

DARK CULLY. A married man that keeps a mistress, whom he visits only at night, for fear of discovery.

DARKMANS. The night. *Cant*. [Cf. the sea-term, *the darks* (moonless nights), popular with the smugglers.B.—In such a word,-*mans* is a covering-up appendage, a purely deceptive amplification: this explanation would fit all the examples in G.]

DARKMANS BUDGE. One that slides into a house in the dark of the evening, and hides himself, in order to let some of the gang in at night to rob it. [Cf. Yorkshire *darkison*, sneak.EDD.]

DART. A straight-armed blow in boxing.

DASH. A tavern drawer. To cut a dash; to make a figure.

DAVID JONES. The devil, the spirit of the sea; called Nekin in the north countries, such as Norway, Denmark, and Sweden. [Smollett, 1751.OD.—Roberts, Voyages, 1726.W.]

DAVID JONES'S LOCKER. The sea. [Soon familiarised

to Davy.—The prophet *Jonah*, formerly *Jonas*, became *Jones* and was suitably graced with a Welsh christian name.W.— The noise of an oncoming wind was formerly described by sailors as "Davy putting the coppers on for the parson."B.]

DAVID'S SOW. As drunk as David's sow; a common saying, which took its rise from the following circumstance: One David Lloyd, a Welchman, who kept an alehouse at Hereford, had a living sow with six legs, which was greatly resorted to by the curious; he had also a wife much addicted to drunkenness, for which he used sometimes to give her due correction. One day David's wife having taken a cup too much, and being fearful of the consequences, turned out the sow, and lay down to sleep herself sober in the stye. A company coming in to see the sow, David ushered them into the stye, exclaiming, There is a sow for you! did any of you ever see such another? all the while supposing the sow had really been there; to which some of the company, seeing the state the woman was in, replied, it was the drunkenest sow they had ever beheld; whence the woman was ever after called David's sow. [The saying is in Ray's *Proverbs*, 1678.EDD.]

DAVY. I'll take my davy of it; vulgar abbreviation of affidavit. [Also dialectal. EDD.]

TO DAWB. To bribe. The cull was scragged because he could not dawb; the rogue was hanged because he could not bribe. All bedawbed with lace; all over lace.

DAY LIGHTS. Eyes. To darken his day lights, or sew up his sees; to close up a man's eyes in boxing.

DEAD CARGO. A term used by thieves, when they are disappointed in the value of their booty.

DEAD HORSE. To work for the dead horse; to work for wages already paid. [Also *pull the dead horse*. C17.F.]

DEAD LOUSE. Vulgar pronunciation of the Dedalus ship of war.

DEAD MEN. A cant word among journeymen bakers, for loaves falsely charged to their masters' customers; also empty bottles. [Of bottles, Swift; in early C19 it became, through the navy, *dead marine*.F, EDD.]

DEADLY NEVERGREEN, that bears fruit all the year round. The gallows, or three-legged mare. See THREE-LEGGED MARE.

DEAR JOYS. Irishmen; from their frequently making use of that expression. [Earliest, 1688. OD.]

DEATH HUNTER. An undertaker, one who furnishes the necessary articles for funerals. See CARRION HUNTER. [In C19 a vendor of 'last dying speeches.' F.—In North Riding dialect, one who, in C19, went from parish to parish, as a death occurred, to carry the corpse.EDD.]

DEATH'S HEAD UPON A MOP-STICK. A poor, miserable, emaciated fellow; one quite an otomy. See OTOMY.— He looked as pleasant as the pains of death.

DECUS. A crown piece. [From the motto *decus et tutamen*.Shadwell, 1688.F.]

DEEP-ONE. A thorough-paced rogue, a sly designing fellow; in opposition to a shallow or foolish one.

DEFT FELLOW. A neat little man. [Also, in dialect, little and pretty; active. G.—And clever.P.]

DEGEN, or DAGEN. A sword. Nim the degen; stealthesword. Dagen is Dutch for a sword. *Cant.*

DELLS. Young buxom wenches, ripe and prone to venery, but who have not lost their virginity, which the *upright man* claims by virtue of his prerogative; after which they become free for any of the fraternity. Also a common strumpet. *Cant.* [The former sense, Harman, 1567.F.]

DEMURE. As demure as an old whore at a christening.

DEMY-REP. Abbreviation of demy-reputation; a woman of doubtful character. ["Whom everybody knows to be what nobody calls her," Fielding; *The Connoisseur*, 1754, "Not to be found in any of our dictionaries"; authorised and sanctified by Thackeray in *Vanity Fair*.F, OD.]

DERBY. To come down with the derbies; to pay the money.

DERRICK. The name of the finisher of the law, or hangman, about the year 1608.—'For he rides his circuit with the Devil, ' and Derrick must be his host, and Tiburne the inne at which 'he will lighte.' Vide Bellman of London, in art. PRIGGING

LAW.—'At the gallows, where I leave them, as to the haven
' at which they must all cast anchor, if Derrick's cables do but
' hold.' Ibid. [The three senses, the hangman, hanging, the
gallows, all occur within the period 1600-1607. The hoisting-
contrivance, a derivative, *ca.* 1740.OD.]

DEUSEA VILLE. The country. *Cant.* [In C19 slang, *daisy-
ville.* EDD.]

DEUSEA VILLE STAMPERS. Country carriers. *Cant.*

DEVIL. A printer's errand-boy. Also a small thread in the
king's ropes and cables, whereby they may be distinguished
from all others. The Devil himself; a small streak of blue thread
in the king's sails. The Devil may dance in his pocket; i.e. he
has no money; the cross on our ancient coins being jocularly
supposed to prevent him from visiting that place, for fear, as it
is said, of breaking his shins against it. To hold a candle to the
Devil; to be civil to any one out of fear; in allusion to the story
of the old woman, who set a wax taper before the image of St
Michael, and another before the Devil, whom that saint is commonly represented as trampling under his feet; being reproved
for paying such honour to Satan, she answered, as it was uncertain which place she should go to, heaven or hell, she chose
to secure a friend in both places. That will be when the Devil
is blind, and he has not got sore eyes yet; said of any thing un-
likely to happen. It rains whilst the sun shines, the Devil is beating his wife with a shoulder of mutton: this phenomenon is also
said to denote that cuckolds are going to heaven; on being in-
formed of this, a loving wife cried out with great vehemence,
'Run, husband, run!'

> The Devil was sick, the Devil a monk would be;
> The Devil was well, the devil a monk was he.

A proverb signifying that we are apt to forget promises made
in time of distress. To pull the Devil by the tail; to be reduced
to one's shifts. The Devil go with you and sixpence, and then
you will have both money and company.

DEVIL. The gizzard of a turkey or foul, scored, peppered, salted, and broiled; it derives its appellation from being hot in the
mouth.

DEVIL'S BOOKS. Cards. [Of Presbyterian origin, this term was coined as a counterblast to *King's books*, from the full description: *The History of the Four Kings*. F. Variants: *Devil's painted, or pictured, books*.EDD.]

DEVIL CATCHER, or DEVIL DRIVER. A parson. See SNUB DEVIL.

DEVIL'S DAUGHTER. It is said of one who has a termagant for his wife, that he has married the Devil's daughter, and lives with the old folks.

DEVIL'S DAUGHTER'S PORTION,

> Deal, Dover, and Harwich,
> The Devil gave with his daughter in marriage;
> And, by a codicil to his will,
> He added Helvoet and the Brill.

A saying occasioned by the shameful impositions practised by the inhabitants of those places, on sailors and travellers.

DEVIL DRAWER. A miserable painter.

DEVIL'S DUNG. Assafœtida. [Obsolete except in dialect.]

DEVIL'S GUTS. A surveyor's chain; so called by farmers, who do not like their land should be measured by their landlords.

DEVILISH. Very: an epithet, which in the English vulgar language is made to agree with every quality of thing; as, devilish bad, devilish good; devilish sick, devilish well; devilish sweet, devilish sour; devilish hot, devilish cold, &c. &c.

DEW BEATERS. Feet. *Cant.* [In C17, pedestrians out and about before the dew has gone; G's sense, derivative; derivative variants, C19: *dew-dusters, dew-treaders*.F.—In dialect, either large boots or clumsily-walking large-footed persons. EDD.]

DEWS WINS, or DEUX WINS. Two-pence. *Cant.* [Cf. *deuce*, the lowest throw in dicing.W.—In the American underworld, the two-dollar bill is ill-omened, perhaps as a reminiscence of dicing, perhaps in allusion to *the deuce!* being popularly considered=*the devil!* I.]

DEWITTED. Torn to pieces by a mob, as that great statesman John de Wit was in Holland, anno 1672. [There were two

De Witts, who, opponents of William of Orange, were massacred by the mob—without subsequent inquiry. The modern equivalent is *lynch*, though *dewit* prevailed for about 150 years. F.]

DICE. The names of false dice:
A bale of bard cinque deuces
A bale of flat cinque deuces
A bale of flat sice aces
A bale of bard cater traes
A bale of flat cater traes
A bale of fulhams
A bale of light graniers
A bale of langrets contrary to the ventage
A bale of gordes, with as many highmen as lowmen for passage
A bale of demies
A bale of long dice for even and odd
A bale of bristles
A bale of direct contraries.

DICK. That happened in the reign of queen Dick, i.e. never; said of any absurd old story. I am as queer as Dick's hatband; that is, out of spirits, or don't know what ails me. [*As Dick's hatband* appears in almost any such phrase; Cheshire C19 dialect had: "All my eye and Dick's hatband." EDD.—Cf *Betty Martin*.]

DICKY. A woman's under-petticoat. It's all Dickey with him; i.e. it's all over with him. ["It's all Dicky with him" should be lower-case: "it's all dick(e)y with him," since *dicky* is dialect for shaky, uncertain, hazardous, critical, ill.EDD.]

DIDDEYS. A woman's breasts or bubbies. [Properly *diddies*. Also of an animal's teats or dugs.EDD.]

DIDDLE. Gin. [Presumably from dialect and slang verb *diddle*, to deceive, trick, swindle.]

DIGGERS. Spurs. *Cant*. [Parker, *Life's Painter*, 1789.F.]

DILDO. (From the Italian *diletto*, q.d. a woman's delight; or from our word *dally*, q.d. a thing to play withal). Penis Succedaneus, called in Lombardy Passo Tempo. *Baily*. [The first edition entry was longer and more explicit: G evidently decided that it were better in its modified form. This *Dildo* is connected with the *dildo* that, occurring so frequently in Jacobean and Caroline refrains, usually constitutes a veiled reference to the phallus—or a representation thereof. The 'locus classicus' on *dildo* is in Burton's *Thousand Nights and a Night*.]

DILIGENT. Double diligent, like the Devil's apothecary; said of one affectedly diligent.

DILLY. (An abbreviation of the word *diligence*.) A public voiture or stage, commonly a post-chaise, carrying three persons: the name is taken from the public stage vehicles in France and Flanders. The dillies first began to run in England about the year 1779.

DIMBER. Pretty. A dimber cove; a pretty fellow. Dimber mort; a pretty wench. *Cant*. [C17.F.]

DIMBER DAMBER. A top man, or prince, among the canting crew; also the chief rogue of the gang, or the completest cheat. *Cant*. [Literally: a skilful chief.F.]

DING. To knock down. To ding it in one's ears: to reproach or tell one something one is not desirous of hearing. Also to throw away or hide: thus a highwayman who throws away or hides any thing with which he robbed, to prevent being known or detected, is, in the canting lingo, styled a Dinger. [The verb is very old and survives in dialect.EDD.—"I'se ding him," C18 Northern for "I shall beat him." G.]

DING BOY. A rogue, a hector, a bully, or sharper. *Cant*.

DING DONG. Helter skelter, in a hasty disorderly manner. [It now means *vigorous(ly)*.F.— In dialect, with variant *d.dang*, it also=in earnest, fast, great, extraordinary, and, as a noun, clatter, confusion.EDD.]

DINGEY CHRISTIAN. A mulatto; or any one who has, as the West Indian term is, a lick of the tar-brush, that is, some negro blood in him.

DINING ROOM POST. A mode of stealing in houses that let lodgings, by rogues pretending to be postmen, who send up sham letters to the lodgers, and, whilst waiting in the entry for the postage, go into the first room they see open, and rob it.

DIP. To dip for a wig. Formerly, in Middle Row, Holborn, wigs of different sorts were, it is said, put into a closestool box, into which, for three-pence, any one might dip, or thrust in his hand, and take out the first wig he laid hold of: if he was dissatisfied with his prize, he might, on paying three half-pence, return it and dip again.

THE DIP. A cook's shop, under Furnival's Inn, where many attornies' clerks, and other inferior limbs of the law, take out the wrinkles from their bellies. *Dip* is also a punning name for a tallow chandler.

DIPPERS. Anabaptists.

DIPT. Pawned or mortgaged. [From the old verb *dip* in these two senses. Dryden in 1693, *The Spectator* in 1711, have it as to mortgage.F,OD,]

DIRTY PUZZLE. A nasty slut.

DISGRUNTLED. Offended, disobliged. [C18-19 dialect and slang, but *ca.* 1880 it became good English.EDD.]

DISGUISED. Drunk. [Fairly common in dialect till *ca.* 1890. EDD.—In Shakespeare, *disguise*=drunkenness, intoxication. O.]

DISHED UP. He is completely dished up; he is totally ruined. To throw a thing in one's dish; to reproach or twit one with any particular matter. [For this, as for numerous other words and phrases, G is the earliest authority. The OD misses this first reference, perhaps because the entry is absent from the first edition.]

DISHCLOUT. A dirty, greasy, woman. He has made a napkin of his dishclout: a saying of one who has married his cook maid. To pin a dishclout to a man's tail; a punishment often threatened by the female servants in a kitchen, to a man who pries too minutely into the secrets of that place. [Used by Shakespeare in depreciatory comparison: "Romeo's a dishclout to him." O.]

DISMAL DITTY. The psalm sung by the felons at the gallows, just before they are turned off. [The origin of *dismal* is *dis mal*, the Old French equivalent of L. *dies mali*, the unlucky days of the medieval calendar. W:MWAM.]

DISPATCHES. A mittimus, or a justice of the peace's warrant for the commitment of a rogue.

DITTO. A suit of ditto: coat, waistcoat, and breeches, all of one colour. [The C19 form was *ditto(e)s*, used occasionally for the trousers alone.]

DIVE. To dive; to pick a pocket. To dive for a dinner; to go down into a cellar to dinner. A dive, is a thief who stands ready to receive goods thrown out to him by a little boy put in at a window. *Cant.* [Whence the American *dive*.]

DIVER. A pickpocket; also one who lives in a cellar. [Variant *dive*. Dekker, 1608, and cf. Jenny Diver in Gay's *Beggar's Opera*. F.]

DIVIDE. To divide the house with one's wife; to give her the outside, and to keep all the inside to one's self, i.e. to turn her into the street.

DO. To do any one; to rob or cheat him. I have done him: I have robbed him. Also to overcome in a boxing match: witness those laconic lines written on the field of battle, by Humphreys to his patron—'Sir, I have done the Jew.' [The corresponding noun, as a fraud, appears in Vaux's *Memoirs*, 1812. F.—The modern slang *do*=event, party, feast, etc., became fully established about 1920, but it was known in dialect, as the EDD tells us, at least as early as 1820.]

TO DO OVER. Carries the same meaning, but is not so briefly expressed; the former having received the polish of the present times. [In C19 cant it also meant to search a victim's pockets unperceived; and in C19 venery, to seduce, to know carnally. F.]

DOASH. A cloak. *Cant.*

DOBIN RIG. Stealing ribbands from haberdashers early in the morning, or late at night; generally practised by women in the disguise of maid servants. [*Dob(b)in*, a ribbon; *rig*, stealing. F.]

TO DOCK. To lie with a woman. The cull docked the dell all the darkmans: the fellow lay with the wench all night. Docked smack smooth; one who has suffered an amputation of his penis, from a venereal complaint. He must go into dock: a sea phrase, signifying that the person spoken of must undergo a salivation. Docking is also a punishment inflicted by sailors on the prostitutes who have infected them with the venereal disease; it consists in cutting off all their clothes, petticoat, shift and all, close to their stays, and then turning them into the street. [*Dock*, literally to deflower, hence to possess sexually, occurs in Harman, 1567 and derives from Gipsy *dukker*, to ravish, to bewitch, cf. Gipsy *duke*, to hurt, to bewitch.F; GB.]

DOCTOR. Milk and water, with a little rum, and some nutmeg; also the name of a composition used by distillers, to make spirits appear stronger than they really are, or, in their phrase, better proof.

DOCTORS. Loaded dice that will run but two or three chances. They put the doctors upon him; they cheated him with loaded dice.

DODSEY. A woman: perhaps a corruption of Doxey. *Cant.* [In Shakespeare, *doxy* is vagabond's cant for a beggar's mistress. O.—G, therefore, has presumably conjectured correctly.]

DOG. An old dog at it; expert or accustomed to anything. Dog in a manger; one who would prevent another from enjoying what he himself does not want: an allusion to the well known fable. The dogs have not dined: a common saying to any one whose shirt hangs out behind. To dog, or dodge; to follow at a distance. To blush like a blue dog, i.e. not at all. To walk the black dog on any one; a punishment inflicted in the night on a fresh prisoner, by his comrades, in case of his refusal to pay the usual footing or garnish. ["I am dog at a catch," *Twelfth Night, II, iii*, 66.O.]

DOG BUFFERS. Dog stealers, who kill those dogs not advertised for, sell their skins, and feed the remaining dogs with their flesh.

DOG IN A DOUBLET. A daring, resolute fellow. In Germany and Flanders the boldest dogs used to hunt the boar, having a kind of buff doublet buttoned on their bodies. Rubens has represented several so equipped, so has Sneyders.

DOG LATIN. Barbarous Latin, such as was formerly used by the lawyers in their pleadings. [Variants: *Kitchen, Bog, Garden,* or *Apothecaries' Latin*.F.—Since *ca.* 1830, *Dog Latin* has meant especially medical Latin. H.—In dialect, the term means slang or some other special form of speech or even dialect itself. EDD.]

DOG'S PORTION. A lick and a smell. He comes in for only a dog's portion; a saying of one who is a distant admirer or dangler after women. See DANGLER.

DOG'S RIG. To copulate till you are tired, and then turn tail to it. [Cf. the C19 slang phrase, *to make a dog's match of it*, to have wayside intercourse.F.]

DOG'S SOUP. Rain water.

DOG VANE. A cockade. *Sea term.*

DOGGED. Surly. [In Shakespeare's *King John*, cruel, malicious.O.]

DOGGESS, DOG'S WIFE or LADY, PUPPY'S MAMMA. Jocular ways of calling a woman a bitch.

DOLL. Bartholomew doll; a tawdry, over-drest woman, like one of the children's dolls sold at Bartholomew fair. To mill doll; to beat hemp at Bridewell, or any other house of correction.

DOLLY. A Yorkshire dolly; a contrivance for washing, by means of a kind of wheel fixed in a tub, which being turned about, agitates and cleanses the linen put into it, with soap and water.

DOMINE DO LITTLE. An impotent old fellow.

DOMINEER. To reprove or command in an insolent or haughty manner. Don't think as how you shall domineer here. [Shakespeare has it to mean, to live riotously.O.]

DOMMERER. A beggar pretending that his tongue has been cut out by the Algerines, or cruel and blood-thirsty Turks, or else that he was born deaf and dumb. *Cant.* [Variants, *dommerar*, *dummerer*. In Harman, 1567.OD.]

DONE, or DONE OVER. Robbed; also, convicted or hanged. *Cant.*—See DO.

DONE UP. Ruined by gaming and extravagances. *Modern term.* [Cf. modern *done-in*, which in soldiers' slang in 1914-1918 signified spoiled; finished, destroyed; dead, killed. F & G.]

DONKEY, DONKEY DICK. A he, or jack ass: called donkey, perhaps, from the Spanish or don-like gravity of that animal, intitled also the king of Spain's trumpeter.

DOODLE. A silly fellow, or noodle: see NOODLE. Also a child's penis. Doodle doo, or Cock a doodle doo: a childish appellation for a cock, in imitation of its notes when crowing. [As=dolt, perhaps first 'dictionaried' by Ash, 1775.F. Used by Ford the dramatist in 1628; cf. Cobden's phrase, 1845: "the Noodles and Doodles of the aristocracy." OD.]

DOODLE SACK. A bagpipe. *Dutch.*—Also the private parts of a woman.

DOPEY. A beggar's trull.

DOSE. Burglary. He was cast for felon and dose; he was found guilty of felony and burglary. *Cant.*

DOT AND GO ONE. To waddle: generally applied to persons who have one leg shorter than the other, and who, as the sea phrase is, go upon an uneven keel. Also a jeering appellation for an inferior writing-master, or teacher of arithmetic. [Scott in *Nigel*, 1822, popularised *dot and carry one*.F.]

DOUBLE. To tip any one the double; to run away in his or her debt. [Also *to give the double.* Apparently first used in Parker's *View of Society*, 1781.F.]

DOUBLE JUGG. A man's backside. *Cotton's Virgil.* [Burton *ca.* 1620.F.]

DOUGLAS. Roby Douglas, with one eye and a stinking breath; the breech. *Sea wit.*

DOVE-TAIL. A species of regular answer, which fits in to the subject, like the contrivance whence it takes its name: ex.Who own(s) this? The dovetail is, Not you by your asking.

DOWDY. A coarse, vulgar-looking woman. [The sense of vulgar disappeared *ca.* 1810; in dialect, however, the word has always connoted slatternliness.EDD.]

DOWDYING. A local joke formerly practised at Salisbury, on large companies, or persons boasting of their courage. It was performed by one Pearce, who had the knack of personating madness, and who, by the direction of some of the company, would burst into a room, in a most furious manner, as if just

128

broke loose from his keeper, to the great terror of those not in the secret. Dowdying became so much the fashion of the place, that it was exhibited before his Royal Highness the Prince of Wales, father of our present sovereign. Pearce obtained the name of Dowdy, from a song he used to sing, which had for its burthen the words *dow de dow*.

DOWN HILLS. Dice that run low.

TO DOWSE. To take down; as, Dowse the pendant. Dowse your dog vane; take the cockade out of your hat. Dowse the glim; put out the candle. [*Dowse* (later *douse*) *the glim* was exalted from cant to normal English by Scott's employment of the phrase. *Punch* welcomed it in 1860, Charles Reade in 1863. OD,F.]

DOWSE ON THE CHOPS. A blow in the face.

DOWSER. Vulgar pronunciation of *douceur*.

DOXIES. She beggars, wenches, whores. [Harman, 1567. A very common C16-17 word. Dyche in 1748 defined as "a she-beggar. . . . the female companion of a foot-soldier, travelling tinker, etc." In late C18 and in C19 the word came occasionally to mean a jade, a girl, even a wife, the last occurring in Mayhew, 1851, in a list of patterer's words.F.—In dialect, *doxy* as early as 1760 signified a young girl, a sweetheart and in C19 a slattern; but also, in C19 dialect, the adjective *doxy*= smart, pretty. EDD.]

DRAB. A nasty, sluttish whore. [C16.OD.]

DRAG. To go on the drag; to follow a cart or waggon, in order to rob it. *Cant*. [In C19, *go on* or *flash the drag* meant to don women's clothes for immoral purposes.F.—In G's phrase there is a play on words, *drag* being a cart, but also a trick, stratagem.]

DRAGGLETAIL, or DAGGLETAIL. One whose garments are bespattered with dag or dew: generally applied to the female sex, to signify a slattern.

DRAGOONING IT. A man who occupies two branches of one profession, is said to dragoon it; because, like the soldier of that denomination, he serves in a double capacity. Such is a physician who furnishes the medicines, and compounds his own prescriptions.

129

DRAM. A glass or small measure of any spirituous liquors, which, being originally sold by apothecaries, were estimated by drams, ounces, &c. Dog's dram; to spit in his mouth, and clap his back. [From Gr. for a handful.W.—In C19 dialect *to dram*=to tipple, *dramming*=tippling.EDD.]

DRAM-A-TICK. A dram served upon credit.

DRAPER. An ale-draper; an alehouse keeper.

DRAUGHT, or BILL, ON THE PUMP AT ALDGATE. A bad or false bill of exchange. See ALDGATE.

DRAW LATCHES. Robbers of houses whose doors are only fastened with latches. *Cant.*

DRAWERS. Stockings. *Cant.* [Very long ones.H.]

DRAWING THE KING'S PICTURE. Coining. *Cant.*

TO DRESS. To beat. I'll dress his hide neatly; I'll beat him soundly. [Usually, as in Mrs Centlivre in 1715, *dress down* (a person).F.]

DRIBBLE. A method of pouring out, as it were, the dice from the box, gently, by which an old practitioner is enabled to cog one of them with his fore-finger. [Cf. Northern C18 *dribble*, "a laborious and diligent servant." G.]

DRIPPER. A gleet.

DROMEDARY. A heavy, bungling thief or rogue. A purple dromedary: a bungler in the art and mystery of thieving. *Cant.* [In C19 dialect, a dull or stupid person.EDD.]

DROMMERARS. See DOMMERER.

DROP. The new drop; a contrivance for executing felons at Newgate, by means of a platform, which drops from under them: this is also called the last drop. See LEAP.

DROP A COG. To let fall, with design, a piece of gold or silver, in order to draw in and cheat the person who sees it picked up; the piece so dropped is called a dropt cog. [For an excellent account of this practice see Borrow's *Romano Lavo-Lil*, where it is called *ring-dropping*.]

DROP IN THE EYE. Almost drunk. [Swift has it.F.— Like the equivalent *drop in the head*, it appears in dialect.EDD.]

TO DRUB. To beat any one with a stick, or rope's end: perhaps a contraction of *dry rub*. It is also used to signify a good beating with any instrument. [More probably from the Barbary states, where the Arabic *daraba*=to beat, to bastinado. OD.—Shakespeare has *dry-beat* (O): this tends to support G.]

DRUMBELO. A dull, heavy fellow. [In Shakespeare, *drumble* =to be sluggish.O.—In C18 Northern dialect, *drumbled*, muddy, could be applied to ale.P.—*Drumbelo* is probably a combinative derivation from *drumble*, dialectal for a dull or inactive person, and *drumbled*, muddy or thick. (EDD.)]

DRUMMER. A jockey term for a horse that throws about his fore legs irregularly: the idea is taken from a kettle drummer, who, in beating, makes many flourishes with his drumsticks.

DRUNK. Drunk as a wheel-barrow. Drunk as David's sow. See DAVID'S SOW.

DRURY LANE AGUE. The venereal disorder.

DRURY LANE VESTAL. A woman of the town, or prostitute: Drury-lane, and its environs ,were formerly the residence of many of those ladies.

DRY BOB. A smart repartee; also copulation without emission; in law Latin, *siccus robertulus*.

DRY BOOTS. A sly humorous fellow.

DUB. A picklock, or master-key. *Cant.*

DUB LAY. Robbing houses by picking the locks.

DUB THE JIGGER. Open the door. *Cant.*

DUB O' TH' HICK. A lick on the head.

DUBBER. A picker of locks. *Cant.*

DUCE. Two-pence. [Cf. *Dews Wins.*]

DUCK. A lame duck; an Exchange-alley phrase for a stock-jobber, who either cannot or will not pay his losses, or differences, in which case he is said to *waddle out of the alley*, as he cannot appear there again till his debts are settled and paid; should he attempt it, he would be hustled out by the fraternity.

DUCKS AND DRAKES. To make ducks and drakes; a school-boy's amusement, practised with pieces of tile, oyster-shells, or flattish stones, which being skimmed along the surface of a pond, or still river, rebound many times. To make ducks and drakes of one's money; to throw it idly away. [The game dates back to the time of Scipio Africanus the Younger. Used semi-figuratively in 1605 by Chapman.F.]

DUCK F-CK-R. The man who has the care of the poultry on board a ship of war.

DUCK LEGS. Short legs. [In several dialects, *duck-legged*. EDD.]

DUDDERS, or WHISPERING DUDDERS. Cheats who travel the country, pretending to sell smuggled goods: they accost their intended dupes in a whisper. The goods they have for sale are old shopkeepers',or damaged; purchased by them of large manufactories. See DUFFER. [In early C19, also *dudsmen*. By 1860 both the term and the practice were nearly obsolete.H.]

DUDDERING RAKE. A thundering rake, a buck of the first head, one extremely lewd.

DUDGEON. Anger. [Out of place: has always been good English.]

DUDS. Clothes. [In 1440 *dudde* was defined as cloth; in Harman, 1567, *duddes*=clothes. In plural has always been low: C16-17, cant; C18-20, slang. OD.]

DUFFERS. Cheats who ply in different parts of the town, particularly about Water-lane, opposite St Clement's Church in the Strand, and pretend to deal in smuggled goods, stopping all country people, or such as they think they can impose on; which they frequently do, by selling them Spitalfields goods at double their current price. [From the cant verb *duff*, to sell goods that—to enhance the idea of their value—one pretends are either stolen or smuggled. Colquhoun, in *Police of the Metropolis*, 1796: "A class of sharpers. . . . duffers, who go about from house to house, and attend public-houses, inns, and fairs, pretending to sell smuggled goods." This sense obtained till late C19.F.—In C19 dialect, pedlars, especially hawkers of women's clothes. EDD.]

DUKE, or RUM DUKE. A queer unaccountable fellow.

DUKE OF LIMBS. A tall, awkward, ill-made fellow.

DUKE HUMPHREY. To dine with Duke Humphrey; to fast. In old St Paul's church was an aisle called Duke Humphrey's walk (from a tomb vulgarly called his, but in reality belonging to John of Gaunt), and persons who walked there, while others were at dinner, were said to dine with Duke Humphrey. [Gabriel Harvey, 1592.OD.]

DULL SWIFT. A stupid, sluggish fellow, one long going on an errand.

DUMB ARM. A lame arm.

DUMB-FOUNDED. Silenced, also soundly beaten. [The dialectal variant *dumbfounder* has caused some confusion in the ranks of those who would write in good English.]

DUMB GLUTTON. A woman's privities.

DUMB WATCH. A venereal bubo in the groin.

DUMPLIN. A short thick man or woman. Norfolk dumplin; a jeering appellation of a Norfolk man, dumplins being a favourite kind of food in that country. [In dialect, *dumpling* means also fool, blockhead.EDD.]

DUMPS. Down in the dumps; low-spirited, melancholy: jocularly said to be derived from Dumpos, a king of Egypt, who died of melancholy. Dumps are also small pieces of lead, cast by schoolboys in the shape of money. [The OD ignores G's fanciful etymology and tentatively proposes Middle Dutch *domp*, haze, mist. More in 1529 has it=melancholy. OD.—In Roxburghshire dialect, *dumps*=mournful tunes. EDD.—Cf. use in Shakespeare: "(Properly) mournful melody or song, (hence) tune in general." O.]

DUN. An importunate creditor. Dunny, in the provincial dialect of several counties, signifies *deaf;* to dun, then, perhaps may mean to deafen with importunate demands: some derive it from the word *donnez*, which dignifies *give*. But the true original meaning of the word, owes its birth to one Joe Dun, a famous bailiff of the town of Lincoln, so extremely active, and so dexterous in his business, that it became a proverb, when a man refused to pay, Why do not you *Dun* him? that is, Why do not you set Dun to arrest him? Hence it became a cant word, and is now as old as since the days of Henry VII. Dun was also the general name for the hangman, before that of Jack Ketch.

And presently a halter got,
Made of the best strong hempen teer [*sic*],
And ere a cut could lick her ear,
Had tied it up with as much art,
As DUN himself could do for's heart.
                    Cotton's Virgil's Trav. book iv.
["It may have been a stock name of the *John Doe......Tommy Atkins* type." W.]

DUNAKER. A stealer of cows and calves. [Frequent in C17. F.]

DUNGHILL. A coward: a cockpit phrase, all but game cocks being styled dunghills. To die dunghill; to repent, or shew any signs of contrition, at the gallows. Moving dunghill: a dirty, filthy man or woman. Dung, an abbreviation of dunghill, also means a journeyman taylor who submits to the law for regulating journeymen taylors' wages, therefore deemed by the flints a coward. See FLINTS. [Dialect has variant *dung-belly*.EDD.]

DUNNOCK. A cow. *Cant.* [Not in this sense in dialect, which, however, has it as the name of two birds, the hedge-sparrow (as in Cotgrave) and the wryneck; as a sweetheart (a woman and only W. Yorks.); and as=dun-coloured (E. Lancs). EDD.]

TO DUP. To open a door: a contraction of *do ope*, or *open*. See DUB. [Harman, 1567; by 1724 it meant also to enter (a house). F.—In Shakespeare it=do up.O.]

DURGEN. A little trifling fellow. [Usually *durgan;* in dialect, a dwarf or a dwarfish person, also an undersized animal.EDD.]

DURHAM MAN. Knocker kneed, he grinds mustard with his knees: Durham is famous for its mustard.

DUST. Money. Down with your dust; deposit the money. To raise or kick up a dust; to make a disturbance or riot: see BREEZE. Dust it away; drink about. [As money, Fuller, 1655. Probably from *gold-dust*. Smollett, 1759, has *kick up a dust*, Henry Brooke in 1766 has *raise a dust*.OD,F.]

DUSTMAN. A dead man: your father is a dustman.

DUTCH COMFORT. Thank God it is no worse. [C19 variant, *Dutch consolation*. To G's four *Dutch* phrases add:—*To do a Dutch*, to run away, to desert; *That beats the Dutch*, a sarcastic superlative, used in 1775; *To talk Dutch, Double Dutch, High Dutch*, to talk gibberish, hence nonsense, Marlowe in *Faustus* having "he speaks Dutch fustian;" *The Dutch have taken Holland*, to impute stale news, an earlier form of "Queen Anne is dead;" *Dutch auction* or *sale*, i.e. at minimum prices, or a mock auction; a *Dutch bargain*, one-sided; *Dutch courage; Dutch defence*, a sham defence (Fielding); *Dutch gleek*, drinks, 1654; *I'm a Dutchman if I do!* a strong refusal; *Dutchman's breeches*, nautical for two blue streaks in a cloudy sky; *Dutchman's drinks*, a draught that empties the glass or pot; *a Dutch treat*, everyone paying; *Dutch uncle*, severe or fierce one, usually in *I'll talk to you like a Dutch uncle*, where we have a fusion of the idea in Horace's *ne sis patruus mihi* and of Dutchmen's former reputation as brutal disciplinarians; *Dutch widow*, a prostitute, Middleton, 1608. OD,F.—In dialect we have these compounds:—*Dutch barn*, one consisting of a pillared roof without sides (Tuke, *Agriculture*, 1800); *Dutch cheese*, the fruit of the dwarf-mallow (Cheshire only); *Dutch cousins*, great friends (Sussex coast); *Dutch doll*, a jointed wooden one (Irish); *Dutch nightingale*, a frog (East Anglia and Norfolk: cf. the Lincolnshire *fen-nightingale*); *Dutch oven*, a tin hastener for roasting food (Yorkshire and Somerset); *Dutch plough*, an ordinary one (North Riding; Tuke, 1801). Also these phrases:—*As Dutch as a mastiff*, in allusion to facial innocence after actual wrongdoing; *To talk as Dutch as Daimport's (Davenport's) bitch*, to talk refinedly, affectedly, or without a provincial accent (Cheshire); in W. Yorkshire the same meaning attaches to *to talk Dutch*, which in Cheshire signifies to speak angrily; in W. Yorks., again, *to Dutch*=to talk mincingly. The noun *Dutch* in the Shetlands=tobacco. Dialect has *Dutchman's corner*, the front of the fire, while the *Dutchman's breeches* already mentioned has in Devonshire dialect the meaning, *seal-flower*. In C19 in Nottinghamshire, *Dutchy*=a toy marble, the word deriving from the times when nearly all coarse earthenware came from Holland. EDD.—In most of these terms and phrases, *Dutch* has a pejorative sense, "a witness, no doubt, to the long-standing hatred engendered by the bitter fight for the supremacy of the seas between England and Holland in the seventeenth century." F.—In the approximate period 1550-1640, *Spanish* had served as the scape-goat; in the C19, *French*, as in *French leave*, *French letter*, to which, by the way, the French responded with *filer à l'anglaise* and *capote anglaise;* in 1914-1918, and for nearly a decade afterwards, *German*, especially in the form *Hun*, assumed the same rôle.]

DUTCH CONCERT. Where everyone plays or sings a different tune. [Variant, *Dutch medley*. F.]

DUTCH FEAST. Where the entertainer gets drunk before his guests. [Noted in 1888 as already obsolete. F.]

DUTCH RECKONING, or ALLE-MAL. A verbal or lump account, without particulars, as brought at spunging or bawdy houses.

DUTCHESS. A woman enjoyed with her pattens on, or by a man in boots, is said to be made a dutchess.

DYE HARD, or GAME. To dye hard, is to shew no signs of fear or contrition at the gallows; not to whiddle or squeak. This advice is frequently given to felons going to suffer the law, by their old comrades, anxious for the honour of the gang. [One of the most picturesque of the many expressions relating directly to the gallows (I have formed a collection numbering nigh on a hundred), is 'to die in a horse's nightcap.']

E ARNEST. A deposit in part of payment, to bind a bargain. [Cooper, 1573, defines L. *arrha* as "an earnest penny, earnest money;" this *earnest*, quite distinct from *earnest*=serious, derives from M.E. *ernes*. W:ROW.]

EASY. Make the cull easy or quiet; gag or kill him. As easy as pissing the bed.

EASY VIRTUE. A lady of easy virtue; an impure or prostitute.

EAT. To eat like a beggar man, and wag his under jaw; a jocular reproach to a proud man. To eat one's words; to retract what one has said.

TO EDGE. To excite, stimulate, or provoke; or, as it is vulgarly called, to egg a man on. Fall back, fall edge; i.e. let what will happen. Some derive to egg on, from the Latin word, *age*, *age*. [Probably the two stimulatory senses of *edge*, i.e. *edge* and *egg*, are of distinct derivation. OD.—Yet *egg* is the Northern form of *edge*.W.]

EIGHT EYES. I will knock out two of your eight eyes; a common Billingsgate threat from one fish nymph to another: every woman, according to the naturalists of that society, having eight eyes; viz. two seeing-eyes, two bub-eyes, a bell-eye, two popes-eyes, and a *** -eye. He has fallen down and trod upon his eye; said of one who has a black eye.

ELBOW GREASE. Labour. Elbow grease will make an oak table shine. [Cf. the French *huile de bras*.F.]

ELBOW ROOM. Sufficient space to act in. Out at elbows; said of an estate that is mortgaged.

ELBOW SHAKER. A gamester, one who rattles Saint Hugh's bones, i.e. the dice. [Dyche, 1748.F.]

ELF. A fairy or hobgoblin, a little man or woman. [Shakespeare has *elf-skin*, a thin slight man.O. In Renfrewshire, *elf* is an opprobrious epithet, as in Picken, *Poems*, 1813.EDD.—In Norfolk and Suffolk, *ca.* 1800, *elvish* signified irritable, spiteful, and could be applied to bees.P.]

ELIZABETHS. A society for commemorating the anniversary of queen Elizabeth, who met at the sign of her head, Hick's Hall, in the room said to be that wherein she received her juvenile education.

EMPEROR. Drunk as an emperor, i.e. ten times as drunk as a lord.

ENGLISH BURGUNDY. Porter.

ENSIGN BEARER. A drunken man, who looks red in the face, or hoists his colours in his drink.

EQUIPT. Rich: also having new clothes. Well equipt; full of money, or well dressed. The cull equipped me with a brace of meggs; the gentleman furnished me with a couple of guineas.

ERIFFS. Rogues just initiated, and beginning to practise. [*New Canting Dictionary*, 1725.OD.—In C19 the word became American thieves' slang.F.]

ESSEX LION. A calf: Essex being famous for calves, and

chiefly supplying the London markets. [Also in Essex dialect. So too the next entry.EDD.]

ESSEX STILE. A ditch: a great part of Essex is low marshy ground, in which there are more ditches than stiles.

ETERNITY BOX. A coffin.

EVANS. Mrs Evans; a name frequently given to a she cat; owing, as it is said, to a witch of the name of Evans, who frequently assumed the appearance of a cat.

EVES. Hen-roosts. [Somerset dialect. Became obsolete *ca.* 1880.EDD.]

EVE'S CUSTOM-HOUSE, where Adam made his first entry. The monosyllable.

EVES DROPPER. One that lurks about to rob hen-roosts; also a listener at doors and windows, to hear private conversations. [Unfortunately, *eavesdropper* belies G's etymology.]

EVIL. A halter. *Cant.* [From the older meanings, an illness, (specifically) a swelling on the neck.EDD.—In C19 slang, a wife, matrimony.F.)

EWE. A white ewe; a beautiful woman. An old ewe, drest lamb fashion; an old woman, drest like a young girl. [I have myself heard a Cockney remark on a woman obviously aged fifty but dressed like a girl of seventeen: "There's a piece of mutton pretending to be lamb." *Mutton dressed up to look like lamb* is more general. Apparently the recession of sheep from London caused the simile to shift from the animal to the animal's flesh.]

EXECUTION DAY. Washing day. [In modern American tramp and underworld slang, it means Monday, i.e. washing-day.I.]

EXPENDED. Killed: alluding to the gunner's accounts, wherein the articles consumed are charged under the title of expended. *Sea phrase.*

EYES AND LIMBS. The foot-guards were formerly so called by the marching regiments, from a favourite execration in use among them, which was, damning their eyes, limbs, and blue breeches.

EYE-SORE. A disagreeable object. It will be an eye-sore as

long as she lives; said by a man whose wife was cut for a fistula in ano. [Also in dialect with variants *eye-list* and *eye-last*, literally of a flaw or deformity, figuratively of a cause for regret. EDD.]

FACE-MAKING. Begetting children. To face it out; to persist in a falsity. No face but his own; a saying of one who has no money in his pocket, or no court cards in his hand. [The second phrase may be compared with the Yorkshire "I hadn't a feeace but t'feeace I leuk'd wi'." EDD.]

FACER. A bumper, a glass filled so full as to leave no room for the lip.

FADGE. It won't fadge; it won't do. A farthing. [In Shakespeare, *fadge*=fit, be suitable. O.—There is a common dialect verb *fadge*, to fit, suit, agree; to succeed. EDD.]

TO FAG. To beat. Fag the bloss; beat the wench. *Cant.* A fag also means a boy of an inferior form or class, who acts as a servant to one of a superior, who is said to fag him—he is my fag; whence, perhaps, fagged out, for jaded or tired. To stand a good fag; not to be soon tired. [*Fag*, to beat, is recorded in B. Martin's *English Dictionary*, 1754. For *fag* as a school term, cf. De Quincey's *faggery*. F.— *Fagged out* comes more probably from the two dialectal words, *fag*, to exhaust oneself in toil, to droop, and *fagged out*, frayed. Likewise, *to stand a good fag* may be due to *fag*, to cut corn to the ground, and *fagging*, a way of so reaping corn as to leave no stubble. EDD.]

FAGGER. A little boy put in at a window to rob the house. [Variants *figger, figure*. See Duncombe's *Sinks of London*, 1848. F.]

FAGGOT. A man hired at a muster to appear as a soldier. To faggot in the canting sense, means to bind: an allusion to the faggots made up by the woodmen, which are all bound. Faggot the culls; bind the men.

FAITHFUL. One of the faithful; a taylor who gives long credit. His faith has made him unwhole; i.e. trusting too much, broke him. [Also C17 slang for a drunkard. F.]

FALLALLS. Ornaments, chiefly women's, such as ribbands,

139

necklaces, &c. [Common in dialect with variant *falderal*, and with senses of nonsense, conceit, humbug; in singular, a gaudily dressed woman. Also, *fallall* may be an adjective. EDD.]

FALLEN AWAY FROM A HORSE LOAD TO A CART LOAD. A saying on one grown fat.

FAM LAY. Going into a goldsmith's shop, under pretence of buying a wedding ring, and palming one or two, by daubing the hand with some viscous matter. [*Lay*=act.F.]

FAMS, or FAMBLES. Hands. Famble cheats; rings or gloves. *Cant.* [Also as *fem*, perhaps from German slang. "A likely etymon is the Swedish and Danish *fem*, five." Harman, 1567. Cf. the old cant verb *fam*, to handle purposively: *to fam for the plant*=to feel for the goods sought-for; *fam a donna* (cf. modern slang *donah*, girl or sweetheart), to take liberties with a woman. F.]

TO FAMGRASP. To shake hands: figuratively, to agree or make up a difference. Famgrasp the cove; shake hands with the fellow. *Cant.* [Also a noun.F.]

FAMILY OF LOVE. Lewd women; also, a religious sect.

TO FAN. To beat any one. I fanned him sweetly; I beat him heartily. [In dialect, to flog an animal.EDD.]

FANTASTICALLY DRESSED, with more rags than ribbands.

FART. He has let a brewer's fart, grains and all; said of one who has bewrayed his breeches.

> Piss and fart,
> Sound at heart.
> *Mingere cum bumbis,*
> *Res saluberrima est lumbis.*

I dare not trust my a-se with a fart; said by a person troubled with a looseness. [Both noun and verb began in M.E.; the noun occurs in Chaucer, Ben Jonson, Fielding, Burns (who writes it f-t), and others. OD,F.—The modern sense, to dawdle, trifle, generally as *fart about*, was already present in C19 dialect.EDD.]

FART CATCHER. A valet or footman, from his walking behind his master or mistress.

FARTING CRACKERS. Breeches.

FARTLEBERRIES. Excrement hanging about the anus.

FASTNER. A warrant.

FASTNESSES. Bogs.

FAT. The last landed, inned, or stowed, of any sort of merchandise: so called by the water-side porters, carmen, &c. All the fat is in the fire; that is, it is all over with us: a saying used in case of any miscarriage or disappointment in an undertaking; an allusion to overturning the frying-pan into the fire. Fat, among printers, means void spaces.

AS FAT AS A HEN IN THE FOREHEAD. A saying of a meagre person.

FAT CULL. A rich fellow.

FAT-HEADED. Stupid. [Shakespeare uses *fat* by itself to mean slow-witted, dull.O.—The noun *fathead* occurs not till 1842, in Barham, OD., though as surname in C13.W.]

FAULKNER. A tumbler, juggler, or shewer of tricks: perhaps because they lure the people, as a faulconer does his hawks. *Cant.* [Evidently a derivative from the original meaning of *falconer* (whence two surnames): a dealer in hawks. "Itinerant vendors of hawks travelled from castle to castle, and it is quite possible that our modern hawker is an extended use of the same name." W:RON.]

FAWNEY. A ring. [Usually *fawny*. Parker in *Life's Painter*, 1789: "an old, stale trick, called ring-dropping." F.—From Irish *fáinne*, a ring.EDD. Cf:]

FAWNEY RIG. A common fraud, thus practised: A fellow drops a brass ring, double gilt, which he picks up before the party meant to be cheated, and to whom he disposes of it for less than its supposed, and ten times more than its real, value. See MONEY DROPPER.

FAYTORS, or FATORS. Fortune tellers. [In Elizabethan times and in Langland, impostors, cheats.O.—Bailey, 1728: "an idle fellow, a vagabond." From Fr. *faiteur*.F.—In slang spelt also *fater*, *fayter*. In the North Riding it used to mean a gipsy, a vagabond.EDD.]

FEAGUE. To feague a horse, to put ginger up a horse's fundament, and formerly, as it is said, a live eel, to make him lively and carry his tail well; it is said, a forfeit is incurred by any horse-dealer's servant, who shall shew a horse without first feaguing him. Feague is used, figuratively, for encouraging or spiriting one up. [Originally to beat, whip, then to 'settle,' both in C17; G earliest example of the sense here given; Scott had *to feague it away*, to work at full stretch.OD.]

TO FEATHER ONE'S NEST. To enrich one's self. [Earliest, 1553.W.]

FEATHER-BED LANE. A rough or stony lane.

FEE, FAW, FUM. Nonsensical words, supposed in childish story-books to be spoken by giants. I am not to be frighted by fee, faw, fum; I am not to be scared by nonsense.

FEEDER. A spoon. To nab the feeder; to steal a spoon.

FEET. To make feet for children's stocking; to beget children. An officer of feet; a jocular title for an officer of infantry.

FEINT. A sham attack on one part, when a real one is meant at another. [Out of place here. Never in this sense colloquial. Originated *ca.* 1680.OD.]

FELLOW COMMONER. An empty bottle: so called at the university of Cambridge, where fellow commoners are not in general considered as over-full of learning. At Oxford an empty bottle is called a gentleman commoner for the same reason.

FEN. A bawd, or common prostitute. *Cant.*

FENCE, or FENCING CULLY. A receiver of stolen goods. To fence; to spend or lay out. He fenced his hog; he spent his shilling. *Cant.* [From good-English *fence*, short for *defence*, from L. *defendere*.W.—As receiver, earliest recording: B.E.'s dictionary, *ca.* 1690. As receiving house, not till 1847. As the related verb, 1610.OD.—In C20 American underworld slang, "a receiver of stolen goods. He may merely buy the goods from the thief, or he may even indicate in advance what he is willing to take." I.]

FENCING KEN. The magazine or warehouse, where stolen goods are secreted. [In C19, *fencing-crib*.F.]

FERME. A hole. *Cant.* [Dekker spells *ferm*. At one period, a prison. Fr. *fermer*, to shut, to close.F.]

FERMERDY BEGGARS. All those who have not the sham sores or clymes.

FERRARA. Andrea Ferrara; the name of a famous sword-cutler: most of the Highland broad-swords are marked with his name; whence an Andrea Ferrara has become the common name for the glaymore or Highland broad-sword. See GLAY-MORE. [The name of an armourer at Ferrara in Italy, or (*Andrea dei Ferrari*) of a sword-maker at Belluno. Not a Scotsman.W:ROW.]

FERRET. A tradesman who sells goods to young unthrifty heirs, at excessive rates, and then continually duns them for the debt. To ferret: to search out or expel any one from his hiding place, as a ferret drives out rabbits; also to cheat. Ferret-eyed; red-eyed: ferrets have red eyes. [In Shakespeare, to worry.O.—Cf. *ferreting*, the act of kind.F.]

FETCH. A trick, wheedle, or invention to deceive. [Thus in Skelton, Shakespeare, Gay, Mrs Cowley (1780), Lowell (1848). OD,O,F.—In Scottish dialect as early as 1631.EDD.]

FEUTERER. A dog-keeper: from the French *vautrier*, or *vaultrier*, one that leads a lime hound for the chase.

TO FIB. To beat. Fib the cove's quarron in the rumpad for the lour in his bung; beat the fellow in the highway for the money in his purse. *Cant.*—A fib is also a tiny lie. [As to beat, Lancashire dialect.EDD.—As a lie, Cotgrave, 1611; as to lie, Dryden, 1690; as a liar, 1568.OD.]

FICE, or FOYSE. A small windy escape backwards, more obvious to the nose than ears; frequently by old ladies charged on their lap-dogs. See FIZZLE.

FID OF TOBACCO. A quid, from the small pieces of tow with which the vent or touch-hole of a cannon is stopped. *Sea term.* [In several Southern dialects, a thick piece of anything. EDD.]

FIDDLE. A writ to arrest.

FIDDLE FADDLE. Trifling discourse, nonsense. A mere fiddle faddle fellow; a trifler. [C16 for the noun; C17 for the verb, to try, trifle.OD.]

FIDDLER'S MONEY. All sixpences: sixpence being the usual sum paid by each couple, for music at country wakes and hops.

FIDDLESTICK'S END. Nothing: the ends of the ancient fiddlesticks ending in a point; hence metaphorically used to express a thing terminating in nothing.

FIDGETS. He has got the fidgets; said of one that cannot sit long in a place.

FIDLAM BEN. General thieves; called also St Peter's sons, having every finger a fish-hook. *Cant.*

FIELD LANE DUCK. A baked sheep's head.

FIERI FACIAS. A red-faced man is said to have been served with a writ of fieri facias. [Nashe, 1594.F.]

FIGGER. A little boy put in at a window to hand out goods to the diver. See DIVER.

FIGGING LAW. The art of picking pockets. *Cant.*

FIGURE DANCER. One who alters figures on bank notes, converting tens to hundreds.

FILCH, or FILEL. A beggar's staff, with an iron hook at the end, to pluck clothes from an hedge, or any thing out of a casement. Filcher; the same as angler. Filching cove; a man thief. Filching mort; a woman thief. [As a hook, in Dekker; as to rob, Harman, 1657; as to pilfer, Awdelay, 1561; therefore originally cant.OD,F.—For *filel* I suggest *filer*.]

FILE, FILE CLOY, or BUNGNIPPER. A pickpocket. To file; to rob or cheat. The file, or bungnipper, goes generally in company with two assistants, the adam tiler, and another called the bulk or bulker, whose business it is to jostle the person they intend to rob, and push him against the wall, while the file picks his pocket, and gives the booty to the adam tiler, who scours off with it. *Cant.* [Connected perhaps with Fr. *filou*, pickpocket, and *filouter*, to pilfer.W.—*File-Cloy*, 1673 (later *file-cly*), is recorded before *file*, but "etymology unknown." OD.—I suspect an origin in *file*, the metal instrument, which appears in a glossary of *ca.* 800. If so, then connected with *file*, a cunning fellow, a rascal. The occasional C19 use of the word as

144

chap, old chap, old fellow, may be a blunted derivative of the rascal sense: cf. *rascal* as an endearment.—In U.S.A., *file* as pickpocket is one of the oldest of crook terms in general use.I.]

FIN. An arm. A one-finned fellow; a man who has lost an arm. *Sea phrase.*

FINE. Fine as five-pence. Fine as a cow turd stuck with primroses. [The finer phrase occurs in Wycherley.F.]

FINGER IN EYE. To put finger in eye; to weep; commonly applied to women. The more you cry the less you'll p-ss; a consolatory speech used by sailors to their doxies. It is as great a pity to see a woman cry, as to see a goose walk barefoot: another of the same kind.

FINGER POST. A parson; so called, because he points out a way to others, which he never goes himself. Like the finger post he points out a way he has never been, and probably will never go, i.e. the way to heaven.

FINISH. The finish; a small coffee-house, in Covent-Garden market, opposite Russel-street, open very early in the morning, and therefore resorted to by debauchees shut out of every other house; it is also called Carpenter's coffee-house.

TO FIRE A SLUG. To drink a dram.

FIRE PRIGGERS. Villains who rob at fires, under pretence of assisting in removing the goods. [The locus classicus is in *Moll Flanders*.]

FIRE SHIP. A wench who has the venereal disease.

FIRE SHOVEL. He or she, when young, was fed with a fire shovel; a saying of persons with wide mouths.

FIRING A GUN. Introducing a story by head and shoulders. A man wanting to tell a particular story, said to the company, Hark! did you not hear a gun?—but now we are talking of a gun, I will tell you a story of one.

FISH. A seaman. A scaly fish; a rough, blunt tar. To have other fish to fry; to have other matters to mind, something else to do. [*Fish* is prominent in the C19 vocabulary of venery.]

FIVE SHILLINGS. The sign of five shillings; i.e. the crown. Fifteen shillings; the sign of the three crowns.

FIZZLE. An escape backward. [In dialect usually *fissle*, to make a whistling sound: Learmont, *Poems*, 1791; Scott, *Antiquary*, 1816.EDD.]

FLABAGASTED. Confounded. [Properly *flabbergasted*, mentioned in a section 'On New Words' in *The Annual Register*, 1772. From *flabby* (or possibly *flap*)+*aghast*.W.]

FLABBY. Relaxed, flaccid, not firm or solid.

FLAG. A groat. *Cant.*—The flag of defiance, or bloody flag, is out; signifying, the man is drunk, and alluding to the redness of his face. *Sea term.* [The coin is recorded by Harman, 1567, the phrase by B. E., 1690.F.]

FLAM. A lie, or sham story; also a single stroke on a drum.To flam; to hum, to amuse, to deceive. Flim flams; idle stories. [As noun and as verb, early C17; as adjective, late C17. From *flim-flams*, which established itself *ca.* 1540.OD.—*Flam* is common in dialect.EDD.—The American underworld uses *flim-flam*=to deceive, cheat, defraud.I.]

FLAP DRAGON. A clap, or pox. [B. E., 1690.F.]

TO FLARE. To blaze, shine, or glare. [Cant in 1690, colloquial in 1790, good English by 1820. (OD,W.)]

FLASH. A periwig. Rum flash; a fine long wig. Queer flash: a miserable weather-beaten caxon.

TO FLASH. To shew ostentatiously. To flash one's ivory; to laugh and shew one's teeth. Don't flash your ivory, but shut your potatoe trap, and keep your guts warm; the Devil loves hot tripes. ["Don't flash your ivory, but shut...." means "Don't laugh, but shut your mouth, and prosper (*or*, be safe): the Devil betrays the talker."]

TO FLASH THE HASH. To vomit. *Cant.*

FLASH KEN. A house that harbours thieves.

FLASH LINGO. The canting or slang language. [Usually just *flash;* the lingo of thieves and their like. *Flash* as an adjective means: relating to criminals, vagabonds, and prostitutes. F, OD.]

FLASH MAN. A bully to a bawdy-house. [Primarily a man talking, or conversant with, *flash*, but in the C18 it came to mean either "one who lives on the hackneyed prostitution of an

146

unfortunate woman of the town" (G. Parker, 1789), she being his *flash-woman;* or as in Grose.F.—In C19 dialect, a *flash-man* was a pedlar or a gipsy.EDD.]

FLAT. A bubble, gull, or silly fellow. [Goldsmith has the word. F.—In C19 Devonshire, simple.EDD.—G's *flatt* is redundant.]

FLAT COCK. A female.

FLATT. A foolish fellow.

FLAWD. Drunk.

FLAYBOTTOMIST. A bum-brusher, or schoolmaster. [Variant *flay-bottom.* An obvious pun on *phlebotomist,* blood-letter. Cotgrave has "*Fesse-cul,* a pedantical whip-arse."F,OD.]

TO FLAY, or FLEA, THE FOX. To vomit.

FLEA BITE. A trifling injury. To send any one away with a flea in his ear; to give any one a hearty scolding. [Burton in 1621 had used *flea bitings.*F.—In dialect, *a flea in the ear (hole)=* a box on the ears; *a flea in the lug,* a scolding, a sharp reproof. EDD.]

TO FLEECE. To rob, cheat, or plunder. [Late C16. As a noun it arose in C17 and had but a short life.OD.—In C19, Yorkshire dialect could show *fleecery,* robbery, deceit.EDD.]

FLEMISH ACCOUNT. A losing, or bad account. [The Flemish *livre* or pound was worth only 12s.: see T. Brown's *The Accurate Accomptant,* 1668.F.]

FLESH BROKER. A match-maker, a bawd. [*Flesh* as generic for the organs of reproduction dates back to the C16; Shakespeare, 1603, has a *flesh-monger,* which like Cowper's *flesh-fly,* 1781, is a whore-master; Florio, 1598, says "to go a fleshing or a wenching;" John Day, 1604, has *flesh-shambles,* a brothel, and Shakespeare in the same year writes: "She would not exchange flesh with one that loved her." F.—Likewise, *flesh-company*=sexual intercourse, as early as 1522. OD.]

FLIBUSTIERS. West India pirates, buccanneers, or free-booters. [The early form. Connected with Dutch *vrijbuiter,* a freebooter.W.—G's definition comes straight from B.E.— Properly, *filibusters* formerly meant piratical adventurers harrying the Spanish West Indies, and now means those who illegally engage in warfare against a foreign state; *buccaneers,* beginning as French hunters in San Domingo, became free-booters on either land or (more generally) sea, and finally pirates —pirates of the Spanish Main; *freebooters* held a roving commission of a piratical kind on either sea or land; *pirates* were sea-robbers, pillaging sea-rovers; *privateers* were author-ised to harry the vessels and ports of foreign nations, and some-times they turned pirates.OD,W; and see my *Pirates, Highway-men, and Adventurers*, 1927, also article in *Everyman* of March 26, 1931.]

FLICKER. A drinking glass. *Cant.* [So in B. E. As a verb it signified to drink, to laugh lewdly, to kiss or wantonly to caress a woman.F.]

FLICKERING. Grinning or laughing in a man's face.

FLICKING. Cutting. Flick me some panam and caffan; cut me some bread and cheese. Flick the peter; cut off the cloak-bag or portmanteau.

TO FLING. To trick or cheat. He flung me fairly out of it; he cheated me out of it.

FLINTS. Journeymen taylors, who on a late occasion refused to work for the wages settled by law. Those who submitted, were, by the mutineers, styled dungs, i.e. dunghills. [Both terms occur in Foote's *The Tailors: a Tragedy for Warm Weather*. F.]

FLIP. Small beer, brandy, and sugar; this mixture, with the addition of a lemon, was, by sailors, formerly called Sir Clouds-ly, in memory of Sir Cloudsly Shovel, who used frequently to regale himself with it.[Cant,1690.F.—Recorded too in 1715 by that versatile lexicographer, John Kersey,who to industry add-ed a very real ability.—Until *ca.* 1880, it used, in Northamp-tonshire dialect, to designate any weak, insipid liquor.EDD.]

FLOATING ACADEMY. See CAMPBELL'S ACADEMY.

TO FLOG. To whip. [Recorded by Coles in 1676; *flogging cove* was described by B.E. in 1690 as cant. Perhaps echoic, perhaps as an arbitrary corruption of L. *flagellare.*OD,W,F.—This B. E., Gent., was a competent fellow, though he included in his dictionary a number of words no more lowly than collo-quialisms; what Harman did for the C16, B.E. did for the C17,

148

Grose for the C18, and Hotten (and, later, Farmer) for the C19.]

FLOGGER. A horsewhip. *Cant.*

FLOGGING COVE. The beadle, or whipper, in Bridewell.

FLOGGING CULLY. A debilitated lecher (commonly an old one), whose torpid powers require stimulating by flagellation.

FLOGGING STAKE. The whipping-post.

FLORENCE. A wench that has been touzed and ruffled. [Cf. the Northants verb *florence*, which became obsolete *ca.* 1900: to go about untidily dressed.EDD.]

FLOURISH. To take a flourish; to enjoy a woman in an hasty manner, to take a flyer. See FLYER.

TO FLOUT. To jeer, to ridicule. [In Shakespeare, to quote with sarcastic intent.O.—In dialect, to scold.EDD.—In G's day, flout may have been a homely word—so many good old English words were homely during the C18!—but it was not strictly a colloquialism.]

FLUMMERY. Oatmeal and water boiled to a jelly; also compliments; neither of which are over-nourishing. [In its primary sense, dialectal.EDD.]

FLUSH IN THE POCKET. Full of money. The cull is flush in the fob; the fellow is full of money. [Earlier, and later: *flush of money*.OD.]

FLUSTERED. Drunk.[1615; from *fluster*, to excite with drink, as in *Othello*.OD,O.]

FLUTE. The recorder of a corporation; a recorder was an ancient musical instrument. [Cant in 1690.F.]

TO FLUX. To cheat, cozen, or over-reach; also to salivate. To flux a wig; to put it up in curl, and bake it.

FLY. A waggon. *Cant.* [In other 'vehicle' senses, good English.]

FLY-BY-NIGHT. You old fly-by-night; an ancient term of reproach to an old woman, signifying that she was a witch, and alluding to the nocturnal excursions attributed to witches, who were supposed to fly abroad to their meetings, mounted on brooms. [In Regency days, a sedan chair on wheels; later, a burglar, a 'spreester,' also a prostitute, the *pudendum muliebre*.F.]

FLYER. To take a flyer; to enjoy a woman with her clothes on, or without going to bed.

FLYERS. Shoes. [Like *flying camps*, it was in 1690 noted as cant.F.]

FLY-FLAPPED. Whipt in the stocks, or at the cart's tail.

FLYING CAMPS. Beggars plying in a body at funerals.

FLYING GIGGERS. Turnpike gates.

FLYING HORSE. A lock in wrestling, by which he who uses it throws his adversary over his head.

FLYING PASTY. Sirreverence wrapped in paper, and thrown over a neighbour's wall.

FLYING PORTERS. Cheats who obtain money by pretending to persons, who have been lately robbed, that they come from a place or party where, and from whom, they may receive information respecting the goods stolen from them, and demand payment as porters.

FLYING STATIONERS. Ballad-singers and hawkers of penny histories. [Cf. the C19 *running patterers*.EDD.]

FLY SLICERS. Life-guard men, from their sitting on horseback, under an arch, where they are frequently observed to drive away flies with their swords.

FOB. A cheat, trick, or contrivance. I will not be fobbed off so; I will not be thus deceived with false pretences. The fob is also a small breeches pocket for holding a watch. [In Shakespeare, *fob*=to cheat and *fobbed off*=put off deceitfully, trickily set aside, in short 'side-tracked.' O.—The verb was much commoner than the noun.EDD.]

FOG. Smoke. *Cant.*

FOGEY. Old fogey; a nick name for an invalid soldier: derived from the French word *fougueux*, fierce or fiery. [W suggests from *foggy*. I believe that G is right, such an adjective being almost 'inevitable' with soldiers; the evidence in OD does not preclude the possibility that even in G's day the stress was laid on the *old*, not on the *fogey*, the spirited soldier, aspect. But one must take into the reckoning the next entry, which is recorded a decade earlier (OD).]

FOGRAM. An old fogram; a fusty old fellow.

FOGUS. Tobacco. Tip me a gage of fogus; give me a pipe of tobacco. *Cant.*

FOOL. A fool at the end of a stick; a fool at one end, and a maggot at the other: gibes on an angler.

FOOL FINDER. A bailiff.

FOOLISH. An expression among impures, signifying the cully who pays, in opposition to a flash man. Is he foolish or flash?

FOOT PADS, or LOW PADS. Rogues who rob on foot. [The Shakespearean equivalent was *foot-land-raker*.O.—On the vocabulary of footpaddery, see my article in *Everyman*, April 9, 1931.]

FOOT WARBLER. A contemptuous appellation for a foot soldier, commonly used by the cavalry. [I.e. *foot-wobbler;* cf. the *foot-slogger* of 1914-1918. B & P. Also my article on 'Some Soldiers' Slang with a Past' in *The Quarterly Review*, April 1931.

FOOTMAN'S MAWND. An artificial sore made with un-slaked lime, soap, and the rust of old iron, on the back of a beggar's hand, as if hurt by the bite or kick of a horse.

FOOTY DESPICABLE. A footy fellow, a despicable fellow; from the French *foutüe*. [In C18-19 *footy* was in general dialectal use throughout England, Scotland and Ireland: mean, base, as in Forbes, *Ulysses*, 1785; indecorous, obscene, as in Finlayson, *Rhymes*, 1815; paltry, worthless, undersized; foolish, affected. *Foutiness*, Scottish: meanness, obscenity. *Footer, Fouter, futer, futor, futter*, as noun: a term of contempt; as verb: to ridicule. *Footer* with its dialectal variations: confusion, a bungler or a shabby fellow; to work clumsily, to potter about. *Footering* ==clumsy, troublesome. A very good example of the richness of English dialect.EDD.]

FOREMAN OF THE JURY. One who engrosses all the talk to himself, or speaks for the rest of the company. [1690.F.]

FORK. A pickpocket. Let us fork him; let us pick his pocket.— 'The newest and most dexterous way, which is, to thrust the 'fingers strait, stiff, open, and very quick, into the pocket, and 'so closing them, hook what can be held between them.' N.B. This was taken from a book, written many years ago: doubtless the art of picking pockets, like all others, must have been much improved since that time. [The verb is remotely but significantly connected with Edinburgh dialect *fork for*, to search for, to look after oneself (Crawford, *Poems*, 1798).EDD.]

FORLORN HOPE. A gamester's last stake. [Cf. Shakespeare's "The forlorn soldier, that so nobly fought," *Cymbeline*, V.v.406.O.—In ordinary English, it meant, in 1799, the leaders of a storming party; and earlier, soldiers in any way imperilled. From obsolete Dutch *verloren hoop*, a lost company of men (cf. the Fr. *enfants perdus*), showing that the *hope* has nothing to do with confident expectation.W:ROW.]

FORTUNE HUNTERS. Indigent men, seeking to enrich themselves by marrying a woman of fortune.

FORTUNE TELLER, or CUNNING MAN. A judge, who tells every prisoner, his fortune, lot, or doom. To go before the fortune teller, lambskin men, or conjurer; to be tried at an assize. See LAMBSKIN MEN. [Cant, 1690.F.]

FOUL. To foul a plate with a man; to take a dinner with him.

FOUL-MOUTHED. Abusive. [Shakespeare has *in foul mouth*, *foul-spoken*.O.]

FOUNDLING. A child dropped in the streets, and found, and educated at the parish expence. [Out of place in G: this very old word has never been other than good English.]

FOX. A sharp, cunning fellow. Also an old term for a sword, probably a rusty one, or else from its being dyed red with blood: some say this name alluded to certain swords of remarkable good temper, or metal, marked with the figure of a fox, probably the sign, or rebus, of the maker. [As a sword, *fox* appears in Shakespeare, where "the wolf on some makes of sword-blade is supposed to have been taken for a fox." O.—Possibly the original maker was one Fox, or again the word may be a corruption of L. *falx*.F.]

FOX'S PAW. The vulgar pronunciation of the French words *faux pas*. He made a confounded fox's paw.

FOXED. Intoxicated. [In Barry's play *Ram Alley*, 1611, and as late as 1891, in *The Sporting Times*.F.—Also W. Yorks. dialect. EDD.]

FOXING A BOOT. Mending the foot by capping it.

FOYST. A pickpocket, cheat, or rogue. See WOTTON'S GANG.

TO FOYST. To pick a pocket. [Modern *foist*, ancient *fyste*. Probably from Dutch *vuist*, a fist: with *foist on* cf. *palm off*. Originally a dicing term. W.—*To foist* was to palm a 'flat' (a false die): *foisted in*, therefore, refers to the 'flat' being surreptitiously introduced into play after being palmed. The various terms were recorded *ca.* 1550. OD.]

FOYSTED IN. Words or passages surreptitiously interpolated or inserted into a book or writing.

FRATERS. Vagabonds who beg with sham patents, or briefs, for hospitals, fires, inundations, &c. [Harman, 1567.F.— From the days when these vagabonds imitated the monks and friars as genuine solicitors of alms. Such words of learned origin are more frequent in cant than in dialect, but from L. *fraternus* or *fraterne* we get, as the EDD informs us, the Herefordshire *fratern* or *fraturn:* literally, to resemble as brothers; derivatively, to resemble in facial appearance.]

FREE. Free of fumbler's hall; a saying of one who cannot get his wife with child.

FREE BOOTERS. Lawless robbers and plunderers; originally soldiers who served without pay, for the privilege of plundering the enemy. [Cf. the C19 pun, *freebookers*, piratical booksellers or publishers.]

FREEHOLDER. He whose wife accompanies him to the alehouse.

FREEZE. A thin, small, hard cider, much used by vintners, and coopers in parting their wines, to lower the price of them, and to advance their gain. A freezing vintner; a vintner who balderdashes his wine.

FRENCH CREAM. Brandy; so called by the old tabbies and dowagers when drank in their tea. [In C19 Wexford, whiskey. In dialectal phrases, *French* is not very frequent, less so than *Dutch* in fact; but in compound names of plants, birds and fishes, it is much commoner than *Dutch*. We may note *French tobacco*, a weed smoked by boys (Norfolk); *to make a French*, i.e. an apple-pie, *bed* (East Anglia); *French*, very bad, in great trouble, is obsolescent East Anglian, but *French*, new, foreign, was widespread and it still lingers on; in Ireland *Frenchman* till *ca.* 1900 meant a foreigner; and *Frenchy*, in various dialects, still signifies any kind of foreigner.EDD.]

FRENCH DISEASE. The venereal disease, said to have been imported from France. French gout; the same. He suffered by a blow over the snout with a French faggot-stick; i.e. he lost his nose by the pox. [Earliest form, *French pox*, Florio, 1598, and Cotgrave, 1611.F.]

FRENCH LEAVE. To take French leave; to go off without taking leave of the company: a saying frequently applied to persons who have run away from their creditors. [Smollett, 1771.OD.]

FRENCHIFIED. Infected with the venereal disease. The mort is Frenchified; the wench is infected.

FRESHMAN. One just entered a member of the university. [Nashe, 1596; as=newcomer, about fifty years earlier.OD.]

FRIBBLE. An effeminate fop: a name borrowed from a celebrated character of that kind, in the farce of Miss in her Teens, written by Mr Garrick. [In 1747. The name from the verb, to trifle, earlier to falter, to stammer.W.]

FRIDAY FACE. A dismal countenance. Before, and even long after the Reformation, Friday was a day of abstinence, or *jour maigre*. Immediately after the restoration of king Charles II a proclamation was issued, prohibiting all publicans from dressing any suppers on a Friday. [Greene, 1592.OD.]

TO FRIG. To be guilty of the crime of self-pollution. Frigging is also figuratively used for trifling. [Florio, Cotgrave, Bailey.F.—In dialect, to wriggle.EDD.]

FRIG PIG. A trifling, fiddle-faddle fellow.

FRIGATE. A well-rigged frigate; a well-dressed wench. [Cant, 1690.F.]

FRISK. To dance the Paddington frisk; to be hanged. [Paddington being in the West of London, this fact may have influenced the 1914-1918 phrase, *to go west*, to die.B & P, and *Quarterly Review, l.c.*]

154

TO FRIZ, or FRISK. Used by thieves to signify searching a person whom they have robbed. Blast his eyes! friz, or frisk him. [In American underworld slang, *frisk* survives: as noun, a search —especially of the person; as verb, to search or ransack—not necessarily for loot. I.]

FROE, or VROE. A woman, wife, or mistress. Brush to your froe, or bloss, and wheedle for crop; run to your mistress, and sooth and coax her out of some money. *Dutch.* [Dekker, 1607.F.]

FROGLANDER. A Dutchman. [Recorded *ca.* 1690.OD.]

FROSTY FACE. One pitted with the small pox.

FRUMMAGEMMED. Choaked, strangled, or hanged. *Cant.* [1671.F.]

FUBSEY. Plump. A fubsey wench; a plump healthy wench. [Properly *fubsy.* Frequent in Yorkshire and Lancashire. Apotheosised by Kipling, 1896.EDD.]

TO F—K. To copulate. [Banned by OD and EDD. Used by Lyndsay *ca.* 1540, and occurring in Florio's definition of *fottere:* "To jape; to sarde, to fucke; to swive; to occupy." One of the last occasions on which it appeared in print, in the ordinary way of publication, was in Burns. As early as 1728, Bailey defines it as *feminam subagitare,* and it would seem to have acquired a bad odour *ca.* 1690.F.—It is extremely doubtful if the efforts of James Joyce in *Ulysses* and D. H. Lawrence in *Lady Chatterley's Lover* have done anything to restore the term to its former place as a language-word, i.e. neither slang nor dialect. B & P.—From Greek *phuteuo,* L. *futuere,* Fr. *foutre,* the medial *c* coming from a Teutonic root. Sir Richard Burton, in his Arabian Nights, attempted a Gallic twist: *futter.*—The synonyms (on the basis of F) are numerous in accredited literature exclusive of slang, euphemism, and conventionalism. Of the transitive verbs, the following writers are operatively responsible for these numbers of different synonyms:—Lyndsay, 3; Shakespeare,9; Florio, 3; Fletcher, 7; Urquhart,4; Durfey,3; Fielding, 2; Burns,1 . Of the intransitive synonyms:—Shakespeare, 5; Marston, 3; Herrick, 2; Urquhart, 12; Rochester, 1; Durfey, 6; Burns, 6; Whitman, 1.—The vivid expressiveness and the vigorous ingenuity of these synonyms bear witness to the fertility of English and to the enthusiastic English participation in the universal fascination of the creative act. The word was very much used by the British Soldier in 1914-1918 (see the Introduction in B & P), when free currency was also given to the adjective formed by the addition of *ing* and to *f—ker;* this latter, in the mouths of the fouler-spoken, meant little more than chap, fellow, and the decent substituted *mucker; mucking* was less frequent.]

F—K BEGGAR. See BUSS BEGGAR.

FUDDLE. Drink. This is rum fuddle: this is excellent tipple, or drink. Fuddled; drunk. Fuddle cap: a drunkard. [An early form is *fuzzed*, e.g. in Burton, 1621. The intransitive verb occurs in 1588, the transitive *ca.* 1600, the reflexive in 1855. As a noun, 1680. OD.—Cf. obsolete *fuzzle*, to make drunk. *Fuddle* is frequent in Pepys, who also has *foxed*. W.—Common in dialect as drink, drinking-bout, intoxication. EDD.]

FULHAMS. Loaded dice are called high and lowmen, or high and low fulhams, by Ben Jonson, and other writers of his time; either because they were made at Fulham, or from that place being the resort of sharpers. [Also in Nashe and Shakespeare. *Fulhams* as shams came later as a natural derivative: Butler in *Hudibras*, "Fulhams of poetic fiction." Fulham long retained its unsavoury reputation, a C19 slang phrase being *Fulham virgin*, a fast woman. F.]

TO FULK. To use an unfair motion of the hand in plumping at taw. *Schoolboy's term.* [In C18-19 dialect a *fulk* was a blow with the fist. EDD.]

FULL OF EMPTINESS. Jocular term for empty.

FUMBLER. An old impotent man. To fumble, also means to go awkwardly about any work, or manual operation. [C17 origin in slang. OD.]

FUN. A cheat, or trick. Do you think to fun me out of it; do you think to cheat me?—Also the breech, perhaps from being the abbreviation of fundament. I'll kick your fun. *Cant.* [B.E's. dictionary, 1690, gives these two senses, also *fun* as verb. F.—Also dialect. EDD.]

FUNK. To smoke; figuratively, to smoke or stink through fear.

I was in a cursed funk. To funk the cobler; a schoolboy's trick, performed with assafoetida, and cotton, which are stuffed into a pipe; the cotton being lighted, and the bowl of the pipe being covered with a coarse handkerchief, the smoke is blown out at the small end, through the crannies of a cobler's stall. [As fear, first in phrase *to be in a funk*, which originated at Oxford *ca.* 1720.W.—The intransitive verb came *ca.* 1735, the transitive not till a century later; also *ca.* 1835, *funky*.OD.]

FURMEN. Aldermen. [Cant. 1690,F.]

FURMITY, or FROMENTY. Wheat boiled up to a jelly. To simper like a furmity kettle: to smile, or look merry about the gills. [Cf. Fr. *froment*. A C19 phrase was *furmity-faced*, white-faced. F.—The commonest spellings are *frumety, frummety*. A dish of 'hulled' wheat, boiled in milk, and flavoured with spice and with currants or sugar or treacle.EDD.—Much has been written on the subject, but see especially OD,EDD, and Harland & Wilkinson's *Folk-Lore*, 1867.]

FUSS. A confusion, a hurry, an unnecessary to do about trifles. [From *ca.* 1700.W.—Now good but not 'literary' English.]

FUSSOCK. A lazy fat woman. An old fussock; a frowzy old woman. [Defined by B.E. as "a lazy, fat-arsed wench." F.— In dialect, also=a stupid person.EDD.]

FUSTIAN. Bombast language. Red fustian; port wine. [Old Fr. *fustaine*, from Fustat, a suburb of Cairo, where the fabric was first made.W:ROW.—As ranting, in Shakespeare. In 1690 B. E. defined *fustian verse* as "verse in words of lofty sound and humble sense." F.]

FUSTY LUGGS. A beastly, sluttish woman. [Variants, *fustilug, fustilugs*.F.—Shakespeare's *fustilarian* is probably a comic variation. O.—Common in C18-19 dialect as a big coarse person; a dirty slattern; a very untidy or dirty child. EDD.—On Exmoor in C18, a big-boned person.G.]

TO FUZZ. To shuffle cards minutely; also, to change the pack.

GAB, or GOB. The mouth. Gift of the gab; a facility of speech, nimble-tongued eloquence. To blow the gab; to confess or peach.[(The verb occurs in Chaucer.) The *gift* phrase originally ended with *gob*, which, also in the sense of mouth, was earlier than *gab* as noun. The second locution became *blow the gaff,ca.* 1810. F,OD.—In American tramp and underworld slang, *gab* still means mouth, also idle talk or chatter.I.— The North Country has the expressive phrase, *all gob and guts*, applied either to greedy children or to ignorant, talkative grown-ups.EDD.]

GAB, or GOB, STRING. A bridle.

GABEY. A foolish fellow. [More usually *gaby*. Also a babbler, a boor. F.—Cf. *Gauby-fair*, a statutory fair at which servants in C18 and early C19 were hired.EDD.]

GAD-SO. An exclamation said to be derived from the Italian word *cazzo*. [A relic of phallicism.F.]

GAG. An instrument used chiefly by housebreakers and thieves, for propping open the mouth of a person robbed, thereby to prevent his calling out for assistance. [1553.OD.]

GAGE. A quart pot, or a pint; also a pipe.*Cant.*

GAGE OF FOGUS. A pipe of tobacco.

GAGGERS, High and Low. Cheats, who by sham pretences, and wonderful stories of their sufferings, impose on the credulity of well-meaning people. See RUM GAGGER.

GALIMAUFREY. A hodgepodge made up of the remnants and scraps of the larder. [In Shakespeare a jumble; a promiscuous assemblage.O.]

GALL. His gall is not yet broken; a saying used in prisons of a man just brought in, who appears dejected. [Ironic, *gall* or *galls* having long stood for courage.—In low American slang, *gall* still means either courage or high spirits.I.]

GALLEY. Building the galley: a game formerly used at sea, in order to put a trick upon a landsman, or fresh-water sailor.It being agreed to play at that game, one sailor personates the builder, and another the merchant or contractor; the builder first begins by laying the keel, which consists of a number of men laid all along on their backs, one after another, that is,

158

head to foot; he next puts in the ribs or knees, by making a number of men sit feet to feet, at right angles to, and on each side of, the keel; he now fixing on the person intended to be the object of the joke, observes he is a fierce-looking fellow, and fit for the lion; he accordingly places him at the head, his arms being held or locked in by the two persons next to him, representing the ribs. After several other dispositions, the builder delivers over the galley to the contractor as complete; but he, among other faults and objections, observes the lion is not gilt; on which the builder, or one of his assistants, runs to the head, and dipping a mop in the excrement, thrusts it into the face of the lion.

GALLEY FOIST. A city barge, used formerly on the lord mayor's day, when he was sworn in at Westminster. [Ben Jonson. F.]

GALLIED. Hurried, vexed, over-fatigued, perhaps like a galley slave. [More likely from dialectal *gally*, to frighten; to scare away; especially, to confuse with noise.EDD.]

GALLIGASKINS. Breeches. [Shakespeare has *gaskins*.O.— In Lincolnshire and Somerset dialect, leggings, gaiters. In Cotgrave.EDD.]

GALLIPOT. A nick name for an apothecary. [Literally a pot conveyed in a galley, once a common name for vessels starting from the Mediterranean. W:MWAM.]

GALLORE, or GOLORE. Plenty. [Irish *go leor*, sufficiently. OD.]

GALLOWS BIRD. A thief, or pickpocket; also one that associates with them. [Often just *gallows* (C16-19).F.]

GAMBS. Thin, ill-shaped legs; a corruption of the French word *jambes*. [Variant *gams*. From Northern Fr. *gambes*, whence direct or through the Lingua Franca of the Mediterranean.F. In American low slang, *gams* always means a girl's legs.I.—As good English, a term in heraldry; in cant, almost always ill-shapen, even bow, legs. The OD says that *gammy* is *gamy*, which in turn is *game*: *a game leg* is not recorded till 1787: it is at least as likely that *gam(b)* in its pejorative sense led to *gammy*.]

GAMBADOES. Leathern cases of stiff leather, used in Devonshire instead of boots; they are fastened to the saddle, and admit the leg, shoe and all; the name was at first jocularly given.

GAMBLER. A sharper, a tricking gamester. [The sense of sharp practice disappeared *ca.* 1840, when the term, originally cant, was a century old. OD. On gambling in C18 London, see Chancellor's *Pleasure Haunts* for a most entertaining and informative account.]

GAME. Bubbles or pigeons drawn in to be cheated. Also, at bawdy-houses, lewd women. Mother, have you any game; mother, have you any girls? To die game; to suffer at the gallows without shewing any signs of fear or repentance. Game pullet; a young whore, or forward girl in the way of becoming one. [As prone to venery, Etherege, 1676; simpleton, and as brothel or a bevy of prostitutes, 1690; courageous, early C18.F,OD.]

GAMON AND PATTER. Common-place talk of any profession; as the gamon and patter of a horse-dealer, sailor, &c. [Also, thieves' cant (C18); a meeting, a palaver (C19). The verb *gammon*, to deceive, to humbug, late C17; the exclamation, early C19.F.]

GAN. The mouth or lips. *Cant.* [Possibly Swedish. EDD.]

GANDER MONTH. That month in which a man's wife lies in: wherefore, during that time, husbands plead a sort of indulgence in matters of gallantry. [Variant, *gander-moon*.OD.]

GANG. A company of men, a body of sailors, a knot of thieves, pickpockets, &c. A gang of sheep trotters; the four feet of a sheep. [In C17-18, cant when not nautical. (OD).]

GAOLER'S COACH. A hurdle: traitors being usually conveyed from the goal, to the place of execution, on a hurdle or sledge.

GAP STOPPER. A whoremaster. [Later, the member.F.]

GAPESEED. Sights: any thing to feed the eye. I am come abroad for a little gapeseed. [Late C16.OD.—In C19 dialect: *have a little gapeseed, gather* or *sow gapeseed*.EDD.]

GARNISH. An entrance fee demanded by the old prisoners of one just committed to gaol. [Abolished temp. George IV.F.— (As a survival?) in Yorkshire, *ca.* 1865, a fine exacted from a new workman to provide drink.EDD.]

GARRET, or UPPER STORY. The head. His garret, or upper story, is empty, or unfurnished; i.e. he has no brains, he is a fool. [Cf. Kentish *not rightly garreted*.EDD.]

GARRET ELECTION. A ludicrous ceremony, practised every new parliament: it consists of a mock election of two members to represent the borough of Garret (a few straggling cot· tages near Wandsworth, in Surry); the qualification of a voter is, having enjoyed a woman in the open air within that district: the candidates are commonly fellows of low humour, who dress themselves up in a ridiculous manner. As this brings a prodigious concourse of people to Wandsworth, the publicans of that place jointly contribute to the expence, which is sometimes considerable.

GAWKEY. A tall, thin, awkward young man or woman. [Dialectal *gawk*, adjective and noun for left-hand(ed), awkward (ness), cognate with Fr. *gauche*. Of the variants, *gawkiness*, as befits an abstract noun, shows the greatest deviation.EDD.]

GAZEBO. An elevated observatory or summer-house. [In Irish dialect, a gaping-stock.EDD.]

GEE. It won't gee; it won't hit or do, it does not suit or fit. [Originally cant.F.—Perhaps $g(o)$: cant sometimes descended to such transparent disguises.]

GELDING. An eunuch.

GELT. Money, *German*.—Also, castrated. [The money sense is probably from the German for payment, tribute.(EDD.)]

GENTLE CRAFT. The art of shoemaking. One of the gentle craft: a shoemaker; so called because once practised by St Crispin.

GENTLEMAN COMMONER. An empty bottle; an university joke, gentleman commoners not being deemed over-full of learning.

GENTLEMAN'S COMPANION. A louse.

GENTLEMAN'S MASTER. A highway robber, because he makes a gentleman obey his commands, i.e. stand and deliver.

GENTLEMAN OF THREE INS. In debt, in gaol, and in danger of remaining there for life; or, in gaol, indicted, and in danger of being hanged in chains.

GENTLEMAN OF THREE OUTS. That is, without money, without wit, and without manners; some add another out, i.e. without credit.

GENTRY COVE. A gentleman. *Cant.*

GENTRY COVE'S KEN. A gentleman's house. *Cant.*

GENTRY MORT. A gentlewoman. [Also cant. The three gentry terms are in Harman. An early variant of *cove* is *cofe*; Blackmore in 1881 has *gentry-man* (Devon). An abbreviation is *gentry-ken*.F.]

GEORGE. A half-crown piece. Yellow George; a guinea. Brown George; an ammunition loaf.

GEORGES. The brethren of the honourable society of Royal Georges; a society which met at the St Luke's Head and Eight Bells, Smithfield.

GERMAN DUCK. Half a sheep's head boiled with onions.

GET. One of his get; one of his offspring, or begetting. [C14. Since *ca.* 1880, only of animals: unless pejorative. (OD).]

GIB CAT. A northern name for a he cat, there commonly called Gilbert. As melancholy as a gib cat; as melancholy as a he cat that has been catterwauling, whence they always return scratched, hungry, and out of spirits. Aristotle says, *Omne animal post coitum est triste;* to which an anonymous author has given the following exception: *preter gallum, gallinaceum, et sacerdotem gratis fornicantem.* [In *Hamlet* as *gib*.O.—In dialect, often a castrated cat, an explanation sharpening the *melancholy* simile, but cf. *gib-fish*, the male fish.EDD.—As to Aristotle, I thought it was some medieval wit and that there were only two exceptions: *gallum* and *feminam* (or *mulierem*).]

GIBBERISH. The cant language of thieves and gypsies, called Pedlars French, & St.Giles's Greek: see ST GILES'S GREEK. Also the mystic language of Geber, used by chymists. Gibberish likewise means a sort of disguised language, formed by inserting any consonant between each syllable of an English word; in which case it is called the gibberish of the letter inserted: if F, it is the F gibberish; if G, the G gibberish; as in the sentence, How do you do? Howg dog youg dog. [*Ca.* 1550: earlier than *gibber*. Cotgrave has "*Jargonnois:* fustian, gibridge, pedlers French." W.—The modern meaning (inarticulate nonsense) is foreshadowed in Dyche, 1748.F.]

GIBLETS. To join giblets; said of a man and woman who cohabit as husband and wife, without being married; also to copulate. [In dialect, merely to enter into partnership or to go halves.EDD.]

GIBSON, or SIR JOHN GIBSON. A two-legged stool, used to support the body of a coach whilst finishing.

GIFTS. Small white specks under the finger nails, said to portend gifts or presents. A stingy man is said to be as full of gifts as a brazen horse of his farts. [In C19 Northants dialect there was the couplet (spoken as one touched thumb and each successive finger),

> A gift, a friend, a foe,
> A lover to come, a journey to go.

In Kent: a present; a friend or a lover; a foe; a visit to pay; a journey to be made. Other counties, other sayings—and other 'items.' EDD.]

GIFT OF THE GAB. A facility of speech.

GIGG. A nose. Snitchel his gigg; fillip his nose. Grunter's gigg; a hog's snout. Gigg is also a high one-horse chaise, and a woman's privities. To gigg a Smithfield hank; to hamstring an overdrove ox, vulgarly called a mad bullock. [Properly *gig*. As nose and female genitals, cant in 1690. Other old colloquial senses are a wanton (Chaucer), a jest (Nashe), fun (Tom Moore).F.]

GIGGER. A latch, or door. Dub the gigger; open the door. Gigger dubber: the turnkey of a gaol.

GILES'S, or ST GILES'S BREED. Fat, ragged, and saucy; Newton and Dyot streets, the grand head-quarters of most of the thieves and pickpockets about London, are in St Giles's parish. St Giles's Greek; the cant language, called also Slang, Pedlar's French, and Flash. [The phrase *a cellar in St Giles's*, in the approximate period 1650-1820, was proverbial for utmost poverty, and until *ca.* 1870 the Dyott Street area was "a low and dirty neighbourhood." Chancellor's *London's Old Latin Quarter*.]

TO GIGGLE. To suppress a laugh. Gigglers; wanton women.

163

[With *gigglers* cf. Shakespearean *giglet*, *giglot*, possibly from *gig* (as in Hamlet), to walk wantonly. O. The earliest form is *gigelot*, 1340. OD.]

GILFLURT. A proud minks, a vain capricious woman. [Properly *gill-flirt*. Also a wanton, a flirt; cf. Shakespeare's *flirt-gill*, a loose woman.F.—Survived in dialect till *ca.* 1900, though obsolescent for some years before.EDD.]

GILL. The abbreviation of Gillian, figuratively used for woman. Every jack has his gill; i.e. every jack has his gillian, or female mate. [And *Gillian=Juliana*. Modern *jill*. In C17-18, three senses: a girl, a sweetheart, a wanton.F.]

GILLS. The cheeks. To look rosy about the gills; to have a fresh complexion. To look merry about the gills; to appear chearful. [In singular, the word in dialect means also lower jaw, mouth, throat.EDD.]

GILLY GAUPUS. A Scotch term for a tall, awkward fellow. [In C19 Scottish, more usually a gaper, a half-wit.EDD.]

GILT, or RUM DUBBER. A thief who picks locks, so called from the gilt or picklock key: many of them are so expert, that, from the lock of a church door to that of the smallest cabinet, they will find means to open it: these go into reputable public houses, where, pretending business, they contrive to get into private rooms, up stairs, where they open any bureaus or trunks, they happen to find there.

GIMBLET-EYED. Squinting, either in man or woman.

GIMCRACK, or JIMCRACK. A spruce wench; a gimcrack also means a person who has a turn for mechanical contrivances. [In C17, a showy simpleton.F.—In dialect the noun, anything novel or showy; the adjective, tawdry, strange, unreliable.EDD.]

GINGAMBOBS. Toys, bawbles; also a man's testicles. See THINGAMBOBS.

GINGERBREAD. A cake made of treacle, flour, and grated ginger; also money. He has the gingerbread; he is rich. [The *cake* sense has never been colloquial.OD.]

GINGERBREAD WORK. Gilding and carving; these terms are particularly applied by seamen on board Newcastle colliers,

164

to the decorations of the sterns and quarters of West-India-men, which they have the greatest joy in defacing. [Smollett, 1748.OD.]

GINGER-PATED, or GINGER-HACKLED. Red haired: a term borrowed from the cockpit, where red cocks are called gingers.

GINGERLY. Softly, gently, tenderly. To go gingerly to work: to attempt a thing gently, or cautiously. [As both adverb and adjective, arose *ca.* 1500, especially in reference to delicate walking.W.]

GINNY. An instrument to lift up a grate, in order to steal what is in the window. *Cant.* [Recorded as cant in 1673, but this probably derives from early dialectal *ginny*, a lifting engine, a kind of primitive crane. (OD,EDD.)]

GIN SPINNER. A distiller.

GIRDS. Quips, taunts, severe or biting reflections.

GIZZARD. To grumble in the gizzard; to be secretly displeas-ed. [The phrase belongs to Yorkshire, which claims also the variant, *to squeak in the gizzard.* EDD.]

GLASS EYES. A nick name for one wearing spectacles. [But Northern *glass-eyed*=wall-eyed.EDD.]

GLAYMORE. A Highland broad-sword: from the Erse *glay,* or *glaive,* a sword; and *more,* great. [Obsolete for *claymore.* Properly a two-edged, not a two-handed, sword.OD.]

GLAZE. A window. *Cant.* [Recorded 1690.F.]

GLAZIER. One who breaks windows and shew-glasses, to steal goods exposed for sale. Glaziers; eyes. *Cant.*—Is your father a glazier; a question asked of a lad or young man, who stands be-tween the speaker and the candle, or fire. If it is answered in the negative, the rejoinder is—I wish he was, that he might make a window through your body, to enable us to see the fire or light. [As eyes, 1567; as thief, 1673.OD.]

GLIB. Smooth, slippery. Glib-tongued; talkative. [Shake-speare was one of the first to use it:

I want that glib and oily art

To speak and purpose not   (*Lear*).

Originally, smooth, slippery, and probably cognate with *glide.*

165

W.—Never colloquial, though the original sense is now dialectal.OD.—Before it meant 'talkative,' it meant 'quick to use one's tongue'; cf. C18-19 Scottish *glibs*, a sharper or a sharp person. EDD.—An interesting sidelight is that in C19 slang, *glib* meant tongue.H.]

GLIM. A candle, or dark lantern, used in housebreaking; also fire. To glim; to burn in the hand. *Cant*. [Like the next three words, recorded by B.E. in 1690.F.—In C19 it became slang, and has long been common in dialect.EDD. G's *glimms* is the same word, a quarter of a century earlier than the OD's first mention.—Survives too in American slang of trampdom and the underworld as a light—an eye—an eye-glass.I.]

GLIMFENDERS. Andirons. *Cant*.

GLIMFLASHY. Angry, or in a passion. *Cant*.

GLIMJACK. A link-boy. *Cant*.

GLIMMER. Fire. *Cant*.

GLIMMERERS. Persons begging with sham licences, pretending losses by fire. [Usually women: Harman, 1567, has *glimmering morte*.OD.]

GLIMMS. Eyes.

GLIMSTICK. A candlestick. *Cant*.

GLOBE. Pewter. *Cant*.

GLOVES. To give any one a pair of gloves; to make them a present or bribe. To win a pair of gloves; to kiss a man whilst he sleeps; for this a pair of gloves is due to any lady who will thus earn them.

GLUEPOT. A parson: from joining men and women together in matrimony.

GLUM. Sullen. [From *glum*, to look sullen, the C14 *gloom*.W. —cf. the Exmoor *glumping*.G.]

GLYBE. A writing. *Cant*.

GO BETWEEN. A pimp or bawd.

GO BY THE GROUND. A little short person, man or woman. [Cf. Lincolnshire *go-by-the-wall*, a slow, creeping, helpless person.EDD.]

GO SHOP. The Queen's Head in Duke's-court, Bow street, Covent-garden; frequented by the under players: where gin

166

and water is sold in three-halfpenny stools, called Goes; the gin is called Arrack. The go; the fashion: as, large hats are all the go.

GOADS. Those who wheedle in chapmen for horse-dealers. [Cant, 1690.OD.]

GOAT. A lascivious person. Goat's jig; making the beast with two backs, copulation. [Cf. the Shakespearean *goatish*.O.]

GOB. The mouth; also a bit or morsel; whence gobbets. Gift of the gob; wide-mouthed, or one who speaks fluently, or sings well. [Cf. *gab*, q.v.]

GOB STRING. A bridle.

GOBBLE P—K. A rampant, lustful woman.

GOBBLER. A turkey cock.

GODFATHER. He who pays the reckoning, or answers for the rest of the company; as, Will you stand godfather, and we will take care of the brat; i.e. repay you another time. Jurymen are also called godfathers, because they name the crime the prisoner before them has been guilty of, whether felony, petit larceny, &c. [As juryman, Shakespeare, 1596.OD.]

GOD PERMIT. A stage coach; from that affectation of piety, frequently to be met with in advertisements of stage coaches or waggons, where most of their undertakings are premised with, "if God permit;" or, "God willing."

GOG. All-a-gog; impatient, anxious, or desirous of a thing.

GOG AND MAGOG. Two giants, whose effigies stand on each side of the clock in Guildhall, London; of whom there is a tradition, that, when they hear the clock strike one, on the first of April, they will walk down from their places.

GOGGLES. Eyes: see OGLES. Goggle eyes; large prominent eyes. To goggle; to stare. [As spectacles, 1715.OD.]

GOING UPON THE DUB. Going out to break open, or pick the locks of houses.

GOLD DROPPERS. Sharpers who drop a piece of gold, which they pick up in the presence of some unexperienced person, for whom the trap is laid; this they pretend to have found, and, as he saw them pick it up, they invite him to a public house to partake of it: when there, two or three of their comrades drop in, as if by accident, and propose cards, or some other game, when they seldom fail of stripping their prey.

GOLD FINDER. One whose employment is to empty necessary houses; called also a tom-turd-man, and night-man: the latter from that business being always performed in the night. [Florio has *gong* and *dung-farmer*; Cotgrave, *jakes-farmer*.F.—In C19 Warwickshire, *gold-digger;* there also *gold-dust*.EDD.]

GOLDEN FLEECE. The knights of this ancient and honourable order, were a society about the year 1749. [If the Golden Fleece Club is meant, it existed *ca.* 1700: "a rattle-brained society." See Timbs, *Club Life*, and Ned Ward's *Secret History of Clubs*, 1709.]

GOLDFINCH. One who has commonly a purse full of gold. Goldfinches; guineas. [Cant, 1690.F.—Also a sovereign.EDD.]

GOLGOTHA, OR THE PLACE OF SCULLS. Part of the Theatre at Oxford, where the heads of houses sit; those gentlemen being, by the wits of the university, called sculls. [Amherst, 1726. OD.—Also note especially James Miller's *Humours of Oxford*, 1730.F.]

GOLLUMPUS. A large, clumsy fellow. [Perhaps from *goll*, a hand.F.]

GOLOSHES, i.e. Goliah's shoes. Large leathern clogs, worn by invalids over their ordinary shoes. [Fr. *galoche*.OD.]

GOOD MAN. A word of various imports, according to the place where it is spoken: in the city it means a rich man; at Hockley in the Hole, or St Giles's, an expert boxer; at a bagnio in Covent Garden, a vigorous fornicator; at an alehouse or tavern, one who loves his pot or bottle; and sometimes, though but rarely, a virtuous man. [Cf. the name *Goodman*, which has these possible origins:— "The A.S. Godman or Godmund, (2) the good 'man,' i.e. servant, (3) the man of *Good*, a common personal name, (4) the 'good man', (5) the 'goodman' of the house, i.e. the master." W:S.]

GOOD WOMAN. A nondescript, represented on a famous sign in St Giles's, in the form of a common woman, but without a head.

GOODYER'S PIG. Like Goodyer's pig; never well but when in mischief.

GOOSE. A taylor's goose; a smoothing iron used to press down the seams, for which purpose it must be heated: hence it is a jocular saying, that a taylor, be he ever so poor, is always sure to have a goose at his fire. He cannot say boh to a goose; a saying of a bashful or sheepish fellow. [Shakespeare has the word in its technical sense.O.]

GOOSE RIDING. A goose, whose neck is greased, being suspended by the legs to a cord tied to two trees or high posts, a number of men on horseback, riding full speed, attempt to pull off the head; which if they effect, the goose is their prize. This has been practised in Derbyshire within the memory of persons now living.

GOOSEBERRY. He played up old gooseberry among them; said of a person who, by force or threats, suddenly puts an end to a riot or disturbance. [*Old Gooseberry* was one of the synonyms and nicknames of the devil.EDD. See my article, "The Devil and his Nicknames," in *John O' London's Weekly*, Summer Reading Number 1931.]

GOOSEBERRY EYED. One with dull grey eyes, like boiled gooseberries.

GOOSEBERRY WIG. A large frizzled wig; perhaps, from a supposed likeness to a gooseberry bush.

GOOSECAP. A silly fellow, or woman. [Nashe, 1589.OD.]

GOREE. Money, chiefly gold: perhaps from the traffic carried on at that place, which is chiefly for gold dust. *Cant.*

GORMAGON. A monster with six eyes, three mouths, four arms, eight legs, five on one side and three on the other, three arses, two tarses, and a **** upon its back; a man on horseback, with a woman behind him.

GOTCH-GUTTED. Pot-bellied: a gotch in Norfolk signifying a pitcher, or large round jug. [Not restricted to Norfolk. EDD.]

TO GOUGE. To squeeze out a man's eye with the thumb: a cruel practice used by the Bostonians in America. [For an excellent account of the word, see R. H. Thornton's *American Glossary*, 1912.]

TO GRABBLE. To seize. To grabble the bit; to seize any one's money. *Cant*. [At first, *ca.* 1580, to grope about, the transitive, to handle roughly, being a century later; neither sense was cant.OD.]

GRAFTED. Cuckolded, i.e. having horns grafted on his head.

GRANNAM. Corn. [*Cant*. In Harman. Cf. *granary* and, for the form, *pannam*.]

GRANNUM'S GOLD. Hoarded money; supposed to have belonged to the grandmother of the possessor.

GRANNY. An abbreviation of grandmother; also the name of an ideot, famous for licking her eye, who died Nov. 14, 1719. Go teach your granny to suck eggs: said to such as would instruct any one in a matter he knows better than themselves.

GRAPPLE THE RAILS. A cant name used in Ireland for whiskey.

GRAVE DIGGER. Like a grave-digger; up to the a-se in business, and don't know which way to turn.

GRAVY-EYED. Blear-eyed, one whose eyes have a running humour.

TO GREASE. To bribe. To grease a man in the fist; to bribe him. To grease a fat sow in the a-se; to give to a rich man. Greasy chin; a treat given to parish officers in part of commutation for a bastard; called also, Eating a child. [First in Skelton, in whom we find so many colloquialisms. (OD.)]

GREAT INTIMATE. As great as shirt and shitten a-se.

GREAT JOSEPH. A surtout. *Cant*.

GREEDY GUTS. A covetous or voracious person. [In Florio. F.]

GREEK. St Giles's Greek; the slang lingo, cant, or gibberish. [First in Dekker, 1600.OD.—Cf. the Scottish dialectal phrase, *to become short of the Greek*, i.e. speechless.EDD.]

GREEN. Doctor Green; i.e. grass; a physician, or rather medicine, found very successful in curing most disorders to which horses are liable. My horse is not well, I shall send him to Doctor Green.

GREEN BAG. An attorney; those gentlemen carry their clients' deeds in a green bag; and, it is said, when they have no deeds to carry, frequently fill them with an old pair of breeches, or any other trumpery, to give themselves the appearance of business.

GREEN GOWN. To give a girl a green gown; to tumble her on the grass. [Late C16. At first, innocently, but soon it came to mean a dress grass-stained, hence an indication of virginity lost. (OD.)—Cf. the dialectal phrase, *get on the green gown*, to be buried.EDD.]

GREEN SICKNESS. The disease of maids occasioned by celibacy. [In Shakespeare.O.—Nowadays chlorosis.]

GREENHEAD. An inexperienced young man. [Cf. dialectal *green-hand*.EDD.]

GREENHORN. A novice on the town, an undebauched young fellow, just initiated into the society of bucks and bloods. [As applied to persons, recorded for 1650-1680, but the surname *Greenhorn* points to an existence beginning at least three centuries before.W:S.—Dialectal *green-horned*=simple, foolish.EDD.]

GREENWICH BARBERS. Retailers of sand from the pits at and about Greenwich, in Kent; perhaps they are styled barber from their constant shaving the sand banks.

GREENWICH GOOSE. A pensioner of Greenwich Hospital.

GREGORIAN TREE. The gallows: so named from Gregory Brandon, a famous finisher of the law; to whom Sir William Segar, garter king of arms (being imposed on by Brooke, a herald), granted a coat of arms. [1641.F.]

GREY BEARD. Earthen jugs formerly used in public houses, for drawing ale; they had the figure of a man with a large beard stamped on them; whence probably they took their name; see *Ben Jonson's Plays, Bartholomew Fair*, &c &c. Dutch earthen jugs, used for smuggling gin on the coasts of Essex and Suffolk, are at this time called grey beards. [Also in dialect, which exhibits the variants *grey-beard jar* or *jug* or *Geordie* or *George*.EDD.]

GREY MARE. The grey mare is the better horse; said of a

woman who governs her husband. [1546, and as a proverb cited by Ray.OD,F.]

GREY PARSON. A farmer who rents the tithes of the rector or vicar. [I.e. a lay impropriator of tithes.]

GRIG. A farthing. A merry grig; a fellow as merry as a grig: an allusion to the apparent liveliness of a grig, or young eel. [Or from the cricket. In Somerset, *so merry's a cricket* is equally common with *so merry's a grig:* though this does not settle the matter.EDD,W.]

GRIM. Old Mr Grim; death.

GRIMALKIN. A cat: mawkin signifies a hare in Scotland. [I.e. *Gray Malkin*, the *malkin* being a familiar diminutive for *Matilda, Mary*, a common name for a she-cat.W.]

GRIN. To grin in a glass case: to be anatomized for murder: the skeletons of many criminals are preserved in glass cases, at surgeons' hall.

GRINAGOG, THE CAT'S UNCLE. A foolish grinning fellow, one who grins without reason. [C16; now, and long, dialect only.OD.]

GRINDERS. Teeth. Gooseberry grinder; the breech. Ask bogey, the gooseberry grinder; ask mine a-se. [Originally the molars.OD.]

GROATS. To save his groats; to come off handsomely: at the universities, nine groats are deposited in the hands of an academic officer, by every person standing for a degree: which if the depositor obtains with honour, the groats are returned to him.

GROG. Rum and water. Grog was first introduced into the navy about the year 1740, by Admiral Vernon, to prevent the sailors intoxicating themselves with their allowance of rum or spirits. Groggy, or groggified; drunk. [Because the Admiral wore a grogram coat: see esp.W:A.—In slang, *groggy* now=in poor health,—in colloquial speech, unsteady (see G's *grogged*). Analogous is the Australianism *crook*, which in 1914-1918 puzzled many an English doctor in military hospitals.]

GROG-BLOSSOM. A carbuncle, or pimple in the face, caused by drinking.

172

GROGGED. A grogged horse; a foundered horse.

GROGHAM. A horse. *Cant.*

GROPERS. Blind men; also midwives.

GROUND SWEAT. A grave. [Cant, 1690.F.—Cynical brutality is a key-characteristic of cant:cf. the Tommy's *cold-meat ticket* for an identity-disc (B & P)and the dialectal *take a ground-sweat about anything*, to worry oneself greatly (EDD).]

GROUND SQUIRREL. A hog, or pig. *Sea term.*

GRUB. Victuals. To grub; to dine. To ride grub; to be sullen, or out of temper. [As food, C17. With the phrase, cf. the equivalent dialectal *be up a grub, the grubs bite (him) hard.*EDD.]

GRUB STREET. A street near Moorfields, formerly the supposed habitation of many persons who wrote for the booksellers: hence a Grub-street writer, means a hackney author, who manufactures books for the booksellers. [Taylor the Water-Poet, 1630.—Since 1830, Milton Street, which, though roughly parallel to Moorfields, runs off from Fore Street. Figurative, of course: the street inhabited by literary 'grubs.' But it is still a narrow, grimy street.OD,W. On the modern counterpart, in one sense, and modern contrast, in most senses, *vide* E. Beresford Chancellor's *Annals of Fleet Street*, 1912. There was, in London, a *Grub Street Journal* that ran from 1730 to 1737.]

GRUB STREET NEWS. Lying intelligence. [B.E., 1690. OD.—In several dialects, *grub*=idle talk, nonsense.EDD.]

TO GRUBSHITE. To make foul or dirty.

GRUMBLE. To grumble in the gizzard; to murmur or repine.

GRUMBLETONIAN. A discontented person; one who is always railing at the times, or ministry. [Late C17.OD.—Cf. dialectal *grumble-belly* or *-dirt* or *-guts*.EDD.]

GRUNTER. A hog; also a shilling. To grunt; to groan, or complain of sickness. [As hog, Brome, 1641, but generic for a grunting animal at least 200 years earlier.OD.—In West Yorkshire, a hedgehog.EDD.]

GRUNTER'S GIG. A smoaked hog's face.

GRUNTING PECK. Pork, bacon, or any kind of hog's flesh.

GUDGEON. One easily imposed on. To gudgeon; to swallow

the bait, or fall into a trap; from the fish of that name, which is easily taken. [As fool, late C16.OD.]

GULL. A simple, credulous fellow, easily cheated. [In 1590-1605 the following senses and variations established themselves: a ninny, a dupe, a trick or fraud; to trick; *gullery*, fraud, whether incidental or persistent; *gullage*, the same, also cajolery. F,OD.— Cf. Shakespeare's *gull-catcher*, a trickster.O.]

GULLED. Deceived, cheated, imposed on.

GULLGROPERS. Usurers who lend money to the gamesters.

GUM. Abusive language. Come, let us have no more of your gum. [East Suffolk, chatter, insolent talk.EDD.]

GUMMY. Clumsy; particularly applied to the ancles of men or women, and the legs of horses.

GUMPTION, or RUM GUMPTION. Docility, comprehension, capacity. [Arose *ca.* 1700 in Scotland, origin unknown. W.—Dialect also has *gumptionless*, tactless, foolish.EDD.]

GUN. He is in the gun; he is drunk: perhaps from an allusion to a vessel called a gun, used for ale in the universities. [*In the gun* was cant in 1690, slang in G's day.F.]

GUNDIGUTS. A fat, pursy fellow. [Sc. *gundie*, greedy.EDD.]

GUNNER'S DAUGHTER. To kiss the gunner's daughter: to be tied to a gun and flogged on the posteriors: a mode of punishing boys on board a ship of war.

GUNPOWDER. An old woman. *Cant.*

GUTS. My great guts are ready to eat my little ones; my guts begin to think my throat's cut; my guts curse my teeth; all expressions signifying the party is extremely hungry.

GUTS AND GARBAGE. A very fat man or woman. More guts than brains; a silly fellow. He has plenty of guts, but no bowels; said of a hard, merciless, unfeeling person. [In Shakespeare, *guts*=a gluttonous or a corpulent person. *More guts than brains* is also dialect; cf. the 1914-1918 army phrase, *more ballocks than brains*, more brawn than brains. With G's second phrase, cf. dialectal *have neither gut nor gall in one*, to be heartless and lazy.EDD.]

GUTFOUNDERED. Exceeding hungry. [In dialect, graver: "diseased from the effects of hunger." EDD.]

GUT SCRAPER, or TORMENTOR OF CATGUT. A fiddler.

GUTTER LANE. The throat, the swallow, the red lane. See RED LANE. [Cant, 1690.F.—Perhaps connected with Gutter Lane, London, as so much of non-gipsy cant was of London origin. The locality may have added point to, or even suggested, the phrase, wherein *gutter* is probably the L. *guttur*, throat, or figuratively, as in Juvenal, gluttony. As in cant and slang in general there is often a bafflingly rich accumulation, or a surprisingly fortuitous concourse, of circumstances, so here there may be hints from Devonshire *gutter* to eat greedily, and the better-known *guttle*, cognate with *guzzle; gutter, guttle*, and *guzzle* all deriving from *gut*. So I conjecture, *pace* the mighty. The interlacing of senses may be illustrated by the fact that, in dialect (EDD), *guzzle*, relevantly to the "argument," means to eat or drink excessively; throat; a glutton; food, but more especially drink, and as drink especially beer, small ale.]

GUTTING A QUART POT. Taking out the lining of it; i.e. drinking it off. Gutting an oyster; eating it. Gutting a house; clearing it of its furniture.

GUZZLE. Liquor. To guzzle; to drink greedily.

GUZZLE GUTS. One greedy of liquor.

GYBE, or JYBE. Any writing or pass with a seal. [Harman, 1567.F.]

GYBING. Jeering or ridiculing.

GYLES, or GILES. Hopping Giles; a nick name for a lame person: St Giles was the tutelar saint of cripples.

GYP. A college runner or errand-boy at Cambridge, called at Oxford a scout. See SCOUT. ["Popularly derived by Cantabs from the Greek *gups, gyps*, a vulture." H.—But probably from C17 *gippo*, Fr. *jupeau*, an article of clothing, hence a varlet; cf. *buttons*.W:WAM.]

GYPSIES. A set of vagrants who, to the great disgrace of our police, are suffered to wander about the country. They pretend that they derive their origin from the ancient Egyptians, who were famous for their knowledge in astronomy, and other sciences; and, under the pretence of fortune-telling, find means to rob or defraud the ignorant and superstitious. To colour their impostures, they artificially discolour their faces, and speak a kind of gibberish peculiar to themselves. They rove up and down the country in large companies, to the great terror of the farmers, from whose geese, turkeys, and fowls, they take very considerable contributions.

When a fresh recruit is admitted into the fraternity, he is to take the following oath, administered by the principal maunder, after going through the annexed forms:

First, a new name is given him, by which he is ever after to be called; then standing up in the middle of the assembly, and directing his face to the dimber damber, or principal man of the gang, he repeats the following oath, which is dictated to him by some experienced member of the fraternity.

I, Crank Cuffin, do swear to be a true brother, and that I will in all things obey the commands of the great tawney prince, and keep his counsel, and not divulge the secrets of my brethren. I will never leave nor forsake the company, but observe and keep all the times of appointment, either by day or by night, in every place whatever.

I will not teach any one to cant, nor will I disclose any of our mysteries to them.

I will take my prince's part against all that shall oppose him, or any of us, according to the utmost of my ability: nor will I suffer him, or any one belonging to us, to be abused by any strange abrams, rufflers, hookers, pailliards, swaddlers, Irish toyles, swigmen, whip jacks, jarkmen, bawdy baskets, dommerars, clapper dogeons, patricoes, or curtals; but will defend him, or them, as much as I can, against all other outliers whatever. I will not conceal aught I win out of libkins, or from the ruffmans, but will preserve it for the use of the company. Lastly, I will cleave to my doxy wap stiffly, and will bring her duds, margery praters, goblers, grunting cheats, or tibs of the buttery, or anything else I can come at, as winnings for her wappings.

The canters have, it seems, a tradition, that from the three first articles of this oath, the first founders of a certain boastful,

176

worshipful fraternity (who pretend to derive their origin from the earliest times) borrowed both the hint and form of their establishment; and that their pretended derivation from the first *Adam* is a forgery, it being only from the first *Adam Tiler:* see ADAM TILER. At the admission of a new brother, a general stock is raised for booze, or drink, to make themselves merry on the occasion. As for peckage, or eatables, they can procure it without money; for while some are sent to break the ruffmans, or woods and bushes, for firing, others are detached to filch geese, chickens, hens, ducks (or mallards), and pigs. Their morts are their butchers, who presently make bloody work with what living things are brought them; and having made holes in the ground, under some remote hedge in an obscure place, they make a fire and boil or broil their food; and when it is enough, fall to work tooth and nail: and having eaten more like beasts than men, they drink more like swine than human creatures, entertaining one another all the time with songs in the canting dialect.

As they live, so they lie, together promiscuously, and know not how to claim a property, either in their goods or children; and this general interest ties them more firmly together than if all their rags were twisted into ropes, to bind them indissolubly from a separation; which detestable union is farther consolidated by the above oath.

They stroll up and down all summer time in droves, and dexterously pick pockets, while they are telling of fortunes; and the money, rings, silver thimbles, &c. which they get, are instantly conveyed from one hand to another, till the remotest person of the gang (who is not suspected because they come not near the person robbed) gets possession of it: so that, in the strictest search, it is almost impossible to recover it: while the wretches with imprecations, oaths, and protestations, disclaim the thievery.

That by which they are said to get the most money, is, when young gentlewomen of good families and reputation have happened to be with child before marriage, a round sum is often bestowed among the gypsies, for some one mort to take the child; and as that is never heard of more by the true mother and family, so the disgrace is kept concealed from the world; and, if the child lives, it never knows its parents.

[*The New Statesman*, November 8th, 1930: "Much nonsense has been invented about the gypsy; children have been taught to fear him and grown-up children have put into force all kinds of unfair and petty laws in order to protect themselves from him; he was for centuries regarded as a heathen, his women as no better than witches, his tribe as a motley of dirty, picturesque, shifty vagabonds of whom it was easy to suspect any crime, from poaching a rabbit to the kidnapping of noblemen's daughters."—For an admirable summary of the history and fortunes of the gipsies, see Borrow's *Romano Lavo-Lil*, 1874; for a description of their life, Frank Cuttriss, *Romany Life*, 1915, and Dr J. Sampson, *The Wind on the Heath*, 1930, a very fine anthology in prose and verse, covering all periods and many countries, while *No 717, the Autobiography of a Gypsy*, edited by F.W. Carew, 1891, should also be read; for Romany, the gipsy lingo, see *Romano Lavo-Lil*, Dr Sampson's anthology, and Smart & Crofton's *Dialect of the English Gypsies*, enlarged 1875, while valuable short notes are to be found in OD,F,W.—As to the word *gipsy, gypsy*, it was in C16 *gypcian* for *Egyptian* because the gipsies were supposed to come from Egypt; other names are *Bohemian, Gitano, Romany, Zingari*.W.—Relating to the superstitions attaching to, and the prejudices against, gipsies, are many curious words and phrases; they provide a happy ramble in the great dictionaries. Among them are:—*Gipsy*, a term of contempt for woman or girl; *gipsy*, to wander about for pleasure or for the sake of a change; *gipsy*, an intermittent spring; *gipsy-nuts*, hips and haws. EDD.—In the American underworld, *gyp* means either to cheat, defraud, or a confidence game or confidence-worker.I.]

HABERDASHER OF PRONOUNS. A schoolmaster, or usher. [In obsolete North Country dialect, *h. of nouns and pronouns*.EDD.]

HACKNEY WRITER. One who writes for attornies or book-sellers. [The riding-horse for general use was, in C17-18, a *hackney* or *hack*: hence a *hackney-writer*, C18, or *hack*, C19-20. *Hack* is now applied to the merely industrious uncreative writer that lacks genius or talent on the one hand and genuine scholar-ship on the other. *Hack*, literal, came in as colloquial *ca.* 1700; as figurative for a servile writer, *ca.* 1774, but not established till *ca.* 1800. OD; W:A.]

HACKUM. Captain Hackum; a bravo, a slasher. [Variant *hackster*, 1690.]

HAD'EM. He has been at Had'em, and come home by Clap-ham; said of one who has caught the venereal disease.

HALBERT. A weapon carried by a serjeant of foot. To get a halbert; to be appointed a serjeant. To be brought to the hal-berts; to be flogged *à la militaire:* soldiers of the infantry, when flogged, being commonly tied to three halberts, set up in a triangle, with a fourth fastened across them. He carries the hal-bert in his face; a saying of one promoted from a serjeant to a commission officer. [*Halbert* itself has never been colloquial, and the weapon was very little used after 1600.]

HALF A HOG. Sixpence.

HALF AN OUNCE. Half a crown: silver being formerly esti-mated at a crown, or five shillings an ounce.

HALF BOARD. Sixpence. *Cant.*

HALF SEAS OVER. Almost drunk. [Cf. dialectal *half-sea.* EDD.]

HAMLET. A high constable. *Cant.* [Cf. Yorkshire *play Hamlet with*, to play the devil with, to scold. EDD.]

HAMS or HAMCASES. Breeches.

HAND. A sailor. We lost a hand; we lost a sailor. Bear a hand; make haste. Hand to fist; opposite: the same as tête-à-tête, or cheek by jowl.

HAND AND POCKET SHOP. An eating house, where ready money is paid for what is called for.

HAND BASKET PORTION. A woman whose husband re-ceives frequent presents from her father, or family, is said to have a hand-basket portion.

HANDLE. To know how to handle one's fists; to be skilful in the art of boxing.

HANDSOME. He is a handsome-bodied man in the face; a jeering commendation of an ugly fellow. Handsome is that handsome does; a proverb frequently cited by ugly women.

HANDSOME REWARD. This, in advertisements, means a horse-whipping.

TO HANG AN ARSE. To hang back, to hesitate. [Late C16, when also *to hang the groin*.OD.]

HANG GALLOWS LOOK. A thievish, or villainous appearance. [The modern *hang-dog look*.]

HANG IN CHAINS. A vile, desperate fellow. Persons guilty of murder, or other atrocious crimes, are frequently, after execution, hanged on a gibbet, to which they are fastened by iron bandages: the gibbet is commonly placed on or near the place where the crime was committed. [Cf. Northumberland, *hang-a-balk*.EDD.]

HANG IT UP. Score it up; speaking of a reckoning. [Cant, 1725.F.]

HANGER ON. A dependant. [Mid-C16.OD.]

HANGMAN'S WAGES. Thirteen pence halfpenny; which, according to the vulgar tradition, was thus allotted: one shilling for the execution, and three halfpence for the rope.—N.B. This refers to former times; the hangmen of the present day having, like other artificers, raised their prices. The true state of this matter is, that a Scottish mark was the fee allowed for an execution, and the value of that piece was settled by a proclamation of James I at thirteen pence halfpenny. [In Shropshire, money paid beforehand for a piece of work.EDD.]

HANK. He has a hank on him; i.e. an ascendancy over him, or a hold upon him. A Smithfield hank: an ox rendered furious by over-driving and barbarous treatment. [In dialect: a rope, the knot or the loop of a rope; cf. *in a hank*, in trouble.EDD.]

HANKER. To hanker after any thing; to have a longing after or for it. [From *ca.* 1600.W.—Dialect has *hankersome*, envious. EDD.]

HANKTELO. A silly fellow. [C16.F.—Also dialect, but obsolete before 1900.EDD.]

HANS IN KELDER. Jack in the cellar, i.e. the child in the womb: a health frequently drank to breeding women or their husbands. [From Dutch; became general *ca*. 1640.F.]

HAP WORTH A COPERAS. A vulgar pronunciation of *habeas corpus*.

HARD. Stale beer, nearly sour, is said to be hard. Hard also means severe; as, hard fate, a hard master. [As sour, cant in 1690; now good English in *hard cider*.F.—Of whiskey, strong, *the hard* meaning whiskey.EDD.]

HARD AT HIS ARSE. Close after him.

HARE. He has swallowed a hare; he is drunk; more probably a *hair*, which requires washing down.

HARK-YE-ING. Whispering on one side to borrow money.

HARMAN. A constable. *Cant*. [Short for *harman beck*. Perhaps *hardman*.OD.—Tentatively, I suggest *har-man*, the man who cries *ha*, in dialect *har*, i.e. stop!—Cf. dialectal *har off!* be off, come along!]

HARMAN BECK. A beadle. *Cant*.

HARMANS. The stocks. *Cant*. [In 1567. The *mans* is the same as in *crackmans, darkmans, lightmans, ruffmans, togemans*.OD.]

HARP. To harp upon; to dwell upon a subject. Have among you, my blind harpers; an expression used in throwing or shooting at random among a crowd. Harp is also the Irish expression for woman, or tail, used in tossing up in Ireland: from Hibernia being represented with a harp on the reverse of the copper coins of that country; for which reason it is, in hoisting the copper, i.e. tossing up, sometimes likewise called music. [The actual words in tossing-up were *head or harp*.EDD.]

HARRIDAN. A hagged[*sic*]old woman; a miserable, scraggy, worn-out harlot, fit to take her bawd's degree: derived from the French word *haridelle*, a worn-out jade of a horse or mare.

HARRY. A country fellow. *Cant*. Old Harry; the Devil.

HARUM SCARUM. He was running harum scarum; said of any one running or walking hastily, and in a hurry, after they know not what. [Perhaps *hare 'em, scare 'em*, from the obsolete *hare*, to harass. Smollett's (1751) form, *hare'um scare'um*, buttresses this. W. (OD.)—The famous American novel, *David Harum*, by Westcott, 1900, develops the idea expressed in its title.]

HASH. To flash the hash; to vomit. *Cant.*

HASTY. Precipitate, passionate. He is none of the Hastings sort: a saying of a slow, loitering fellow: an allusion to the Hastings pea, which is the first in season. [In G's day, on the borderline between colloquialism and good English.]

HASTY PUDDING. Oatmeal and milk boiled to a moderate thickness, and eaten with sugar and butter. Figuratively, a wet muddy road: as, The way through Wandsworth is quite a hasty pudding. To eat hot hasty pudding for a laced hat, or some other prize, is a common feat at wakes and fairs.

HAT. Old hat; a woman's privities: because frequently felt. [*Hat* is connected with the biggest 'brick' that Browning or any other great poet ever dropped: I suspect that some antiquarian pulled Browning's leg. With *old hat*, cf. *bad hat*, a person of dubious morals.]

HATCHES. Under the hatches; in trouble, distress, or debt. [Cf. *under the weather.*]

HATCHET FACE. A long thin face.

HAVIL. A sheep. *Cant.*

HAVY CAVY. Wavering, doubtful, shilly shally. [A Nottingham anglicising of L. *habe, cave.* G.]

HAWK. Ware hawk; the word to look sharp, a bye-word when a bailiff passes. Hawk also signifies a sharper, in opposition to pigeon. See PIGEON. [Both phrase and word go back to C16 vagabondage. OD.]

HAWKERS. Licensed itinerant retailers of different commodities, called also pedlars; likewise the sellers of newspapers. Hawking; an effort to spit up the thick phlegm, called *oysters:* whence it is wit upon record to ask the person so doing whether he has a licence; a punning allusion to the Act of hawkers and pedlars.

TO HAZEL GILD. To beat any one with a hazel stick.

HEAD CULLY OF THE PASS, or PASSAGE BANK. The

top tilter of that gang throughout the whole army, who demands and receives contribution from all the pass banks in the camp. A 1690 variant was *head bully of the pass*. F.]

HEAD RAILS. Teeth. *Sea phrase.*

HEARING CHEATS. Ears. *Cant.* [Harman, 1567. F.]

HEART'S EASE. A twenty-shilling piece; also one of the names for gin. [Cant, 1690. F.]

HEARTY CHOAK. He will have a hearty choak and caper sauce for breakfast: i.e. he will be hanged.

HEATHEN PHILOSOPHER. One whose breech may be seen through his pocket-hole: this saying arose from the old philosophers, many of whom despised the vanity of dress to such a point, as often to fall into the opposite extreme. [Cant, 1690. F.]

TO HEAVE. To rob. To heave a case; to rob a house. To heave a bough; to rob a booth. *Cant.* [Harman, 1567. F.]

HEAVER. The breast. *Cant.* [B. E., 1690. F.]

HEAVERS. Thieves who make it their business to steal tradesmen's shop-books. *Cant.*

HECTOR. A bully, a swaggering coward. To hector; to bully; probably from such persons affecting the valour of Hector, the Trojan hero.

HEDGE. To make a hedge; to secure a bet, or wager, laid on one side, by taking the odds on the other, so that, let what will happen, a certain gain is secured, or hedged in, by the person who takes this precaution; who is then said to be on velvet. [Shakespeare has *hedge*, to shuffle, to evade. O.]

HEDGE ALEHOUSE. A small obscure alehouse. [1690 variant, *hedge tavern*. F.]

HEDGE CREEPER. A robber of hedges. [Recorded for 1548. OD.]

HEDGE PRIEST. An illiterate unbeneficed curate, a patrico. [1550. The next term came a little later. *Hedge* was a pejorative, which Johnson called a detrimental prefix. OD, F.]

HEDGE WHORE. An itinerant harlot, who bilks the bagnios and bawdy-houses, by disposing of her favours on the wayside, under a hedge; a low beggarly prostitute.

HEELS. To be laid by the heels; to be confined, or put in prison. Out at heels; worn, or diminished; his estate or affairs are out at heels. To turn up his heels; to turn up the knave of trumps at the game of all fours. [These three phrases were established by *ca.* 1600. OD.—G's explanation of the third illustrates what we may describe as society-cant.]

HEEL TAP. A peg in the heel of a shoe, taken out when it is finished. A person leaving any liquor in his glass, is frequently called upon by the toast-master to take off his heel-tap.[In dialect, also the last or the end of anything; and as a plural, gossip or scandal.EDD.]

HELL. A taylor's repository for his stolen goods, called cabbage: see CABBAGE. Little hell; a small dark covered passage, leading from London-wall to Bell-alley. [A C16 term; cf. Shakespeare's *hell*, a "place of confinement for debtors." O.]

HELL-BORN BABE. A lewd graceless youth, one naturally of a wicked disposition.

HELL CAT. A termagant, a vixen, a furious scolding woman. See TERMAGANT and VIXEN.

HELL HOUND. A wicked abandoned fellow. [In Shakespeare, a fiendish person; cf. *hell-kite*, a person of hellish cruelty.O.]

HELTER SKELTER. To run helter skelter, hand over head, in defiance of order. [The etymology remains a mystery. Possibly a corruption of *helter* (a halter, to put a halter on, to hang) +*kelter* (order): i.e. in defiance of order.G.]

HEMP. Young hemp; an appellation for a graceless boy.

HEMPEN FEVER. A man who was hanged is said to have died of a hempen fever; and, in Dorsetshire, to have been stabbed with a Bridport dagger; Bridport being a place famous for manufacturing hemp into cords. [Cf. Skelton's *hempen snare* and Nashe's *hempen circle*.O.—Cf. also *hemp-string*, Gascoigne, 1566, and *hemp-seed*, Shakespeare, 1598.F.—Like *hempen widow* most such terms were cant.]

HEMPEN WIDOW. One whose husband was hanged.

HEN-HEARTED. Cowardly.

HEN HOUSE. A house where the woman rules: called also a

she house, and *hen frigate:* the latter a sea phrase, originally applied to a ship, the captain of which had his wife on board, supposed to command him.

HENPECKED. A husband governed by his wife, is said to be henpecked. [In B. E., 1690.F.]

HERE AND THEREIAN. One who has no settled place of residence.

HERRING. The devil a barrel the better herring; all equally bad.

HERRING-GUTTED. Thin, as a shotten herring.

HERRING POND. The sea. To cross the herring pond at the king's expence; to be transported. [As Atlantic, 1686.W.—In Cornish, *herring-pool*.EDD.]

HERTFORDSHIRE KINDNESS. Drinking twice to the same person. [Fuller, 1661.OD.]

HICCOBITES. The brethren of this most ancient and joyous order, held their general court, Dec. 5, 1750, at the Sun-tavern, Fish-street-hill. [Presumably *hiccup-ites*.]

HICK. A country hick; an ignorant clown. *Cant*. [Not cant, but colloquial. A familiar by-form of *Richard*, as *Bob* of *Robert*. Most people think it is an Americanism.—In American low slang, *hick* means, derisively, a farmer; also one ignorant of what impends.I.]

HICKENBOTHOM. Mr Hickenbothom; a ludicrous name for an unknown person, similar to that of Mr Thingambob. Hickenbothom is a corruption of the German word *ickenbaum*, i.e. oak tree. [The derivation is obviously nonsense.]

HICKEY. Tipsey; quasi, hickupping. [Dialect *hick*, to hiccup. EDD.]

HICKSIUS DOXIUS. Drunk. [Properly *hiccius doccius*. As noun, a juggler or a trickster. Either a nonsense formula simulating Latin, or a corruption of *hicce est doctus*, lo! the learned man. Originally, jugglers' cant, or rather part of their patter. OD.]

HIDE AND SEEK. A childish game. He plays at hide and seek; a saying of one who is in fear of being arrested for debt, or apprehended for some crime, and therefore does not chuse to

185

appear in public, but secretly skulks up and down. See SKULK. [The term has at least thirteen variants in dialect.EDD.]

HIDEBOUND. Stingy, hard of delivery; a poet poor in invention, is said to have a hidebound muse. [I.e. "a costive muse." EDD.—In the *Dictionarium Rusticum*, 1717, we find that the word indicated a distemper in horses and a defect in trees. The figurative sense occurs as early as the Tudor authors.W:MW AM.]

HIGGLEDY PIGGLEDY. Confusedly mixed.

HIGH EATING. To eat skylarks in a garret.

HIGH FLYERS. Tories, Jacobites. [The modern sense dates back to C17.F.]

HIGH JINKS. A gambler at dice, who, having a strong head, drinks to intoxicate his adversary, or pigeon. [Also a country drinking-game obsolete by *ca.* 1800.F.]

HIGH LIVING. To lodge in a garret or cock loft.

HIGH PAD. A highwayman. *Cant.* [From *high pad*, the highway. Harman, 1567.F.]

HIGH ROPES. To be on the high ropes; to be in a passion.

HIGH SHOON, or CLOUTED SHOON. A country clown.

HIGH WATER. It is high water with him; he is full of money. [Cf. *high-tide* in B.E., 1690.F.]

HIGHGATE. Sworn at Highgate—a ridiculous custom formerly prevailed at the public houses in Highgate, to administer a ludicrous oath to all travellers of the middling rank who stopped there. The party was sworn on a pair of horns, fastened on a stick; the substance of the oath was never to kiss the maid when he could kiss the mistress, never to drink small beer when he could get strong, with many other injunctions of the like kind to all which was added the saving clause of "unless you like it best." The person administering the oath was always to be called father by the juror; and he, in return, was to style him son, under the penalty of a bottle. [*Sworn in at Highgate*=sharp, clever.EDD.]

HIKE. To hike off; to run away. *Cant.* [So too in dialect.EDD. —Like *hick*, it went to America and has returned to England as a stock phrase of American films and Wild-West novels.]

HIND LEG. To kick out a hind leg; to make a rustic bow.

HINNEY, MY HONEY. A north country hinney, particularly a Northumbrian: in that country, hinney is the general term of endearment. [*Hinny* itself, of course, means honey.]

HISTORY OF THE FOUR KINGS, or CHILD'S BEST GUIDE TO THE GALLOWS. A pack of cards. He studies the history of the four kings assiduously; he plays much at cards.

HOAXING. Bantering, ridiculing. Hoaxing a quiz; joking an odd fellow. *University wit.*

HOB, or HOBBINOL. A clown. [Cf. Northern *hobbil, hobgobbin*, "a natural fool a blockhead." G.]

HOB or NOB. Will you hob or nob with me? a question formerly in fashion at polite tables, signifying a request or challenge to drink a glass of wine with the proposer; if the party challenged answered Nob, they were to chuse whether white or red. This foolish custom is said to have originated in the days of good queen Bess, thus: When great chimnies were in fashion, there was at each corner of the hearth, or grate, a small elevated projection, called the hob: and behind it a seat. In winter time the beer was placed on the hob to warm; and the cold beer was set on a small table, said to have been called the nob: so that the question, Will you have hob or nob? seems only to have meant, Will you have warm or cold beer? i.e. beer from the hob, or beer from the nob. [In Shakespeare, *hob, nob*, a variant of *hab, nab* (i.e. *ne habe*): have, have not. O.—In C18 Northern dialect, an adverb: "*Hob-nob* (sometimes pronounced *hab-nab*), at a venture, rashly." G.—the *hab, nab* origin was influenced by reduplicated *Hob*, a familiar by-form of *Robert*.W.—Several dialects have *hob-nobble*. EDD.]

HOBBERDEHOY. Half a man and half a boy; a lad between both. [Many spellings. Earliest record, *hobbledehoye*, Palsgrave, 1540. A puzzling word, the best account occurring in W.—G's definition comes straight from Ray's *Proverbs* (EDD); in Norfolk, one used to say: "Hobbledehoy, neither man nor boy."F.]

HOBBLED. Impeded, interrupted, puzzled. To hobble; to walk lamely.

HOBBLEDYGEE. A pace between a walk and a run, a dog-trot.

HOBBY. Sir Posthumous's hobby: one nice or whimsical in his clothes.

HOBBY HORSE. A man's favourite amusement, or study, is called his hobby horse. It also means a particular kind of small Irish horse; and also a wooden one, such as is given to children. [*Hobby*, like *Dobbin*, is from *Robert* and is likewise an old name for a horse. Cf. Fr. *enfourcher un dada*. W:ROW.—Shakespeare, a wanton; in Jonson, a witless, uncouth lout.F.—In dialect, a hoyden; a butt (figurative). EDD.]

HOBBY-HORSICAL. A man who is a great keeper or rider of hobby horses; one that is apt to be strongly attached to his systems of amusement.

HOBNAIL. A country clodhopper; from the shoes of country farmers and ploughmen being commonly stuck full of hobnails, and even often clouted, or tipped with iron. The Devil ran over his face with hobnails in his shoes; said of one pitted with the small-pox.

HOBSON'S CHOICE. That or none; from old Hobson, famous carrier of Cambridge, who used to let horses to the students; but never permitted them to chuse, always allotting each man the horse he thought properest for his manner of riding and treatment. [Originally *Hodgson's choice*, proverbial fourteen years before the famous carrier died and thereby distorted the phrase.W:ROW.]

HOCKS. A vulgar appellation for the feet. You have left the marks of your dirty hocks on my clean stairs; a frequent complaint from a mop-squeezer to a footman.

HOCKEY. Drunk with strong stale beer, called old hock. See HICKSIUS DOXIUS, and HICKEY. [This is cryptic. G means that *hockey*, i.e. a harvest-home or harvest-supper or even the last load of a harvest, is celebrated with *old hock*, a sour ale sold cheap to the employer of the harvesters. Note the analogous *hockey-supper; hockey-cart* (in Herrick *hock-cart*), that which carries the *hockey-load*, the last load; *hockey-cake*, offered as largesse to the poor at harvest time. Cf. *hopken*, Kentish for a supper given to the workers when the hop-picking is finished. EDD.]

HOCKING, or HOUGHING. A piece of cruelty practised by the butchers of Dublin, on soldiers, by cutting the tendon of Achilles: this has been by law made felony.

HOCUS POCUS. Nonsensical words used by jugglers, previous to their deceptions, as a kind of charm, or incantation. A celebrated writer supposes it to be a ludicrous corruption of the words, *hoc est corpus*, used by the popish priests in consecrating the host. Hocus is also used to express drunkenness; as he is quite hocus; he is quite drunk. [In C17 a conjuror; also, to hoax. The *corpus* theory may be the right one. W. See also G & K.]

HOD. Brother hod; a familiar name for a bricklayer's labourer; from the hod which is used for carrying bricks and mortar.

HODDY DODDY, ALL A-SE AND NO BODY. A short clumsy person, either male or female. [In a C16 play. F.]

HODGE. An abbreviation of Roger; a general name for a country booby.

HODGE PODGE. An irregular mixture of numerous things. [From Fr. *hochepot*, the scale being *hotch-pot*, *hotch-potch*, *hodge-potch*, *hodge-podge*. W:MWAM.]

HODMANDODS. Snails in their shells.

HOG. A shilling. To drive one's hogs; to snore; the noise made by some persons in snoring, being not much unlike the notes of that animal. He has brought his hogs to a fine market; a saying of any one who has been remarkably successful in his affairs, and is spoken ironically to signify the contrary. A hog in armour; an awkward or mean looking man or woman, finely dressed, is said to look like a hog in armour. To hog a horse's mane; to cut it short, so that the ends of the hair stand up like hog's bristles. Jonian hogs; an appellation given to the members of St John's College, Cambridge.

HOG GRUBBER. A mean stingy fellow. [Cant, 1690. F.]

HOGGISH. Rude, unmannerly, filthy.

HOGO. Corruption of *haut goust*, high taste, or flavour; commonly said of flesh somewhat tainted. It has a confounded hogo; it stinks confoundedly. [In C19 slang, *fogo*. H.]

HOIST. To go upon the hoist; to get into windows accidentally left open; this is done by the assistance of a confederate, called the hoist, who leans his head against the wall, making his back a kind of step or ascent.

HOISTING. A ludicrous ceremony formerly performed on every soldier, the first time he appeared in the field after being married; it was thus managed: As soon as the regiment, or company, had grounded their arms to rest a while, three or four men of the same company to which the bridegroom belonged, seized upon him, and putting a couple of bayonets out of the two corners of his hat, to represent horns, it was placed on his head, the back part foremost. He was then hoisted on the shoulders of two strong fellows, and carried round the arms, a drum and fife beating and playing the pioneers call, named Round Heads and Cuckolds, but on this occasion styled the Cuckold's March; in passing the colours, he was to take off his hat; this, in some regiments, was practised by the officers on their brethren. Hoisting, among pickpockets, is, setting a man on his head, that his money, watch, &c. may fall out of his pockets; these they pick up, and hold to be no robbery. See REVERSED.

HOITY-TOITY. A hoity-toity wench; a giddy, thoughtless, romping girl. ["The earliest record, *upon the hoyty-toyty* (1668), suggests the *high ropes* and *tight rope*, or simply a jingle on *high*." W. Also an article in W:MWAM.— The dialectal sense, uppish, has prevailed.EDD.]

HOLBORN HILL. To ride backwards up Holborn hill; to go to the gallows: the way to Tyburn, the place of execution for criminals condemned in London, was up that hill. Criminals going to suffer, always ride backwards; as some conceive, to increase the ignominy, but more probably to prevent their being shocked with the distant view of the gallows, as, in amputations, surgeons conceal the instruments with which they are going to operate. The last execution at Tyburn, and consequently of this procession, was in the year 1784, since which the criminals have been executed near Newgate.

HOLIDAY. A holiday bowler; a bad bowler. Blind man's holiday; darkness, night. A holiday is any part of a ship's bottom, left uncovered in paying it. *Sea term*. It is all holiday; see

ALL HOLIDAY. [With the sea term, cf. Cornish *holiday*: indicating parts left undusted, unswept, uncleaned, unpainted. EDD.]

HOLLOW. It was quite a hollow thing; i.e. a certainty, or decided business.

HOLY FATHER. A butcher's boy of St Patrick's Market, Dublin, or other Irish blackguard; among whom the exclamation, or oath, By the Holy Father (meaning the Pope), is common. [*Holy* used pejoratively is fairly common in dialect, and cf. the colloquialisms *holy show, holy lance, holy poker(s)*! EDD.]

HOLY LAMB. A thorough-paced villain. *Irish*.

HOLY WATER. He loves him as the Devil loves holy water; i.e. hates him mortally. Holy water, according to the Roman Catholics, having the virtue to chase away the Devil and his imps.

HONEST MAN. A term frequently used by superiors to inferiors. As honest a man as any in the cards when all the kings are out: i.e. a knave. I dare not call thee rogue for fear of the law, said a quaker to an attorney; but I will give thee five pounds, if thou canst find any creditable person who will say thou art an honest man.

HONEST WOMAN. To marry a woman with whom one has cohabited as a mistress, is termed, making an honest woman of her.

HONEY MOON. The first month after marriage. A poor honey; a harmless, foolish, good-natured fellow. It is all honey or all t—d with them; said of persons who are either in the extremity of friendship or enmity, either kissing or fighting. [Dialect also has *honey month*. EDD. For an article on the word, see W:MWAM.]

HOOD-WINKED. Blindfolded by a handkerchief, or other ligature, bound over the eyes.

HOOF. To beat the hoof; to travel on foot. He hoofed it, or beat the hoof, every step of the way from Chester to London. [Shakespeare has *plod away ith' hoof*, also *o' the hoof*, on foot. O.— In G. by printer's error, *heat the hoof*.]

HOOK AND SNIVEY, WITH NIX THE BUFFER. This rig consists in feeding a man and a dog for nothing, and is carried on thus: Three men, one of whom pretends to be sick and unable to eat, go to a public house; the two well men make a bargain with the landlord for their dinner, and when he is out of sight, feed their pretended sick companion and dog gratis. [Later, *hookum snivey*, imposture, impostor.F.]

HOOKED. Over-reached, tricked, caught; a simile taken from fishing. **** hooks; fingers.

HOOKERS. See ANGLERS. [Harman, 1567.—Cf. modern American underworld slang, *hooker*, a harlot or a drink of liquor.I.]

HOOP. To run the hoop; an ancient marine custom. Four or more boys having their left hands tied fast to an iron hoop, and each of them a rope, called a nettle, in their right, being naked to the waist, wait the signal to begin; this being made by a stroke with a cat of nine tails, given by the boatswain to one of the boys, he strikes the boy before him, and every one does the same; at first the blows are but gently administered; but each irritated by the strokes from the boy behind him, at length lays it on in earnest. This was anciently practised when a ship was wind-bound.

TO HOOP. To beat. I'll well hoop his or her barrel. I'll beat him or her soundly.

TO HOP THE TWIG. To run away. *Cant.*

HOP MERCHANT. A dancing master. See CAPER MERCHANT. [Slang, but in B.E., 1690.OD.]

HOP-O-MY-THUMB. A diminutive person, man or woman. She was such a hop-o-my-thumb, that a pigeon, sitting on her shoulder, might pick a pea out of her a-se. [In 1530, *hoppe upon my thombe*.W.—In C19 W. Somerset, fop, dandy. EDD.]

HOPKINS. Mr Hopkins; a ludicrous address to a lame or limping man, being a pun on the word *hop*.

HOPPER-ARSED. Having large projecting buttocks; from their resemblance to a small basket, called a hopper, or hoppet, worn by husbandmen for containing seed corn, when they sow the land. [C17; as *hopper-hipped*, C16.F.]

HOPPING GILES. A jeering appellation given to any person who limps, or is lame; St Giles was the patron of cripples, lepers, &c. Churches dedicated to that saint commonly stand out of town, many of them having been chapels to hospitals. See GYLES.

HORNS. To draw in one's horns; to retract an assertion through fear; metaphor borrowed from a snail, who, on the apprehension of danger, draws in his horns, and retires to his shell.

HORN COLIC. A temporary priapism. [Actually in EDD.]

HORN FAIR. An annual fair held at Charlton, in Kent, on St Luke's day, the 18th of October. It consists of a riotous mob, who, after a printed summons dispersed through the adjacent towns, meet at Cuckold's Point, near Deptford, and march from thence in procession, through that town and Greenwich to Charlton, with horns of different kinds upon their heads; and at the fair there are sold rams' horns, and every sort of toy made of horn; even the gingerbread figures have horns. The vulgar tradition gives the following history of the origin of this fair: King John, or some other of our ancient kings, being at the palace of Eltham, in this neighbourhood, and having been out a hunting one day, rambled from his company to this place, then a mean hamlet; when entering a cottage to enquire his way, he was struck with the beauty of the mistress, whom he found alone; and having prevailed over her modesty, the husband returning suddenly, surprised them together; and threatening to kill them both, the king was obliged to discover himself, and to compound for his safety by a purse of gold, and a grant of the land from this place to Cuckold's Point, besides making the husband master of the hamlet. It is added, that, in memory of this grant, and the occasion of it, this fair was established, for the sale of horns, and all sorts of goods made with that material. A sermon is preached at Charlton church on the fair day.

HORN MAD. A person extremely jealous of his wife, is said to be horn mad. Also a cuckold, who does not cut or breed his horns easily. [At first of horned beasts; derivatively of persons,

stark mad or furious and sometimes, by a play on words, 'mad'
at being cuckolded, both personal senses occurring in Shake-
speare.O.—In C19 venery, extremely lecherous.F.]

HORN WORK. Cuckold-making. [In Sterne, 1759.OD.]

HORNIFIED. Cuckolded.

HORSE BUSS. A kiss with a loud smack; also a bite.

HORSE COSER. A dealer in horses; vulgarly and corruptly
pronounced *horse courser*. The verb *to cose* was used by the Scots,
in the sense of bartering or exchanging. [The usual Scottish,
even in G's day, was *horse-couper*.EDD. The earliest form of
G's term was *horse-courser*, variously spelt, C16.OD.]

HORSE GODMOTHER. A large masculine woman, a gen-
tlemanlike kind of a lady.

HORSE LADDER, A piece of Wiltshire wit, which consists
in sending some raw lad, or simpleton, to a neighbouring farm
house, to borrow a horse ladder, in order to get up the horses,
to finish a hay-mow.

HORSE'S MEAL. A meal without drinking.

HOSTELER, i.e. oat stealer. Hosteler was originally the
name for an inn-keeper; inns being in old English styled hostels,
from the French signifying the same. [From Old Fr. *hostel*.OD.]

HOT POT. Ale and brandy made hot. [So in dialect. The
famous Lancashire *hot pot* (meat and potatoes baked together)
is not recorded till 1854.OD.]

HOT STOMACH. He has so hot a stomach, that he burns all
the clothes off his back; said of one who pawns his clothes to
purchase liquor.

HOUSE, or TENEMENT, TO LET. A widow's weeds; also
an atchievement marking the death of a husband, set up on
the outside of a mansion; both supposed to indicate that the
dolorous widow wants a male comforter. [In American low
slang, *house for rent*.I.]

HOYDON. A romping girl. [Originally ca. 1600 applied to a
boor and probably connected with *heathen*.W.—Cf. Kentish
hoyden about, to romp.EDD.]

HUBBLE-BUBBLE. Confusion. A hubble-bubble fellow; a
man of confused ideas, or one thick of speech, whose words

sound like water bubbling out of a bottle. Also an instrument used for smoaking through water in the East Indies, called likewise a caloon, and hooker. [Reduplication of course: on which word, uncertain.]

HUBBLE DE SHUFF. Confusedly. To fire hubble de shuff; to fire quick and irregularly. *Old military term.*

HUBBUB. A noise, riot, or disturbance. [Perhaps from Gaelic *ubub!* contemptuous interjection.W.]

HUCKLE MY BUFF. Beer, egg, and brandy, made hot.

HUCKSTERS. Itinerant retailers of provisions. He is in hucksters' hands; he is in a bad way. [From Dutch.W.—In C17, colloquial.F.—Common in dialect for a small tradesman not necessarily itinerant.EDD.]

TO HUE. To lash. The cove was hued in the naskin; the rogue was soundly lashed in bridewell. *Cant.*

TO HUFF. To reprove, or scold at any one; also to bluster, bounce, ding, or swagger. A captain huff; a noted bully. To stand the huff; to be answerable for the reckoning in a public house. [In C16, *huff*=to play the braggart.W.—"She huffed me and laughed at me." D.]

HUG. To hug brown bess; to carry a firelock, or serve as a private soldier. He hugs it as the Devil hugs a witch; said of one who holds any thing as if he was afraid of losing it.

HUGGER MUGGER. By stealth, privately, without making an appearance. They spent their money in a hugger mugger way. [In the *Paston Letters* as *hedermoder*, i.e. *hudder-mudder*. In C16, (*in*) *hucker-mucker*. C19 sense, confusion as well as secrecy. In dialect as noun, adverb, and verb. W,EDD.—Among sailors: slovenly.B.]

HUGOTONTHEONBIQUIFFINARIANS. A society existing in 1748.

HULKY, or HULKING. A great hulky fellow; an overgrown clumsy lout, or fellow. [Dyche, 1748, defines *hulk* as "a lazy, dronish fellow." F.]

HULVER-HEADED. Having a hard impenetrable head; hulver, in the Norfolk dialect, signifying holly, a hard and solid wood.

TO HUM, or HUMBUG. To deceive, or impose on one by some story or device. A humbug; a jocular imposition, or deception. To hum and haw; to hesitate in speech, also to delay, or be with difficulty brought to consent to any matter or business. [The verb *humbug* did not become general till C19; the noun was in 1754, in *The Connoisseur*, described as new-coined and nonsensical. *Hum* as both noun and verb came about the same time, 1750.F,OD. The best account is in OD, but the most readable is in H.]

HUMBUGS. The brethren of the venerable society of humbugs was held at brother Hallam's, in Goodman's Fields.

HUMS. Persons at church. There is a great number of hums in the autem; there is a great congregation in the church.

HUM BOX. A pulpit. [*Cant.* So to the next.F.]

HUM CAP. Very old and strong beer, called also stingo. See STINGO.

HUM DRUM. A hum drum fellow; a dull tedious narrator, a bore; also a set of gentlemen, who (Bailey says) used to meet near the Charter House, or at the King's Head in St John's street, who had more of pleasantry, and less of mystery, than the free masons. ["Reduplication on *hum*, with reminiscence of *drum*." W.—C16 for both noun and adjective.OD.]

HUM DURGEON. An imaginary illness. He has got the hum durgeon, the thickest part of his thigh is nearest his a-se; i.e. nothing ails him except low spirits.

HUMMER. A great lye, a rapper. See RAPPER. [Like the next entry, cant, F.]

HUMMING LIQUOR. Double ale, stout Pharaoh. See PHARAOH.

HUMMUMS. A bagnio, or bathing-house. [As the former (a brothel), slang; as the latter, good English, from Arabic *hammam*, a hot bath.OD. In addition to the regular brothels, there were, in the C18, three classes of place partly affected to such uses. "Some of the so-called coffee houses were frankly brothels kept by women who had a regular *clientèle;* others were taverns whose upstairs rooms were used for the same purpose, although their ground floors were apparently innocent of anything except drunkenness; while....the Bagnios or Baths formed a third series of places for prostitution." The name *Bagnio* was "a cloak, and that this was so is proved by the fact that not a few of the disorderly houses....gave themselves this title," and "they appear to have been indicated by a bunch of grapes hanging at the door." Beresford Chancellor's *Covent Garden*, whence we learn further that one hostelry, afterwards an hotel, was called the Hummums, from its original capacity.]

HUMP. To hump; once a fashionable word for copulation. [In American criminal and vagabond slang, this verb survives; there, too, one may hear *hump* as the corresponding noun.I.]

HUMPTY DUMPTY. A little humpty dumpty man or woman; a short clumsy person of either sex: also ale boiled with brandy. [Perhaps a reduplication on a corruption or endearment of *Humphrey*.W.]

HUMSTRUM. A musical instrument made of a mopstick, a bladder, and some packthread, thence also called bladder and string, and hurdy gurdy; it is played on like a violin, which is sometimes ludicrously called a humstrum: sometimes, instead of a bladder, a tin canister is used.

TO HUNCH. To jostle, or thrust. [In dialect, gore or butt. EDD.]

HUNCH-BACKED. Hump-backed.

HUNKS. A covetous miserable fellow, a miser; also the name of a famous bear mentioned by Ben Jonson.[Dekker, 1602.OD. —And as late as Trollope, 1857, and Sir Theodore Martin, 1893.F. The word is still heard occasionally.]

HUNT'S DOG. He is like Hunt's dog, will neither go to church nor stay at home. One Hunt, a labouring man at a small town in Shropshire, kept a mastiff, who on being shut up on Sundays, whilst his master went to church, howled so terribly as to disturb the whole village; wherefore his master resolved to take him to church with him: but when he came to the church door, the dog having perhaps formerly been whipped out by the sexton, refused to enter; whereupon Hunt exclaimed loudly against the dog's obstinacy, who would neither go to church nor stay at home. This shortly became a bye-word for discontented and whimsical persons.

HUNTING. Drawing in unwary persons to play or game. *Cant.*

HUNTING THE SQUIRREL. An amusement practised by post-boys and stage-coachmen, which consists in following a one-horse chaise, and driving it before them, passing close to it, so as to brush the wheel, and by other means terrifying any woman or person that may be in it. A man whose turn comes for him to drink, before he has emptied his former glass, is said to be hunted. [In C19 Somerset, *hunt-the-squirrel* was a kind of country dance.EDD.]

HUNTSUP. The reveillier of huntsmen, sounded on the French horn, or other instrument. [In Shakespeare. From *The Hunt Is Up*, a song sung to rouse huntsmen from sleep.O.]

HURDY GURDY. A kind of fiddle, made perhaps out of a gourd: at present it is confounded with the humstrum. See HUMSTRUM.

HURLY BURLY. A rout, riot, bustle, or confusion. [Riming reduplication, from *hurling and burling*, where *hurling*=a commotion and *burling* is reduplicative.W:ROW.—C16 and Shakespeare.OD.]

HUSH. Hush the cull; murder the fellow.

HUSH MONEY. Money given to hush up or conceal a robbery, theft, or any other offence, or to take off the evidence from appearing against a criminal. [Steele in 1709, Swift in 1731.OD.]

HUSKYLOUR. A guinea, or job. *Cant.*

HUSSAR-LEG ROLL UP. A meeting of a club so called, was advertised A.D. 1747.

HUSSY. An abbreviation of housewife, but now always used as a term of reproach; as, How now, hussy? or, She is a light hussy. [Cf. the degeneration of *quean* and *wench*, as of Fr. *garce* and *fille*.W:ROW.—In dialect: a housewife; a woman of any age; especially and generally a young girl, with or without pejorative sense according to context. Scottish *hizzie*. EDD.]

HUZZA. Said to have been originally the cry of the huzzars, or Hungarian light horse; but now the national shout of the English, both civil and military, in the sea phrase termed a cheer; to give three cheers being to huzza thrice.

HYP, or HIP. A mode of calling to one passing by. Hip, Michael, your head's on fire; a piece of vulgar wit to a redhaired man.

HYP. The hypochondriac; low spirits. He is hypped; he has got the blue devils.&c, [As *hyps* in Berkeley, 1705, in Swift, 1731; as *hips*, 1710 in *The Tatler*; as *hyp* in Gray, 1736; and as *hip* in C. Johnston, 1762. *Hypo*, 1711, and *hippo*, 1725. *Hypped*, 1710, and *hipped*, 1712.OD.]

IDEA POT. The knowledge box, the head. See KNOWLEDGE BOX.

ILL-FORTUNE, or THE PICTURE OF ILL-LUCK. A ninepenny piece. [B.E., 1690; so too the next entry.F.]

IMPOST TAKERS. Usurers who attend the gaming-tables, and lend money at great premiums.

IMPUDENT STEALING. Cutting out the backs of coaches, and robbing the seats.

IMPURE. A modern term for a lady of easy virtue. [First recorded for 1784.OD.]

INCHING. Encroaching. [B.E., 1690.F.—Cf. *Inching and pinching* in Hardy's *Two in a Tower*.EDD.]

INDIES. Black Indies; Newcastle.

INDIA WIPE. A silk handkerchief.

INDORSER. A sodomite. To indorse with a cudgel; to drub or beat a man over the back with a stick, to lay *cane* upon Abel.

INEXPRESSIBLES. Breeches. [Cf. *indescribables*, 1794; *indispensables*, 1841; *ineffables*, 1823; *inexplicables*, Dickens, 1836; *innominables*, ca. 1840. Also *unmentionables*, 1830 in U.S.A. and 1836 (Dickens) in England; *unutterables*, 1843; *unwhisperables*, 1837. The terms from F, also H; dates, OD.]

INKLE WEAVERS. Supposed to be a very brotherly set of people; 'as great as two inkle-weavers' being a proverbial saying. [A cant synonymous simile of 1725 was *as great as cup and can*.F.—Very frequent in dialect, which has also *as thick, kind, loving, close as inkle-weavers*. Weavers of this fabric (an inferior, coarse kind of tape) had to sit close together.EDD.]

INLAID. Well inlaid; in easy circumstances, rich, or well to pass. [Cf. W. Yorkshire *inlaid for*, provided with.EDD.]

INNOCENTS. One of the innocents; a weak or simple person, man or woman. [With especial reference to the mind.]

IRISH APRICOTS. Potatoes. It is a common joke against the Irish vessels, to say they are loaded with fruit and timber, that is, potatoes and broomsticks. Irish assurance; a bold forward behaviour: as being dipt in the river Styx was formerly supposed to render persons invulnerable, so it is said, that a dipping in the river Shannon totally annihilates bashfulness; whence arises the saying of an impudent Irishman, that he has been dipt in the Shannon.

IRISH BEAUTY. A woman with two black eyes.

IRISH EVIDENCE. A false witness.

IRISH LEGS. Thick legs, jocularly styled the Irish arms. It is said of the Irish women, that they have a dispensation from the Pope to wear the thick end of their legs downwards.

IRISH TOYLES. Thieves who carry about pins, laces and other pedlars ware, and under the pretence of offering their goods to sale, rob houses, or pilfer any thing they can lay hold of. [Cant, C16-18.OD.—From *ca.* 1690, *Irish* was a frequent 'derogatory prefix.' In addition to G's five examples, note *Irishman's dinner*, a fast; *Irish fortune*, pudend and pattens; *Irishman's harvest*, the London costermongers' phrase for the orange season; *Irishman's hurricane*, nautical for a dead calm; *Irish pennants*, fag-ends of rope; *Irishman's reef*, nautical for a sailhead tied up; *Irish rifle*, a small toothcomb; *Irish rise* or *promotion*, a reduction in pay or position; *Irish root*, the member; *Irish theatre*, a guard-room; *Irish toothache*, a priapism; *Irish wedding*, the emptying of a cesspool; *Irish whist*, coition. Most of these terms belong to C19.F.—In dialect:—*Irish blackguard*, a variety of snuff; *Irish cry*, funeral mourners' lamentation; *Irish daisy*, the dandelion; *Irish mahogany*, the common alder; *Irishman*, the work of the hay-harvest; *Irishman's fire*, one that burns only atop; *Irish nightingale*, the sedge-warbler; *Irish ortolan*, the stormy petrel, esteemed a delicacy in 1756; *Irish stone*, one that, brought from Ireland, was reputed to possess curative properties; *Irish vine*, the honeysuckle; *Irish*, anger, now slang with synonym *paddy*; a C19 Warwickshire gibe, *You are Irish and the top of your head's poison.*EDD.]

IRON. Money in general. To polish the king's iron with one's eyebrows; to look out of grated or prison windows, or, as the Irishman expressed them, the iron glass windows. Iron doublet; a prison. See STONE DOUBLET. [In American low slang, *iron man* is a silver dollar, a piece of hard cash; *iron house*, a prison.I.]

IRONMONGER'S SHOP. To keep an ironmonger's shop by the side of a common, where the sheriff sets one up: to be hanged in chains. Iron-bound; laced. An iron-bound hat; a silver-laced hat.

ISLAND. He drank out of the bottle till he saw the island: the island is the rising bottom of a wine bottle, which appears like an island in the centre, before the bottle is quite empty.

ITCHLAND, or SCRATCHLAND. Scotland. [The 1690 cant dictionary says Wales; that of 1725, Scotland.F.]

IVY BUSH. Like an owl in an ivy bush; a simile for a meagre or weasel-faced man, with a large wig, or very bushy hair.

JABBER. To talk thick and fast, as great praters usually do, to chatter like a magpye; also to speak a foreign language. He jabbered to me in his damned outlandish parlez vouz, but I could not understand him; he chattered to me in French, or some other foreign language, but I could not understand him. [Cf. *jabber(k)nowl, jobber(k)nowl*, a prating blockhead.EDD.]

JACK. A farthing, a small bowl serving as the mark for bowlers, an instrument for pulling off boots. [These three senses established themselves in C17.F.—With this sense of *jack*, cf. old dialectal sense: a quarter-pint.P.]

JACK ADAMS. A fool. Jack Adam's parish; Clerkenwell.
[Like the next four entries, slang in C17.F.—Among sailors:a
stubborn seaman.B.]

JACK AT A PINCH. A poor hackney parson.

JACK IN A BOX. A sharper, or cheat.

JACK IN AN OFFICE. An insolent fellow in authority.

JACK KETCH. The hangman: vide DERRICK & KETCH.

JACK NASTY FACE. A sea term, signifying a common
sailor. ["In the old Merchant Service, the cook's assistant, but
latterly anybody who happens to be ugly." B.]

JACK OF LEGS. A tall long-legged man; also a giant, said
to be buried in Weston church, near Baldock, in Hertfordshire,
where there are two stones fourteen feet distant, said to be the
head and feet stones of his grave. This giant, says Salmon, as
fame goes, lived in a wood here, and was a great robber, but a
generous one; for he plundered the rich to feed the poor: he
frequently took bread for this purpose from the Baldock bakers,
who catching him at an advantage, put out his eyes, and afterwards hanged him upon a knoll in Baldock field. At his death
he made one request, which was, that he might have his bow
and arrow put into his hand, and on shooting it off, where the
arrow fell, they would bury him; which being granted, the
arrow fell in Weston churchyard. About seventy years ago, a
very large thigh bone was taken out of the church chest, where
it had lain many years for a show, and was sold by the clerk to
Sir John Tradescant, who, it is said, put it among the rarities
of Oxford.

JACK PUDDING. The merry andrew, zany, or jester to a
mountebank. [Milton, 1650.Cf. Fr. *Jean Potage*.F.—Derivatively, the self-appointed jester of an assembly or a party.EDD.]

JACK ROBINSON. Before one could say Jack Robinson; a
saying to express a very short time, originating from a very
volatile gentleman of that appellation, who would call on his
neighbours, and be gone before his name could be announced.

JACK SPRAT. A dwarf, or diminutive fellow. [C16.F.]

JACK TAR. A sailor. [1781, in readable George Parker.OD.]

JACK WHORE. A large masculine overgrown wench. [Also,

in C18 Cornwall and Hampshire, the strong trull that Jack Tar liked best.EDD.—*Jack* is common as a pejorative: cf. *Jack of all trades, Jack Straw,* etc.F.—See also G & K.]

JACK WEIGHT. A fat man.

JACKANAPES. An ape; a pert, ugly, little fellow. ["The earliest record....is in a satirical song on the unpopular William de la Pole, Duke of Suffolk, who was beheaded at sea in 1450. He is called *Jack Napes,* the allusion being apparently to his badge, an ape's clog and chain. But there also seems to be association with Naples; cf. *fustian-anapes* for Naples fustian. A poem of the 15th century mentions among our imports from Italy—'apes and japes and marmusettes tayled.' " W:ROW. More fully in W:MWAM.]

JACKED. Spavined. A jacked horse. [Cf. the modern *jacked up,* exhausted.W.]

JACKMEN. See JARKMEN.

JACOB. A ladder; perhaps from Jacob's dream.*Cant.* Also the common name for a jay, jays being usually taught to say, Poor Jacob! a cup of sack for Jacob.

JACOBITES. Sham or collar shirts. Also partizans for the Stuart family: from the name of the abdicated king, i.e. James or Jacobus. It is said by the whigs, that God changed Jacob's name to Israel, lest the descendants of that patriarch should be called Jacobites. [Cf. C19 Lincolnshire *Jacobines,* disorderly persons, malcontents.EDD.]

JADE. A term of reproach to women. [Also to men, in Shakespeare.O.]

JAGUE. A ditch; perhaps from jakes.

JAIL BIRDS. Prisoners.

JAKES. A house of office, a cacatorium. [Early C16, and in Florio.F.—Perhaps *Jack's* (house, place).O.D.—Used at the older English universities with the (Oxford) variant *bogs**.—In S.W. dialects, human excrement, and, figuratively, dirty mess, confusion.EDD.— The most famous book on the subject is Sir John Harington's *Metamorphosis of Ajax,* ed. by Jack Lindsay, 1928. *Add *rear(s),* Oxford; *fourth,* Cambridge.]

JAMMED. Hanged. *Cant.*

JANIZARIES. The mob, sometimes so called; also bailiffs, their setters and followers. [Cant, 1690.F.]

JAPANNED. Ordained. To be japanned; to enter into holy orders, to become a clergyman, to put on the black cloth; from the colour of the japan ware, which is black.

JARK. A seal. [Cant, in Harman as is *jarkman*.F.]

JARKMEN. Those who fabricate counterfeit passes, licences, and certificates for beggars.

JARVIS. A hackney coachman. [In C19, *Jarvey*.H.]

JASON'S FLEECE. A citizen cheated of his gold. [Cant, 1690.F.]

JAW. Speech, discourse. Give us none of your jaw; let us have none of your discourse. A jaw-me-dead; a talkative fellow. Jaw work; a cry used in fairs by the sellers of nuts. [As noun and as verb in Smollett, 1748.F.]

JAZEY. A bob wig. [From *Jersey* (*flax*).H.]

JEFFY. It will be done in a jeffy; it will be done in a short space of time, in an instant. [The C18 also had modern *jiffy*.F.]

JEHU. To drive jehu-like; to drive furiously: from a king of Israel of that name, who was a famous charioteer, and mentioned as such in the Bible. [In Dryden, Congreve, etc.OD.]

JEM. A gold ring. *Cant.*

JEMMY FELLOW. A smart spruce fellow.

JENNY. An instrument for lifting up the grate or top of a showglass, in order to rob it. *Cant.* [Cant, 1690.—Now a *jemmy*, in U.S.A. *jimmy*.I.]

JERRYCUMMUMBLE. To shake, towzle, or tumble about.

JERRY SNEAK. A henpecked husband; from a celebrated character in one of Mr Foote's plays, representing a man governed by his wife. [*The Mayor of Garratt*.H.]

JESSAMY. A smart jemmy fellow, a fopling. [Cf. *jemmy fellow*, supra. In 1753, the ascending order of masculine fashionableness was "greenhorn, jemmy, jessamy, honest fellow, joyous spirit, buck, and blood," *The Adventurer*, no. 100.F.]

JESUIT. See TO BOX THE JESUIT.

JESUITICAL. Sly, evasive, equivocal. A jesuitical answer; an equivocal answer.

JET. A lawyer. Autem jet; a parson. [Cant, 1725.F.]

JEW. An over-reaching dealer, or hard, sharp fellow; an extortioner; the brokers behind St Clement's church in the Strand were formerly called Jews by their brethren the taylors. [As term of opprobrium, in print from *ca.* 1600, but obviously in use much earlier. *Jew* is often a 'derogatory prefix,' as in *jew's harp*. OD.]

JEW BAIL. Insufficient bail: commonly Jews, who for a sum of money will bail any action whatsoever, and justify, that is, swear to their sufficiency; but, when called on, are not to be found.

JEW'S EYE. That's worth a Jew's eye, a pleasant or agreeable sight; a saying taken from Shakespeare.

JIBBER THE KIBBER. A method of deceiving seamen, by fixing a candle and lantern round the neck of a horse, one of whose fore feet is tied up; this at night has the appearance of a ship's light. Ships bearing towards it, run on shore, and being wrecked, are plundered by the inhabitants. This diabolical device is, it is said, practised by the inhabitants of our western coasts.

JIG. A trick. A pleasant jig; a witty arch trick. Also a lock or door. The feather-bed jig; copulation.

JIGGER. A whipping-post. *Cant.* [In Harman, cant for a door. F.]

JILT. A tricking woman, who encourages the addresses of a man whom she means to deceive and abandon. [Both noun and verb came in *ca.* 1670.OD.]

JILTED. Rejected by a woman who has encouraged one's advances.

JINGLE BOXES. Leathern jacks tipped with silver, and hung with bells, formerly in use among fuddle caps. *Cant.*

JINGLE BRAINS. A wild, thoughtless, rattling fellow.

JINGLERS. Horse cosers, frequenting country fairs. *Cant.*

JOB. A guinea. [Cant, 1690.F.]

TO JOB. To reprove or reprehend. *Cambridge term.*

JOB'S COMFORT. Reproof instead of consolation. [Cf. the pejorative *Job's news, Job's post* (messenger), *as poor as Job's turkey, Job's wife, Job's ward* (for 'venereals').F.]

JOB'S COMFORTER. One who brings news of some additional misfortune.

JOB'S DOCK. He is laid up in Job's dock; i.e. in a salivation. The apartments for the foul or venereal patients in St Bartholomew's hospital, are called Job's ward.

JOBATION. A reproof. [Late C17.OD.]

JOBBERNOLE. The head.

JOCK, or CROWDY-HEADED JOCK. A jeering appellation for a north-country seaman, particularly a collier; Jock being a common name, and crowdy the chief food, of the lower order of the people in Northumberland.

TO JOCK, or JOCKUM CLOY. To enjoy a woman. [Cant, 1690.F.—Cf. dialectal *jock*, to jolt.EDD.]

JOCKUM GAGE. A chamber-pot, jordan, looking-glass, or member-mug. *Cant.* [*Jockum* or *jock*=membrum virile; also in C18 the "private parts of a man or woman," Potter, 1790.F.—Cf. the *jock-strap* of athletes and footballers.]

JOGG-TROT. To keep on a jogg-trot; to get on with a slow but regular pace.

JOHNNY BUM. A he or jack ass; so called by a lady that affected to be extremely polite and modest, who would not say jack because it was vulgar, nor ass because it was indecent. [As contrasted with *Jack*, *John(ny)* imports a favourable or a neutral note, as in *John-a-dreams*, *John-among-the-maids* (a ladies' man), *John Barleycorn*, *John Blunt*, *John Company*, *Johnny Raw*, *John Trot* (a clown).F.]

JOINT. To hit a joint in carving, the operator must think of a cuckold. To put one's nose out of joint; to rival one in the favour of a patron or mistress.

JOLLY, or JOLLY NOB. The head. I'll lump your jolly nob for you; I'll give you a knock on the head.

JOLLY DOG. A merry facetious fellow; a *bon vivant*, who never flinches from his glass, nor cries to go home to bed.

JOLTER HEAD. A large head; metaphorically a stupid fellow.

JORDAIN. A great blow, or staff. I'll tip him a jordain if I transnear; i.e. I'll give him a blow with my staff, if I come near him. *Cant.*

JORDAN. A chamber-pot. [Short for *Jordan bottle*, a memory of the Crusades. In Chaucer, Pope, Shakespeare, Goldsmith. F.]

JORUM. A jug, or large pitcher. [In C19-20, especially a bowl of punch. From the Biblical Joram's collection, "vessels of silver, and vessels of gold, and vessels of brass." Cf. the derivation of *jeroboam*. EDD.]

JOSEPH. A woman's great coat. Also, a sheepish bashful young fellow: an allusion to Joseph who fled from Potiphar's wife. You are Josephus rex; you are jo-king, i.e. joking. [*Joseph* is cant in origin, but by *ca.* 1810 it had become good English. F.]

JOWL. The cheek. Cheek by jowl; close together, or cheek to cheek. [Out of place in G: never merely colloquial.]

JUG. See DOUBLE JUG.

JUGGLER'S BOX. The engine for burning culprits in the hand. *Cant.*

JUKRUM. A licence. [Cant, 1690; so too the next entry. F.]

JUMBLEGUT LANE. A rough road or lane.

JUMP. The jump, or dining-room jump: a species of robbery effected by ascending a ladder placed by a sham lamp-lighter, against the house intended to be robbed. It is so called, because should the lamp-lighter be put to flight, the thief who ascended the ladder has no means of escape but that of jumping down.

JUMPERS. Persons who rob houses by getting in at the windows. Also a set of Methodists established in South Wales.

JUNIPER LECTURE. A round scolding bout. [In dialect, a curtain lecture, but obsolete by 1900. EDD.]

JURY LEG. A wooden leg: allusion to a jury mast, which is a temporary substitute for a mast carried away by a storm, or any other accident. *Sea phrase.* [Influenced by *jury rudder*: vide Ansted, *Sea terms*, 1898. EDD.]

JURY MAST. A *journière* mast; i.e. a mast for the day or occasion. [Derivation incorrect.]

JUST-ASS. A punning appellation for a justice.

KATE. A picklock. 'Tis a rum kate; it is a clever picklock. *Cant*.

KEEL BULLIES. Men employed to load and unload the coal vessels. [Cant, 1690.F.]

KEELHAULING. A punishment in use among the Dutch seamen, in which, for certain offences, the delinquent is drawn once, or oftner, under the ship's keel; ludicrously defined, undergoing a great hard-ship. [Recorded, 1666, adumbrated in 1626. Like so many of our nautical terms, from the Dutch.OD, W.—In dialect and derivatively, the verb means to treat roughly.EDD.]

TO KEEP. To inhabit. Lord, where do you keep? i.e. where are your rooms? *Academical phrase*. [So, thrice, in Shakespeare. O.]

TO KEEP IT UP. To prolong a debauch. We kept it up finely last night: metaphor drawn from the game of shuttlecock.

KEEPING CULLY. One who keeps a mistress, as he supposes, for his own use, but really for that of the public. [Cant, 1690; so also the next two entries.F.]

KEFFEL. A horse. *Welsh*.

KELTER. Condition, order.Out of kelter; out of order. [Common in dialect, where it also=money, property, rubbish, nonsense.EDD.]

KEMP'S MORRIS. William Kemp, said to have been the original Dogberry in Much ado about Nothing, danced a morris from London to Norwich in nine days; of which he printed the account,A.D.1600, intitled Kemp's Nine Days Wonder,&c.

KEMP'S SHOES. Would I had Kemp's Shoes to throw after you. *Ben Jonson*. Perhaps Kemp was a man remarkable for his good luck or fortune; throwing an old shoe, or shoes, after any one going on an important business, being by the vulgar deemed lucky.

KEN. A house. A bob ken, or a bowman ken; a well-furnished house, also a house that harbours thieves. Biting the ken; robbing the house. *Cant*. [Harman, 1567.F.—In Romany, a house, properly a nest, cf. Hebrew *kin*.GB.]

KEN MILLER, or KENCRACKER. A housebreaker. *Cant.*

KENT-STREET EJECTMENT. To take away the street door: a method practised by the landlords in Kent-street, Southwark, when their tenants are above a fortnight's rent in arrear.

KERRY SECURITY. Bond, pledge, oath, and keep the money.

KETCH. Jack Ketch; a general name for the finishers of the law, or hangmen, ever since the year 1682, when the office was filled by a famous practitioner of that name, of whom his wife said, that any bungler might put a man to death, but only her husband knew how to make a gentleman die sweetly. This officer is mentioned in Butler's Ghost, p. 54, published about the year 1682, in the following lines:

> *Till Ketch observing he was chous'd,*
> *And in his profits much abus'd,*
> *In open hall the tribute dunn'd,*
> *To do his office, or refund.*

Mr Ketch had not long been elevated to his office, for the name of his predecessor Dun occurs in the former part of this poem, page 29:

> *For you yourself to act squire Dun,*
> *Such ignominy ne'er saw the sun.*

The addition of 'squire,' with which Mr Dun is here dignified, is a mark that he had beheaded some state criminal for high treason: an operation which, according to custom for time out of mind, has always entitled the operator to that distinction. The predecessor of Dun was Gregory Brandon, from whom the gallows was called the Gregorian tree, by which name it is mentioned in the prologue to Mercurius Pragmaticus, a tragicomedy acted at Paris, &c. 1641:

> *This trembles under the black rod, and he*
> *Doth fear his fate from the Gregorian tree.*

Gregory Brandon succeeded Derrick. See DERRICK.

KETTLE DRUMS. Cupid's kettle drums; a woman's breasts, called by sailors chest and bedding.

KETTLE OF FISH. When a person has perplexed his affairs

in general, or any particular business, he is said to have made a fine kettle of fish of it. [The variants: *a pretty* (or *fine* or *nice* or *rare*) *kettle* (or *kiddle*, basket) *of fish*, or simply *a fine kettle*.F, OD.]

KHAJBAR. The worthy brethren of this order met, A.D. 1749, at the Nag's Head, Tothill-street, Westminster.

KICKS. Breeches. A high kick; the top of the fashion. It is all the kick; it is the present mode. Tip us your kicks, we'll have them as well as your lour; pull off your breeches, for we must have them as well as your money. A kick; sixpence. Two and a kick; half-a-crown. A kick in the guts; a dram of gin, or any other spirituous liquor. A kick up: a disturbance, also a hop or dance. An odd kick in one's gallop; a strange whim or peculiarity. [As breeches and as fashion, cant, 1690; as sixpence, cant, 1725,—*two and a kick* being still current in slang.F.—Dialect has *kicking*, smartly dressed; *kicky*, noun and adjective, (in) the height of fashion; and *kick-out*, fashionable clothes. EDD.—In pre-War Liverpool slang *kicks* meant trousers: an example of cant becoming localised and surviving as a local slang.]

TO KICK THE BUCKET. To die. He kicked the bucket one day; he died one day. [Cf. Yorkshire *kick one's clog(s)*, *kick up the heels*, and East Anglian *kick stiff*.EDD.]

KICKERAPOO. Dead. *Negro word.*

KICKSHAWS. French dishes: corruption of *quelque chose*. [In Shakespeare. Florio spells it *quelque chose*, Cotgrave *quelk-chose(s)*. In dialect: novelty, oddity, trumpery.EDD.]

KID. A child. [Arose as cant in late C16; by 1748, slang; by *ca.* 1850, colloquial.F.OD,—The verb *kid*, to hoax, came in *ca.* 1810; *kidnapper* and *kidnap*, *ca.* 1680. OD, and especially W: MWAM.]

KID LAY. Rogues who make it their business to defraud young apprentices, or errand-boys, of goods committed to their charge, by prevailing on them to execute some trifling message, pretending to take care of their parcels till they come back; these are, in cant terms, said to be on the kid lay.

KIDDER. A forestaller: see CROCKER. Kidders are also persons employed by the gardeners to gather peas.

KIDDEYS. Young thieves. [Properly *kiddies*, as in that very strange poem, Tomlinson's *Slang Pastoral*, 1780. Not necessarily young thieves.F.]

KIDDEY NIPPERS. Taylors out of work, who cut off the waistcoat pockets of their brethren, when cross-legged on the board, thereby grabbling their bit. *Cant.*

KIDNAPPER. Originally one who stole or decoyed children or apprentices from their parents or masters, to send them to the colonies; called also spiriting: but now used for all recruiting crimps for the king's troops, or those of the East India company, and agents for indenting servants for the plantations, &c.

KIDNEY. Disposition, principles, humour. Of a strange kidney; of an odd or unaccountable humour. A man of a different kidney; a man of different principles. [Shakespeare: "a man of my kidney." Cf. Cornish *to kidney*, to agree together, to confederate.EDD.]

KILKENNY. An old frize coat.

KILL CARE CLUB. The members of this club, styled also the Sons of Sound Sense and Satisfaction, met at their fortress, the Castle-tavern, in Pater-noster-row.

KILL DEVIL. New still-burnt rum. [Cant, 1690.F.]

KILL PRIEST. Port wine. [Cf. Irish *kill-the-beggar*, a sort of whiskey.EDD.]

TO KIMBAW. To trick, cheat, or cozen: also to beat or to bully. Let's kimbaw the cull; let's bully the fellow. To set one's arms a-kimbaw, vulgarly pronounced a-kimbo, is to rest one's hands on the hips, keeping the elbows square, and sticking out from the body; an insolent bullying attitude. *Cant.* [*Akimbo* is not cant, *to kimbow* was in 1690.F.—In M.E. *in kenebowe*, probably *in can-bow*, i.e. *in* (after the fashion of) *a can-handle*: cf. Plautus's *ansatus homo* with its allusion to braggartry. See the brilliant exposition by W in ROW and, at greater length, WAM.]

KINCHIN. A little child. Kinchin coes; orphan beggar boys, educated in thieving. Kinchin morts; young girls under the like circumstances and training. Kinchin morts, or coes in slates; beggar's children carried at their mothers' backs in sheets. Kinchin cove; a little man. *Cant.* [Harman.F.]

KING'S BAD BARGAIN. One of the king's bad bargains; a malingeror, or soldier who shirks his duty.

KING'S HEAD INN, or CHEQUER INN, IN NEWGATE-STREET. The prison of Newgate.

KING JOHN'S MEN. He is one of king John's men, eight score to the hundred; a saying of a little undersized man.

KING OF THE GYPSIES. The captain, chief, or ringleader of the gang of misrule; in the cant language called also the upright man.

KING'S PICTURES. Coin, money. [C17 cant.F.]

KINGDOM COME. He is gone to kingdom come; he is dead.

KIP. The skin of a large calf, in the language of the Excise-office. [In 1914-1918, much used by the soldiers for sleep, sleeping-place, a bed. B & P. Probably the term *kip*, a bed, arose from the old-time bed of skins.I.—Sleeping-place would come next, either in sense of a brothel (Goldsmith) or of a lodging-house (C19).OD.— As sleep, C20 and recorded by neither OD nor W.—As brothel, obsolete except in Dublin, where it has become slang.]

KISS MINE A-SE. An offer, as Fielding observes, very frequently made, but never, as he could learn, literally accepted. A kiss mine a-se fellow; a sycophant.

KISSING CRUST. That part where the loaves have touched in the oven.

KIT. A dancing-master; so called from his kit or cittern, a small fiddle, which dancing-masters always carry about with them, to play to their scholars. The kit is likewise the whole of a soldier's necessaries, the contents of his knapsack: and is used also to express the whole of different commodities; as, Here, take the whole kit, i.e. take all. [Cant, 1725.F.]

KIT-CAT CLUB. A society of gentlemen, eminent for wit and learning, who in the reign of queen Anne and George I. met at a house kept by one Christopher Cat. The portraits of most of the members of this society were painted by Sir Godfrey Kneller, of one size; thence still called the kit-cat size. [A Whig Club, founded under James II. The man's name was Kat or Catling (probably Dutch). A portrait, half-length, including hands, and of fixed dimensions.W.—Beresford Chancellor's *Annals of Fleet Street* contains an excellent short account of the club.]

KITCHEN PHYSIC. Food, good meat roast or boiled. A little kitchen physic will set him up; he has more need of a cook than a doctor.[C16; cf. the C17 *kitchen-stuff*, a female servant.F.]

KITTLE PITCHERING. A jocular method of hobbling, or bothering a troublesome teller of long stories: this is done by contradicting some very immaterial circumstance at the beginning of the narration, the objections to which being settled, others are immediately started to some new particular of like consequence; thus impeding, or rather not suffering him to enter into, the main story. Kittle pitchering is often practised in confederacy, one relieving the other, by which the design is rendered less obvious.

KITTYS. Effects, furniture; stock in trade. To seize one's Kittys; to take his sticks.

KNACK SHOP. A toy-shop, a nick-nack-atory. [In Shakespeare, knack=a trifle, a knick-knack.O.]

KNAPPER'S POLL. A sheep's head. *Cant.*

KNAVE IN GRAIN. A knave of the first rate: a phrase borrowed from the dyehouse, where certain colours are said to be in grain, to denote their superiority, as being dyed with cochineal, called grain. Knave in grain is likewise a pun applied to a cornfactor or miller.

KNIGHT OF THE BLADE. A bully. [These *knight* phrases are mostly cant. A few belong to C16 many to C17.Those added by C19 were numerous, but were slang or colloquialisms.]

KNIGHT OF THE POST. A false evidence, one that is ready to swear any thing for hire.

KNIGHT OF THE RAINBOW. A footman: from the variety of colours in the liveries and trimming of gentlemen of that cloth.

KNIGHT OF THE ROAD. A highwayman.

KNIGHT OF THE SHEERS. A taylor.

KNIGHT OF THE THIMBLE, or NEEDLE. A taylor or staymaker.

KNIGHT OF THE TRENCHER. A great eater.

KNIGHT AND BARROW PIG, more hog than gentleman. A saying of any low pretender to precedency.

KNOB. The head. See NOB.

KNOCK. To knock a woman; to have carnal knowledge of her. To knock off; to conclude: phrase borrowed from the blacksmith. To knock under; to submit. [Both the verb and the noun (act of coition; the male member) were in print in C16. Derivatives: *knocking-house* or *shop*, the latter being frequently used by the soldiers of 1914-1918, who considered the verb quite respectable; *knocking-jacket*, night-dress or -gown; *knocker*, the member, also either party to the act. The word may be a variant of *nock*, which appears in Florio for the pudend and which Ash in his Dictionary, 1775, gives as a verb: "*Nock*, to perform the act of generation on a female," Florio having already defined the Italian *cunnata* as "a woman nocked."F.]

KNOCK ME DOWN. Strong ale or beer, stingo. [*Knock-'em-down*, 1515, and *knockdown* in 1698.F.]

KNOT. A crew, gang, or fraternity. He has tied a knot with his tongue, that he cannot untie with his teeth; i.e. he is married. [Shakespeare has *knot*, to assemble in a cluster.O.]

KNOWING ONES. Sportsmen on the turf, who, from experience and an acquaintance with the jockies, are supposed to be in the secret, that is, to know the true merits or powers of each horse; notwithstanding which it often happens that the knowing ones are taken in. [*Knowing*, like *sly*, was once a compliment. W.]

KNOWLEDGE BOX. The head. [In low American slang, a school.I.]

KNUCKLES. Pickpockets who attend the avenues to public places, to steal pocket books, watches, &c. a superior kind of pickpockets. To knuckle to; to submit.

TO KNUCKLE ONE'S WIPE. To steal his handkerchief.

KNUCKLE DABS, or KNUCKLE-CONFOUNDERS. Ruffles. [The former meant also handcuffs.F.]

LACED MUTTON. A prostitute. [So in Shakespeare. O.]
LACING. Beating. I'll lace your jacket handsomely. [Late
C16. OD.—In low American slang, "to punch, beat or man-
handle." I.]

LADDER. To go up the ladder to rest; to be hanged. [C16. F.]

LADY. A crooked or hump-backed woman.

LADY OF EASY VIRTUE. A woman of the town, an impure, a prostitute.

LADYBIRDS. Light or lewd women. [C16, or two centuries
earlier than the preceding.]

TO LAG. To drop behind, to keep back. Lag last; the last of a
company.

LAGE. Water. *Cant.* [*Lag* in Harman, who also has *lage*, to
drink, and the next entry.]

LAGE OF DUDS. A buck of linen.

LAID ON THE SHELF, or LAID UP IN LAVENDER.
Pawned. [The second is the earlier.]

TO LAMB or LAMBASTE. To beat. Lamb pye; a beat-
ing: from *lambo*. [Properly *lam*. Cf. *lambeake*, 1555; *lamback*,
1589; *lambskin*, 1589; *lambaste*, 1637, this probably being *lam*+
baste, perhaps on analogy of *bumbaste*, 1596, when *lamme* is recorded first, though implied earlier in *belam*. OD.—From Old
Norse *lemja*, to flog, thrash. EDD.]

LAMB'S WOOL. Apples roasted and put into strong ale.

LAMBSKIN MEN. The judges: from their robes lined and
bordered with ermine.

LAND. How lies the land? how stands the reckoning? Who
has any land in Appleby? a question asked the man at whose
door the glass stands long, or who does not circulate it in due
time.

LAND LOPERS, or LAND LUBBERS. Vagabonds lurking
about the country, who subsist by pilfering. [Also *land leapers*,
the earliest of the three and general till *ca.* 1620. Derivatively,
adventurers. F, EDD.]

LAND PIRATES. Highwaymen. [Dekker, 1609. OD.]

LANK SLEEVE. The empty sleeve of a one-armed man. A
fellow with a lank sleeve; a man who has lost an arm.

215

LANSPRISADO. One who has only two-pence in his pocket. Also a lance, or deputy corporal; that is, one doing the duty without the pay of a corporal. Formerly a lancier, or horseman who being dismounted by the death of his horse, served in the foot, by the title of lansprisado, or *lancepesato*, a broken lance. [Usual forms, *lancepesade* from French, and *lanceprisado* from Italian.C16.OD.]

LANTHORN-JAWED. Thin-visaged; from their cheeks being almost transparent. Or else, lenten jawed; i.e. having the jaws of one emaciated by a too rigid observation of Lent. Dark lanthorn; a servant or agent at court, who receives a bribe for his principal or master.

LAP. Butter-milk or whey. *Cant.* [In Harman.F.]

LARK. A boat.

[LARKING. In first edition: "Larking, a lascivious practice that will not bear explanation." Irrumation, cunnilingism.]

LARRY DUGAN'S EYE WATER. Blacking: Larry Dugan was a famous shoe-black at Dublin.

LATCH. Let in. [Cant, 1725.F.]

LATHY. Thin, slender. A lathy wench; a girl almost as slender as a lath.

LATITAT. A nick-name for an attorney; from the name of a writ. [In Cooper's *Thesaurus*, 1565.OD.]

LAUGH. To laugh on the wrong side of the mouth; to cry. I'll make him laugh on the wrong (or t'other) side of his mouth.

LAUNCH. The delivery, or labour, of a pregnant woman; a crying out or groaning.

LAVENDER. Laid up in lavender; pawned.

LAW. To give law to a hare; a sporting term, signifying to give the animal a chance of escaping, by not setting on the dogs till the hare is at some distance; it is also more figuratively used for giving any one a chance of succeeding in a scheme or project.

LAY. Enterprise, pursuit, or attempt: to be sick of the lay. It also means a hazard, or chance: he stands a queer lay: i.e. he is in danger. *Cant.* [As hazard, in Farquhar, 1707.OD.]

LAYSTALL. A dunghill about London, on which the soil brought from necessary houses is emptied; or, in more technical terms, where the old gold collected at weddings by the Tom t—d man, is stored. [G's sense and that of a burial-place, C16.OD.]

LAZY. As lazy as Ludlam's dog, who leaned against the wall to bark. As lazy as the tinker who laid down his budget to f—t. [The former proverb is in Ray.F.]

LAZYBONES. An instrument like a pair of tongs, for old or very fat people to take any thing from the ground without stooping. [More generally a loafer, from *ca.* 1590.F.]

LAZY MAN'S LOAD. Lazy people frequently take up more than they can safely carry, to save the trouble of coming a second time.

LEAF. To go off with the fall of the leaf; to be hanged: criminals in Dublin being turned off from the outside of the prison by the falling of a board, propped up, and moving on a hinge, like the leaf of a table. *Irish term.*

TO LEAK. To make water. [Shakespeare, 1596.O.]

LEAKY. Apt to blab: one who cannot keep a secret is said to be leaky. [Late C17.OD.]

LEAPING OVER THE SWORD. An ancient ceremonial said to constitute a military marriage. A sword being laid down on the ground, the parties to be married joined hands, when the corporal or serjeant of the company repeated these words:

Leap rogue, and jump whore,
And then you are married for evermore.

Whereupon the happy couple jumped hand in hand over the sword, the drum beating a ruffle; and the parties were ever after considered as man and wife.

LEAST IN SIGHT. To play least in sight; to hide, keep out of the way, or make one's self scarce.

LEATHER. To lose leather; to be galled with riding on horseback, or, as the Scotch express it, to be saddle-sick. To leather also means to beat, perhaps originally with a strap; I'll leather you to your heart's content. Leather-headed; stupid. Leathern conveniency; term used by quakers for a stage-coach. [*Leather-headed,* ironic from *leatherhead,* 1690 cant for a swindler.F.—

217

Leather, to beat, is early C17, a period rich in colloquial 'coinings.' (OD).]

LEERY. On one's guard. See PEERY. [From *lear*, a look; and cf. C19 slang *leery*, sly, somewhat wild.]

LEFT-HANDED WIFE. A concubine; in allusion to an ancient German custom, according to which, when a man married his concubine, or a woman greatly his inferior, he gave her his left hand. [Cf. *left-handed bridegroom*, Killigrew, 1663.F.]

LEG.To make a leg;to bow.To give leg-bail and land security; to run away. To fight at the leg; to take unfair advantages: it being held unfair by back-sword players to strike at the leg. To break a leg; a woman who has had a bastard, is said to have broken a leg. [In dialect, *to give one leg-bail* meant to escape somebody,while *to take leg-bail* meant to run away from the consequences; *to fight at the leg*, to beat down in a bargain; *to get one's leg dressed*, to fornicate.EDD.—In C17-19 slang there are some scabrously vivid locutions. We may, however, quote a C17 proverb from Ray: *More belongs to marriage than four bare legs in a bed*.F.]

LEGGERS. Sham leggers; cheats who pretend to sell smuggled goods, but in reality only deal in old shop-keepers' or damaged goods.

LENTEN FARE. Spare diet. [In Hamlet, *lenten entertainment*. O.]

LETCH. A whim of the amorous kind, out of the common way. [In dialect, lust, strong desire, or an absurd fancy.EDD.]

LEVITE. A priest or parson. [A contemptuous term, C17; in Macaulay.OD.]

TO LIB. To lie together. *Cant*. [As a noun, sleep.F.]

LIBBEGE. A bed. *Cant*.

LIBBEN. A private dwelling-house. *Cant*.

LIBKEN. A house to lie in. *Cant*.

TO LICK. To beat; also to wash, or to paint slightly over. I'll give you a good lick o' the chops; I'll give you a good stroke or blow on the face. Jack tumbled into a cow t—d, and nastied his best clothes, for which his father stept up, and licked him neatly.—I'll lick you! the dovetail to which is, If you lick me all over, you won't miss—.[Harman, 1567. Popularised by Fielding.F.]

LICKSPITTLE. A parasite, or talebearer. [Forty years before the OD record, as it appeared in first edition.—Dialectal variants, *lick-ma-doup*, *lick-pan*, *lick-plate*, *lick-spit*, *lick-trencher*. EDD.]

LIFT. To give one a lift; to assist. A good hand at a dead lift; a good hand upon an emergency. To lift one's hand to one's head; to drink to excess, or to drink drams. To lift or raise one's elbow; the same.

LIFT. See SHOPLIFTER, &c.

LIFTER. A crutch. [B.E., 1690.F.—This kind of word is typically cant.]

LIG. A bed. See LIB. [Cf. Northern *lig*, to lie. G.—In American criminal slang, a *lig-robber* is a thief that hides under a bed (or in a closet) until the woman is alone in the house, and then robs and perhaps assails her.I.]

LIGHT BOB. A soldier of the light infantry company.

LIGHT FINGERED. Thievish, apt to pilfer. [C16: in North and earlier.OD.]

LIGHT-HEELED. Swift in running. A light-heeled wench; one who is apt, by the flying up of her heels, to fall flat on her back, a willing wench. [The wench was, by 1710 or earlier, known as *light heels*, *light o' love*, and *light skirts*.F.]

LIGHTMANS. The day. *Cant*. [Harman. OD.]

LIGHTNING. Gin.

LILLIPUTIAN. A diminutive man or woman; from Gulliver's Travels, written by Dean Swift, where an imaginary kingdom of dwarfs of that name is described.

LILY WHITE. A chimney-sweeper. [Cant, 1690.F.—In American tramp and underworld slang, *lilies*=the hands.I.]

LIMBS. Duke of limbs; a tall awkward fellow.

LIMB OF THE LAW. An inferior or pettyfogging attorney.

LIMBO. A prison, confinement. [*Limbo patrum*, the abode of those just men who died B.C.; *limbo infantum*, that of infants who have died unbaptised. Shakespeare twice uses *limbo* for hell, and in the sense of prison he has *limbo* and also *Limbo Patrum*.O.]

TO LINE. A term for the act of coition between dog and bitch. [In use C14-19, but neither cant, slang, colloquial nor dialect, therefore out of place here. (OD).]

LINE OF THE OLD AUTHOR. A dram of brandy.

LINEN ARMOURERS. Taylors. [Cant, 1690.F.]

LINGO. Language. An outlandish lingo; a foreign tongue. The parlezvous lingo; the French language. [A C17 nautical word from the Mediterranean; from Provençal *lengo, lingo*, or Gascon *lengo*: L. *lingua*.W.—Possibly a corruption of *Lingua* (*Franca*), for *lingua* itself=a lingo about as early as *lingo* is recorded.OD.—Durfey's words, "We teach them their lingua, to crave and to cant," 1719, are significant.F.]

LION. To tip the lion; to squeeze the nose of the party tipped, flat to his face with the thumb. To shew the lions and tombs; to point out the particular curiosities of any place, to act the ciceroni: an allusion to Westminster Abbey, and the Tower, where the tombs and lions are shewn. A lion is also a name given by the gownsmen of Oxford to an inhabitant or visitor. It is a standing joke among the city wits to send boys and country folks, on the first of April, to the Tower-ditch, to see the lions washed. [*To see the lions* is a very early phrase: C16 at least.F.]

LIQUOR. To liquor one's boots; to drink before a journey; among Roman Catholics, to administer the extreme unction. [In Gloucestershire, to oil, to anoint.EDD.]

LITTLE BARBARY. Wapping. [Cant, 1690.F.]

LITTLE BREECHES. A familiar appellation used to a little boy.

LITTLE CLERGYMAN. A young chimney-sweeper.

LITTLE EASE. A small dark cell in Guildhall, London, where disorderly apprentices are confined by the city Chamberlain: it is called Little Ease, from its being so low that a lad cannot stand upright in it. [Also, as early as C16, prison, pillory, stocks.F.—In dialect, with variant *little-years*, a gaol, a lock-up, EDD.]

LITTLE SNAKESMAN. A little boy who gets into a house through the sink-hole, and then opens the door for his accomplices; he is so called, from writhing and twisting like a snake, in order to work himself through the narrow passage.

LIVE LUMBER. A term used by sailors, to signify all landsmen on board their ships. [In C19 also cattle.B.]

LIVE STOCK. Lice or fleas. [So too in 1914-1918.]

LOAF. To be in bad loaf; to be in a disagreeable situation, or in trouble.

LOB. Going on the lob; going into a shop to get change for gold, and secreting some of the change.

LOB'S POUND. A prison. Dr Grey, in his notes on Hudibras, explains it to allude to one Doctor Lob, a dissenting preacher, who used to hold forth when conventicles were prohibited, and had made himself a retreat by means of a trap-door at the bottom of his pulpit. Once being pursued by the officers of justice, they followed him through divers subterraneous passages, till they got into a dark cell, from whence they could not find their way out, but calling to some of their companions, swore they had got into Lob's Pound. [Late C16.OD.—Also in C17 the pudend.F.]

LOBCOCK. A large relaxed penis; also a dull inanimate fellow. [Shakespeare has *lob*, to droop.O.—In dialect, *lob*=a country clown, a clumsy fellow.EDD.]

LOBKIN. A house to lie in; also a lodging.

LOBLOLLEY BOY. A nick name for the surgeon's servant on board a man of war, sometimes for the surgeon himself: from the water-gruel prescribed to the sick, which is called loblolley. [As gruel, *loblolly* is late C16; as boor, early C17.OD.—In Devonshire *l.boy* is errand boy.EDD.In the Navy, a sick-bay attendant. In the Merchant Service one of the few printable old names for a steward. Also a boy at sea without very much 'go' in him.B.]

LOBONIAN SOCIETY. A society which met at Lob Hall,

at the King and Queen, Norton Falgate, by order of Lob the Great.

LOBSCOUSE. A dish much eaten at sea, composed of salt beef, biscuit, and onions, well peppered, and stewed together. [In Smollett as *lob's-course*. Dana in 1840 speaks of *scouse*, "biscuit pounded fine, salt beef cut into small slices, and a few potatoes, boiled up together and seasoned with pepper." F.]

LOBSTER. A nick name for a soldier: from the colour of his clothes. To boil one's lobster; for a churchman to become a soldier; lobsters, which are of a bluish black, being made red by boiling. I will not make a lobster-kettle of my ****; a reply frequently made by the nymphs of the Point at Portsmouth, when requested by a soldier to grant him a favour. [Originally, i.e. in the Civil War, *lobster* was employed of a regiment of dragoons "so prodigiously armed that they were called by the other side 'lobsters,' because of their bright iron shells with which they were covered" (Clarendon's *History of the Great Rebellion*).W:MWAM.— With *lobster-kettle* cf. the C19 term in venery: *lobster-pot*.F.]

LOCK. Character. He stood a queer lock; he bore but an indifferent character. A lock is also a buyer of stolen goods, as well as the receptacle for them. [As character, cant in 1725; as conduct and as line-of-business, mainly a C18 word; as a 'fence,' cant in 1690 with variant *lock-all-fast*, both meaning also the receiving warehouse. In C18-19 venery, with variant *lock of all locks* (the latter in, e.g., G. A. Stevens, 1772), the pudend; the corresponding term is *key*.F.]

LOCK HOSPITAL. An hospital for venereal patients.

LOCK UP HOUSE. A spunging-house; a public house kept by sheriffs' officers, to which they convey the persons they have arrested, where they practise every species of imposition and extortion with impunity. Also houses kept by agents or crimps, who enlist, or rather trepan, men to serve the East India or African Company as soldiers.

LOCKERAM-JAWED. Thin-faced, or lanthorn-jawed. See LANTHORN-JAWED.

LOCKSMITH'S DAUGHTER. A key.

LOGE. A watch. He filed a cloy of a loge, or scout; he picked a pocket of a watch. See SCOUT. [Cant, in B.E. Presumably from Fr. *horloge*.F.]

LOGGERHEAD. A blockhead, or stupid fellow. We three loggerheads be; a sentence frequently written under two heads, and the reader by repeating it makes himself the third. A loggerhead is also a double-headed or bar shot of iron. To go to loggerheads; to fall to fighting. [As blockhead in Shakespeare. F.]

LOLL. Mother's loll; a favourite child, the mother's darling. [From *loll*, to lounge, to sprawl, as in Langland, Spenser, Dryden. The origin of *lollop*.F.]

LOLL TONGUE. He has been playing a game at loll tongue; he has been salivated.

LOLLIPOPS. Sweet lozenges purchased by children.

TO LOLLOP. To lean with one's elbows on a table.

LOLPOOP. A lazy, idle drone.

LOMBARD FEVER. Sick of a lombard fever; i.e. of the idles. [Probably nothing to do with the lombard bankers and usurers, except for the form. *Lombard fever*, which occurs in Ray's *Proverbs*, 1678, is connected with dialectal *lomber*, to idle, and represents folk-etymology for *fever-lurden,-lurgan,-lurgy,-largie*, that tired feeling.OD.]

LONG. Great. A long price; a great price.

LONG GALLERY. Throwing, or rather trundling, the dice, the whole length of the board.

LONG MEG. A jeering name for a very tall woman: from one famous in story, called Long Meg of Westminster. [Like the next, cant in 1690.]

LONG SHANKS. A long-legged person.

LONG SHILLING. This among hackney coachmen, before the alteration in the fares, was from the Royal Exchange to the east corner of Catherine-street, in the Strand.

LONG STOMACH. A voracious appetite.

LONG-TONGUED. Loquacious, not able to keep a secret. He is as long-tongued as Granny: Granny was an ideot who could lick her own eye. See GRANNY.

LONG-WINDED. A long-winded parson; one who preaches long, tedious sermons. A long-winded paymaster; one who takes long credit. [C16; the *paymaster* phrase is cant.F.]

LOO. For the good of the loo; for the benefit of the company or community. [As *loo* was used of a party playing at the game of loo, so by a further extension to a set of people, hence to a community. (OD).]

LOOBY. An awkward, ignorant fellow. [Langland: "Great loubies and long, that loth were to swinke." F.]

LOOKING AS IF ONE COULD NOT HELP IT. Looking like a simpleton, or as if one could not say boh! to a goose.

LOOKING GLASS. A chamber-pot, jordan, or member mug. [Wright, *mirabile dictu*, tells a good story of the consequent inevitable ambiguity.]

LOON, or LOUT. A country bumkin, or clown. [In Shakespeare (with variant *lown*), a clumsy, stupid fellow, also a man of low birth.O.—*To play the loon* originally meant to misbehave sexually.EDD.]

LOONSLATE. Thirteen pence halfpenny. [Cant, 1690.F.]

LOOPHOLE. An opening, or means of escape. To find a loophole in an act of parliament; i.e. a method of evading it.

LOP-SIDED. Uneven, having one side larger or heavier than the other: boys' paper kites are often said to be lop-sided.

TO LOPE. To leap, to run away. He loped down the dancers; he ran down stairs. [Old Norse *hlaupa*, to leap, run, with perhaps an influencing by Sp. *lobo*, a wolf.W.]

LORD. A crooked or hump-backed man. These unhappy people afford great scope for vulgar raillery; such as, 'Did you 'come straight from home? if so, you have got confoundedly 'bent by the way.' 'Don't abuse the gemman,' adds a by-stander, 'he has been grossly insulted already: don't you see his 'back's up?' Or some one asks him if the show is behind; 'because I see,' adds he, 'you have the drum at your back.' Another piece of vulgar wit is let loose on a deformed person: If met by a party of soldiers on their march, one of them observes that that gentleman is on his march too, for he has got his knapsack at his back. It is said in the British Apollo, that the title of Lord was first given to deformed persons in the reign of Richard III. from several persons labouring under that misfortune being created peers by him; but it is more probably derived from the Greek word *lordos*, crooked. [Cant, B.E, 1690.F. —The Greek, more precisely, means bent backward. It is a technical and medical word: Aristotle and Hippocrates have it; Suidas glosses it interestingly; E. A. Sophocles does not record it.]

LORD MANSFIELD'S TEETH. The chevaux de frize round the top of the wall of the King's Bench prison.

LOUNGE. A loitering place or gossiping shop. ['The London Literary Lounge' is the name given to a well-known West End bookseller's downstairs room, the haunt of many discerning bibliophiles.]

LOUSE. A gentleman's companion. He will never louse a grey head of his own; he will never live to be old.

LOUSE BAG. A black bag worn to the hair or wig.

LOUSE HOUSE. The round house, cage, or any other place of confinement.

LOUSE LADDER. A stitch fallen in a stocking.

LOUSE LAND. Scotland.

LOUSE TRAP. A small-toothed comb. [In B.E., *Scotch lousetrap*.F.—Dialect has several vivid if homely phrases: *not worth a louse('s liver)*, worthless; *to skin a louse* or *to drive a louse to London for the hide and tallow*, to be exceedingly greedy and grasping; *within two tumbles of a louse*, very near or close.EDD.]

LOUT. A clumsy stupid fellow.

LOVE-BEGOTTEN CHILD. A bastard.

LOW PAD. A footpad.

LOW TIDE, or LOW WATER. When there is no money in a man's pocket.

LOWRE. Money. *Cant.* [In Harman; other C16-17 forms, *lour(e)*, *lower*. Either from Fr. *louer* (F) or from Wallachian Romany *lowe*, coined money (H).]

LUBBER. An awkward fellow: a name given by sailors to

landsmen. [In Shakespeare, a clumsy, stupid fellow, with adjective *lubberly*.O.—In Langland, Shakespeare, Milton, Smollett.F.—Cf. *looby*.W.]

LUCK, or GOOD LUCK. To tread in a sirreverence, to be bewrayed: an allusion to the proverb, Sh-tt-n luck is good luck.

LUD'S BULWARK. Ludgate prison. [Cant, 1690.F.— "Hardly any London name has been so repeatedly and inconclusively discussed" as *Ludgate*, and at an allusion to King Lud does W (in W:A) leave it. Lud Gate was one of the old gates of London, and *Lud*, I rashly suggest, may be from Norwegian *ludden*, thick, broad.—In connection with the prison, one notes that *to take Ludgate*, already in Higgins, 1585, means to go bankrupt (OD).]

LUGS. Ears or wattles. See WATTLES.

LULLABY CHEAT. An infant. *Cant.*

LULLIES. Wet linen. *Cant.*

LULLY PRIGGERS. Thieves who steal wet linen. *Cant.*

LUMB. Too much. [Cant, 1725.F.]

LUMBER. Live lumber; soldiers or passengers on board a ship are so called by the sailors.

LUMBER TROOP. A club or society of citizens of London.

TO LUMP. To beat; also to include a number of articles under one head. [The colloquialism, *like it or lump it*, which is cognate with G's second definition, is recorded in 1577.W:A.]

TO LUMP THE LIGHTER. To be transported.

LUMPERS. Persons who contract to unload ships; also thieves who lurk about wharfs to pilfer goods from ships, lighters, &c. [Nowadays chiefly in *coal-lumpers*.]

LUMPING. Great. A lumping pennyworth; a great quantity for the money, a bargain. He has got a lumping pennyworth; frequently said of a man who marries a fat woman. [Cf. dialectal *lumping weight*, good weight or measure, hence a good bargain.EDD.]

LUN. Harlequin. [Is *lun* (omitted by the OD) in any way cognate with the Shakespearean *lunes*, mad freaks?]

LURCH. To be left in the lurch; to be abandoned by one's confederates or party, to be left in a scrape. [This phrase comes

from the old game of lurch, which resembled backgammon.S·
—In C16-17, *lurch*, in cant, signified a cheat, a trick, also to
cheat (F), the last occurring also in Shakespeare (O).]
LURCHED. Those who lose a game of whist, without scoring
five, are said to be lurched.
LURCHER. A lurcher of the law; a bum bailiff, or his setter.
[In C16 a rogue.F.—In dialect, *lurch*=to lurk, slink about.
EDD.]
LURRIES. Money, watches, rings, or other moveables. [Per-
haps from dialectal *lurry*, to carry (EDD).]
LUSH. Strong beer. ["First in slang dictionaries of late 18th
century. ?f om Shelta *lush*, to eat and drink." W. *Lushington*, a
drunkard, may be from Lushington the brewer, or suggested
by *lush* (H,W). *Lushy* was early C19 cant for drunk, while in
dialect *lush*, besides denoting strong drink, meant to drink
freely of an intoxicant (F,EDD). In American low slang, *lush*
still means drunkard, the drink, and to drink (I). Sailors occasionally say *lush* for liquor, and B observes that in the North
Country *lush*=to splash.]
LYE. Chamber lye; urine.

MACCARONI. An italian paste made of flour and eggs.
Also a fop: which name arose from a club, called the Maccaroni Club, instituted by some of the most dressy travelled
gentlemen about town, who led the fashions; whence a man
foppishly dressed, was supposed a member of that club, and by
contraction styled a Maccaroni. [The dandies were so styled
in 1760-1775.F.]
MACE. The mace is a rogue assuming the character of a gentleman, or opulent tradesman, who under that appearance
defrauds workmen, by borrowing a watch, or other piece of
goods, till one that he bespeaks is done. *Cant.*
MACHINES. Mrs Philip's ware. See CUNDUM.
MACKEREL. A bawd: from the French *maquerel*. Mackerel-
backed; long-backed. [Rather Fr. *maquereau*, a pander. In
English as early as 1426, and applied to a pimp.OD.—In Amer-

ican criminal slang, *mac* is a pander, also a lover or an associate of a lewd woman. I.]

MAD TOM, or TOM OF BEDLAM, otherwise an Abram Man. A rogue that counterfeits madness. *Cant.*

MADAM. A kept madam; a kept mistress. [In 1719 Durfey calls Hyde Park the *market of madams*.OD.—In dialect as in slang, a hussy.EDD.]

MADAM VAN. A whore. *Cant.*

MADE. Stolen. *Cant.* [In the Great War, soldiers used *make* in just the same way, also with sense: acquire not quite lawfully. For the *steal* group of Army slang words see my essay in *A Martial Medley*, by various hands, 1931.]

MADGE. The private parts of a woman. [Variant, *madge-howlet*.F.—Cf. the Scottish *madge* as a playful or a contemptuous term for a woman.EDD.]

MADGE CULLS. Sodomites. *Cant.*

MAGGOT BOILER. A tallow chandler.

MAGGOTTY. Whimsical, capricious. [B.E., 1690, defines it as freakish; *maggot*,"a whimsicall Fellow, full of strange Fancies and caprichio's." Both words refer to "the old belief in internal parasites as cause of mental or bodily disturbance." W.—The adjective in dialect=fractious, queer- or ill-tempered, irritable.EDD.]

MAHOMETAN GRUEL. Coffee: because formerly used chiefly by the Turks.

MAIDEN SESSIONS. A sessions where none of the prisoners are capitally convicted.

MAKE. A halfpenny. *Cant.*

MAKE WEIGHT. A small candle: a term applied to a little slender man.

MALINGEROR. A military term for one who, under pretence of sickness, evades his duty. [Hardly colloquial. Perhaps from Old Fr. *malingreux*, a beggar with artificial sores.W.]

MALKIN, or MAULKIN. A general name for a cat: also a parcel of rags fastened to the end of a stick, to clean an oven; also a figure set up in a garden to scare the birds; likewise an awkward woman.

MALKINTRASH. One in a dismal garb. [Cant, 1690.F.]

MALMSEY NOSE. A red pimpled snout, rich in carbuncles and rubies. [In Shakespeare.O.]

MALTOUT. A nick name for a marine, used by sailors and soldiers of other corps: probably a corruption of *matelot*, the French word for a sailor.

MAN OF THE TOWN. A rake, a debauchee.

MAN OF THE TURF. A horse racer, or jockey.

MANOEUVERING THE APOSTLES. Robbing Peter to pay Paul, i.e. borrowing of one man to pay another.

MAN TRAP. A woman's commodity.

MANUFACTURE. Liquors prepared from materials of English growth.

MARE'S NEST. He has found a mare's nest, and is laughing at the eggs; said of one who laughs without any apparent cause. [*Mare's Nest* is early C17, but the obsolete *horse-nest* dates back to 1583: the former in Fletcher, the latter in Stanyhurst.W.]

MARGERY PRATER. A hen. *Cant.* [In Harman.F.]

MARINATED. Transported to some foreign plantation. [Head, 1673. Cant.OD.]

MARINE OFFICER. An empty bottle: marine officers being held useless by the seamen. *Sea wit*. [From *ca.* 1850 always *dead marine*. King William IV apologised for using *marine officer* in a wardroom by saying that, like the officer, the bottle had done its duty once and was ready to do it again. B.]

MARRIAGE MUSIC. The squalling and crying of children.

MARRIED. Persons chained or handcuffed together, in order to be conveyed to gaol, or on board the lighters for transportation, are in the cant language said to be married together.

MARROW BONES. The knees. To bring any one down on his marrow bones; to make him beg pardon on his knees: some derive this from Mary's bones, i.e. the bones bent in honour of the Virgin Mary; but this seems rather far-fetched. Marrowbones and cleavers; principal instruments in the band of rough music; these are generally performed on by butchers, on marriages, elections, riding skimmington, and other public or joy-

229

ous occasions. [In C16-17 *marquess of marrowbones* denoted a lackey.F.]

MARTINET. A military term for a strict disciplinarian: from the name of a French general, famous for restoring military discipline to the French army. He first disciplined the French infantry, and regulated their method of encampment; he was killed at the siege of Doesbourg, in the year 1672. [Wycherley has the word in 1676, "about forty years before Martinet's death. Moreover, this application of the name is unknown in French, which has, however, a word *martinet* meaning a kind of cat-o'-nine-tails. In English *martinet* means the leech-end of a sail, hence, possibly, rope's end, and Wycherley applies the term to a brutal sea-captain." W:ROW.]

MASON'S MAUND. A sham sore above the elbow, to counterfeit a broken arm by a fall from a scaffold.

MASTER OF THE MINT. A gardener.

MASTER OF THE ROLLS. A baker.

MASTER OF THE WARDROBE. One who pawns his clothes to purchase liquor.

MATRIMONIAL PEACE-MAKER. The sugar-stick, or arbor vitae.

MAUDLIN DRUNK. Crying drunk: perhaps from Mary Magdalene, called Maudlin, who is always painted in tears.

MAULED. Extremely drunk, or soundly beaten. [The former meaning was cant, the latter a colloquialism already in 1690. *Mauley*, a fist, established itself *ca.* 1800 (F), the dialectal equivalent being *mauler* (EDD). The early senses were to stun, to belabour, to batter; the present, to pull about, even to lacerate. From L. *malleus*, a heavy hammer. W:WAM.]

MAUNDERING BROTH. Scolding. [Cf. dialectal *maunder*, to grumble, to threaten *sotto voce.* EDD.]

MAUNDING. Asking or begging. *Cant.* [*Maund*, to beg, probably from either *mendier* or *quémander*, to beg, or from a confusion of the two words. Possibly *maund*, a large basket, may have entered into the popular conception of the words, just as amateur etymologists derive *beg* from *bag.* W.]

MAWKES. A vulgar slattern. [Also in C18 a whore. F.]

MAW-WALLOP. A filthy composition, sufficient to provoke vomiting.

MAY BEES. May bees don't fly all the year long; an answer to any one who prefaces a proposition with, It may be.

MEALY-MOUTHED. Over-modest or backward in speech. [At first *meal-mouthed*, meaning rather fair-spoken, flattering; the *meal* is perhaps cognate with L.*mel*, honey.W:MWAM.]

MEDLAR. A fruit, vulgarly called an open a-se; of which it is more truly than delicately said, that it is never ripe till it is as rotten as a t—d, and then it is not worth a f—t.

MEGGS. Guineas. We forked the rum cull's meggs to the tune of fifty; we picked the gentleman's pocket of full fifty guineas. *Cant.* [The half-guinea was a *smelt*, as Shadwell tells us in the underworld play, *The Squire of Alsatia*.F.—In American low slang, *meig*=a five-cent piece, also one cent when used in the plural.I.—In Liverpool, one may still hear a halfpenny called a *meg*.]

MELLOW. Almost drunk. [So in Burns.EDD.—In 1690, as a noun it signified "a smooth, soft drink" (B.E.), not a soft-drink!]

TO MELT. To spend. Will you melt a borde? will you spend a shilling? The cull melted a couple of decusses upon us; the gentleman spent a couple of crowns upon us. *Cant.*

MEMBER MUG. A chamber pot. [*Member*, the membrum virile, occurs in C13; *privy member* also in late C13; *carnal member*, early C15; *dearest member*, in Burns.OD,F.]

MEN OF KENT. Men born east of the river Medway, who are said to have met the Conqueror in a body, each carrying a green bough in his hand, the whole appearing like a moving wood; and thereby obtaining a confirmation of their ancient privileges. The inhabitants of Kent are divided into Kentish Men and Men of Kent. Also a society held at the Fountain Tavern, Bartholomew Lane, A.D. 1743.

MERCURIANS. A convivial society held in London.

MERKIN. Counterfeit hair for women's privy parts. See *Bailey's Dict*. [Also=the pudendum.F.]

MERRY ANDREW, or Mr MERRYMAN. The jack pudding, jester, or zany of a mountebank, usually dressed in a par-ty-coloured coat. [*Andrew* is a frequent name for a manservant. W:WAM.]

MERRY-BEGOTTEN. A bastard.

MESSJOHN. A Scotch presbyterian teacher or parson.

MESSMATE. One who eats at the same mess, companion, or comerade. [In 1st edition, *camerade*.]

METTLE. The semen. To fetch mettle; the act of self-pollu-tion. Mettle is also figuratively used for courage. [Cf. the two senses of *spunk*.]

METTLESOME. Bold, courageous.

MICHAEL. Hip, Michael, your head's on fire. See HYP.

MIDSHIPMAN'S WATCH AND CHAIN. A sheep's heart and pluck.

MILCH COW. One who is easily tricked out of his property: a term used by gaolers, for prisoners who have money and bleed freely.

MILK AND WATER. Both ends of the busk.

TO MILK THE PIGEON. To endeavour at impossibilities.

MILL. A chisel.

TO MILL. To rob; also to break, beat out, or kill. I'll mill your glaze; I'll beat out your eye. To mill a bleating cheat; to kill a sheep. To mill a ken; to rob a house. To mill doll; to beat hemp in Bridewell. *Cant*. [As noun, *mill* in C18 meant a fight (F); in C19-20 America, "a free-for-all fight" (I).]

MILL LAY. To force open the doors of houses in order to rob them. *Cant*.

MILLER. A murderer.

MINE A-SE ON A BANDBOX. An answer to the offer of any thing inadequate to the purpose for which it is wanted, just as a bandbox would be if used for a seat.

MINE UNCLE'S. A pawnbroker's shop; also a necessary house. Carried to mine uncle's; pawned. New-married men are also said to go to their uncle, when they leave their wives soon after the honey moon. [In second sense, C19-20 have *my aunt's;* cf. the colloquial Fr. *chez ma tante*.]

MINIKIN. A little man or woman: also the smallest sort of pin.

MINOR CLERGY. Young chimney sweepers.

MINT. Gold. A mint of money; common phrase for a large sum.

MISCHIEF. A man loaded with mischief, i.e. a man with his wife on his back. [Cf. Ashley Dukes' brilliant comedy, *The Man with a Load of Mischief*, published in 1924, staged in 1925.]

MISH. A shirt, smock, or sheet. *Cant.* [See *camesa.*]

MISH TOPPER. A coat, or petticoat.

MISS. A miss, or kept mistress; a harlot. [Evelyn on January 9, 1662, uses the word and adds: "as at this time they begin to call lewd women"; B.E., 1690: "a whore of quality"; Ash, 1775: "a strumpet, a whore, a concubine." F.]

MISS LAYCOCK. The monosyllable.

MITE. A nick name for a cheesemonger: from the small insect of that name found in cheese.

MIX METAL. A silversmith.

MOABITES. Bailiffs, or Philistines. [First in B.E., 1690.OD.]

MOB, or MAB. A wench, or harlot.

MOBILITY. The mob: a sort of opposite to nobility. [*Mob* being short for *mobile*, which itself represented the L. *mobile vulgus.*W.—In *The Maccaroni and Theatrical Magazine* for January 1773 appeared this notice:—"Pantheons: the *Nobility's*, Oxford Road; the *Mobility's*, Spawfields." Chancellor, *Pleasure Haunts.*]

MOHAIR. A man in the civil line, a townsman, or tradesman: a military term, from the mohair buttons worn by persons of those descriptions, or any others not in the army, the buttons of military men being always of metal: this is generally used as a term of contempt, meaning a bourgeois, tradesman, or mechanic. [Cf. the Fr. *pékin.*]

MOIETY. Half, but vulgarly used to signify a share or portion: as, he will come in for a small moiety. [Both the loose and the strict sense occur in Shakespeare.O.]

MOLL. A whore. [Bee, in his *Dictionary of the Turf*, 1823, describes molls as "the female companions of low thieves, at bed, board, and business." F.—In American slang of trampdom and the underworld, "a woman, regardless of character or con-

233

dition. Seldom used to designate a prostitute or a disorderly female." I.—In English dialect, likewise, it may denote a wench, a sweetheart (EDD), a usage not unknown in the British Army in 1914-1918. The word is familiarly short for *Mary*, always an exceedingly common name.]

MOLL PRATLY'S GIG. A rogering bout.

MOLL THOMPSON'S MARK. M.T. i.e. empty: as, Take away this bottle, it has Moll Thompson's mark upon it.

MOLLY. A Miss Molly; an effeminate fellow, a sodomite. [In 1900-1914, the former was often called a *Gussie;* in post-War days, the latter is frequently alluded to as a *Nancy*, a *Nancy Boy*, a *Cissy*, this last in both senses.]

MONDAY. Saint Monday. See SAINT.

MONEY. A girl's private parts, commonly applied to little children: as, Take care Miss, or you will show your money. [Cf. C19 slang *money-box,-maker,-spinner*.F.]

MONEY DROPPERS. Cheats who drop money, which they pretend to find just before some country lad; and by way of giving him a share of their good luck, entice him into a public house, where they and their confederates cheat or rob him of what money he has about him.

MONGREL. A hanger on among cheats, a spunger; also a child whose father and mother are of different countries.

MONKS AND FRIARS. Terms used by printers: monks are sheets where the letters are blotted, or printed too black; friars, those letters where the ink has failed touching the type, which are therefore white or faint.

MONKEY. To suck the monkey; to suck or draw wine, or any other liquor, privately out of a cask, by means of a straw, or small tube. Monkey's allowance; more kicks than halfpence. Who put that monkey on horseback without tying his legs? vulgar wit on a bad horseman. [*To suck the monkey* (the operation mentioned by G is sometimes described as *tapping the admiral*, as B tells us) also means to drink rum out of coco-nuts, and again to drink out of the bottle. In the old Navy, *monkey* was a wooden vessel for grog. It is also the general nautical diminutive, as in *monkey gaff*, *monkey poop*, *monkey jacket*.B.—

Urquhart used *monkey's money* to mean words, fair words. F.]
MONOSYLLABLE. A woman's commodity. [Omitted by
OD. The first example in F belongs to 1714. *Monosyllable* was
the polite slang word throughout the approximate period
1720-1880 (just as *c—t* has been the plain-spoken word ever
since *ca.* 1600), and was usually preceded by *the*: "therefore,"
says Bee in 1823, "do some men call it 'the article,' 'my article,'
and 'her article', as the case may be." No word, unless it be
article, which is, however, more frivolous, has in C20 usage re-
placed *the monosyllable*. F gives an imposing list of synonyms
(some are mere euphemisms) employed in literature or noted
by such lexicographers as Florio and Cotgrave. Operative
origins of English synonyms are accounted for thus:—Chaucer
3, Dunbar 3, Shakespeare 5, Florio 5, Donne 5, Carew 4, Herrick 5, Urquhart 15, Rochester 7, Durfey 14, Cleland 5,
Stevens 6, Burns 12. And there are many, many others in this
list, which is valid to the end of the 19th century; since 1900, I
believe, extremely few synonyms have been coined. Not that
any more are needed, for the 20 or so recorded by F range from
the learned appositeness of Urquhart's *contrapunctum* to the
learned prettiness of Herrick's *postern gate to the Elysian fields:*
from the terse Latin suitability of Urquhart's *pudend* to the
'Saxon' ineptitude of *what do you call it:* from the native brutality of Durfey's *gap* to the 'foreign' delicacy of Donne's *centrique
part:* from the crass inadequacy of *fleshly part*, or Shakespeare's
circle to the offensive adequacy of Florio's *brat-getting place:*
from the erudite ingenuity of Urquhart's *aphrodisaical tennis
court* or the same writer's *solution of continuity* to the insipid conventionalism of *temple of Venus* or Marston's *love's paradise:* and
from the technical cleverness of G.A. Stevens' *book-binder's
wife* ("manufacturing in sheets") or Lord Coke's *star over the
garter* to the obviousness of the *thing* or *it* variety and of the
orifice variety.]
MOON CURSER. A link-boy: link-boys are said to curse the
moon, because it renders their assistance unnecessary; these
gentry frequently, under colour of lighting passengers over
kennels, or through dark passages, assist in robbing them.*Cant.*

MOON-EYED HEN. A squinting wench.

MOON MEN. Gypsies. [So in derision by others, for, as Dekker remarks, the term denotes madmen; Dekker adds that "by a by-name they are called gypsies, they call themselves Egyptians." F.—Cf. note at *gypsies*.]

MOON RAKERS. Wiltshire men: because it is said that some men of that county, seeing the reflection of the moon in a pond, endeavoured to pull it out with a rake. [Wiltshire people have a more complimentary version, but Blackmore in *Lorna Doone* uses *moon-raking* to indicate wool-gathering.F.—In C18 and early C19 dialect, *moon-raking* euphemised smuggling.EDD.]

MOONSHINE. A matter or mouthful of moonshine; a trifle, nothing. The white brandy smuggled on the coasts of Kent and Sussex, and the gin in the north of Yorkshire, are also called moonshine. ["Contraband spirits, a phrase that seems to have been used at sea quite as early as on land." B.— In American low slang, both *shine* and its original, *moonshine*, designate liquor, usually that manufactured illicitly; the term was used in America first by the local distillers of the Blue Ridge Mountains.I.]

MOP. A kind of annual fair in the west of England, where farmers usually hire their servants. [The girls carried a mop or a broom to indicate the kind of job they wanted: whence we see that *mop*, an habitual drunkard (H), and (*to be*) *mops and brooms*, half-drunk, arose probably from the drinking customary at such fairs.OD.—For modern allusive passages see Buckman, *Darke's Sojourn*, 1890, and Gibbs, *Cotswold Village*, 1898. EDD.]

MOPED. Stupid, melancholy for want of society. [From C16 *mope*, to despond, to be bewildered.]

MOPSEY. A doudy, or homely woman.

MOPSQUEEZER. A maid servant, particularly a house maid.

MOPUSSES. Money. [The singular meant a small coin ($\frac{1}{4}$d or $\frac{1}{2}$d according to B.E., 1690), perhaps a corruption from *Mompesson*, Sir Charles, a notorious monopolist of the C17.F.]

MORE-ISH. This wine has but one fault, and that is, it is more-ish: i.e. more of it is wanted, or there is too little of it. [The *-ish* words so frequent in post-War colloquial speech show the influence of dialect, especially Northern: in the North these *-ish* words were well established at least as early as 1860. (EDD).]

MORGLAG. A brown bill, or kind of halbert, formerly carried by watchmen; corruption of *more*, great or broad, and *glave*, blade.

MORRIS. Come, morris off; dance off, or get you gone:allusion to morris, i.e. *morisco*, or moorish dancing.

MORT. A woman or wench; also a yeoman's daughter. To be taken all a-mort; to be confounded, surprised, or motionless through fear. [As a girl or a woman, chaste or not, C16, the harlot sense occurring in Harman (OD): in either sense, cant, as GB makes quite clear in his definition of *mort* as "woman, concubine; a cant word." *Walking* or *strolling mort*=a female tramp.]

MOSES. To stand Moses; a man is said to stand Moses when he has another man's bastard child fathered upon him, and he is obliged by the parish to maintain it. [Contrast the dialectal *say Moses*, to make an offer of marriage. EDD.]

MOSS. A cant term for lead, because both are found on the tops of buildings.

MOSSY FACE. The mother of all saints.

MOT. A girl, or wench. See MORT. [Or *mott*, as used by Sir Richard Burton in 1885 to denote a whore. F.]

MOTHER, or THE MOTHER. A bawd. Mother abbess; the same. Mother midnight; a midwife. Mother in law's bit; a small piece, mothers in law being supposed not apt to overload the stomachs of their husband's children.

MOTHER OF ALL SAINTS. The monosyllable.

MOTHER OF ALL SOULS. The same.

MOTHER OF THE MAIDS. A bawd.

MOUCHETS. Small patches worn by ladies: from the French word *mouches*.

MOUSE. To speak like a mouse in a cheese; i.e. faintly, or indistinctly.

MOUSETRAP. The parson's mousetrap; the state of matrimony. [In old cant, *mousetrap* is the pudend, whence G's term, itself current by 1690.F.]

MOUTH. A noisy fellow. Mouth half cocked; one gaping and staring at every thing he sees. To make any one laugh on the wrong or t'other side of his mouth; to make him cry or grieve. [As a noisy fellow, in Shakespeare; contemptuous also in dialect, which possesses *mouthy*, saucy, abusive.F,EDD.]

MOVEABLES. Rings, watches, or any toys of value.

TO MOW. A Scotch word for the act of copulation. [And for the noun.EDD.]

MOW HEATER. A drover: from their frequent sleeping on hay mows. *Cant.*

MOWER. A cow. [Cant.F.]

MUCK. Money; also dung. [Both established by *ca.* 1300.OD.]

MUCKINDER. A child's handkerchief tied to the side. [Properly *muckender*, though *muckinger* was also frequent. Not specially a child's.OD.]

MUCKWORM. A miser. [Also *muck-grub(ber)*.EDD.]

MUD. A fool, or thick-sculled fellow; also, among printers, the same as dung among journeymen taylors. See DUNG.

MUD LARK. A hog.

MUFF. The private parts of a woman. To the well wearing of your muff, mort: to the happy consummation of your marriage, girl; a health.

MUFFLING CHEAT. A napkin. [Cant, C16.F.]

MUGGLETONIANS. The sect or disciples of Lodowick Muggleton.

MULLIGRUBS. Sick of the mulligrubs with eating chopped hay; low-spirited, having an imaginary sickness. [In C17 also *mouldy grubs*. The oldest meaning, stomach-ache, persisted till late in C19 in slang (H) and still persists in dialect, where, with variant *mullygrum(ph)s*, it signifies also any imaginary ailment, ill-temper, dejection (EDD). *Grub* was once the usual word for a worm, and in Latin the same discomfort is *verminatio*, from *vermis*, a worm.W:ROW.]

MUM. An interjection directing silence. Mum for that; I shall

238

be silent as to that. As mute as Mumchance, who was hanged for saying nothing; a friendly reproach to any one who seems low-spirited and silent.

MUMCHANCE. An ancient game like hazard, played with dice: probably so named from the silence observed in playing at it.

MUM GLASS. The monument erected on Fish-street Hill, London, in memory of the great fire in 1666.

MUMBLE A SPARROW. A cruel sport practised at wakes and fairs, in the following manner: A cock sparrow whose wings are clipped, is put into the crown of a hat; a man having his arms tied behind him, attempts to bite off the sparrow's head, but is generally obliged to desist, by the many pecks and pinches he receives from the enraged bird.

MUMMER. The mouth. [This sense, C18. As actor, C19; as actor in a dumb show, *ca.* 1500.OD.—Perhaps cognate with *Momus*.W.]

MUMPERS. Originally beggars of the genteel kind, but since used for beggars in general. [C17, from *mump*, to beg.F.]

MUMPERS' HALL. An alehouse where beggars are harboured.

MUNDUNGUS. Bad or rank tobacco: from *mondongo*, a Spanish word signifying tripes, or the uncleaned entrails of a beast, full of filth. [From *ca.* 1640.OD.]

MUNS. The face, or rather the mouth: from the German word *mund*, the mouth. Toute his muns; look at his face. [*Mun*= mouth, *muns*=face, from Norwegian dialectal *munn*, the mouth. EDD.]

MUNSTER PLUMS. Potatoes. *Irish.*

MURDER. He looked like God's revenge against murder; he looked angrily.

MUSHROOM. A person or family suddenly raised to riches and eminence: an allusion to that fungus which starts up in a night. [Bacon very satirical in 1622.F.—Cf. *mushroom-hall*, a house built hastily to establish a claim to the site.EDD.]

MUSIC. The watch-word among highwaymen, signifying the person is a friend, and must pass unmolested. Music is also an

239

Irish term, in tossing up, to express the harp side, or reverse, of a farthing or halfpenny, opposed to the head.

MUTE. An undertaker's servant, who stands at the door of a person lying in state: so named from being supposed mute with grief. [In Shakespeare, a silent spectator.O.]

MUTTON-HEADED. Stupid.

MUTTON MONGER. A man addicted to wenching. [Cotgrave, 1611: "A noteable smel-smocke, or muttonmonger, a cunning solicitor of a wench." F.—*Mutton* as food for lust, hence a prostitute or a loose woman, was established early in C16.OD.]

MUZZLE. A beard.

MYNT. See Mint.

MYRMIDONS. The constable's assistants, watchmen, &c.

NAB, or NAB CHEAT. A hat. Penthouse nab; a large hat. [Related to *nab*, *nob*, head, Swedish dialect *nobb*, head. EDD.—Originally C17 cant as hat, and C16 cant as head.F, OD.]

TO NAB. To seize, or catch unawares. To nab the teize; to be privately whipped. To nab the stoop; to stand in the pillory. To nab the rust; a jockey term for a horse that becomes restive. To nab the snow; to steal linen left out to bleach or dry. *Cant.* [As either to catch in general, or to arrest, late C17.OD.—In American criminal slang, both senses survive (I), as that of arrest survived among soldiers in 1914-1918.]

NAB GIRDER, or NOB GIRDER. A bridle. [Late C17 cant.F.]

NACK. To have a nack; to be ready at any thing, to have a turn for it.

NACKY. Ingenious.

NAILED. Secured, fixed. He offered me a decus, and I nailed him; he offered me a crown, and I struck or fixed him. [This sense has persisted in slang, where, in C19-20, it means also to steal.]

NANNY HOUSE. A brothel. [C17-18 cant.F.]

TO NAP. To cheat at dice by securing one chance. Also to catch the venereal disease. You've napt it; you are infected.

NAPPING. To take any one napping; i.e. to come upon him unexpectedly, to find him asleep: as, He caught him napping, as Morse caught his mare. [Later, *catch napping*. C16, and in Shakespeare.F.]

NAPPER. The head; also a cheat or thief.

NAPPER OF NAPS. A sheep stealer. *Cant.*

NAPPY ALE. Strong ale. [In dialect, of any liquor.EDD.]

NASK, or NASKIN. A prison or Bridewell. The new nask; Clerkenwell bridewell. Tothil-fields nask; the bridewell at Tothil-fields. *Cant.* [Earliest record 1686.OD.—Perhaps cognate with obsolete Scottish *nask*, a withe (EDD).]

NATION. An abbreviation of damnation; a vulgar term used in Kent, Sussex, and the adjacent counties, for very. Nation-good; very good. A nation long way; a very long way. [In C18 also=a) great; and b) a large number of, as in "The French had a nation of hedges," Sterne.F.—In dialect, *nation-sized*=very bad, extremely unpleasant, and *nationish, nationly*=very.EDD. —Another piece of dialect that has been whole-heartedly welcomed by the U.S.A. with variant *tarnation*.]

NATTY LADS. Young thieves or pickpockets. *Cant.* [*Natty* is perhaps a corruption of *neat*.W.]

NATURAL. A mistress, a child; also an idiot. A natural son or daughter; a love or merry-begotten child, a bastard.

NAY-WORD. A bye-word, a proverb. ["No obvious connexion with either *nay* or *ay*." OD—In Shakespeare as byword and as watchword.O.]

NAZARENE FORETOP. The foretop of a wig made in imitation of Christ's head of hair, as represented by the painters and sculptors.

NAZY. Drunken. Nazy cove or mort; a drunken rogue or harlot. Nazy nabs; drunken coxcombs. [C16 cant.F.]

NEB, or NIB. The bill of a bird, and the slit of a pen. Figuratively, the face and mouth of a woman; as, She holds up her neb; she holds up her mouth to be kissed. [Dialect.]

NECK STAMPER. The boy who collects the pots belonging

to an alehouse, sent out with beer to private houses. [Like the next, C17-18 cant.F.]

NECK VERSE. Formerly the persons claiming the benefit of clergy were obliged to read a verse in a Latin manuscript psalter; this saving them from the gallows, was termed their neck verse: it was the first verse of the fifty-first psalm, *Miserere mei, &c.*

NECK WEED. Hemp.

NEEDLE POINT. A sharper.

NEGLIGEE. A woman's undressed gown, vulgarly termed a neggledigee.

NEGRO. A black-a-moor: figuratively used for a slave. I'll be no man's negro; I will be no man's slave.

NEGROES' HEADS. Brown loaves delivered to the ships in ordinary.[Cf. *Brown George*, q.v.]

NETTLED. Teized, provoked, out of temper. He or she has pissed on a nettle; said of one who is peevish or out of temper.

NEW COLLEGE STUDENTS. Golden scholars, silver bachelors, and leaden masters.

NEW DROP. The scaffold used at Newgate for hanging criminals; which dropping down, leaves them suspended. By this improvement, the use of that vulgar vehicle, a cart, is entirely left off.

NEWGATE BIRD. A thief or sharper, frequently caged in Newgate. [Dekker, 1607; cf. *Newgate nightingale*, Copland, *ca.* 1530. Already by 1592, *Newgate* was a common name for all prisons. By 1740 *Newgate* also meant to imprison. *Newgate fashion* and *N. terms* were in use by 1600.F,OD. The New Gate, already so called in C12, was in the western wall of the city of London; through it passed *Newgate Street*. The famous gaol, so named from C13 onward, was reconstructed on several occasions before, being completed, it outmoded Tyburn as a place of execution. Newgate was finally demolished only in 1902. W: A. —Defoe, 1721, speaks thus emphatically: "(Newgate) ruined more young people than all the town besides," and again: "There are more thieves and rogues made by that one prison of

Newgate than by all the clubs and societies of villains in the nation."]

NEWGATE SOLICITOR. A pettyfogging and roguish attorney, who attends the gaols to assist villains in evading justice.

NEW LIGHT. One of the new light; a methodist. [In C19, the term belonged much rather to Scotland and Presbyterianism than to England and Methodism. The epithet can be applied to the liberal-minded and progressive party in any church. EDD.]

TO NICK. To win at dice, to hit the mark just in the nick of time, or at the critical moment. [Shakespeare has *in the nick*. O.]

NICK. Old Nick; the Devil. [C17. F.]

NICK NAME. A name given, in ridicule or contempt; from the French *nom de nique*. *Nique* is a movement of the head to mark a contempt for any person or thing. [As *an ewt* became *a newt*, so *an eke-name* became *a nickname*. W: ROW.—Shakespeare has the verb: to name wrongly; to mention by mistake. O.]

NICK NINNY. A simpleton. [Like the next, in B.E., 1690. F. —*Ninny* is related to *innocent* as *Ned* is to *Edward*. W: A.]

NICKIN, NIKEY, or NIZEY. A soft simple fellow; also a diminutive of Isaac.

NICKNACKS. Toys, baubles, or curiosities.

NICKNACKATORY. A toyshop.

NICKUMPOOP, or NINCUMPOOP. A foolish fellow; also one who never saw his wife's ****. [The former is the earlier. A formation similar to *tomfool*. W.]

NIFFYNAFFY FELLOW. A trifler. [Cf. dialect *niff-naff*, a trifle, to trifle. EDD.]

NIG. The clippings of money. Nigging: clipping. Nigler; a clipper. *Cant.*

NIGGLING. Cutting awkwardly, trifling; also accompanying with a woman. [To trifle, early C17; to copulate, in Harman. Cf. *niggler*, a lascivious person of either sex, C17 only. OD.—Cf. also the East Anglian *niggle*, to cuddle. EDD.—In American low slang, to have sexual intercourse. I.]

NIGHT MAGISTRATE. A constable.

NIGHTINGALE. A soldier who, as the term is, sings out at the halberts. It is a point of honour in some regiments, among the grenadiers, never to cry out, or become nightingales, whilst under the discipline of the cat of nine tails; to avoid which, they chew a bullet.

NIGHTMAN. One whose business it is to empty necessary houses in London, which is always done in the night: the operation is called a wedding. See WEDDING.

NIGIT. A fool: seemingly a corruption and contraction of the words *an idiot*. [Dialectal variants *nidget, nidyard, nidyed*.EDD.]

NIGMENOG. A very silly fellow.

TO NIM. To steal or pilfer: from the German *nemen*, to take. Nim a togeman; steal a cloak. [Cognate with the German but derived from A.S. *niman*, to take. Now obsolete in dialect.EDD. —A good English word that fell on evil days in C16: cant also had *nimmer*, a thief, and *nimming*, theft, robbery.F.—Hence Shakespeare's Nym.H.]

NIMGIMMER. A physician or surgeon, particularly those who cure the venereal disease. [C17 cant.F.]

NINE LIVES. Cats are said to have nine lives, and women ten cats' lives.

NINE SHILLINGS. Corruption of *nonchalance*.

NINNY, or NINNYHAMMER. A simpleton.

NIP. A cheat. Bung nipper; a cutpurse. [Harman has *nyp a boung*, to cut a purse. *Nip*, to steal, is also C16.F.—In American cant, *nip* is "to open a locked door by means of a pair of hollow-nosed nippers, which grasp the end of the old-fashioned key, allowing it to be turned in the lock. To steal a stud or other piece of jewellery from the person, especially with the aid of the nipper." I.]

NIP CHEESE. A nick name for the purser of a ship; from those gentlemen being supposed sometimes to nip, or diminish, the allowance of the seamen, in that and every other article. It is also applied to stingy persons in general. [The purser's steward, says B.—Generically, dialectal variants are *nip-corn, -farthing,-fig,-prune,-raisin,-screed,-screw,-skin,-skitter*.EDD.]

NIPPERKIN. A small measure.

NIPPS. The sheers used in clipping money.

NIT SQUEEGER, i.e. SQUEEZER. A hair-dresser.

NO CATCHY NO HAVY. If I am not caught, I cannot be hurt. *Negro saying.*

NOB. The head.

NOB THATCHER. A peruke-maker.

NOCK. The breech; from *nock*, a notch.

NOCKY BOY. A dull simple fellow.

NOD. He is gone to the land of Nod; he is asleep.

NODDLE. The head. [C16. Earlier, the back of the head. OD.]

NODDY. A simpleton or fool. Also a kind of low cart, with a seat before it for the driver, used in and about Dublin, in the manner of a hackney coach: the fare is just half that of a coach, for the same distance; so that for sixpence one may have a set down, as it is called, of a mile and a half, and frequently a tumble down into the bargain: it is called a noddy from the nutation of its head. Knave noddy; the old-fashioned name for the knave of trumps. [The first is in Shakespeare. O.]

NOKES. A ninny, or fool. John-a-Nokes and Tom-a-Stiles; two honest peaceable gentlemen, repeatedly set together by the ears by lawyers of different denominations: two fictitious names formerly used in law proceedings, but now very seldom, having for several years past been supplanted by two other honest peaceable gentlemen, namely, John Doe and Richard Roe. ["With *John Doe* and *Richard Roe*, fictitious plaintiff and defendant in ejection action (abolished 1852), cf. *John a' Nokes* and *John a' Stiles*, i.e. John of the oaks and John of the stiles." W.—The earlier terms existed by 1531 and went out of fashion just about two centuries later (OD). Any one of these four representative names serves to particularise the generality of men into an individual.]

NOLL. Old Noll; Oliver Cromwell. [As *Nell* for *Ellen*, so *Noll* for *Oliver*. W.—There is a pun on *noll*=a simpleton.]

NON-CON. A nonconformist, presbyterian, or any other dissenter.

NONE-SUCH. One that is unequalled: frequently applied ironically.

NONSENSE. Melting butter in a wig.

NOOZED. Married, hanged.

NOPE. A blow: as, I took him a nope on the costard. [Northern dialect. In London, cant—recorded 1725.OD.]

NORFOLK CAPON. A red herring.

NORFOLK DUMPLING. A nick name, or term of jocular reproach to a Norfolk man; dumplings being a favourite food in that county.

NORTH ALLERTONS. Spurs; that place, like Rippon, being famous for making them.

NORTHUMBERLAND. Lord Northumberland's arms; a black eye; so called in the last century. [The phrase survives in Northumberland. Either from the dark-colour fusils carried by the Percys' retainers or from the black and red predominant in the spectacles-resembling badge of this powerful family.EDD.]

NORWAY NECKCLOTH. The pillory, usually made of Norway fir.

NOSE. As plain as the nose on your face; evidently to be seen. He is led by the nose; he is governed. To follow one's nose; to go straight forward. To put one's nose out of joint; to rival one in the favour of any person. To make a bridge of any one's nose; to pass by him in drinking. To nose a stink; to smell it. He cut off his nose to be revenged of his face; said of one who, to be revenged on his neighbour, has materially injured himself. [*Led by the nose*, C17, was probably first applied to tame bears. W:A. —In C18 cant, *nose*=an informer, a paid spy. *To nose*, C17-18, =to suspect, *to nose upon* being the C19 form.F.]

TO NOSE. To bully.

NOSE BAG. A bag fastened to the horse's head, in which the soldiers of the cavalry put the oats given to their horses: whence the saying of, I see the nosebag in his face; i.e. he has been a private man, or rode private.

NOSE GENT. A nun. [Cant *ca.* 1550-1850.F.—Harman spells it as *nosegent.*]

NOSTRUM. A medicine prepared by particular persons only, a quack medicine. ['Our' remedies are always the best.W: ROW.—Like *note* (see below), hardly in place here.]

NOTCH. The private parts of a woman.

NOTE. He changed his note; he told another sort of a story.

NOZZLE. The nose of a man or woman. [Cf. *nuzzle*, to push with the nose.]

NUB. The neck; also coition. [Like next entry, C17 cant. F,OD.]

NUBBING. Hanging. Nubbing cheat; the gallows. Nubbing cove; the hangman. Nubbing ken; the sessions house.

NUG. An endearing word: as, My dear nug; my dear love. [The key to this and the next two entries is the old cant *nug*, to fondle, to know carnally.F.]

NUGGING DRESS. An out-of-the-way old-fashioned dress, or rather a loose kind of dress, denoting a courtesan.

NUGGING HOUSE. A brothel.

TO NULL. To beat: as, He nulled him heartily. [Probably short for *annul*.]

NUMBERS. To consult the book of numbers; a term used in the House of Commons, when, instead of answering or confuting a pressing argument, the minister calls for a division, i.e. puts the matter to the vote.

NUMBSCULL. Stupid fellow. [Usually *numskull*. Colloquial in C18, good English in C19, 'literary' in C20.]

NUMMS. A sham collar, to be worn over a dirty shirt. [C17 cant.F.]

NUNNERY. A bawdy house. [As early as Nashe, 1593.OD.]

NUPSON. A cully, a fool. [Or *nup*. Both occur in the anonymous play, *Lingua*, 1607; *nupson* however is recorded in Jonson in 1598.OD.]

TO NURSE. To cheat: as, They nursed him out of it. An estate in the hands of trustees, for the payment of debts, is said to be at nurse.

NUTS. It was nuts for them; i.e. it was very agreeable to them.

NUTCRACKERS. The pillory: as, The cull peeped through the nutcrackers. [C17 cant.F.]

NUTMEGS. Testicles.

NYP, or NIP. A half pint, a nip of ale: whence the nipperkin, a small vessel.

NYP SHOP. The Peacock in Gray's Inn Lane, where Burton ale is sold in nyps.

NYPPER. A cut-purse: so called by one Wotton, who in the year 1585 kept an academy for the education and perfection of pickpockets and cut-purses: his school was near Billingsgate, London. As in the dress of ancient times many people wore their purses at their girdles, cutting them was a branch of the light-fingered art, which is now lost, though the name remains. Maitland, from Stow, gives the following account of this Wotton: This man was a gentleman born, and sometime a merchant of good credit, but fallen by time into decay: he kept an alehouse near Smart's Key, near Billingsgate, afterwards for some misdemeanor put down. He reared up a new trade of life, and in the same house he procured all the cut-purses about the city, to repair to his house; there was a school-house set up to learn young boys to cut purses: two devices were hung up; one was a pocket, and another was a purse; the pocket had in it certain counters, and was hung about with hawks' bells, & over the top did hang a little sacring bell. The purse had silver in it; and he that could take out a counter, without noise of any of the bells, was adjudged a judicial *nypper:* according to their terms of art, a *foyster* was a pick-pocket; a *nypper* was a pick-purse, or cut-purse.

OAF. A silly fellow. [Earlier *auph, ouph*, variants of *elf.* Originally of a changeling. W.—Daringly used by Kipling, whose pre-War audacity undoubtedly lost him the laureateship.]

OAFISH. Simple.

OAK. A rich man, a man of good substance and credit. To sport oak; to shut the outward door of a student's room at college. An oaken towel; an oaken cudgel. To rub a man down with an oaken towel; to beat him. [In American cant, an *oak towel* is a policeman's club. I.]

OAR. To put in one's oar; to intermeddle, or give an opinion unasked: as, To be sure, you must put in your oar! [In Florio as *have an oar in*.F.]

OATS. He has sowed his wild oats; he is staid, or sober, having left off his wild tricks. ["With *wild oats*, typical, from C16, of crop that one will regret sowing, cf. figurative use of Fr. *folle avoine*." W.]

O BE JOYFUL. I'll make you sing O be joyful on the other side of your mouth; a threat, implying the party threatened will be made to cry. To sing O be easy: to appear contented when one has cause to complain, and dare not.

OBSTROPULOUS. Vulgar misnomer of *obstreperous*: as, I was going my rounds, and found this here gemmem very obstropulous, whereof I comprehended him as an auspicious parson. ["Genuine London dialect," remarked Halliwell in 1847. F.]

OCCUPY. To occupy a woman; to have carnal knowledge of her. [Twice thus in Shakespeare. Dr Onions, with the pertinence and economy that characterise his remarkable lexicography: "In consequence of its vulgar use in this sense, this verb was little used in literature in the 17th and 18th century; cf. the *Second Part of King Henry IV*, at II, iv, 159, 'as odious as the word *occupy*.'"]

OCTOGONIANS. This ancient and honourable order met, Nov. 16, 1750, at the Ship and Anchor, Temple Bar.

ODDS PLUT AND HER NAILS. A Welch oath, frequently mentioned in a jocular manner by persons, it is hoped, ignorant of its meaning; which is, By God's blood, and the nails with which he was nailed to the cross.

ODD-COME-SHORTLYS. I'll do it one of these odd-come-shortlys; I will do it some time or another. [Swift, Scott.OD,F.]

OGLES. Eyes. Rum ogles; fine eyes.

OIL OF BARLEY, or BARLEY BROTH. Strong beer.

OIL OF GLADNESS. I will anoint you with the oil of gladness; ironically spoken for, I will beat you. [Dialect has also *oil of birch, hazel, oak, strap*.EDD.]

OIL OF STIRRUP. A dose the cobler gives his wife whenever she is obstropulous.

OLD. Ugly. *Cant.* [In the *old* entries, the word mostly means expert, cunning, experienced, or is an intensive meaning great, wonderful, or extremely objectionable.]

OLD DOG AT IT. Expert, accustomed.

OLD HAND. Knowing or expert in any business. [Cf. the Yorkshire *old-hand*, to deceive, delude, and the War and post-War phrase *come the old soldier* (*over*), to deceive (trans. and intransitive), from *old soldier*, a knowing one. EDD; B & P.]

OLD HARRY. A composition used by vintners to adulterate their wines; also the nick-name for the Devil.

OLD LING. See OLD HAT. [G means "see *Hat.*" But in dialect *old ling* and its synonyms *old lant* or *Mary* or *wash*=stale urine. EDD.]

OLD Mʀ GORY. A piece of gold.

OLD NICK. The Devil: from *Neken*, the evil spirit of the north. [From *Nicholas.*W.—Dialect has about forty *old* synonyms for the Devil (EDD).]

OLD ONE. The Devil.

OLD PEG. Poor Yorkshire cheese, made of skimmed milk.

OLD ROGER. The Devil.

OLD STAGER. One accustomed to business, one who knows mankind.

OLD TOAST. A brisk old fellow. *Cant.*

OLIVER'S SCULL. A chamber pot. [In derision of Cromwell. Possibly in the American cant *Oliver*, the moon, there is another reference to Cromwell. (See my terminal essay on the English thieves'-cant antecedents of American low slang in I.)]

OLLI COMPOLLI. The name of one of the principal rogues of the canting crew. *Cant.*

OMNIUM GATHERUM. The whole together: jocular imitation of law Latin. [In C15 *omnigatherum*, mock-Latin from *gather.*W.]

ONE IN TEN. A parson: an allusion to his tithes.

ONE OF US, or ONE OF MY COUSINS. A woman of the town, a harlot.

OPEN ARSE. A medlar. See MEDLAR.

ORGAN. A pipe. Will you cock your organ? will you smoke your pipe?

ORTHODOXY AND HETERODOXY. Somebody explained these terms by saying, the first was a man who had a doxy of his own, the second a person who made use of the doxy of another man.

OSCHIVES. Bone-handled knives. *Cant.*

OSMANIANS. A society held at Tunbridge Wells.

OSTLER. Oatstealer. [One of G's little jokes.—From Old Fr. *hostelier*, a hotel-keeper, whence, by modification, the English meaning: stable-man at an inn. W.]

OTTOMY. The vulgar word for a skeleton. [Like *atomy*, *natomy*, *notomy*, a vulgar variant of *anatomy*, colloquial and dialectal for a skeleton, derivatively a very thin person or animal, a very small person, a contemptible person, and a diminished particle. EDD.]

OTTOMISED. To be ottomised; to be dissected. You'll be scragged, ottomised, and grin in a glass case; you'll be hanged, anatomised, and your skeleton kept in a glass case at Surgeons' Hall.

OUT AT HEELS, or OUT AT ELBOWS. In declining circumstances.

OUTRUN THE CONSTABLE. A man who has lived above his means, or income is said to have outrun the constable.

OUTS. A gentleman of three outs. See GENTLEMAN.

OVEN. A great mouth. The old woman would never have looked for her daughter in the oven, had she not been there herself.

OVERSEER. A man standing in the pillory, is, from his elevated situation, said to be made an overseer.

OWL. To catch the owl; a trick practised upon ignorant country boobies, who are decoyed into a barn under pretence of catching an owl, where, after divers preliminaries, the joke ends in their having a pail of water poured upon their heads.

OWL IN AN IVY BUSH. He looks like an owl in an ivy

bush; frequently said of a person with a large frizzled wig, or a woman whose hair is dressed a-la-blowze.

OWLERS. Those who smuggle wool over to France. [B defines *owling* as "one of the earliest forms of smuggling—running wool out of England to the Continent without the payment of dues or against the royal embargo that was constantly being imposed."]

OX HOUSE. He must go through the ox house to bed; a saying of an old fellow who marries a young girl. [Late C17 cant. F.—Signifying, of course, that he has horns, is in short a cuckold.]

OYES. Corruption of oyez, proclaimed by the crier of all courts of justice.

OYSTER. A gob of thick phlegm, spit by a consumptive man; in law Latin, *unum viridum gobbum*.

P'S. To mind one's P's and Q's; to be attentive to the main chance. [The modern sense, not to say or do 'the wrong thing,' is petty by comparison. Note too the C19 dialectal *to be P and Q*, to be of prime quality. EDD.]

P.P.C. An inscription on the visiting cards of our modern fine gentlemen, signifying that they have called *pour prendre congé*, i.e. 'to take leave.' This has of late been ridiculed by cards inscribed D.I.O. i.e. 'Damme, I'm off.'

PACKET. A false report. [Cf. *to sell a packet to*, to hoax.]

PACKTHREAD. To talk packthread; to use indecent language well wrapt up. [In the North Country, merely to talk nonsense. EDD.]

PAD. The highway, or a robber thereon; also a bed. Foot pads; foot robbers. To go out upon the pad; to go out in order to commit a robbery. [Harman has *high pad*, the highway; as robber, established *ca.* 1600. In sense of bed, it may be a variant of *pod*, cant for a pillow, hence a bed. F.—This last sense survives in American cant. I.]

PAD BORROWERS. Horse stealers.

TO PAD THE HOOF. See TO BEAT THE HOOF. [American tramps' slang for travelling afoot.I.—*Pad it* was fairly general C19 slang for to walk any considerable distance. EDD.]

PADDINGTON FAIR DAY. An execution day, Tyburn being in the parish or neighbourhood of Paddington. To dance the Paddington frisk; to be hanged. [Cf. *Paddington spectacles*, the cap pulled over a criminal's eyes at his hanging.]

PADDY. The general name of an Irishman: being the abbreviation of Patrick, the name of the tutelar saint of that island.

PAINTER. I'll cut your painter for you; I'll send you off; the painter being the rope that holds the boat fast to the ship. *Sea term.*

PAIR OF WINGS. Oars. *Cant.*

TO PALAVER. To flatter: originally an African word for a treaty, talk, or conference. [From Portuguese *palavra*, word or speech. "Used by Portuguese travellers of parleys with natives in West Africa, and brought thence by English sailors." W.— Whereas modern colloquial English has returned to the noun in the sense that was *démodé* in G's time, dialect has preserved G's sense of the verb with the corresponding substantival sense and with the allied sense of a wearisome talker, a person of foolish and showy manners (EDD).]

PALLIARDS. Those whose fathers were clapperdogeons, or beggars born, and who themselves follow the same trade: The female sort beg with a number of children, borrowing them, if they have not a sufficient number of their own, and making them cry by pinching, in order to excite charity; the males make artificial sores on different parts of their bodies, to move compassion. [Fr. *paillards;* C16 cant. F.]

PAM. The knave of clubs. [Short for Fr. *pamphile*, a card-game and especially the knave of clubs. W.]

PANNAM. Bread. [Cant C16-18. Through Lingua Franca, from L. *panis*, bread; cf. *pannam-struck*, starving. Variant *pan(n)-um*. F.—In current French slang, *(du)panam*=bread.]

PANNIER MAN. A servant belonging to the Temple and Gray's Inn, whose office is to announce the dinner. This, in the Temple, is done by blowing a horn; and in Gray's Inn, proclaiming the word Manger, Manger, Manger, in each of the three courts.

PANNY. A house. To do a panny; to rob a house. See the Sessions Papers. Probably, panny originally meant the butler's pantry, where the knives and forks, spoons, &c. are usually kept. *Cant*. [Not in OD.]

PANTER. A hart: that animal is, in the Psalms, said to pant after the fresh water-brooks. Also the human heart, which frequently pants in time of danger. *Cant*.

PANTILE SHOP. A presbyterian, or other dissenting meeting-house, frequently covered with pantiles; called also a cockpit. [Mrs Centlivre, 1715, has *pantile* as an adjective=dissenting.OD.]

PANTLER. A butler.

PAP. Bread sauce; also the food of infants. His mouth is full of pap; he is still a baby. ["In many languages, *papa, mamma*, both occur in the sense of 'breast,' the former surviving in English in the archaic *pap*. . . . and also in the sense of baby-food, the latter passing from Latin into modern languages as the recognised scientific name of the maternal breast, and the basis of a whole zoological nomenclature." W:A.—Cf. North Country *pap-mouth*, a soft or effeminate man.EDD.]

PAPER SCULL. A thin-scull'd foolish fellow.

PAPLER. Milk pottage.

PARELL. Whites of eggs, bay salt, milk, and pump water, beat together, and poured into a vessel of wine to prevent its fretting.

PARENTHESIS. To put a man's nose into a parenthesis; to pull it, the fingers and thumb answering the hooks or crotchets.

PARINGS. The chippings of money. *Cant*.[Error for *clippings*.]

PARISH. His stockings are of two parishes; i.e. they are not fellows. [Two interesting *parish* compounds are *parish-candles*, the stars, and *parish-lamp* or *-lantern*, the moon.EDD.]

PARISH SOLDIER. A jeering name for a militia man: from substitutes being frequently hired by the parish from which one of its inhabitants is drawn.

PARSON. A guide post, hand or finger post by the road side

for directing travellers; compared to a parson, because, like him, it sets people in the right way. See GUIDE POST. He that would have luck in horse-flesh, must kiss a parson's wife.

PARSON PALMER. A jocular name, or term of reproach, to one who stops the circulation of the glass by preaching over his liquor; as it is said was done by a parson of that name whose cellar was under his pulpit. [Cf. the C16-18 *remember parson Mallum:* pray drink about, Sir! F.]

PARTIAL. Inclining more to one side than the other, crooked all o' one hugh. [G's *all o' one hugh* is elucidated by H, who defines *all of a hugh* as "all on one side; falling with a thump; the word *hugh* being pronounced with a grunt. Suffolk."]

PASS BANK. The place for playing at passage, cut into the ground almost like a cock-pit. Also the stock or fund.

PASSAGE. A camp game with three dice; doublets, making up ten or more, to pass or win; any other chances lose.

PAT. Apposite, or to the purpose.

PATE. The head. Carotty-pated; red-haired. [In Shakespeare. Jocular or derisive.F.—Adam Rudipat, i.e. Ruddy-Pate, occurs in the Rolls of *ca.* 1200.W:A.]

PATRICO, or PATER COVE. The fifteenth rank of the canting tribe; strolling priests that marry people under a hedge without gospel or common prayer book; the couple standing on each side of a dead beast, are bid to live together till death them does part; so shaking hands, the wedding is ended. Also any minister or parson. [*Ca.* 1550, *patryng cove; patriarke co,* Awdelay, 1561; 1567, Harman, *patrico.* Either *pater+cove,* or *patter+cove,* or *patter+co,* a lad.OD,F.]

PATTERING. The maundering or pert replies of servants; also talk or pallaver in order to amuse one intended to be cheated. Pattering of prayers; the confused sound of a number of persons praying together. [*Patter* is probably from *paternoster,* which, with the *Ave Maria,* is the most famous of all prayers, and often appears as simply *pater* (cf. *ave*). Prayers being often repeated or mumbled. . . . But there is perhaps a reference to the pattering of rain.W.—Cf. *patter flash,* which=to talk cant: so does *flash the patter.*]

TO PAUM. To conceal in the hand. To paum a die; to hide a die in the palm of the hand. He paums; he cheats. Don't pretend to paum that upon me. [I.e. *palm;* French influence.]

PAUNCH. The belly. Some think Paunch was the original name of that facetious prince of puppets, now called Mr Punch, as he is always represented with a very prominent belly; though the common opinion is, that both the name and character were taken from a celebrated Italian comedian, called Polichenello.

PAVIOURS' WORKSHOP. The street. [From *paviour, pavior, paver*, a paving-stone, still in dialectal use. EDD.]

PAW. A hand or foot; look at his dirty paws. Fore paw; the hand. Hind paw; the foot. To paw; to touch or handle clumsily.

PAW PAW TRICKS. Naughty tricks; an expression used by nurses, &c. to children. [First recorded in G. Perhaps a reduplication on the 'dirty' implication in *paw*.]

TO PAY. To smear over. To pay the bottom of a ship or boat; to smear it over with pitch: The devil to pay, and no pitch hot or ready. *Sea term.*—Also to beat; as, I will pay you as Paul paid the Ephesians, over the face and eyes, and all your d—d jaws. To pay through the nose; to pay an extravagant price.

TO PEACH. To impeach; called also to blow the gab, squeak, or turn stag. [Twice thus in Shakespeare. O.—Literary in C16-17, colloquial in C18-19, slang in C20.]

PEAK. Any kind of lace.

PEAL. To ring a peal in a man's ears; to scold at him: his wife rang him such a peal! [Cf. dialectal *to be, to get into a peal*, i.e. a temper, and *to keep, to lead a peal*, to make a noise or disturbance. EDD.]

PECCAVI. To cry peccavi; to acknowledge one's self in an error, to own a fault: from the Latin *peccavi*, I have sinned.

PECK. Victuals. Peck and booze; victuals and drink. [Cant C16-17, colloquial C18. (OD).]

PECKISH Hungry.

PECULIAR. A mistress. [Early C17 as wife, late C17 as here. OD.]

PED. A basket. *Cant.* [G says cant, so too B.E.; but it is a very old dialectal word (OD,EDD).]

PEDLAR'S FRENCH. The cant language. Pedlar's pony; a walking-stick. [As cant in Harman; in C19 sometimes=unintelligible jargon.OD.]

TO PEEL. To strip: allusion to the taking off the coat or rind of an orange or apple.

PEEPER. A spying-glass; also a looking-glass. Track up the dancers, and pike with the peeper; whip up stairs, and run off with the looking-glass. *Cant.* [The various senses of *peeper(s)* verged on cant in C17-18 and have been slang since *ca.* 1800.F.]

PEEPERS. Eyes. Single-peeper, a one-eyed man.

PEEPING TOM. A nick name for a curious prying fellow; derived from an old legendary tale, told of a taylor of Coventry, who, when Godiva, countess of Chester, rode at noon quite naked through that town, in order to procure certain immunities for the inhabitants (notwithstanding the rest of the people shut up their houses) slily peeped out of his window, for which he was miraculously struck blind. His figure, peeping out of a window, is still kept up in remembrance of the transaction.

PEEPY. Drowsy. [In B.E., 1690. Also dialect.F,EDD.]

TO PEER. To look about, to be circumspect.

PEERY. Inquisitive, suspicious. The cull's peery; that fellow suspects something. There's a peery, 'tis snitch; we are observed, there's nothing to be done. [First recorded in B.E., 1690 OD.]

PEG. Old Peg; poor hard Suffolk or Yorkshire cheese. A peg is also a blow with a straight arm; a term used by the professors of gymnastic arts. A peg in the day-light, the victualling office, or the haltering-place; a blow in the eye, stomach, or under the ear.

PEG TRANTUM'S. Gone to Peg Trantum's; dead. [In E. Anglia *Peg Trantum*=a hoyden, a tomboy.EDD.]

PEGO. The penis of man or beast. [Perhaps from Gr. *pegë*, a spring.F.]

PELL-MELL. Tumultuously, helter skelter, jumbled together.

PELT. A heat, chase, or passion: as, What a pelt he was in!

Pelt is also the skin of several beasts. [Cf. Shakespeare's *pelt*, to utter angry words.O.]

PENANCE BOARD. The pillory.

PENNY WISE AND POUND FOOLISH. Saving in small matters, and extravagant in great.

PENNYWORTH. An equivalent. A good pennyworth; a cheap bargain.

PENTHOUSE NAB. A broad-brimmed hat. [*Nab* is a mark of cant.]

PEPPERED. Infected with the venereal disease. [Earlier, seriously hurt.F.]

PEPPERY. Warm, passionate.

PERKIN. Water cyder. [I.e. the washing left after the best cider has been made.EDD.]

PERRIWINKLE. A wig.[Deliberate corruption of *perruque*.F.]

PERSUADERS. Spurs. [First record.]

PET. In a pet; in a passion or miff. [Dialect has also *in the pet*, *at pet*.EDD.]

PETER. A portmanteau or cloke-bag. Biter of peters; one that makes it a trade to steal boxes and trunks from behind stage coaches or out of waggons. To rob Peter to pay Paul; to borrow of one man to pay another; styled also manœuvring the apostles. [*Peter* is an old English cant word, which has survived in American low slang as a safe.I.]

PETER GUNNER, will kill all the birds that died last summer. A piece of wit commonly thrown out at a person walking through a street or village near London, with a gun in his hand.

PETER LAY. The department of stealing portmanteaus, trunks, &c. [Like next entry, cant.F.]

PETER LUG. Who is Peter Lug? who lets the glass stand at his door, or before him?

PETTICOAT HOLD. One who has an estate during his wife's life, called the apron-string hold.

PETTICOAT PENSIONER. One kept by a woman for secret services. [Cf. *petticoat affair*, one involving a woman, as in Dryden, 1690; *petticoat government*, as in the *Fool of Quality*, 1766; *petticoat merchant*, *petticoat-hunting*, *petticoat-led* established themselves in early C19; *petticoat loose*, compliant (of a woman); *petticoat*, a woman, appears in Prior and Smollett.F,OD.]

PETTISH. Passionate. [In Shakespeare, ill-humoured.O.]

PETTYFOGGER. A little dirty attorney, ready to undertake any litigious or bad cause; it is derived from the French word *petit vogue*, of small credit, or little reputation. [C16. The second element may be obsolete Dutch *focker*, monopolist, cognate with Flemish cant *focken*, to cheat.W.]

PHARAOH. Strong malt liquor. [Earlier, *old Pharaoh*, later *stout Pharaoh*.OD.]

PHILISTINES. Bailiffs, or officers of justice; also drunkards. ["The Philistines are upon thee," *Judges*, xvi.W. In dialect, insects, especially earwigs.EDD.]

PHILO DRACO SANGUINARIANS. A club that met in London.

PHOENIX MEN. Firemen belonging to an insurance office, which gave a badge charged with a phoenix; these men were called likewise firedrakes.

PHRASE OF PAPER. Half a quarter of a sheet. See VESSEL. [*Phrase* or *fraze* is Northern, *vessel* Southern.P.]

PHYZ. The face. Rum phyz; an odd face or countenance.

PICAROON. A pirate; also a sharper. [Also, in obsolete literary English, a plunderer of wrecks, from Sp. *picarón*, a thorough rogue.EDD.]

PICKANINY. A young child, an infant. *Negro term.* [From C17 Negro diminutive of Sp. *pequeño* or Port. *pequeno*, small; cf. Port. *pequenino*, very small.W.]

PICKING. Pilfering, petty larceny.

PICKLE. An arch waggish fellow. In pickle, or in the pickling tub; in a salivation. There are rods in brine, or pickle, for him; a punishment awaits him, or is prepared for him. Pickle herring; the zany or merry andrew of a mountebank. See JACK PUDDING. [Cf. Smollett's title. *Rods in brine* was sometimes *rods in piss*.F.]

PICKT HATCH. To go to the manor of pickt hatch; a cant name for some part of the town noted for bawdy-houses in Shakespeare's time, and used by him in that sense.

PICKTHANK. A tale-bearer or mischief-maker. [In Shakespeare a flatterer or sycophant.O.—In dialect, as in G and as fault-finder.EDD.—Like terminal *monger*, initial *pick* is pejorative, as in *pickpenny*, a medieval name for a miser, *pickpurse* in Chaucer, and *pickharness* in Langland for a stripper of the slain.W:MWAM.]

PICTURE FRAME. The sheriff's picture frame; the gallows or pillory. [As gallows still in American cant.I.]

TO PIDDLE. To make water; a childish expression; as Mammy, I want to piddle. Piddling also means trifling, or doing any thing in a small degree: perhaps from peddling.

PIECE. A wench. A damned good or bad piece; a girl who is more or less active and skilful in the amorous congress. [This word in C19-20 is less derogatory and was a favourite with the soldiers in 1914-1918 for a sweetheart or the girl with whom one walked out.—In dialect as in Middle English, occasionally of a man (F,EDD).]

PIG. Sixpence, a sow's baby. Pig-widgeon; a simpleton. To pig together; to lie or sleep together, two or more in a bed. Cold pig; a jocular punishment inflicted by the maid servants, or other females of the house, on persons lying over long in bed: it consists in pulling off all the bed clothes, and leaving them to pig or lie in the cold. To buy a pig in a poke; to purchase any thing without seeing it. Pig's eyes; small eyes. Pigsnyes; the same: a vulgar term of endearment to a woman. He can have boiled pig at home; a mark of being master of his own house: an allusion to a well-known poem and story. Brandy is Latin for pig and goose; an apology for drinking a dram after either.

PIG-HEADED. Obstinate.

PIG RUNNING. A piece of game frequently practised at fairs, wakes, &c. A large pig, whose tail is cut short, and both soaped and greased, being turned out, is hunted by the young men and boys, and becomes the property of him who can catch and hold him by the tail, above the height of his head.

PIGEON. A weak silly fellow easily imposed on. To pigeon; to cheat. To milk the pigeon; to attempt impossibilities, to be put to shifts for want of money. To fly a blue pigeon; to steal

260

lead off a church. [Cf. Thackeray's *Captain Rook and Mr Pigeon.*
F.]

PIGEONS. Sharpers, who, during the drawing of the lottery,
wait ready mounted near Guildhall, and, as soon as the first
two or three numbers are drawn, which they receive from a
confederate on a card, ride with them full speed to some distant insurance office, before fixed on, where there is another of
the gang, commonly a decent looking woman, who takes care
to be at the office before the hour of drawing; to her he secretly
gives the number, which she insures for a considerable sum;
thus biting the biter. [In American criminal slang a *pigeon-joint*
is either a store where burglars' tools may be purchased, or a
resort specialising in the supply of such tools.I.]

PIGEON'S MILK. Boys and novices are frequently sent on
the first of April, to buy pigeon's milk. [The root-idea may be
traced to Aristophanes (F), and the general vocabulary of
April-foolery is treated in my *All Fools' Day* in *The New Statesman and Nation* of March 28, 1931.—In dialect, *pigeon's milk* is
used as in G, but, by extension, it means also a novice, a green-
horn.EDD.]

TO PIKE. To run away. Pike off; run away. [*Pike off*, in cant,
=to die, and in dialect *pike* by itself signifies merely to go.F,
EDD.]

PILGRIM'S SALVE. A sirreverence, human excrement.

PILL, or PEELE GARLICK. Said originally to mean one
whose skin or hair had fallen off from some disease, chiefly the
venereal one; but now commonly used by persons speaking of
themselves: as, There stood poor pill garlick; i.e. there stood I.
[*Pill garlick* in frequent use from *ca.* 1450 to 1800. *Pill* or *peele*=
pilled, i.e. peeled; humorous for a bald-headed person and
often spelt *pilgarlic*.W.—In dialect, usually a weakling or a
simpleton.EDD.]

PILLALOO. The Irish cry or howl at funerals. [Also in several
English dialects.EDD.]

PIMP. A male procurer, or cock bawd; also a small faggot
used about London for lighting fires, named from introducing
the fire to the coals. [Obscure origin. Recorded in 1607.OD.—

Never slang and hardly colloquial, but, like all words convey-
ing a 'strong' idea, it has been avoided by the fastidious and
therefore regarded by them as vulgar. Many vulgarisms that
are perfectly good English are in general considered as colloquial: especially those indicative of bodily functions or parts.]
PIMP WHISKIN. A top trader in pimping. [Ford, 1638;
pimp-whisk, ca. 1700. Both often meant merely a pimp.OD.]
PIN. In or to a merry pin; almost drunk: an allusion to a sort
of tankard, formerly used in the north, having silver pegs or
pins set at equal distances from the top to the bottom; by the
rules of good fellowship, every person drinking out of one of
these tankards, was to swallow the quantity contained between two pins; if he drank more or less, he was to continue
drinking till he ended at a pin: by this means persons unaccus-
tomed to measure their draughts were obliged to drink the
whole tankard. Hence, when a person was a little elevated
with liquor, he was said to have drunk to a merry pin. [G misses several colloquial *pin* phrases that were in general use in C18.]
PIN BASKET. The youngest child.
PIN MONEY. An allowance settled on a married woman for
her pocket expences. [This phrase was popularised by the
playwrights of 1670-1710. (F,OD).]
PINCH. At a pinch; on an exigency. [C15.OD.]
TO PINCH ON THE PARSON'S SIDE. To defraud the
parson of his tithes.
PINCHERS. Rogues who, in changing money, by dexterity of
hand frequently secrete two or three shillings out of the change
of a guinea. This species of roguery is called the pinch, or pinching lay.
TO PINK. To stab or wound with a small sword: probably
derived from the holes formerly cut in both men and women's
clothes, called pinking. Pink of the fashion; the top of the mode.
To pink and wink; frequently winking the eyes through a
weakness in them. [Shakespeare has *pinked*, ornamented with
perforations; and *pink of courtesy*.O.]
PINKING DINDEE. A sweater or mohawk. *Irish.*

PINNERIANS. A society formerly held at the Sun in Clare-market.

PINTLE SMITH, or PINTLE TAGGER. A surgeon. [From A.S. *pintel*, the male-member, hence the Yorkshire *pintle-twister*, a whore.EDD.]

PIPER. A broken winded horse. [Perhaps connected with *pipers*, the lungs.F. Also called a *roarer*.]

PISCINARIANS. A club or brotherhood, A.D. 1743.

PISS. He will piss when he can't whistle; he will be hanged. He shall not piss my money against the wall; he shall not have my money to spend in liquor.

> *He who once a good name gets,*
> *May piss a-bed, and say he sweats.*

[Good and current English till *ca.* 1760, when the word began to be avoided. This avoidance led to an obsessive imputation of grossness, hence of vulgar colloquialism. Cf. note on *pimp*.—Dialect has many quaint phrases, of which these may be noted: —*piss by the pot*, to commit adultery (of a married man); *piss in a pot*, to plan mischief; *piss in the sheath*, of oats unable to emerge from their grass covering; *piss out at the tap*, of a liquid passing through any narrow passage.EDD.]

PISS-BURNED. Discoloured: commonly applied to a discoloured grey wig.

PISSING DOWN ANY ONE'S BACK. Flattering him.

PISSING PINS AND NEEDLES. To have a gonorrhea.

PISS MAKER. A great drinker, one much given to liquor.

PISS POT HALL. A house at Clopton, near Hackney, built by a potter chiefly out of the profits of chamber-pots, in the bottom of which the portrait of Dr Sacheverel was depicted.

PISS PROPHET. A physician who judges of the diseases of his patients solely by the inspection of their urine. [Recorded 1625.OD.]

PISS-PROUD. Having a false erection. That old fellow thought he had an erection, but his——was only piss-proud; said of any old fellow who marries a young wife.

PIT. To lay pit and boxes into one; an operation in midwifery

263

or copulation, whereby the division between the anus and vagina is cut through, broken, and demolished; a simile borrowed from the playhouse, when, for the benefit of some favourite player, the pit and boxes are laid together. The pit is also the hole under the gallows, where poor rogues unable to pay the fees are buried.

PITT'S PICTURE. A window stopt up on the inside, to save the tax imposed in that gentleman's administration. *Party wit.*

PIT-A-PAT. The palpitation of the heart: as, My heart went pit-a-pat. Pintledy-pantledy; the same.

PITCHER. The miraculous pitcher, that holds water with the mouth downwards: a woman's commodity. She has cracked her pitcher or pipkin; she has lost her maidenhead.

PITCH-KETTLED. Stuck fast, confounded.

PIZZY CLUB. A society held, A.D. 1744, at the sign of the tower, on Tower-hill: president, Don Pizzaro.

PLAISTER OF WARM GUTS. One warm belly clapped to another: a receipt frequently prescribed for different disorders.

PLANT. The place in the house of the fence, where stolen goods are secreted. [Like the next, has survived in thieves' slang.]

TO PLANT. To lay, place, or hide. Plant your wids and stow them: be careful what you say, or let slip. Also to bury: as, He was planted by the parson.

PLATE. Money, silver, prize. He is in for the plate; he has won the *heat*, i.e. is infected with the venereal disorder: a simile drawn from horse-racing. When the plate fleet comes in; when money comes to hand. [*Plate* in Shakespeare, a piece of money. O.]

PLATTER-FACED. Broad-faced.

PLAY. To play booty; to play with an intention to lose. To play the whole game; to cheat. To play least in sight; to hide or keep out of the way. To play the devil; to be guilty of some great irregularity or mismanagement.

PLUCK. Courage. He wants pluck; he is a coward. Against the pluck; against the inclination. Pluck the ribbon; ring the bell. To pluck a crow with one; to settle a dispute, to reprove one for some past transgression. To pluck a rose; an expression said to be used by women for going to the necessary-house, which in the country usually stands in the garden. To pluck also signifies to deny a degree to a candidate at one of the universities, on account of insufficiency. [As courage, adopted in C18 by the Ring: it had meant an animal's viscera; in the sense of courage, "blackguardly" says Scott, and not used by ladies before the Crimean War (H). Cf. modern *guts*, courage.W.]

PLUG TAIL. A man's penis.

PLUMB. An hundred thousand pounds.

PLUMP. Fat, full, fleshy. Plump in the pocket; full in the pocket. To plump; to strike or shoot. I'll give you a plump in the bread basket, or the victualling office; I'll give you a blow in the stomach. Plump his peepers, or daylights; give him a blow in the eyes. He pulled out his pops and plumped him; he drew out his pistols and shot him. A plumper; a single vote at an election. Plump also means directly, or exactly: as, It fell plump upon him; it fell directly upon him.

PLUMP CURRANT. I am not plump currant; I am out of sorts.

PLUMPERS. Contrivances said to be formerly worn by old maids, for filling out a pair of shrivelled cheeks.

PLYER. A crutch; also a trader. [The former, cant.F.]

POGY. Drunk. [Almost certainly cant.]

POINT. To stretch a point; to exceed some usual limit, to take a great stride. Breeches were usually tied up with points, a kind of short laces, formerly given away by the churchwardens at Whitsuntide, under the denomination of tags; by taking a great stride these were stretched.

POISONED. Big with child: that wench is poisoned, see how her belly is swelled. Poisoned-pated; red-haired. [Doubtless one should read *poison-pated*.]

POKE. A blow with the fist: I'll lend you a poke. A poke likewise means a sack: whence, to buy a pig in a poke, i.e. to buy any thing without seeing or properly examining it. [Also a pocket, Fr. *poche*.]

POKER. A sword. Fore pokers; aces and kings at cards.

POLE. He is like a rope-dancer's pole, lead at both ends; saying of a stupid sluggish fellow.

POLISH. To polish the king's iron with one's eyebrows; to be in gaol, and look through the iron grated windows. To polish a bone, to eat a meal. Come and polish a bone with me; come and eat a dinner or supper with me. [Cf. Irish *polish*, to eat up completely (EDD), and the modern slang, *polish it off*.]

POLL. The head, jolly nob, napper, or knowledge box; also a wig. [As wig obviously derivative.—Also a woman, especially a prostitute: Horace Walpole accused the ladies of his time of *pollyhood*: that they were "more fond than virtuous." F.—And *pretty poll*, of a parrot, dates back to early C17.OD.]

POLT. A blow. Lend him a polt in the muns; give him a knock in the face. [Common in dialect, which has also *polt*, to strike. EDD.]

TO POMMEL. To beat; originally confined to beating with the hilt of a sword; the knob being, from its similarity to a small apple, called *pomelle;* in Spanish it is still called the apple of the sword. As the clenched fist likewise somewhat resembles an apple, perhaps that might occasion the term pommelling to be applied to fistycuffs.

POMP. To save one's pomp at whist, is to score five before the adversaries are up, or win the game: originally derived from *pimp,* which is Welch for five; and should be, I have saved my pimp.

POMPAGINIS. Aqua pompaginis; pump water. See AQUA.

POMPKIN. A man or woman of Boston in America: from the number of pompkins raised and eaten by the people of that country. Pompkinshire; Boston and its dependencies.

PONTIUS PILATE. A pawnbroker. Pontius Pilate's guards; the first regiment of foot, or royal Scots: so entitled from their supposed great antiquity. Pontius Pilate's counsellor; one who like him can say, *Non invenio causam,* I can find no cause.

POPE. A figure burned annually every fifth of November, in memory of the gunpowder plot, which is said to have been carried on by the Papists. [Cf. Kentish *pope*, to go about on November the fifth with a 'Guy Fawkes.' *Pope* was often used pejoratively as in the Dorsetshire *pope*, an oddly-dressed person. EDD.—Cf. *what a pope of a thing; as drunk as a pope* (cf. *bibamus papaliter*); *pope-holy*, C14-16 for a hypocrite or its adjective; *to know no more than the pope*, to be ignorant (Ray's *Proverbs*, 1670); *poperine pear*, the male member.F.—Religious prejudice.]

POPE'S NOSE. The rump of a turkey.

POPS. Pistols. Pop shop; a pawnbroker's shop. To pop: to pawn; also to shoot. I popt my tatler; I pawned my watch. I popt the cull; I shot the man. His means are two pops and a galloper; that is, he is a highwayman.

POPLERS. Pottage. *Cant.* [Milk-porridge.F.]

PORK. To cry pork; to give intelligence to the undertaker of a funeral: metaphor borrowed from the raven, whose note sounds like the word *pork*. Ravens are said to smell carrion at a distance.

PORKER. A hog; also a Jew.

PORRIDGE. Keep your breath to cool your porridge; i.e. hold your tongue. [In Shakespeare as pottage, soup; the modern sense is post-Shakespearean.O.—"Seems to be combined from *pottage* and Middle English *porrets*, plural of *porret*, leek." W:ROW.]

PORRIDGE ISLAND. An alley leading from St Martin's church-yard to Round-court, chiefly inhabited by cooks, who cut off ready-dressed meat of all sorts, and also sell soup.

POSEY or POESY. A nosegay. I shall see you ride backwards up Holborn-hill, with a book in one hand and a posey in t'other; i.e. I shall see you go to be hanged. Malefactors who piqued themselves on being properly equipped for that occasion, had always a nosegay to smell to, and a prayer book, although they could not read. [From the verses or motto accompanying the gift of a bunch of flowers.EDD.]

POSSE MOBILITATIS. The mob. [On the analogy of *posse comitatus*, a sheriff's potential band for the suppression of riots. Dialectally, *posse* and its variants had early come to mean a great muster or company of people.EDD.]

POST MASTER GENERAL. The prime minister who has the patronage of all posts and places.

POST NOINTER. A house painter, who occasionally paints or anoints posts. Knight of the post; a false evidence, one ready to swear any thing for hire. From post to pillar; backwards and forwards.

POSTILLION OF THE GOSPEL. A parson who hurries over the service.

POT. The pot calls the kettle black a-se; one rogue exclaims against another.

POT CONVERTS. Proselytes to the Romish church, made by the distribution of victuals and money.

POT HUNTER. One who hunts more for the sake of the prey than the sport. Pot valiant; courageous from drink. Pot-wallopers; persons intitled to vote in certain boroughs by having boiled a pot there. [In dialect, *pot-walloper*=a scullion or a toper.EDD.]

POTATOE TRAP. The mouth. Shut your potatoe trap and give your tongue a holiday; i.e. be silent. *Irish wit.*

POTHOOKS AND HANGERS. A scrawl, bad writing. [Cf. dialectal *pot hooks and ladles*, the letters *p* and *q*.EDD.]

POT-WABBLERS. Persons entitled to vote for members of parliament in certain boroughs, from having boiled their pots therein. These boroughs are called pot-wabbling boroughs. [Such qualification was abolished in 1832.F.]

POULAIN. A bubo. *French.*

POUND. A prison. See LOB'S POUND. Pounded; imprisoned. Shut up in the parson's pound; married. [The modern sense is in Shakespeare.O.]

POWDER MONKEY. A boy on board a ship of war, whose business it is to fetch powder from the magazine.

POWDERING TUB. The same as pickling tub. See PICKLING TUB. [The reference should be to PICKLE.]

PRAD LAY. Cutting bags from behind horses. *Cant.* [*Prad* is either the old cant for a horse or A.S. *praet*, craft, a trick.F,EDD.]

PRANCER. A horse. Prancer's nab; a horse's head, used as a seal to a counterfeit pass. At the sign of the prancer's poll, i.e. the nag's head.[Cant.F.—In dialect, prancer=a dancer.EDD.]

PRATE ROAST. A talkative boy. *Cant.* [In cant, *prate*= tongue.F.—G's term occurs also in dialect.EDD.]

PRATING CHEAT. The tongue.

PRATTS. Buttocks; also a tinder box. *Cant.* [Also thighs, and in venery the singular denotes the pudend.F.—In American low slang, *pratts* still=the buttocks and derivatively a hip-pocket.I.]

PRATTLE BROTH. Tea. See CHATTER BROTH, SCANDAL BROTH, &c.

PRATTLING BOX. The pulpit.

PRAY. She prays with her knees upwards; said of a woman much given to gallantry and intrigue. At her last prayers; saying of an old maid.

PREADAMITE QUACABITES. This great and laudable society (as they term themselves) held their grand chapter at the Coal-hole.

PREY. Money. [Cant.F.]

PRICK. The virile member. [At least as early as 1592 in written record and probably much earlier in speech. *Prick* would seem to have become a low word *ca.* 1700. In the C16 it was, though even then a vulgarism in this sense, used as a woman's endearment for a man: an equivalent to 'sweetheart.' OD.— In Shakespeare it is employed "often with an indelicate quibble;" in Shakespeare, too, *pillicock*=the member; and in Elizabethan times *pillicock*, like *prick*, was an endearment, with this difference, that *pillicock* was directed to a young boy (Florio, Cotgrave, Urquhart).O. In Florio, Minsheu, Jonson, Heywood, Beaumont & Fletcher, Massinger, Rochester, Cotton, Aubrey, Etherege, the Earl of Cork, Hanbury Williams, Burns. In 1885 Sir Richard Burton uses *prickle*, which dates back to *ca.* 1550.F.—*Penis* is technical; literary English demands *member* or *membrum virile.* Of the synonyms quoted by F, the following are the chief operative sources:—Shakespeare 7, Florio 4, Rochester 4, Urquhart 28, Durfey 3, Cleland 3, Burns 2, and Whitman 3.—*Prick* is still a very common word, but it now ranks definitely as, not a vulgarism but a vulgar colloquialism, and *you silly prick* is an expression of considerable contempt:

except in this phrase, the male member does not convey contempt, and even *you silly p—k* is much less frequently heard than the phrases in which *c—t* and *twat* constitute the insulting or abusive element; moreover, while *you p—k!* does not exist, *you c—t* and *you twat* do exist and were, in fact, frequently used by the soldiers in 1914-1918. There is some psychological reason for this, and I put it forward as a mere suggestion that, in the vivid vocabulary of venery, it is perhaps natural that, in the act of kind, the passive (strictly, the relatively passive) organ, like most 'sufferers,' receives a certain amount of scorn, not necessarily and not usually overt but implied or latent or rather subconscious.]

PRICK-EARED. A prick-eared fellow; one whose ears are longer than his hair; an appellation frequently given to puritans, who considered long hair as the mark of the whore of Babylon. [In Shakespeare, having erect ears.O.]

PRICKLOUSE. A taylor. [C16. Dialectal variants *prick-a-louse, prick-the-louse; prick-the-clout-loon*.EDD.]

PRIEST-CRAFT. The art of awing the laity, managing their consciences, and diving into their pockets.

PRIEST-LINKED. Married.

PRIEST-RIDDEN. Governed by a priest, or priests.

PRIG. A thief, a cheat; also a conceited coxcomical fellow. [In Shakespeare. In first two senses, a cant word.O.—As a 'superior' person, *prig* established itself, 1670-1700, thanks to the dramatists of the period.F.]

PRIG NAPPER. A thief taker.

PRIGGERS. Thieves in general. Priggers of prancers; horse stealers. Priggers of cacklers; robbers of hen-roosts. [The word itself and the two phrases are wholly cant.]

PRIGGING. Riding; also lying with a woman. [The second meaning is derivative, both being cant: but cf. Yorkshire *prig*, to move along, to ride (EDD), which I feel to be cognate with the archaic *prick*, to ride, current at least as early as 1400,—appearing in the famous first line of *The Faerie Queene*, "A gentle Knight was pricking on the plaine,"—used by Milton in *Paradise Lost*,—and revived by Scott in *Marmion*. (OD).]

270

PRIGSTAR. A rival in love.

PRIMINARY. I had like to be brought into a priminary; i.e. into trouble, from *premunire*. [In dialect (variants *priminery*, *primminnerry*, *primanaire*) also confusion, perplexity.EDD.]

PRINCE PRIG. A king of the gypsies; also the head thief or receiver general.

PRINCES. When the majesty of the people was a favourite term in the House of Commons, a celebrated wit, seeing chimney sweepers dancing on a May day, styled them the young princes.

PRINCOD. A pincushion. *Scotch.*—Also a round plump man or woman.

PRINCOX. A pert, lively, forward fellow. [In Shakespeare, a pert saucy boy.O.—In dialect, the North Country form of *princock*, same meaning.EDD.]

PRINCUM PRANCUM. Mrs Princum Prancum; a nice, precise, formal madam. [Obviously from verbs *prink* and *prank*. EDD.]

PRINKING. Dressing over nicely: prinked up as if he came out of a bandbox, or fit to sit upon a cupboard's head. [Dialectal variant, *prinky*. EDD.—Late C18 Exmoor had *prinked* in this sense.G.]

PRINT. All in print; quite neat or exact, set, screwed up. Quite in print; set in a formal manner. [Twice in Shakespeare *in print*=with exactness, to a nicety.O.]

PRISCIAN. To break Priscian's head; to write or speak false grammar. Priscian was a famous grammarian, who flourished at Constantinople in the year 525; and who was so devoted to his favourite study, that to speak false Latin in his company, was as disagreeable to him as to break his head. [The phrase appears early in C16 (Skelton); from *diminuere Prisciani caput*.F. —Shakespeare has *Priscian a little scratched*.O.]

PRITTLE PRATTLE. Insignificant talk: generally applied to women and children.

PROG. Provision. Rum prog; choice provision. To prog; to be on the hunt for provision: called in the military term to forage. [C17 slang, perhaps cant.OD.—Cf. dialectal *progger*, a beggar, also food, and *on the progging order*, able to forage for oneself. EDD.]

PROPERTY. To make a property of any one; to make him a conveniency, tool, or cat's paw; to use him as one's own. [In Shakespeare also, a mere means to an end, with verb *property* in same sense. O.]

PROPHET. The prophet; the Cock at Temple Bar: so called in 1788, by the bucks of the town, of the inferior order.

PROPS. Crutches.

PROUD. Desirous of copulation. A proud bitch; a bitch at heat, or desirous of a dog. [Shakespeare uses it as sensually excited, lascivious. O.—Dialect employs the word also of a sow (EDD), and in Northern dialect of *ca.* 1800 it also meant large. P.]

PROVENDER. He from whom any money is taken on the highway: perhaps providor, or provider. *Cant.*

PRUNELLA. Mr Prunella; a parson: parsons' gowns being frequently made of prunella.

TO PRY. To examine minutely into a matter or business. A prying fellow; a man of impertinent curiosity, apt to peep and inquire into other men's secrets. [The word is here out of place, for it has from M.E. times been good English.]

PUBLIC LEDGER. A prostitute: because, like that paper, she is open to all parties.

PUCKER. All in a pucker; in a dishabille. Also in a fright: as, She was in a terrible pucker. [The latter, frequent in dialect; cf. Lancashire *puckerashun*, vexation or a state of excitement. EDD.]

PUCKER WATER. Water impregnated with alum, or other astringents, used by old experienced traders to counterfeit virginity.

PUDDINGS. The guts: I'll let out your puddings. [The sense survives in dialect; cf. *black pudding*. Of Pudding Lane, London, Stow, 1598, remarks that it was so called "because the butchers of Eastcheap have their scalding-house for hogs there, and their puddings, with other filth of beasts, are voided down that way to their dung-boats, on the Thames." W.]

PUDDING-HEADED FELLOW. A stupid fellow, one whose brains are all in confusion.

PUDDING SLEEVES. A parson.

PUDDING TIME. In good time, or at the beginning of a meal: pudding formerly making the first dish. To give the crow a pudding; to die. You must eat some cold pudding, to settle your love. [The first phrase, C16.OD.]

PUFF, or PUFFER. One who bids at auctions, not with an intent to buy, but only to raise the price of the lot; for which purpose many are hired by the proprietor of the goods on sale. [Other early senses of *puff* are a sham, an impostor, a false promise, a gambler's confederate.F.—Cf. dialectal *puff and lal*, mere verbiage, utter nonsense, empty boasting.EDD.]

PUFF GUTS. A fat man.

PUFFING. Bidding at an auction, as above; also praising any thing above its merits, from interested motives. The art of puffing is, at present, greatly practised, and essentially necessary, in all trades, professions, and callings. To puff and blow; to be out of breath.

PUG. A Dutch pug: a kind of lap-dog, formerly much in vogue; also a general name for a monkey. [Also in C17 a whore.F.— As an adjective it implies smallness or inferiority (OD).]

PUG CARPENTER. An inferior carpenter, one employed only in small jobs.

PUG DRINK. Watered cyder.

PUGNOSED, or PUGIFIED. A person with a snub or turned up nose.

PULLY HAWLY. To have a game at pully hawly; to romp with women. [Colloquially, *pully hauly* by itself=a rough-and-tumble and *to play at pully hauly*=to copulate.F.—In Norfolk and Suffolk in C18 and early C19, *pulling-time* was "the evening of a fair, when the country fellows pull the wenches about. Called *pulling and hauling time* in Yorkshire." P.—Likewise, in C19 Sussex *dragging time* was that at which, not necessarily in the evening, the lads pulled the lasses about.EDD.—For a vivid picture of an old Northern fair, see Hugh Walpole's remarkable novel, *Rogue Herries*, 1930.]

PUMP. A thin shoe. To pump; to endeavour to draw a secret from any one without his perceiving it. Your pump is good, but your sucker is dry: said by one to a person who is attempting to pump him. Pumping was also a punishment for bailiffs, who attempted to act in privileged places, such as the Mint, Temple, &c. It is also a piece of discipline administered to a pickpocket caught in the fact, when there is no pond at hand. To pump ship; to make water, and sometimes to vomit. *Sea phrase.* [The first sense appears in Nashe and Shakespeare.F.]

PUMP-WATER. He was christened in pump water; commonly said of a person that has a red face.

PUNCH. A liquor called by foreigners Contradiction, from its being composed of spirits to make it strong, water to make it weak, lemon juice to make it sour, and sugar to make it sweet. Punch is also the name of the prince of puppets, the chief wit and support of a puppet show. To punch it, is a cant term for running away. Punchable; old passable money, anno 1695. A girl that is ripe for man, is called a punchable wench. [As a blow, C16; as a drink, early C17; *Punch*, ca. 1700, earlier *Punchinello* (*ca.* 1660) with variant *Polichinello*. The last sense in G comes from the instrument, from *ca.* 1500.OD.—With *to punch it* cf. *to beat it.*]

PUNK. A whore; also a soldier's trull. See TRULL. [A very frequent word in Elizabethan and in Restoration plays.— Derivatives: *punker*, a wencher, and *punkish*, meretricious.F.]

PUNY. Weak. A puny child; a weak little child. A puny stomach; a weak stomach. Puny, or puisne judge; the last made judge.

PUPIL MONGERS. Persons at the universities who make it their business to instruct and superintend a number of pupils.

PUPPY. An affected or conceited coxcomb.

PURBLIND. Dim-sighted. [Should not be here. Has always been good English.]

PURE. A harlot, or lady of easy virtue.

PUREST PURE. A courtezan of high fashion.

PURL. Ale in which wormwood has been infused, or ale and bitters drunk warm. [In Pepys, 1680.F.]

PURL ROYAL. Canary wine, with a dash of tincture of wormwood.

PURSE PROUD. One that is vain of his riches.

PURSENETS. Goods taken up at thrice their value, by young spendthrifts, upon trust. [Cf. *purse-net* (sometimes called a tunnel-pipe), the moveable net in which ducks are snared.EDD.]

PURSER'S PUMP. A bassoon: from its likeness to a syphon, called a purser's pump.

PURSY, or PURSIVE. Short-breathed, or foggy, from being over fat. [So in Shakespeare, who has it = fat.O.—Fr. *poussif*, L. *pulsus* (throbbing). Often in C17-18 of horses.W:ROW.]

PUSHING SCHOOL. A fencing school; also a brothel. [Cf. the soldiers' 1914-1918 *square-pushing*, usually just walking out with a girl, rarely fornicating, and as an adjective, derivatively, smart. B & P.]

PUT. A country put; an ignorant awkward clown. To put upon any one; to attempt to impose on him, or to make him the butt of the company. [The noun was originally C17 slang; not always with *country*.OD.]

PUZZLE-CAUSE. A lawyer who has a confused understanding. [In M.E., *puzzle* was *opposaile*, something put before one, a 'poser.' Such abridgement is common in English.W:ROW.]

PUZZLE-TEXT. An ignorant blundering parson.

Q **UACK.** An ungraduated ignorant pretender to skill in physic, a vendor of nostrums. [The word is echoic. As doctor, short for *quacksalver*, C16, one who sells his salves by his quacking, his noisy patter.W.]

QUACK-SALVER. A mountebank; a seller of salves.

QUACKING CHEAT. A duck. [Cant, C16.F.]

QUAG. Abbreviation of quagmire; marshy, moorish ground. [Probably from dialect.(EDD).]

QUAIL-PIPE. A woman's tongue; also a device to take birds of that name, by imitating their call. Quail-pipe boots; boots resembling a quail-pipe, from the number of plaits: they were much worn in the reign of Charles II. [The device from *ca.*

1400; as throat or voice in Dryden, 1693; as a woman's tongue in B.E., 1690.OD.]

QUAKERS. A religious sect: so called from their agitations in preaching. ["The nickname *Quaker* was given (*ca* 1650) to the Society of Friends, by whom it is not recognized." W.]

QUAKING CHEAT. A calf or sheep. [C16 cant.F.]

QUANDARY. To be in a quandary; to be puzzled. Also one so over-gorged, as to be doubtful which he should do first, sh—e or spew. Some derive the term quandary from the French phrase *qu'en dirai je?* what shall I say of it? others from an Italian word signifying a conjuror's circle. [First in Lyly's *Euphues*, 1579. "It is explained (1582) by Mulcaster as 'of a Latin form used English-like,' and it seems possible that the second element is L. *dare*, to give." W.—The OD offers no explanation, but rejects G's, M.E. *wandreth*, and abbreviated *hypochondry*.— Quite independently of W, I had, long ago, noted the possibilities of any one of the Latin phrases *quam dare?*, *quando dare?* and, less probably, *quantum dare?* There may have been either a combination, or a confusion, or even an accumulation, though *quandary* is more likely, of course, to have come from some one phrase.]

QUARREL-PICKER. A glazier; from the small squares in casements, called *carreaux*, vulgarly quarrels. [C17 pun.F.]

QUARROMES, or QUARRON. A body. *Cant.* [C16 cant.F.]

QUARTERED. Divided into four parts. To be hanged, drawn, and quartered, is the sentence on traitors and rebels. Persons receiving part of the salary of an office from the holder of it, by virtue of an agreement with the donor, are said to be quartered on him. Soldiers billetted on a publican are likewise said to be quartered on him.

TO QUASH. To suppress, annul, or overthrow; vulgarly pronounced *squash:* they squashed the indictment.

QUEAN. A slut, a worthless woman, a strumpet. [In Shakespeare a jade, a hussy.O.—Primarily a woman, but, as in *hussy* and *wench*, the pejorative use set-in early. Cf. *to play the quean*, the whore; *queanery*, woman kind, harlotry.F.—In some dialects *quean* still=a woman, in others it is an endearment. Note too the dialectal *queanish*, effeminate (cf. pre-Warslang, *queanie*, a sodomite); *quean-bairn*, a female child, and *quean-lassie*, a young girl; *quean-crazed* or *-fond* or *-strucken*, of a man infatuated with a woman; *quean-house*, a brothel; *quean-hefted*, beset with women (lewd sense).EDD.]

QUEEN DICK. To the tune of the life and death of Queen Dick. That happened in the reign of Queen Dick; i.e. never.

QUEEN STREET. A man governed by his wife, is said to live in Queen-street, or at the sign of the Queen's Head.

QUEER, or QUIRE. Base, roguish, bad, naught, or worthless. How queerly the cull touts; how roguishly the fellow looks. It also means odd, uncommon. *Cant.* [In Awdelay, 1560, *quire*, and in Harman, 1567, *quyer*, both cant. Earlier still in Scottish (W). One of the first examples of the modern sense is seen in 1712 in *The Spectator:* "a queer fellow." F.—In American cant, *queer* as noun=counterfeit money and as adjective: crooked; criminal; and sexually perverted (men or boys).I.]

QUEER AS DICK'S HATBAND. Out of order, without knowing one's disease.

TO QUEER. To puzzle or confound. I have queered the old full bottom; i.e. I have puzzled the judge. To queer one's ogles among bruisers; to darken one's day-lights.

QUEER BAIL. Insolvent sharpers, who make a profession of bailing persons arrested: they are generally styled Jew bail, from that branch of business being chiefly carried on by the sons of Juda. The lowest sort of these, who borrow or hire clothes to appear in, are called Mounters, from their mounting particular dresses suitable to the occasion. *Cant.*

QUEER BIRDS. Rogues relieved from prison, and returned to their old trade. [C16 cant.F.]

QUEER BIT-MAKERS. Coiners. *Cant.*

QUEER BITCH. An odd out-of-the-way fellow.

QUEER BLUFFER. The master of a public house, the resort of rogues and sharpers, a cut-throat inn or alehouse keeper.

QUEER BUNG. An empty purse. [Cant.]

QUEER CHECKERS. Among strolling players, door-keepers who defraud the company, by falsely checking the number of people in the house.

QUEER COLE FENCER. A putter off, or utterer, of bad money. [This and all the other *queer* terms are cant of either C16 or C17 origin.]

QUEER COLE MAKER. A maker of bad money.

QUEER COVE. A rogue. *Cant.*

QUEER CUFFIN. A justice of the peace; also a churl.

QUEER DEGEN. An ordinary sword, brass or iron hilted.

QUEER KEN. A prison. *Cant.*

QUEER KICKS. A bad pair of breeches.

QUEER MORT. A diseased strumpet. *Cant.*

QUEER NAB. A felt hat, or other bad hat.

QUEER PLUNGERS. Cheats who throw themselves into the water, in order that they may be taken up by their accomplices, who carry them to one of the houses appointed by the humane society for the recovery of drowned persons, where they are rewarded by the society with a guinea each; and the supposed drowned person, pretending he was driven to that extremity by great necessity, is also frequently sent away with a contribution in his pocket.

QUEER PRANCER. A bad, worn-out, foundered horse; also a cowardly or faint-hearted horse-stealer.

QUEER ROOSTER. An informer that pretends to be sleeping, and thereby overhears the conversation of thieves in night cellars.

QUEER WEDGES. Large buckles.

TO QUIBBLE. To make subtle distinctions; also to play upon words. [Has always been good English.]

QUICK AND NIMBLE. More like a bear than a squirrel. Jeeringly said to any one moving sluggishly on a business or errand that requires dispatch.

QUID. The quantity of tobacco put into the mouth at one time. To quid tobacco; to chew tobacco. *Quid est hoc? hoc est* quid; also a shilling. [With the noun and the verb, as they relate to tobacco, cf. the dialectal noun and verb *quid*, the cud, to chew the cud. *Quid* and *cud* are basically the same word.EDD.

—As money, never, I think, a shilling, but in C17 a guinea and later a pound (W).]

QUIDS. Cash, money. Can you tip me any quids? can you lend me some money? [In B. E., 1690.OD.]

QUIDNUNC. A politician: from a character of that name in the farce of the Upholsterer. [L. *quid nunc*, what's the news? Hence a news-monger, a gossip. First, apparently, in 1709 in Steele, who had probably heard it 'about town.'OD.—The play referred-to was Murphy's, 1758.F.]

QUIFFING. Rogering. See TO ROGER. [Not in OD.— Durfey, *ca.* 1709.F.]

QUILL DRIVER. A clerk, scribe, or hackney writer. [*Ca.* 1760, though the adjective *quill-driving* goes back to *ca.* 1720, *quill-men* a decade earlier. OD.— *Knight of the quill, ca.* 1690, and *brother of the quill, ca.* 1680.F.]

QUIM. The private parts of a woman: perhaps from the Spanish *quemar*, to burn. [From *ca.* 1600. Variants *queme, quin, quimbox, quimsby*.F.—There may be a reference to the A.S. verb *cweman*, to please, and the dialect *quim*, pleasant, and, as verb, to fit closely (EDD). The word was often used in the Army in 1914-1918. The OD, which admits *twat*, excludes *quim:* this tends to show that it was always cant.]

QUINSEY. Choked by a hempen quinsey; hanged.

QUIPPS. Girds, taunts, jests. ["In common use circa 1530-1650; revived in the 19th century," O. This explains why the word is in G.]

QUIRE, or CHOIR BIRD. A complete rogue, one that has sung in different choirs or cages, i.e. gaols. *Cant.* [*Quire bird* is actually the earlier form of G's *queer bird*.]

QUIRKS AND QUILLETS. Tricks and devices. Quirks in law; subtle distinctions and evasions. [Cf. the C19-20 *quips and quirks*.]

QUI TAM. A qui tam horse; one that will both carry and draw. *Law wit.*

QUIZ A strange-looking fellow, an odd dog. *Oxford.* [Arose *ca.* 1780, arbitrary origin.W.]

QUOD. Newgate, or any other prison. The dab's in quod; the

poor rogue is in prison. [In B. E., 1690. Perhaps from *quadrangle*, that of a prison.W.]

QUOTA. Snack, share, part, proportion, or dividend. Tip me my quota; give me part of the winnings, booty, or plunder. *Cant.* [In this sense colloquial but not cant. Earliest record, in strict sense, 1688.OD.]

R ABBIT. A Welch rabbit; bread and cheese toasted, i.e. a Welch rare bit. Rabbits were also a sort of wooden canns to drink out of, now out of use. [*Rare bit* is wrong.]

RABBIT CATCHER. A midwife.

RABBIT SUCKERS. Young spendthrifts taking up goods on trust at great prices. [In Shakespeare, very young rabbits.O.]

RACK RENT. Rent strained to the utmost value. To lie at rack and manger; to be in great disorder. [*R.-r.* is out of place here. *To lie at r. and m.* also meant to live hard.F.—In dialect *rack and manger*=mismanagement, heedless extravagance, abundance.EDD.]

RACKABACK. A gormagon. See GORMAGON.

RAFFS. An appellation given by the gownsmen of the university of Oxford to the inhabitants of that place.

RAG. A farthing. [In Shakespeare a 'scrap' of money.O.]

TO RAG. To abuse, and tear to rags the characters of the persons abused. She gave him a good ragging, or ragged him off heartily.

RAGAMUFFIN. A ragged fellow, one all in tatters, a tatterdemallion. [In Shakespeare. "Originally the name of a demon." O.—As a demon in Langland. *Ragged*, i.e. shaggy, is a frequent M.E. epithet for demons.W.]

RAG CARRIER. An ensign. [G was perhaps the greatest C18 authority on military slang and on military antiquities, and the eighty-or-so military terms and phrases in this dictionary may be considered lexicographically impeccable.]

RAG FAIR. An inspection of the linen and necessaries of a company of soldiers, commonly made by their officers on Mondays or Saturdays.

RAG WATER. Gin, or any other common dram: these liquors seldom failing to reduce those that drink them to rags.

RAILS. See HEAD RAILS. A dish of rails; a lecture, jobation, or scolding from a married woman to her husband.

RAINBOW. Knight of the rainbow; a footman: from being commonly clothed in garments of different colours. A meeting of gentlemen styled of the most ancient order of the rainbow, was advertised to be held at the Foppington's Head, Moorfields.

RAINY DAY. To lay up something for a rainy day; to provide against a time of necessity or distress. [*Ca.* 1580.OD.]

RAKE, RAKEHELL, or RAKESHAME. A lewd, debauched fellow. ["*Rake*, a debauchee, is a shortened form of the old word *rakel*, 'reckless,' perhaps from old Norse *reikall*, 'vagrant,' which is from *reika* 'to rove,' whence the old verb *rake*,'wander.' Popular etymology made *rakel* into *rakehell* and slang shortened [*rakehell*] to *rake*. *To rake* in the sense of 'live dissolutely' is from the noun." G & K.]

RALPH SPOONER. A fool. [In B.E., 1690.F.—In Suffolk, so *Ralph* or *Rafe* alone .EDD.]

RAM CAT. A he cat.

RAMMER. The arm. The busnapper's kenchin seized my rammer; i.e. the watchman laid hold of my arm. *Cant.*

RAMMISH. Rank. Rammish woman; a sturdy virago. [As rank in Chaucer. As lustful, cf. Stanyhurst, 1577, "Rutting wives make often rammish husbands." OD.—In C19 venery, *ram*=coition, *to ram*=to possess a woman.F.—In Scotland and the North Country *rammish*, in C19 and still, means possessing strong sexual instincts or a highly developed sexuality.EDD.]

RAMSHACKLED. Out of repair. A ramshackled house; perhaps a corruption of *ransacked*, i.e. plundered. [In C19 the *d* was dropped. *Ransackle*, corrupted to *ranshackle*, later *ramshackle*, is the frequentative of *ransack*.W:MWAM.—In Scottish and N. Country dialect one still occasionally hears *ramshackle* as to ransack.EDD.]

RANDLE. A set of nonsensical verses, repeated in Ireland by school-boys, and young people, who have been guilty of breaking wind backwards before any of their companions; if they neglect this apology, they are liable to certain kicks, pinches, and fillips, which are accompanied with divers admonitory couplets.

RANDY. Obstreperous, unruly, rampant. [As wanton or lewd, not recorded till 1847 in Halliwell, whose evidence, along with that of EDD, tends to show that it is, in nearly all its senses, a typically dialect word.]

RANGING. Intriguing with a variety of women. [In Shakespeare, *range*=to be inconstant.O.]

RANK. Stinking, rammish, ill-flavoured; also strong, great. A rank knave; a rank coward: perhaps the latter may allude to an ill savour caused by fear. [In the American underworld, *rank* is a poorly handled crime.I.]

RANK RIDER. A highwayman. [So in B.E., 1690; but a century before it meant a reckless and daring rider, in fact a rough-rider.OD.]

RANTALLION. One whose scrotum is so relaxed as to be longer than his penis, i.e. whose shot pouch is longer than the barrel of his piece.

RANTIPOLE. A rude romping boy or girl; also a gadabout dissipated woman. To ride rantipole; the same as riding St George. See ST GEORGE. [In dialect, also a see-saw, and, as adjective, wild, noisy, rough.EDD.]

RANTUM SCANTUM. Playing at rantum scantum; making the beast with two backs.

TO RAP. To take a false oath; also to curse. He rapped out a volley; i.e. he swore a whole volley of oaths. To rap, means also to exchange or barter: a rap is likewise an Irish halfpenny. Rap on the knuckles; a reprimand. [The coin was an Irish counterfeit halfpenny current about 1700-1750; apparently from a German penny on which was engraved an eagle so crude that the bird was called *Rabe*, a raven; presumably introduced from Germany by Irish soldiers of fortune.W:WAM.]

RAPPAREES. Irish robbers, or outlaws, who in the time of Oliver Cromwell were armed with short weapons, called in Irish *rapiers*, used for ripping persons up. [The derivation is

Irish *rapaire*, a noisy fellow, and the weapon was a pike.EDD.]

RAPPER. A swinging great lie. [Many colloquial and slang nouns for and adjectives indicative of a lie are cussive, verberant, resonant: e.g. *swinger, whopper, thumping, thundering, spanking, rattling, clinking*.]

RAREE SHEW MEN. Poor Savoyards, who subsist by shewing the magic lantern and marmots about London. [Their pronunciation of *rare-show*. From *ca.* 1680.OD.]

RASCAL. A rogue or villain: a term borrowed from the chase; a rascal originally meaning a lean shabby deer, at the time of changing his horns, penis, &c. whence in the vulgar acceptation, rascal is conceived to signify a man without genitals: the regular vulgar answer to this reproach, if uttered by a woman, is the offer of an ocular demonstration of the virility of the part so defamed. Some derive it from *rascaglione*, an Italian word signifying a man without testicles, or an eunuch. [In Shakespeare a young, a lean, or an inferior deer.O.—In Lancashire still, a lean animal, and in Scotland a young deer. EDD.—Applied to persons from C15, to animals from C14.W.]

RAT. A drunken man or woman taken up by the watch, and confined in the watch-house. *Cant.*—To smell a rat; to suspect some intended trick, or unfair design.

RATS. Of these there are the following kinds: a black rat and a grey rat, a py-rat and a cu-rat.

RATTLE. A dice box. To rattle; to talk without consideration, also to move off or go away. To rattle one off; to rate or scold him.

RATTLE-PATE. A volatile, unsteady, or whimsical man or woman. [Dialect has also *rattle-cap*.EDD.]

RATTLE-TRAPS. A contemptuous name for any curious portable piece of machinery, or philosophical apparatus.

RATTLER. A coach. Rattle and pad; a coach and horses. [The single noun and the noun-phrase both sound extremely like C17 cant, as does *rattle*, dice-box.—In dialect *rattler* is a noisy, talkative person or a roisterer.EDD.]

RATTLING COVE. A coachman. *Cant.*

RATTLING MUMPERS. Beggars who ply coaches. *Cant.*

RAW HEAD AND BLOODY BONES. A bull beggar, or scarechild, with which foolish nurses terrify crying brats. [In Florio.F.]

READER. A pocket-book. *Cant.*

READER MERCHANTS. Pickpockets, chiefly young Jews, who ply about the Bank to steal the pocket-books of persons who have just received their dividends there.

READY. The ready rhino; money. *Cant.* [*Ready money* as early as C15. *Ready coin* and *ready gold* are common in C16-17. *Ready* by itself is in Shadwell, 1688, *ready rhino* in T. Brown, 1697.W.]

REBUS. A riddle or pun on a man's name, expressed in sculpture or painting, thus: a bolt or arrow, and a tun, for Bolton; death's head, and a ton, for Morton. [Literally a word or phrase represented 'by things,' though the word comes through the French, especially *rébus de Picardie*.W:ROW.]

RECKON. To reckon without one's host; to make an erroneous judgment in one's own favour. To cast up one's reckoning or accounts; to vomit.

TO RECRUIT. To get a fresh supply of money. [In old cant, *recruits*=money in prospect.F.]

RED FUSTIAN. Port wine.

RED LANE. The throat. Gone down the red lane; swallowed. [Dialectal variants *red close, red loanin', red lone*.EDD.]

RED LATTICE. A public house. [An actual inn was called *The Red Lattice;* it stood in Butcher's Row, on the north side and forming an integral part of the Strand; Steele mentions it in *The Spectator*. E. Beresford Chancellor, *The Annals of the Strand*, 1912.]

RED LETTER DAY. A saint's day or holiday, marked in the calendars with red letters. Red letter men; Roman Catholics: from their observation of the saint's days marked in red letters.

RED RAG. The tongue. Shut your potatoe trap, and give your red rag a holiday; i.e. shut your mouth, and let your tongue rest. Too much of red rag; too much tongue.

RED SAIL-YARD DOCKERS. Buyers of stores stolen out of the royal yards and docks.

RED SHANK. A duck. *Cant.*—Also a Scotch highlander.

RELIGIOUS HORSE. One much given to prayer, or apt to be down upon his knees.

RELIGIOUS PAINTER. One who does not break the commandment which prohibits the making of the likeness of any thing in heaven or earth, or in the waters under the earth.

THE RELISH. The sign of the Cheshire cheese.

REMEDY CRITCH. A chamber pot, or member mug.

REMEMBER PARSON MELHAM. Drink about: A Norfolk phrase.

RENDEZVOUS. A place of meeting. The rendezvous of the beggars were, about the year 1638, according to the Bellman, St Quinton's, the Three Crowns in the Vintry, St Tybs, and at Knapsbury: these were four barns within a mile of London. In Middlesex were four other harbours, called Draw the Pudding out of the Fire, the Cross Keys in Craneford parish, St Julian's in Isleworth parish, and the House of Pettie in Northall parish. In Kent, the King's Barn near Dartford, and Ketbrooke near Blackheath. [In Shakespeare *rendezvous*=a retreat, a refuge, a last resort.O.—Wiltshire has, or very recently had, the quaint *rumsey-voosey*, to keep a rendezvous.EDD.]

REP. A woman of reputation. [Also=reputation itself, as in Fielding.F.]

REPOSITORY. A lock-up or spunging-house, a gaol. Also livery-stables, where horses and carriages are sold by auction.

RESCOUNTERS. The time of settlement between the bulls and bears of Exchange-alley, when the losers must pay their differences, or become lame ducks, and waddle out of the Alley.

RESURRECTION MEN. Persons employed by the students in anatomy to steal dead bodies out of church-yards. [In C19 Scottish, *resurrector*.EDD.—See that curious book, *The Diary of a Resurrectionist*, by J. B. Bailey, 1896.F.]

REVERENCE. An ancient custom, which obliges any person easing himself near the highway or foot-path, on the word *reverence* being given him by a passenger, to take off his hat with his teeth, and without moving from his station to throw it over his head, by which it frequently falls into the excrement: this was considered as a punishment for the breach of delicacy. A person refusing to obey this law, might be pushed backwards. Hence, perhaps, the term, *sir-reverence*.

REVERSED. A man set by bullies on his head, that his money may fall out of his breeches, which they afterwards by accident pick up. See HOISTING. [In B. E., 1690, but probably the slang of the riotous C17 rakes rather than genuine cant.(F).]

REVIEW OF THE BLACK CUIRASSIERS. A visitation of the clergy. See CROW FAIR.

RHINO. Money. *Cant.* [See note at *ready*. *Rhino* by itself is current in American cant for money, cash.I.]

RHINOCERICAL. Rich: the cull is rhinocerical. *Cant.*

RIB. A wife: an allusion to our common mother Eve, made out of Adam's rib. A crooked rib; a cross-grained wife. [Common in Scottish poets, e.g. Fergusson, Galloway, Picken.EDD.]

RIBALDRY. Vulgar abusive language, such as was spoken by ribalds. Ribalds were originally mercenary soldiers, who travelled about, serving any master for pay, but afterwards degenerated into a mere banditti. [Probably from a proper name *Ribaud* (C12) from old Fr. *riber*, to wanton. Cotgrave glosses *ribauld* as "a rogue, ruffian....; also, a ribauld, fornicator."W.]

RIBBIN. Money. The ribbin runs thick, i.e. there is plenty of money.*Cant.*

TO RIBROAST. To beat: I'll ribroast him to his heart's content. [North, 1570.OD.]

RICH FACE, or NOSE. A red pimpled face.

RICHARD SNARY. A dictionary. A country lad, having been reproved for calling persons by their christian names, being sent by his master to borrow a dictionary, thought to shew his breeding by asking for a Richard Snary.

RIDER. A person who receives part of the salary of a place or appointment from the ostensible occupier, by virtue of an agreement with the donor, or great man appointing. The rider is said to be quartered upon the possessor, who often has one or more persons thus riding behind him. See QUARTERED.

RIDGE. A guinea. Ridge cully; a goldsmith. *Cant.* [If manufactured, gold; but if specie, a guinea. C17 cant has also *ridge-*

montra, a gold watch, and *cly full of ridge*, a pocketful of money. F.]

RIDING ST GEORGE. The woman uppermost in the amorous congress; that is, the dragon upon St George. This is said to be the way to get a bishop.

RIDING SKIMMINGTON. A ludicrous cavalcade, in ridicule of a man beaten by his wife. It consists of a man riding behind a woman, with his face to the horse's tail, holding a distaff in his hand, at which he seems to work, the woman all the while beating him with a ladle; a smock displayed on a staff is carried before them as an emblematical standard, denoting female superiority: they are accompanied by what is called the *rough music*, that is, frying pans, bulls' horns, marrow-bones, and cleavers, &c. A procession of this kind is admirably described by Butler in his Hudibras. He rode private, i.e. was a private trooper. [The custom survived in some parts of Southern England till at least 1900. Hardy in *The Mayor of Casterbridge* refers to it as *skimmity-ride*. Other variants are *skymington, skiverton, skymaton, skimmety* (Devon); *skimitin(g)* and *skimmenton* (Wiltshire); *skimity, skimmerton* (Somerset); *skimmiting* (Hampshire). In Kent *skimmington*=a virago.EDD.]

RIFF RAFF. Low vulgar persons, mòb, tag-rag and bobtail. [This sense dates from C15, from C14 *riff and raff*, every bit, scrap, piece, etc.; Old Fr. *rif et raf*, Cotgrave having also *rifle et rafle*.W.—Cf. *raffish*, disreputable, from *ca*. 1800 (OD), and *raff, raffle* (both colloquial)=to live filthily (F).]

RIG. Fun, game, diverson, or trick. To run one's rig upon any particular person; to make him a butt. I am up to your rig; I am a match for your tricks. [In these senses, a typical C18 word, cognate with the C16 *rig*, a (female) wanton (cf. Shakespeare's *riggish*, wanton), itself the original or the derivative of *rig*, to romp about, transitively to deflower. OD,W.— Survives in dialect in all these senses.EDD.]

RIGGING. Clothing. I'll unrig the bloss; I'll strip the wench. Rum rigging; fine clothes. The cull has rum rigging, let's ding him and mill him, and pike; the fellow has good clothes, let's knock him down, rob him, and scour off, i.e. run away. [C17;

dialectal and C19-20 nautical *rig*, clothing, is a shortening. OD,EDD,B.]

RIGMAROLE. Roundabout, nonsensical. He told a long rig-marole story. [First defined in 1736 by Samuel Pegge the elder as "a long story, a 'tale of a tub.' " It is the rambling-verse game of *ragmanroll*, current at least as early as C13, and not the judicial rolls so called, that gave rise to the word.W:MWAM.]

RING. Money procured by begging: beggars so called it from its ringing when thrown to them. Also a circle formed for box-ers, wrestlers, and cudgel-players, by a man styled Vinegar; who, with his hat before his eyes, goes round the circle, striking at random with his whip to prevent the populace from crowd-ing in.

TO RING A PEAL. To scold: chiefly applied to women. His wife rung him a fine peal!

RIP. A miserable rip; a poor, lean, worn-out horse. [As dis-solute fellow, late C18.OD.]

RIPPONS. Spurs: Rippon is famous for a manufactory of spurs, both for men and fighting cocks. [Properly *Ripon*.]

ROARATORIOS AND UPROARS. Oratorios and operas. [Cf. Northamptonshire *roratory*, an oratorio.EDD.]

ROARING BOY. A noisy, riotous fellow. ["The 'roaring boys,' or Mohocks, of the 17th century, who succeeded the 'roarers' of the 16th century, were not named from their voices but from their tumultuous behaviour. As early as 1311 one Simon Brandan....was indicted in London as 'noctivagus et rorere,' i.e. as a night-prowler and disturber of the peace." W: WAM.—Roaring is here from *roar*, to make an uproar, not from the quite distinct *roar*, to roar (as a lion).W.—*Roaring*, as in *roaring blades* and *lads* and *ruffians* and as in *roaring girls* (all C17 terms), means riotous; *roaring drunk* is therefore riotously drunk.F.]

ROARING TRADE. A quick trade.

TO ROAST. To arrest. I'll roast the dab; I'll arrest the ras-cal.—Also to jeer, ridicule, or banter. He stood the roast; he was the butt.—Roast meat clothes; Sunday or holiday clothes.

To cry roast meat; to boast of one's situation. To rule the roast; to be master or paramount. [As butt, from Scottish *roast*=a rough jest, recorded at least as early as 1685.EDD.—It is uncertain whether *roast* or *roost* is the earlier in G's last phrase.]

ROAST AND BOILED. A nick name for the life guards, who are mostly substantial housekeepers, and eat daily of roast and boiled.

ROBERT'S MEN. The third old rank of the canting crew, mighty thieves, like Robin Hood. [Cf. *Roberd's knaves* in Langland.F.]

ROBY DOUGLAS, with one eye and a stinking breath. The breech.

ROCHESTER PORTION. Two torn smocks, and what nature gave. [In B.E., *ca.* 1690.]

ROCKED. He was rocked in a stone kitchen; a saying meant to convey the idea that the person spoken of is a fool, his brains having been disordered by the jumbling of his cradle.

ROGER. A portmanteau; also a man's yard. *Cant.*

ROGER, or TIB OF THE BUTTERY. A goose. *Cant.*— Jolly Roger; a flag hoisted by pirates.

TO ROGER. To bull, or lie with a woman: from the name of Roger being frequently given to a bull. [As in Robertson of Struan, Burns, Sir Richard Burton.F.—Still in fairly frequent use with variant spelling *rodger*.]

ROGUES. The fourth order of canters. A rogue in grain; a great rogue, also a corn chandler. A rogue in spirit; a distiller or brandy merchant. [In C16 cant, *rogue*=a vagabond, perhaps connected with L.*rogare*.W.—Shakespeare has it for rascal, vagabond, and thrice as an endearment, also *roguing* and *roguish*=vagrant.O.—Cf. *rogue*, to live or act as a rascal or a vagrant, common 1570-1650, and to swindle, C19.OD.— Dialect has *rogue-handled*, cheated, and *rogue's-roost*, an accumulation of dirty odds and ends.EDD.]

ROGUM POGUM, or DRAGUM POGRAM. Goat's beard, eaten for asparagus; so called by the ladies who gather cresses, &c. who also deal in this plant.

ROMAN. A soldier in the foot guards, who gives up his pay to his captain for leave to work; serving, like an ancient Roman, for glory, and the love of his country.

ROMBOYLES. Watch and Ward. Romboyled; sought after with a warrant.

ROME MORT. A queen. [Cant. See *Rum Mort.*]

ROMEVILLE. London. *Cant.*

ROMP. A forward wanton girl, a tomrig. Grey, in his notes to Shakespeare, derives it from arompo, an animal found in South Guinea, that is a man eater. See HOYDEN. [The word has noticeably weakened. In B. E., *ramp* in precisely same sense. From verbal sense, to climb vigorously.F,W.]

ROOK. A cheat: probably from the thievish disposition of the birds of that name. Also the cant name for a crow used in house-breaking.—To rook; to cheat, particularly at play. [As a cheat is slightly earlier than the verb, but both arose in C16.OD.]

ROOM. She lets out her fore room and lies backwards: saying of a woman suspected of prostitution.

ROPES. Upon the high ropes; elated, in high spirits, cock-a-hoop.

ROSE. Under the rose; privately or secretly. The rose was, it is said, sacred to Harpocrates, the God of Silence, and therefore frequently placed in the ceilings of rooms destined for the receiving of guests; implying, that whatever was transacted there, should not be made public. [*Ca.* 1540.OD.]

ROSY GILLS. One with a sanguine or fresh-coloured countenance.

ROTAN. A coach, cart, or other wheeled carriage. [Probably cant. Recorded in the dictionary of 1725.OD.]

ROT GUT. Small beer; called beer-a-bumble—will burst one's guts before 'twill make one tumble. [C16.F.—Dialect uses also for inferior food, e.g. unripe fruit.EDD.]

ROUGH. To lie rough; to lie all night in one's clothes: called also roughing it. Likewise to sleep on the bare deck of a ship, when the person is commonly advised to chuse the softest plank. [*Rough it*, C18, was likewise originally nautical.W.]

ROUGH MUSIC. Saucepans, frying-pans, poker and tongs,

marrow-bones and cleavers, bulls' horns, &c. beaten upon and sounded in ludicrous processions. [In dialect, with variant *r. band*, indicates disapproval.EDD.]

ROULEAU. A number of guineas, from twenty to fifty or more, wrapped up in paper, for the more ready circulation at gaming-tables: sometimes they are inclosed in ivory boxes, made to hold exactly 20, 50, or 100 guineas. [Good English.]

ROUND DEALING. Plain, honest dealing.

ROUND HEADS. A term of reproach to the puritans and par-tizans of Oliver Cromwell, and the Rump Parliament, who it is said made use of a bowl as a guide to trim their hair.

ROUND ROBIN. A mode of signing remonstrances prac-tised by sailors on board the king's ships, wherein their names are written in a circle, so that it cannot be discovered who first signed it, or was, in other words, the ringleader. [For a helpful but cautiously inconclusive article on this tricky phrase, see W: MWAM.]

ROUND SUM. A considerable sum. [In Shakespeare.O.]

ROUT. A modern card meeting at a private house; also an order from the Secretary at War, directing the march and quartering of soldiers.

ROVERS. Pirates, vagabonds. [*Rove* originally meant to shoot, in archery, at unspecified marks and distances; cf. *roving glance*, 1470.W:A.—As pirate, *rover* dates from C14.OD.]

ROW. A disturbance: a term used by the students at Cam-bridge. [In G's 1st edition, 1785, which is slightly earlier than the OD record. Perhaps G preferred Oxford to Cambridge.—Probably cognate with *rouse*, aphetic for *carouse*.W.]

ROW. To row in the same boat; to be embarked in the same scheme.

ROWLAND. To give a Rowland for an Oliver: to give an equivalent. Rowland and Oliver were two knights famous in romance: the wonderful achievements of the one could only be equalled by those of the other. [Often in M.E.—W.]

ROWLANDS. A fraternity, by the title of the ancient and hon-ourable family of the Rowlands, held their annual meeting at the Prince and Princess of Orange, Whitechapel Fields.

ROYAL SCAMPS. Highwaymen who never rob any but rich persons, and that without ill treating them. See SCAMP.

ROYAL STAG SOCIETY. Was held every Monday evening, at seven o'clock, at the Three Tuns, near the Hospital Gate, Newgate-street.

ROYSTER. A rude boisterous fellow; also a hound that opens on a false scent. [From *reister* (old Fr. *reistre*), a German trooper, with intrusive *s* grafted on G. *reiter*, rider.W.]

TO RUB. To run away. Don't rub us to the whit; don't send us to Newgate. *Cant.*—To rub up; to refresh: to rub up one's memory. A rub; an impediment. A rubber; the best two out of three. [As impediment, from game of bowls.]

RUBY-FACED. Red-faced.

RUFF. An ornament formerly worn by men and women round their necks. Wooden ruff; the pillory. [In Yorkshire, *ruff*=a halo round the moon.EDD.]

RUFFIAN. The devil. *Cant.*—May the Ruffian nab the cuffin queer, and let the harmanbeck trine with his kinchins about his colquarron; may the Devil take the justice, and let the constable be hanged with his children about his neck. The ruffian cly thee; the Devil take thee. Ruffian cook ruffian, who scalded the Devil in his feathers; a saying of a bad cook. Ruffian sometimes also means a justice. [Earliest *ca.* 1530, in English, as low and brutal fellow, a cut-throat, as swaggering bully or a dissolute, *ca.* 1560; as a whore's 'bully', *ca.* 1610.OD.—Influenced by *rough*.W.—In C17-18 *to ruffian*=to pimp, to bully, to maul.F.—As the Devil in Harman, 1567, but this form may be due to *ruffian*=cut-throat, for *Ruffin* as name of a fiend is recorded more than three centuries earlier.OD.]

RUFFLES. Handcuffs. *Cant.*

RUFFLERS. The first rank of canters; also notorious rogues pretending to be maimed soldiers or sailors.

RUFFMANS. The woods, hedges, or bushes. *Cant.*

RUG. It is all rug; it is all right and safe, the game is secure. *Cant.* [C17 cant.F.]

RUM. Fine, good, valuable. [Cant, as are, all the *rum* phrases. Variant forms *rome*, *room*(*e*). Every single one of G's *rum* phrases

292

occurs in one or another of the following specialists in cant:—
Awdelay, Harman, Rowlands, Head, B.E., this last having 52
such compounds (W).—*Rum* in G's three senses and in that of
the implied 'excellent,' is rare in dialect, and of all G's *rum*
terms only *rum duke* appears in dialect (EDD).—In cant and in
C19 slang combined, the meanings of *rum* fall into three groups.
1. Appreciative,—G's three senses, plus excellent and strong;
this group is cant and it prevailed from 1560 to *ca.* 1810. 2. Odd,
singular, strange, eccentric, queer, from *ca.* 1770 but not common till *ca.* 1800; slang, and showing a development from 1,
especially from G's *rum cove*, a great rogue. 3. Inferior, bad,
questionable, and somewhat strangely silly; C19 and slang or
colloquial. Of the clear instances in G, 40 belong to group 1,
2 to group 2, and 1 to group 3; several of G's compounds are
either border-line or irrelevant. The third group did not last
long, but the 'questionable' sense links up with those in the
second group. Neither the OD nor W essay a derivation, but
H may be right in suggesting a connection with *Rome*; a less
likely alternative is offered by the dialectal *ram-*, very or strong.]
RUM BECK. A justice of the peace. *Cant.*
RUM BITE. A clever cheat, a clean trick.
RUM BLEATING CHEAT. A fat wether sheep. *Cant.*
RUM BLOWER. A handsome wench. *Cant.*
RUM BLUFFER. A jolly host. *Cant.*
RUM BOB. A young apprentice; also a sharp trick.
RUM BOOZE. Wine, or any other good liquor. Rum booz-
ing welts; bunches of grapes. *Cant.*
RUM BUBBER. A dexterous fellow at stealing silver tankards
from inns and taverns.
RUM BUGHER. A valuable dog. *Cant.*
RUM BUNG. A full purse. *Cant.*
RUM CHUB. Among butchers, a customer easily imposed
on, as to the quality and price of meat. *Cant.*
RUM CHANT. A song.
RUM CLOUT. A fine silk, cambric, or holland handkerchief.
Cant.
RUM COD. A good purse of gold. *Cant.*

RUM COE. See COE. [G refers to *Coe*, which does not appear in G.—*Co* or *Coe*=a lad, and is C16 cant.OD.]

RUM COLE. New money, or medals.

RUM COVE. A dexterous or clever rogue.

RUM CULL. A rich fool, easily cheated, particularly by his mistress.

RUM DEGEN. A handsome sword. *Cant.*

RUM DELL. See RUM DOXY.

RUM DIVER. A dexterous pickpocket. *Cant.*

RUM DOXY. A fine wench. *Cant.*

RUM DRAWERS. Silk, or other fine stockings. *Cant.*

RUM DROPPER. A vintner. *Cant.*

RUM DUBBER. An expert picklock.

RUM DUKE. A jolly handsome fellow; also an odd eccentric fellow; likewise the boldest and stoutest fellows lately among the Alsatians, Minters, Savoyards, and other inhabitants of privileged districts, sent to remove and guard the goods of such bankrupts as intended to take sanctuary in those places. *Cant.*

RUM FILE. See RUM DIVER.

RUM FUN. A sharp trick. *Cant.*

RUM GAGGERS. Cheats who tell wonderful stories of their sufferings at sea, or when taken by the Algerines. *Cant.*

RUM GHELT. See RUM COLE. *Cant.*

RUM GLYMMER. King or chief of the link-boys. *Cant.*

RUM GUTTLERS. Canary wine. *Cant.*

RUM HOPPER. A drawer at a tavern. Rum hopper, tip us presently a boozing cheat of rum guttlers; drawer, bring us presently a bottle of the best canary. *Cant.*

RUM KICKS. Breeches of gold or silver brocade, or richly laced with gold or silver. *Cant.*

RUM MAWND. One that counterfeits a fool. *Cant.*

RUM MORT. A queen, or great lady. *Cant.*

RUM NAB. A good hat.

RUM NANTZ. Good French brandy. *Cant.*

RUM NED. A very rich silly fellow. *Cant.*

RUM PAD. The highway. *Cant.*

RUM PADDERS. Highwaymen well mounted & armed. *Cant.*

RUM PEEPERS. Fine looking-glasses. *Cant.*

RUM PRANCER. A fine horse. *Cant.*

RUM QUIDS. A great booty. *Cant.*

RUM RUFF PECK. Westphalia ham. *Cant.*

RUM SNITCH. A smart fillip on the nose.

RUM SQUEEZE. Much wine, or good liquor, given among fiddlers. *Cant.*

RUM TILTER. See RUM DEGEN.

RUM TOL. See RUM DEGEN.

RUM TOPPING. A rich commode, or woman's head-dress.

RUM VILLE. See ROMEVILLE.

RUM WIPER. See RUM CLOUT.

RUMBO. Rum, water, and sugar; also a prison. [The drink occurs in Smollett, 1751; the prison in 1725.OD.]

RUMBOYLE. A ward or watch.

RUMBUMTIOUS. Obstreperous. [Belongs to a group of colloquialisms formed with *rum*, good, fine, etc., or with *ram*, very strong.F.]

RUMFORD. To ride to Rumford to have one's backside new bottomed; i.e. to have a pair of new leather breeches. Rumford was formerly a famous place for leather breeches. A like saying is current in Norfolk and Suffolk, of Bungay, and for the same reason.—Rumford lion; a calf. See ESSEX LION.

RUMP. To rump any one; to turn the back to him: an evolution sometimes used at court. Rump and dozen; a rump of beef and a dozen of claret: an Irish wager, called also buttock and trimmings. Rump and kidney men; fiddlers that play at feasts, fairs, weddings, &c. and live chiefly on the remnants.

RUMPUS. A riot, quarrel, or confusion. [From *ca.* 1760, in earliest examples *riot and rumpus*.OD.]

RUN GOODS. A maidenhead, being a commodity never entered. [In nautical speech, contraband. B.]

RUNNING HORSE, or NAG. A clap, or gleet.

RUNNING SMOBBLE. Snatching goods off a counter, and throwing them to an accomplice, who brushes off with them.

RUNNING STATIONERS. Hawkers of newspapers, trials, and dying speeches.

RUNT. A short squat man or woman: from the small cattle called Welsh runts. [A breed common also in Scotland. Dialect has *runty*, squat or undersized; *runt* as a fool or a simpleton; and *to runt*, to pass the age of fifty if a woman, to approach old age if a man.EDD.]

RUSHERS. Thieves who knock at the doors of great houses in London, in summer time, when the families are gone out of town, and on the door being opened by a woman, rush in and rob the house; also housebreakers who enter lone houses by force.

RUSSIAN COFFEE-HOUSE. The Brown Bear in Bow-street, Covent-Garden, a house of call for the thief-takers and runners of the Bow-street justices.

RUSTY. Out of use. To nab the rust; to be refractory: properly applied to a restive horse, and figuratively to the human species. To ride rusty; to be sullen: called also to ride grub. [*Reasty*, applied to meat left too long 'standing,' is the same as *restive*, properly of a horse that is sluggish (also one that is obstinate, hence refractory). *Rusty* bacon is almost certainly folk-etymology for *reasty* bacon.W.]

RUSTY GUTS. A blunt surly fellow: a jocular misnomer of *rusticus*.

RUTTING. Copulating. Rutting time; the season when deer go to rut. [*Rut*, the recurring sexual excitement of male deer, from *ca.* 1400, ultimately from L.*rugire*, to roar.OD.—*Rutting* occurs as fornication in Shakespeare, who also has *rut-time* and *ruttish*, lewd, lascivious.O.]

S ACHEVEREL. The iron door, or blower, to the mouth of a stove: from a divine of that name, who made himself famous for blowing the coals of dissention in the latter end of the reign of queen Ann.

SACK. A pocket. To buy the sack; to get drunk. To dive into the sack; to pick a pocket. To break a bottle in an empty sack; a bubble bet, a sack with a bottle in it not being an empty sack. [As pocket, cant.F.—*Give, get the sack*, from the French, did not become established till *ca.* 1830. In *to buy the sack*, the wine is meant, *sack* being the "general name for a class of white wines formerly imported from Spain and the Canaries." O.]

SAD DOG. A wicked debauched fellow: one of the ancient family of the sad dogs. Swift translates it into Latin by the words *tristis canis*. [Popularised in the first third of the C18 by such writers as Farquhar, Steele, Swift.F.]

SADDLE. To saddle the spit; to give a dinner or supper. To saddle one's nose; to wear spectacles. To saddle a place or pension; to oblige the holder to pay a certain portion of his income to some one nominated by the donor. Saddle sick; galled with riding, having lost leather.

SAINT. A piece of spoilt timber in a coach maker's shop, like a saint, devoted to the flames.

SAINT GEOFFREY'S DAY. Never, there being no saint of that name: to-morrow-come-never, when two Sundays come together.

SAINT LUKE'S BIRD. An ox: that Evangelist being always represented with an ox.

SAINT MONDAY. A holiday most religiously observed by journeymen shoemakers, and other inferior mechanics: a profanation of that day, by working, is punishable by a fine, particularly among the gentle craft. An Irishman observed, that this saint's anniversary happened every week. [Dialectal variant *saint's day*, idle workmen spending in drink on Monday their Saturday's wages.EDD.—Cf. the modern *Mondayish*, lazy, tired, peevish.]

SAINTONGE. A society formerly held at the Excise Coffeehouse, Old Broad-street.

SAL. An abbreviation of *salivation*. In a high sal: in the pickling tub, or under a salivation.

SALAMANDERS. The worthy members of the society of Salamanders met at the Bull and Anchor, near Hammersmith.

SALESMAN'S DOG. A barker. Vide BARKER.

SALMON-GUNDY. Apples, onions, veal or chicken, and pickled herrings, minced fine, and eaten with oil and vinegar: some derive the name of this mess from the French words *selon mon goust*, because the proportions of the different ingredients are regulated by the palate of the maker; others say it bears the name of the inventor, who was a rich Dutch merchant: but the general and most probable opinion is, that it was invented by the countess of Salmagondi, one of the ladies of Mary de Medicis, wife of king Henry IV. of France, and by her brought into France. [Usually *salmagund(i)(y)*, probably from Rabelais's *salmigondis*, a characteristically fantastic coinage. W.]

SALMON, or SALAMON. The beggars' sacrament or oath. [As *salmon* in Copland's *Spyttel-hous, ca.* 1536; as *salomon* in Middleton's *Roaring Girl*, 1611; Overbury, in his character of A Canting Rogue, 1614, has *saloman*. F.—Usually *by (the) salmon, so help me salmon*; Harman explains the word as cant for an altar, a mass,—which is more probable than the derivation, by corruption, from Fr. *serment*, an oath. OD.]

SALT. Lecherous. A salt bitch; a bitch at heat, or proud bitch. Salt eel; a rope's end, used to correct boys, &c. at sea: you shall have a salt eel for supper. [The sexual sense appears in Shakespeare, who has *salt imagination, salt hours, salt and most hidden loose affection*, etc. "Originally *to go assaut*=to be in heat." O.]

SANDWICH. Ham, dried tongue, or some other salted meat, cut thin, and put between two slices of bread and butter, said to be a favourite morsel with the Earl of Sandwich. [Recorded in 1762, the explanation occurring as early as 1770 in Grosley's *Londres*. OD, W.]

SANDY PATE. A red-haired man or woman.

SANGAREE. Rack punch was formerly so called in bagnios.

SANK, SANKY, or CENTIPEE'S. A taylor employed by clothiers in making soldiers' clothing.

SAPSCULL. A simple fellow. Sappy: foolish. [Head in 1665 defines a *cull* as *a sap-headed fellow*. F.]

SATYR. A libidinous fellow: those imaginary beings are by poets reported to be extremely salacious.

SAUCE BOX. A term of familiar raillery, signifying a bold or forward person. [In C18, *saucy* was stronger than in C20; but weaker than in Shakespeare's time, when it was often seriously condemnatory of insolence or impertinence; Shakespeare also has it to mean wanton, lascivious.O.]

SAUNTERER. An idle lounging fellow: by some derived from *sans terre*; applied to persons who, having no lands or home, lingered and loitered about. Some derive it from persons devoted to the Holy Land, *sainte terre*, who loitered about, as waiting for company. ["Of doubtful origin," OD.—From *ca.* 1660, *saunter*=to roam, to loiter. C17 etymologists derive from *sainte-terre:* "although now derided, it may be partly true. I suggest Sp. *santero*," a hermit or a hermit's 'questing' companion.W.—The only support for the *sans terre* theory that I can find is that in the Hundred Rolls, 1273, is the name John Sansterre, which has yielded the surname Santer (W:S)!]

SAVE-ALL. A kind of candlestick used by our frugal forefathers, to burn snuffs and ends of candles. Figuratively, boys running about gentlemen's houses in Ireland, who are fed on broken meats that would otherwise be wasted: also a miser. [These three senses appear in dialect, which has also:—an overall (Cornwall); a pan or box for the storing of candle-ends (Berkshire); a money-box (N. Cy); a sickly sheep living in fallows (Essex); a boys' game (London). Variants of *save-all*, a miser, are *save-brass* and *save-penny*. EDD.]

SAW. An old saw; an ancient proverbial saying.

SAWNY, or SANDY. A general nick-name for a Scotchman, as Paddy is for an Irishman, or Taffy for a Welchman; Sawny or Sandy being the familiar abbreviation or diminutive of Alexander, a very favourite name among the Scottish nation. [As *sawney*, a fool or a soft, good-natured fellow, the word is common in English and Irish dialects, but not in Scottish.EDD.]

SCAB. A worthless man or woman. [Frequent from *ca.* 1570.F. —Cf. dialectal *scabby*, dirty, mean, worthless, and Yorkshire *scab-Andrew*, a worthless fellow.EDD.]

SCALD MISERABLES. A set of mock masons, who, A.D. 1744, made a ludicrous procession in ridicule of the Free Masons.

SCALY FISH. An honest, rough, blunt sailor. [In C19-20 nautical slang, *scaly back*.B.]

SCAMP. A highwayman. Royal scamp; a highwayman who robs civilly. Royal foot scamp; a footpad who behaves in like manner. [From earlier *scamp*, to go on the highway (whence *scamper*): "recorded for C16 in *scampant*, used in imitation of *rampant* in a rogue's burlesque coat of arms." W.—In cant, *scamp* also=highway robbery and the highway itself.F.]

TO SCAMPER. To run away hastily.

SCANDAL BROTH. Tea. [Cf. Burns's *scandal potion*.EDD.]

SCANDAL PROOF. One who has eaten shame and drank after it, or would blush at being ashamed.

SCANDALOUS. A perriwig. *Cant.*

SCAPEGALLOWS. One who deserves and has narrowly escaped the gallows, a slip-gibbet, one for whom the gallows is said to groan.

SCAPEGRACE. A wild dissolute fellow. [Earliest OD record, 1809.—The etymological sense is "one who escapes the grace of God," as in *scapethrift*, C15, and *want-grace*, also early. *Scapegoat* was coined by Tyndale to render *caper emissarius* (Fr. *bouc émissaire*) of the Vulgate.W:A.]

SCARCE. To make one's self scarce; to steal away.

SCARLET HORSE. A high-red, hired or hack horse: a pun on the word *hired*.

SCAVEY. Sense, knowledge. "Massa, me no scavey;" master, I don't know (*negro language*): perhaps from the French *scavoir*. [Also comprehension. From Sp. *sabe usted*, do you know? G&K.]

SCHEME. A party of pleasure. [Cf. the dialectal sense: an amusement.EDD.]

SCHISM MONGER. A dissenting teacher.

SCHISM SHOP. A dissenting meeting-house.

SCHOOL OF VENUS. A bawdy-house.

SCHOOL BUTTER. Cobbing, whipping.

SCONCE. The head, probably as being the fort and citadel of a man; from *sconce*, an old name for a fort, derived from a Dutch word of the same signification. To build a sconce; a military term for bilking one's quarters. To sconce or skonce; to impose a fine. *Academical phrase*. [The derivation, probably correct, is in Minsheu, who notices the verb as well.W.—In dialect, *sconce*=to guard, protect.EDD.]

SCOTCH BAIT. A halt and a resting on a stick, as practised by pedlars. [Cf. *Scotch casement*, the pillory; *Scotch coffee*, hot water flavoured with burnt biscuit; *Scotch greys*, lice; *Scotch hobby*, "a little sorry, scrubbed, low Horse of that country," B.E., 1690; *Scotch ordinary*, "the house of office" (Ray); *Scotch pint*, a bottle holding two quarts; *Scotch prize*, a capture made by mistake; *Scotch seamanship*, showing more of brawn than of brains. Note too *answer Scotch fashion*, to reply to one question with another.F.]

SCOTCH CHOCOLATE. Brimstone and milk.

SCOTCH FIDDLE. The itch.

SCOTCH MIST. A sober soaking rain: a Scotch mist will wet an Englishman to the skin.

SCOTCH WARMING PAN. A wench; also a fart.

SCOUNDREL. A man void of every principle of honour.

SCOUR. To scour or score off; to run away: perhaps from *score*, i.e. full speed, or as fast as legs would carry one.—Also to wear: chiefly applied to irons, fetters, or handcuffs, because wearing scours them. He will scour the darbies; he will be in fetters. To scour the cramp ring; to wear bolts or fetters, from which, as well as from coffin hinges, rings supposed to prevent the cramp are made.[In C18 *scouring*=imprisonment.D.]

SCOURERS. Riotous bucks, who amuse themselves with breaking windows, beating the watch, and assaulting every person they meet: called scouring the streets. [Thus B.E., 1690.F. —Dissolute young fellows formed themselves into "Clubs and Associations for committing all sorts of excesses in the public streets, and alike attacking ordinary pedestrians and defenceless women. At the Restoration they were 'Mums' and 'Tityre-Tus.' They were succeeded by the 'Hectors' and 'Scourers'... Then came the 'Nickers,' whose delight it was to smash windows with showers of halfpence; next were the 'Hawkabites'; and lastly, the 'Mohocks.'" The Mohocks held together till *ca.* 1715, and were described by Swift, *The Spectator*, and, in *Trivia*, by Gay, who refers also to the Nickers and Scourers. Timbs, *Club Life*.]

SCOUT. A college errand-boy at Oxford, called a gyp at Cambridge. Also a watchman or a watch. *Cant.* [As watchman, slang; as watch, cant. Another C17-18 cant sense was: a mean fellow.F.]

SCRAGGED. Hanged. [From *scrag*, to throttle, to break the neck. EDD.—Modern colloquial *scrag*=to handle roughly. But the hanging terms are all cant: *scrag* or *crag*, a neck; *scrag-boy*, hangman; *scrag*, *scrag-squeezer*, *scragging-post*, the gallows; *scrag'em Fair*, a public execution.F.]

SCRAGGY. Lean, bony.

SCRAN. Victuals. [In C18 also, and in this order of development: refuse, broken victuals, food.F.—In C19-20 *scran* among soldiers and sailors meant both food and a meal. B & P, B.— Cf. dialectal *scrannish*, hungry.EDD.]

SCRAP. A villainous scheme or plan. He whiddles the whole scrap; he discovers the whole plan or scheme. [Cant.F.—Cognate with:]

SCRAPE. To get into a scrape; to be involved in a disagreeable business.

SCRAPER. A fiddler; also one who scrapes plates for mezzotinto prints.

SCRAPING. A mode of expressing dislike to a person, or sermon, practised at Oxford by the students, in scraping their feet against the ground during the preachment; frequently done to testify their disapprobation of a proctor, who has been, as they think, too rigorous.

SCRATCH. Old Scratch; the Devil: probably from the long and sharp claws with which he is frequently delineated.

SCRATCH LAND. Scotland. [From *scratch*, the itch.F.—Cf. the American cant *scratch house*.]

SCRATCH PLATTER, or TAYLOR'S RAGOUT. Bread sopt in the oil & vinegar in which cucumbers have been sliced.

TO SCREW. To copulate. A female screw; a common prostitute. To screw one up; to exact upon one in a bargain or reckoning. [*To screw* is transitive and is operatively male. Not in

302

OD nor EDD. In 1914-1918 it was often used by soldiers, who further employed it to mean coition (a sense holding also in American cant), a sexually-accessible woman or as woman *qua* a means to a pleasurable end.—*To screw one up* is probably cant.F.]

SCREW JAWS. A wry-mouthed man or woman.

SCRIP. A scrap or slip of paper. The cully freely blotted the scrip, and tipt me forty hogs; the man freely signed the bond, and gave me forty shillings.—Scrip is also a Change Alley phrase for the last loan or subscription. What does scrip go at for the next rescounters? what does scrip sell for delivered at the next day of settling? [In Shakespeare, any piece of paper written-upon.O.—As written document, a letter or a bill, *scrip* was, in dialect, obsolescent in 1900 (EDD), but it is not yet obsolete.]

SCROBY. To be tipt the Scroby; to be whipt before the justices.

SCROPE. A farthing. *Cant.*

SCRUB. A low mean fellow, employed in all sorts of dirty work. [In B.E., "a Ragamuffin." F.]

SCRUBBADO. The itch. [C17 cant.F.]

SCULL. A head of a house, or master of a college, at the universities.

SCULL, or SCULLER. A boat rowed by one man with a light kind of oar, called a scull; also a one-horse chaise or buggy.

SCULL THATCHER. A peruke-maker.

SCUM. The riff-raff, tag-rag and bobtail, or lowest order of the people. [So in Marlowe, 1586.OD.]

SCUT. The tail of a hare or rabbit; also that of a woman. [In Shakespeare, of a deer.O.]

SCUTTLE. To scuttle off; to run away. To scuttle a ship; to make a hole in her bottom, in order to sink her. [In C19 venery *scuttle a ship*=to deflower a woman.F.]

SEA CRAB. A sailor.

SEALER, or SQUEEZE WAX. One ready to give bond and judgement for goods or money.

SECRET. He has been let into the secret; he has been cheated at gaming or horse-racing. He or she is in the grand secret; i.e. dead.

SEEDY. Poor, pennyless, stiver-cramped, exhausted. [In C19-20, in bad health.F.]

SEES. The eyes. See DAYLIGHTS. [Cant.]

SERAGLIO. A bawdy-house; the name of that part of the Great Turk's palace where the women are kept. [By B.E. called cant, but this is extremely doubtful. The term came into general use *ca.* 1750 with Mrs Goadby, 'the great Goadby,' who had a very well conducted house in Berwick Street, Soho. Chancellor, *Pleasure Haunts*.]

SET. A dead set; a concerted scheme to defraud a person by gaming. [This phrase was cant.W.]

SETTER. A bailiff's follower, who, like a setting dog, follows and points out the game for his master. Also sometimes an exciseman. [In Shakespeare, one who decoys persons to be robbed. As a C18 cant term, *setters* or *sett:.g dogs* are those who entice dupes to meet gamesters that will cheat them.O.]

TO SETTLE. To knock down or stun any one. We settled the cull by a stoter on his nob; we stunned the fellow by a blow on the head. [In dialect it means also to kill.EDD.]

SEVEN-SIDED ANIMAL. A one-eyed man or woman, each having a right side and a left side, a fore side and a backside, an outside, an inside, and a blind side. [Also in Somerset dialect. EDD.—A C19 American variant was *seven-sided son of a bitch*.F.]

SHABBAROON. An ill-dressed shabby fellow; also a mean-spirited person. [From *shab*, a low fellow (1637) on probable analogy of *picaroon*.OD.—Usually *shabaroon* or *shabroon*.—Cf. dialectal *shab*, to grow shabby, derivatively to act meanly. EDD.]

SHAFTSBURY. A gallon pot full of wine, with a cock.

TO SHAG. To copulate. He is but bad shag; he is no able woman's man. [Also, the act of kind. Probably from obsolete *shag*, to shake, to toss about; or the equally obsolete sense, to render rough. (OD, EDD.) In frequent use among soldiers in 1914-1918 as both verb and, less frequently, noun.—The latter has crossed to the U.S.A., where it is more or less confined to cant.I. In English public schools *ca.* 1900, certainly for many years before and presumably for some years after, the verb *shag* meant to masturbate.]

SHAG-BAG, or SHAKE-BAG. A poor sneaking fellow, a man of no spirit; a term borrowed from the cock-pit. [Earlier *shag-rag*, as in Marlowe, while Scot in 1616 has *shakerag*.F. In dialect *shag-bag* or *-rag* also =a ragged vagabond.EDD.]

SHAKE. To shake one's elbow; to game with dice. To shake a cloth in the wind; to be hanged in chains.

SHALLOW PATE. A simple fellow.

SHAM. A cheat, or trick. To cut a sham; to cheat or deceive. Shams; false sleeves to put on over a dirty shirt, or false sleeves with ruffles to put over a plain one. To sham abram; to counterfeit sickness. [Late C17 slang, generally held to be the Northern form of *shame* and perhaps originating in the contempt felt for any insincere assumption of shame or modesty.W.—"Don't go to sham your stories off upon me." D.]

TO SHAMBLE. To walk awkwardly. Shamble-legged; one that walks wide, and shuffles about his feet.

SHANKER. A venereal wart. [Long obsolete for *chancre*, cf. *cancer* and *canker*.]

SHANKS. Legs, or gams. [In common use from C14. Same as *Shanks's nag* or *mare*.F.]

SHANKS NAGGY. To ride shanks naggy; to travel on foot. *Scotch.*

SHANNON. A river in Ireland: persons dipped in that river are perfectly, and for ever, cured of bashfulness.

SHAPES. To shew one's shapes; to be stript, or made peel, at the whipping-post. [Or....*one's shape*.F.]

SHAPPO, or SHAP. A hat: corruption of *chapeau*. Cant. [B.E.: "The newest Cant, *Nab* being very old and grown too common." Variants *shappeau, shoppo, shopo, shapo*.F.]

SHARK. A sharper; perhaps from his preying upon any one he can lay hold of. Also a custom-house officer, or tide-waiter. Sharks; the first order of pickpockets. *Bow-street term*, A.D. 1785. [Cf. the C18 Exmoor *sharking* or *sherking*, "an eager desire to cheat or defraud another." G.— "*Shark* was used of a sharper or greedy parasite before it was applied to the fish. This, in the records of the Elizabethan voyagers, is more often called by its Spanish name *tiburon*...The origin of *shark* is unknown, but it appears to be identical with *shirk*...earlier *sherk*. We find Italian *scrocco* (whence Fr. *escroc*), German *Schurke*, Dutch *schurk*, rascal, all rendered 'shark' in early dictionaries, but the relationship of these words is not clear." W: ROW.—In American cant, *shark* is an employment agent and rarely a sharper, though ordinary American slang accepts the latter as the correct meaning.I.]

SHARP. Subtle, acute, quick-witted; also a sharper or cheat, in opposition to a flat, dupe, or gull. Sharp's the word and quick's the motion with him: said of any one very attentive to his own interest, and apt to take all advantages. Sharp set; hungry.

SHARPER. A cheat: one that lives by his wits. Sharpers' tools; a fool and false dice. [From *ca.* 1680.OD.]

SHAVER. A cunning shaver; a subtle fellow, one who trims close, an acute cheat. A young shaver; a boy. *Sea term.*[Originally cant, from cant *shave*, to steal, to.swindle; cf. *nipper*, q.v.W. —Relevantly recorded as early as 1534; as fellow, chap, in Marlowe, 1592, *an old shaver*.OD.—Since *shaver*=barber dates from *ca.* 1400 (OD), it would seem that, as barbers have always been 'cute fellows, knowing the latest news and the tips and bets about anything from bear-baiting to dirt-track racing and 'the dogs,' the senses, keen at a bargain, cunning, humorous, odd or eccentric, follow naturally enough.]

SHAVINGS. The clippings of money. [Probably cant.]

SHE HOUSE. A house where the wife rules, or, as the term is, wears the breeches. [*She* by itself as girl or woman was, until *ca.* 1780, good English. Shakespeare uses it, e.g. *the shes of Italy*.O.]

SHE LION. A shilling.

SHE NAPPER. A woman thief-catcher; also a bawd or pimp.

SHEEP'S HEAD. Like a sheep's head, all jaw; saying of a talkative man or woman. [Also, since C16, a blockhead.F.]

SHEEPISH. Bashful, A sheepish fellow; a bashful or shame-faced fellow. To cast a sheep's eye at any thing; to look wishfully at it.

SHERIFF'S BALL. An execution. To dance at the sheriff's ball, and loll out one's tongue at the company; to be hanged, or go to rest in a horse's night-cap, i.e. a halter. [Cf. *sheriff's journeyman*, the hangman. F.]

SHERIFF'S BRACELETS. Handcuffs.

SHERIFF'S HOTEL. A prison.

SHERIFF'S PICTURE FRAME. The gallows.

TO SHERK. To evade or disappoint; to sherk one's duty. [Obsolete for *shirk*, cognate with *shark*. W.—In G's day, *sh(e)(i)rk* denoted a cheat, sharper, or an unreliable, and dialect has a wealth of related senses. EDD.]

TO SHERRY. To run away; sherry off. [Perhaps from an offensive-nationality idea, *sherry* being the wine, early *sherris*, from *Xeres* (*Caesaris urbs*) in Spain; or there may be a corruption of Fr. *charrier*, to carry off; or again it may be cognate with *sheer* (*off*). "These are conjectures!" Precisely, but the third is the OD's.—Yorkshire and Lincolnshire still use the verb. (EDD).]

SHIFTING BALLAST. A term used by sailors, to signify soldiers, passengers, or any landsmen on board.

SHILLALEY. An oaken sapling, or cudgel; from a wood of that name famous for its oaks. *Irish*. [Properly *shillelagh*, from a Co. Wicklow barony with splendid oaks. EDD.]

SHILLY-SHALLY. Irresolute. To stand shilly-shally; to hesitate, or stand in doubt. [*Stand shill I, shall I* is the earliest form (Congreve, 1700): reduplication on *shall I?* OD.]

SHINE. It shines like a shitten barn door.

SHIP SHAPE. Proper, as it ought to be. *Sea phrase.*

SH—T SACK. A dastardly fellow; also a non-conformist. This appellation is said to have originated from the following story:—After the restoration, the laws against the non-conformists were extremely severe. They sometimes met in very obscure places: and there is a tradition that one of their congregations were assembled in a barn, the rendezvous of beggars and other vagrants, where the preacher, for want of a ladder or tub, was suspended in a sack fixed to the beam. His discourse that day, being on the last judgment, he particularly attempted to describe the terrors of the wicked at the sounding of the trumpet; on which a trumpeter to a puppet-show, who had taken refuge in that barn, and lay hid under the straw, sounded a charge. The congregation, struck with the utmost consternation, fled in an instant from the place, leaving their affrighted teacher to shift for himself. The effects of his terror are said to have appeared at the bottom of the sack, and to have occasioned that opprobrious appellation by which the non-conformists were vulgarly distinguished. [Not cant, nor slang, nor colloquialism, this word is a genuine vulgarism, i.e. good English but not in decent use. *Shit* and *shite* are both noun and verb, though the latter form is not, except in dialect, often used of the noun. The verb dates from *ca.* 1300; the noun from *ca.* 1500, since when, indeed, it has been a term of contempt for a man.OD.—In 1914-1918 the soldiers used either *shit* or *shit-house* of any unpopular person (very rarely of a woman); they used it also as an expletive, cf. Fr *merde!* But both these uses had been pre-War. Pre-War was *in the shit*, in trouble; but a specifically military application was: in the mud and slush, in mud and danger, in great or constant danger; and *shit* meant also shelling, especially shelling with shrapnel.—Dialect has many expressive senses and phrases, as e.g. *shitten, shitten-like, shit-arsed fellow*, paltry, contemptible; *to be always either of height or of shite*, to be extremely variable of temper and spirits.EDD. —The OD itself admits *shit-house, shit-fire*, (a hot-tempered person: pejorative), and the obsolete *shit-word* (abuse), all now ranking as vulgarisms.]

SH-T-NG THROUGH THE TEETH. Vomiting. Hark ye, friend, have you got a padlock on your a-se, that you sh-te through your teeth? vulgar address to one vomiting.

SHOD ALL ROUND. A parson who attends a funeral is said to be shod all round, when he receives a hat-band, gloves, and scarf: many shoeings being only partial.

SHOEMAKER'S STOCKS. New or strait shoes. I was in the shoemaker's stocks; i.e. had on a new pair of shoes that were too small for me. [Cf. *shoemaker's pride*, the creaking of new shoes.EDD.]

TO SHOOLE. To go skulking about. [Usually *shool*, dialectal and colloquial, to drag the feet, to shuffle, to saunter (from *shool*, a shovel), hence to go about begging, to beg (as in Smollett), whence *shooler*, a beggar.F,EDD.]

TO SHOOT THE CAT. To vomit from excess of liquor; called also catting.

SHOP. A prison. Shopped; confined, imprisoned. [Cant.F.]

SHOPLIFTER. One that steals whilst pretending to purchase goods in a shop. [Originally (C17) slang if not cant.W.]

SHORT-HEELED WENCH. A girl apt to fall on her back.

SHOT. To pay one's shot; to pay one's share of a reckoning. Shot betwixt wind and water; poxed or clapped. [*Shot*=share, popularised in the decade 1590-1599, is hardly in place here. Analogous is the modern slang *the whole shoot*.W.—Cf. dialectal *shot-flagon*, a drink offered free by the (e.g.) inn-keeper to a guest that has had over a certain amount.EDD.]

SHOTTEN HERRING. A thin meagre fellow.

SHOULDER CLAPPER. A bailiff, or member of the catch club. Shoulder-clapped; arrested. [Shakespeare, 1590.OD.]

SHOULDER SHAM. A partner to a file. See FILE. [Cant.F.]

TO SHOVE THE TUMBLER. To be whipped at the cart's tail. [Cant.F.]

SHOVEL. To be put to bed with shovel; to be buried. He or she was fed with a fire-shovel! a saying of a person with a large mouth.

SHRED. A taylor.

SHRIMP. A little diminutive person. [As early as Chaucer. OD.]

TO SHUFFLE. To make use of false pretences, or unfair shifts. A shuffling fellow; a slippery shifting fellow. [From the card-sharper's practice of 'fixing' the cards; cf. *pack a jury*. W:A.]

SHY COCK. One who keeps within doors for fear of bailiffs.

SICE. Sixpence. [C17 slang, *sice* being 6 on the die.OD.]

SICK AS A HORSE. Horses are said to be extremely sick at

their stomachs, from being unable to relieve themselves by vomiting. Bracken, indeed, in his Farriery, gives an instance of that evacuation being procured, but by a means which he says would make the Devil vomit. Such as may have occasion to administer an emetic either to the animal or the fiend, may consult his book for the recipe. [Bracken's book appeared in 1738.]

SIDE POCKET. He has as much need of a wife as a dog of a side pocket: said of a weak old debilitated man. He wants it as much as a dog does a side pocket: a simile used for one who desires any thing by no means necessary.

SIDLEDYWRY. Crooked.

SIGN OF A HOUSE TO LET. A widow's weeds.

SIGN OF THE FIVE SHILLINGS. The crown.

SIGN OF THE TEN SHILLINGS. The two crowns.

SIGN OF THE FIFTEEN SHILLINGS. The three crowns.

SILENCE. To silence a man; to knock him down, or stun him. Silence in the court, the cat is pissing; a gird upon any one requiring silence unnecessarily.

SILENT FLUTE. See PEGO, SUGAR STICK, &c.

SILK SNATCHERS. Thieves who snatch hoods or bonnets from persons walking in the streets.

SIMKIN. A foolish fellow. [Since ca. 1890 obsolete in dialect, where formerly it was common. EDD.]

SIMON. Sixpence. Simple Simon; a natural, a silly fellow; Simon Suck-egg, sold his wife for an addle duck egg.

TO SIMPER. To smile: to simper like a furmity kettle.

SIMPLETON. Abbreviation of simple Tony, or Anthony, a foolish fellow. [Jocular formation on *simple;* cf. *singleton.* W.]

SIMPLES. Physical herbs; also follies. He must go to Battersea to be cut for the simples—Battersea is a place famous for its garden grounds, some of which were formerly appropriated to the growing of simples for apothecaries, who at a certain season used to go down to select their stock for the ensuing year, at which time the gardeners were said to cut their simples; whence it became a popular joke to advise young people to go to Battersea, at that time, to have their simples cut, or to be cut for the simples. [As medicinal herbs, *simples* "is a special use of *simple*, medicament of one ingredient only. Hence obsolete *to simple*, gather remedies." W.]

TO SING SMALL. To be humbled, confounded, or abashed, to have little or nothing to say for one's self.

SINGLE PEEPER. A person having but one eye. [Grose has *have*.]

SINGLETON. A very foolish fellow; also a particular kind of nails.

SINGLETON. A corkscrew, made by a famous cutler of that name, who lived in a place called Hell, in Dublin; his screws are remarkable for their excellent temper.

SIR JOHN. The old title for a country parson: as Sir John of Wrotham, mentioned by Shakespeare. [Frequent of any parson from C14 to the Restoration.F.]

SIR JOHN BARLEYCORN. Strong beer. [Usually without *sir*.]

SIR LOIN. The sur, or upper loin. [Early etymologists believed that an English king had knighted a loin of beef. "The belief in the knightly origin....was so strong that we find it playfully called the *baronet* (*Tom Jones*). Hence, no doubt, the name *baron* of beef for the double sirloin." W:ROW.]

SIR REVERENCE. Human excrement, a t—d. [From late C16.OD.]

SIR TIMOTHY. One, who, from a desire of being the head of the company, pays the reckoning, or, as the term is, stands squire. See SQUIRE.

SITTING BREECHES. One who stays late in company, is said to have his sitting breeches on, or that he will sit longer than a hen. [Cf. the Yorkshire phrase, *sit eggs*, to outstay one's welcome.EDD.]

SIX AND EIGHT-PENCE. An attorney, whose fee on several occasions is fixed at that sum.

SIX AND TIPS. Whisky and small beer. *Irish*.

SIX POUNDER. A servant maid, from the wages formerly given to maid servants, which was commonly six pounds.

SIXES. Small beer, formerly sold at six shillings the barrel.

SIXES AND SEVENS. Left at sixes and sevens; i.e. in confusion: commonly said of a room where the furniture, &c. is scattered about; or of a business left unsettled. [From the dicing phrase, *to set on six and seven*, probably a fanciful alteration of *to set on cinque and sice*, the two highest numbers.W.]

SIZE OF ALE. Half a pint. Size of bread and cheese; a certain quantity. Sizings; Cambridge term for the college allowance from the buttery, called at Oxford battles. [Usually *battels*.]

SIZER. A poor or inferior student on the college establishment at Cambridge, called at Oxford a servitor.[Properly *sizar*.]

SKEW. A cup, or beggar's wooden dish. [Cant.F.]

SKEWVOW, or ALL A SKEW. Crooked, inclining to one side.

SKIN. In a bad skin; out of temper, in an ill humour. Thin-skinned; touchy, peevish.

SKIN FLINT. An avaricious man or woman.

SKINK. To skink, is to wait on the company, ring the bell, stir the fire, and snuff the candles; the duty of the youngest officer in a military mess. See BOOTS. [From *ca.* 1600, a drawer or tapster, short for the slightly earlier *skinker*.OD.]

SKINS. A tanner.

SKIP JACKS. Youngsters that ride horses on sale, horse-dealers' boys. Also a plaything made for children with the breastbone of a goose.

SKIP KENNEL. A footman. [Almost certainly cant.]

SKIPPER. A barn. *Cant.*—Also the captain of a Dutch vessel. [Literally shipper. "The captain, properly only of a small boat." B.]

TO SKIT. To wheedle. *Cant.* [The modern sense for both verb and noun became established *ca.* 1750, though as a literary or artistic production (light satire) not till *ca.* 1820.OD.]

SKRIP. See SCRIP.

SKULKER. A soldier who by feigned sickness, or other pretences, evades his duty: a sailor who keeps below in time of danger; in the civil line, one who keeps out of the way, when any work is to be done. To skulk; to hide one's self, to avoid labour or duty. [Cf. the dialectal verb *skulk*, to dodge quickly, to sulk, to steal.EDD.—Shakespeare has *skulking*, cowering, lurking.O.]

SKY BLUE. Gin.

SKY FARMERS. Cheats who pretend they were farmers in the isle of Sky, or some other remote place, and were ruined by a flood, hurricane, or some such public calamity; or else called sky farmers from their farms being *in nubibus*, 'in the clouds.' [Cant; first recorded 1753.OD.]

SKY PARLOUR. The garret, or upper story.

SLABBERING BIB. A parson or lawyer's band.

SLAG. A slack-mettled fellow, one not ready to resent an affront.

SLAM. A trick; also a game at whist lost without scoring one. To slam to a door; to shut it with violence.

SLAMKIN. A female sloven, one whose clothes seem hung on with a pitch-fork, a careless trapes. [Also *slammerkin* and *slammocks*, the latter originating the modern slang adjective, *slummocky*, slovenly.F.]

SLANG. Cant langugage. [Originally cant and perhaps cognate with *sling**: cf. the colloquial *sling the bat*, talk the vernacular (Kipling), *sling language* or *words*, to talk. Some regard the word as an argotic corruption of Fr. *langue*, language.W.—As noun it dates from *ca.* 1750, as adjective from about same time. OD.—In dialect, impertinence, abusive language.EDD.*Note that *to sling off* at a person is *to slang* him.]

SLAP-BANG SHOP. A petty cook's shop where there is no credit given, but what is had must be paid *down with the ready slap-bang*, i.e. immediately. This is a common appellation for a night cellar frequented by thieves, and sometimes for a stage coach or caravan.

SLAPDASH. Immediately, instantly, suddenly. [Now rather means happy-go-lucky, (less frequently) impetuous.]

SLASHER. A bullying riotous fellow. *Irish*. [From *ca.* 1550. Not Irish.OD.]

SLAT. Half a crown. *Cant*.

SLATE. A sheet. *Cant.*

SLATER'S PAN. The gaol at Kingston in Jamaica: Slater is the deputy provost martial.

SLATTERN. A woman sluttishly negligent in her dress.

SLEEPING PARTNER. A partner in a trade, or shop, who lends his name and money, for which he receives a share of the profit, without doing any part of the business. [Now perfectly good English; in modern slang, *sleeping partner*=a bed-fellow.]

SLEEPY. Much worn; the cloth of your coat must be extremely sleepy; for it has not had a nap this long time.

SLEEVELESS ERRAND. A fool's errand, in search of what it is impossible to find. [Recorded for 1546 and very common *ca.* 1580-1700. *Sleeveless answer*, an unsatisfactory one, as early as 1387 and frequently used *ca.* 1570-1600.OD.—By a strange irony, a novel entitled *Sleeveless Errand*, which was to have been published in February 1929, was suppressed the night before publication.]

SLICE. To take a slice; to intrigue, particularly with a married woman, because a slice of a cut loaf is not missed. [? *off.*]

SLIPGIBBET. See SCAPEGALLOWS.

SLIPPERY CHAP. One on whom there can be no dependance, a shuffling fellow.

SLIPSLOPS. Tea, water-gruel, or any innocent beverage taken medicinally.

SLIPSLOPPING. Misnaming and misapplying any hard word; from the character of Mrs Slipslop, in Fielding's Joseph Andrews. [Cf. *Malapropism.*]

SLOPS. Wearing apparel and bedding used by seamen. [Palsgrave, *La Langue Francoyse*, 1530: "Payre of sloppe hoses, *braiettes a marinier*." F.—Shakespeare has *slop*=loose breeches.O.]

SLOP SELLER. A dealer in those articles, who keeps a slop shop.

SLOUCH. A stooping gait, a negligent slovenly fellow. To slouch; to hang down one's head. A slouched hat; a hat whose brims are let down.

SLUBBER DE GULLION. A dirty nasty fellow. [Properly one word. Elaboration on *slu(o)bber;* cf. *tatterdemalion.*W.]

314

SLUG. A piece of lead of any shape, to be fired from a blunderbuss. To fire a slug; to drink a dram.

SLUG-A-BED. A drone, one that cannot rise in the morning. From *slug*, glossed by the *Promptorium Parvulorum*, 1440, as *desidio*, *torpeo*, while Cotgrave has: "To slugge it, to laze it, to live idly." F.]

SLUICE YOUR GOB. Take a hearty drink.

SLUR. To slur is a method of cheating at dice; also to cast a reflection on any one's character, to scandalize. [The former from *ca*. 1640 (OD) and probably cant.]

SLUSH. Greasy dish water, or the skimmings of a pot where fat meat has been boiled.

SLUSH BUCKET. A foul feeder, one that eats much greasy food.

SLY BOOTS. A cunning fellow, under the mask of simplicity.

SMABBLED, or SNABBLED. Killed in battle. [This sense is not recorded in the OD. Probably cant. In 1725 *s(m)(n)abble* meant to despoil, to knock down, to half-stun, also to arrest. OD.]

TO SMACK. To kiss. I had a smack at her muns; I kissed her mouth. To smack calves skin; to kiss the book, i.e. to take an oath. The queer cuffin bid me smack calves skin, but I only bussed my thumb; the justice bid me kiss the book, but I only kissed my thumb. [The three illustrative phrases are cant.]

SMACK SMOOTH. Level with the surface, every thing cut away.

SMACKING COVE. A coachman. [Cant.]

SMALL CLOTHES. Breeches: a gird at the affected delicacy of the present age; a suit being called, coat, waistcoat, and articles, or small clothes. [But especially the tight-fitting knee-breeches of C18 and early C19. Tom Hood and Dickens usually wrote *smalls*.F,W.]

SMART. Spruce, fine: as smart as a carrot new scraped. [First applied to dress *ca*. 1700; in C19 restricted to a kitchen-maid in her Sunday best. The word 'came upstairs' *ca*. 1885.W:A.]

SMART MONEY. Money allowed to soldiers or sailors for the loss of a limb, or other hurt received in the service. ["Involuntary contributions to the old Chatham Chest, for the benefit of hurt or wounded naval ratings." B.]

SMASH. Leg of mutton and smash; a leg of mutton and mashed turnips. *Sea term.* [Cf. *s-plash, s-quash, s-crunch.*W.]

TO SMASH. To break; also to kick down stairs. *Cant.*[From *ca.* 1800, *smash* as cant acquired the further sense, to utter base coin.F.]

SMEAR. A plasterer.

SMEAR GELT. A bribe. *German.*

SMELLER. A nose. Smellers; a cat's whiskers. [In April of this year a well-known novelist wrote to me that he had got "a rap on the smeller of a criticism" from a certain London periodical.]

SMELLING CHEAT. An orchard or garden; also a nosegay. *Cant.* [Also, in C16-17, the nose.F.]

SMELTS. Half guineas. *Cant.*

SMICKET. A smock, or woman's shift. [Also, in Cheshire, a term of contempt for girl or woman.EDD.]

SMIRK. A finical spruce fellow. To smirk; to smile, or look pleasantly. [The noun is cant, the verb good English; the modern sense of *to smirk* must have arisen just about the time of Grose's death.(OD).]

SMITER. An arm. To smite one's tutor; to get money from him. *Academic term.* [The noun is cant.F.]

SMITHFIELD BARGAIN. A bargain whereby the purchaser is taken in. This is likewise frequently used to express matches or marriages contracted solely on the score of interest, on one or both sides, where the fair sex are bought and sold like cattle in Smithfield. [The former is recorded for 1662, the market dating from *ca.* 1645.W:A.]

SMOCK-FACED. Fair-faced. [It is tempting to refer to the dialectal adjective *smock*, smooth, but the OD says from *smock*, a shift, a chemise; presumably from the whiteness of the garment. *Smock* occurs in many picturesque senses and phrases: in Shakespearean times typical for a woman (cf. the modern slang use of *skirt*, a girl or woman), and Shakespeare himself has *a shirt and a smock*, i.e. a man and a woman.O.—"In allusive

316

terms, usually suggestive of loose conduct or immorality in, or in relation to, women." OD.—E.g. *smockage, smock-hunting,* wenching; *smock-loose,* wanton; *smock-secret,* an amour.F.]

TO SMOKE. To observe, to suspect. [Used by Shakespeare in the analogous sense, to find a person out.O.]

SMOKER. A tobacconist. [I.e., a smoker! OD.W.]

SMOKY. Curious, suspicious, inquisitive. [Dialectally, low, mean. EDD.]

SMOUCH. Dried leaves of the ash tree, used by the smugglers for adulterating the black or bohea teas.

SMOUS. A German Jew. [Direct from the Dutch; the usual English forms are *smouse* and, later, *smouch*. Sewel in 1708 suggests derivation from *Moses*.W.]

SMUG. A nick name for a blacksmith; also neat and spruce. [The noun is cant.F.]

SMUGGLING KEN. A bawdy-house. [Cant.F.—Cf. dialectal *smuggle*, to hug violently, to smother with caresses.EDD.]

TO SMUSH. To snatch, or seize suddenly. [In good English but long obsolete as *smuss*.(OD).]

SMUT. Bawdy. Smutty story; an indecent story. [From C17 in its various senses; Pepys, 1668, has *smutty*.W.—In American tramp slang, obscene pictures, post-cards and 'literature,' especially those which are peddled, are known as *smuts*.I.]

TO SNABBLE. To rifle or plunder; also to kill. [See *Smabbled*.]

SNACK. A share. To go snacks; to be partners.

TO SNAFFLE. To steal. To snaffle any one's poll; to steal his wig. [Related to *snabble*.W.—*Snaffle* is either cant or dialect (OD,EDD).]

SNAFFLER. A highwayman. Snaffler of prancers; a horse-stealer.

SNAGGS. Large teeth: also snails. [Latter, *snags*; cant.F.]

SNAKESMAN. See LITTLE SNAKESMAN.

SNAP DRAGON. A christmas gambol; raisins and almonds being put into a bowl of brandy, and the candles extinguished, the spirit is set on fire, and the company scramble for the raisins.

TO SNAP THE GLAZE. To break shop windows, or show glasses. [Cant.]

SNAPPERS. Pistols. [Late C16. OD.]

SNAPT. Taken, caught. [C16, common in C17. OD.]

SNATCH CLY. A thief who snatches women's pockets. [Cant.]

SNEAK. A pilferer. Morning sneak; one who pilfers early in the morning, before it is light. Evening sneak; an evening pilferer. Upright sneak; one who steals pewter pots from the alehouse boys employed to collect them. To go upon the sneak; to steal into houses whose doors are carelessly left open. *Cant.* [See especially Vaux's *Memoirs*, 1819.F.—In American cant, to steal.I.]

SNEAKER. A small bowl. [Usually of punch.EDD.—Perhaps from Northern *sneak*, to smell.P.]

SNEAKING BUDGE. One that robs alone. [Cant.]

SNEAKSBY. A mean-spirited fellow, a sneaking cur.

SNEERING. Jeering, flickering, laughing in scorn. [Always good English, therefore out of place here. The same holds of *to snicker*.]

SNICKER. A glandered horse.

TO SNICKER or SNIGGER. To laugh privately, or in one's sleeve.

TO SNILCH. To eye, or look at any thing attentively: the cull snilches. *Cant.*

SNIP. A tailor.

SNITCH. To turn snitch, or snitcher; to turn informer. [In dialect, also as verb, to betray; to tell tales. EDD.—In American cant, a tale-bearer, a spy; also to inform against one's partner or one's associates: "The unforgivable sin in the underworld, and the cause of more killings than any other underworld breach of custom or habit." I.]

TO SNITE. To wipe, or slap. Snite his snitch; wipe his nose, i.e. give him a good knock. [Very old word and good English; *snite his snitch* is, however, colloquial—very!]

TO SNIVEL. To cry, to throw the snot or snivel about. Snivelling; crying. A snivelling fellow; one that whines or complains. [*To snivel* and *snivelling* are good though not elevated English.]

TO SNOACH. To speak through the nose, to snuffle. [Very old dialect.EDD.]

SNOB. A nick name for a shoemaker. [Became in C19 common in English and Scottish dialects.EDD.—As used in the C20 army it might be rather considered a colloquialism. B&P.]

TO SNOOZE, or SNOODGE. To sleep. To snooze with a mort; to sleep with a wench. *Cant.*

SNOUT. A hogshead. *Cant.*

SNOWBALL. A jeering appellation for a negro.

TO SNUB. To check, or rebuke. [Good English. So is *snub nose*, a phrase containing the basic sense of Grose's *to snub*, i.e. to shorten.W.]

SNUB DEVIL. A parson.

SNUB NOSE. A short nose turned up at the end.

SNUDGE. A thief who hides himself under a bed, in order to rob the house. [Cant.F.]

SNUFF. To take snuff; to be offended. [In Shakespeare as noun: huff, resentment.O.]

TO SNUFFLE. To speak through the nose.

SNUFFLES. A cold in the head, attended with a running at the nose.

SNUG. All's snug; all's quiet.

TO SOAK. To drink. An old soaker; a drunkard, one that moistens his clay to make it stick together. [In Goldsmith.F.]

SOCKET MONEY. A whore's fee, or hire, also money paid for a treat, by a married man caught in an intrigue. [Cf. *socketer*, a blackmailer.F.—In dialect, *socket*=money paid by a man about to be married so that his companions may drink his health, *socket-brass*=hush-money, and *socketing-brass*=a fine paid by a man found courting (especially outside his own district). EDD.—The radical idea resides in *socket*, the common C17 word for the pudend.F.]

SOLDIER'S BOTTLE. A large one. [The pejorative sense appears especially in nautical slang:—*Sogering* is acting like a soldier aboard ship, i.e. 'loafing'; *soldier*, an inferior seaman; *soldier's masts* was "during the transition period from sail to steam in the Navy, the old seaman's term of contempt for pole

319

masts without sails;" *soldier-walking*, land-operations carried out by bluejackets; *soldier's wind*, one that is fair either way.B. —In C19 colloquialism and dialect, *soldier's thigh*=an empty pocket, and *soldier's bite* a big bite.F,EDD.]

SOLDIER'S MAWND. A pretended soldier, begging with a counterfeit wound, which he pretends to have received at some famous siege or battle.

SOLDIER'S POMATUM. A piece of tallow candle.

SOLFA. A parish clerk.

SOLO PLAYER. A miserable performer on any instrument, who always plays alone, because no one will stay in the room to hear him.

SOLOMON. The mass. *Cant.* [Cf. *Salmon*,q.v.]

SON OF PRATTLEMENT.A lawyer. [Also *son of parchment*. F.]

SONG. He changed his song: he altered his account or evidence. It was bought for an old song, i.e. very cheap. His morning and his evening song do not agree; he tells a different story.

SOOTERKIN. A joke upon the Dutch women, supposing that by their constant use of stoves, which they place under their petticoats, they breed a kind of small animal in their bodies, called a sooterkin, of the size of a mouse, which when mature slips out.

SOP. A bride. A sop for Cerberus; a bribe for a porter, turnkey, or gaoler.

SORREL. A yellowish red. Sorrel pate; one having red hair.

SORROW SHALL BE HIS SOPS. He shall repent this. Sorrow go by me; a common expletive used by the presbyterians in Ireland.

SORRY. Vile, mean, worthless. A sorry fellow, or hussy; a worthless man or woman. [Good English.]

SOSS BRANGLE. A slatternly wench. [Cant, though *soss* itself is dialectal for a slattern, originally a mess of food, hence a mess; a C19 Lancashire variant was *soss-midden*.EDD.]

SOT WEED. Tobacco.

SOUL CASE. The body. He made a hole in his soul case; he wounded him.

SOUL DOCTOR, or DRIVER. A parson.

SOUNDERS. A herd of swine. [In good English, *sounder*=a herd of wild swine; a noun of assembly.OD.]

SOUSE. Not a souse; not a penny. *French.*

SOUSE CROWN. A silly fellow.

SOUTH SEA. Mountain, gin.

SOW. A fat woman. He has got the wrong sow by the ear; he mistakes his man. Drunk as David's sow; see DAVID'S SOW.

SOW'S BABY. A sucking pig.

SOW CHILD. A female child. [Cf. the dialectal *sow cat*, a female cat, and *sow waps*, the queen wasp.EDD.]

SPADO. A sword. *Spanish.*

SPANISH. The Spanish; ready money.

SPANISH COIN. Fair words, and compliments. [In 1570-1650 (especially), *Spanish* was a derogatory 'prefix.' Note also *Spanish pike*, a needle; *Spanish plague*, building; *to walk Spanish*, to walk under compulsion; *to ride the Spanish mare*, an old nautical punishment.E.—Seldom, pejoratively, in dialect: or rather, perhaps, very little has been recorded, the period preceding that at which dialect began to be at all fully 'documented.']

SPANISH FAGGOT. The sun.

SPANISH GOUT. The pox.

SPANISH PADLOCK. A kind of girdle contrived by jealous husbands of that nation, to secure the chastity of their wives.

SPANISH, or KING OF SPAIN'S, TRUMPETER. An ass when braying. [Don Key.F.]

SPANISH WORM. A nail: so called by carpenters when they meet with one in a board they are sawing.

SPANKING. Large. [Also, of course, excellent, dashing.]

SPANKS, or SPANKERS. Money; also blows with the open hand. [The former from obsolete dialectal *spank*, to sparkle or shine, hence *spanker*, a gold coin (Devonshire, 1777).EDD.]

SPARK. A spruce, trim, or smart fellow. A man that is always thirsty, is said to have a spark in his throat. [In C17 a *spark* was a courageous fellow, cf. the C18 *gallant spark*, now archaic and 'literary.' F,W.]

SPARKISH. Fine, gay. [For a well-illustrated, authoritative

account of the social life in G's day, see Chancellor's *The XVIIIth Century in London.*]

SPARRING BLOWS. Blows given by cocks before they close, or, as the term is, mouth it; used figuratively for words previous to a quarrel.

SPARROW. Mumbling a sparrow; a cruel sport frequently practised at wakes and fairs: for a small premium, a booby having his hands tied behind him, has the wing of a cock sparrow put into his mouth; with this hold, without any other assistance than the motion of his lips, he is to get the sparrow's head into his mouth: on attempting to do it, the bird defends itself surprisingly, frequently pecking the mumbler till his lips are covered with blood, and he is obliged to desist: to prevent the bird from getting away, he is fastened by a string to a button of the booby's coat.

SPARROW-MOUTHED. Wide-mouthed, like the mouth of a sparrow: it is said of such persons, that they do not hold their mouths by lease, but have it from year to year: i.e. from ear to ear. One whose mouth cannot be enlarged without removing their ears, and who when they yawn have their heads half off. [In dialect, *sparrow* occurs in some homely-vivid phrases and compounds, e.g. *sparrow-blasted*, dumbfounded, and *at sparrow-fart*, at daybreak. EDD.]

SPATCH COCK. (Abbreviation of *dispatch cock*.) A hen just killed from the roost, or yard, and immediately skinned, split, and broiled: an Irish dish upon any sudden occasion.

TO SPEAK WITH. To rob. I spoke with the cull on the cherry-coloured prancer; I robbed the man on the black horse. *Cant.* [Cf. Shakespeare's *speak*, to exchange blows, to fight (*Coriolanus*, I, iv, 4). O.]

SPECKED WIPER. A coloured handkerchief. *Cant.*

SPIDER-SHANKED. Thin-legged.

TO SPIFLICATE. To confound, silence, or dumbfound. [Perhaps an elaborately arbitrary analogy to, or formation on, *suffocate*: cf. dialectal *smothercate*. W.]

SPILL. A small reward, or gift of money.

SPILT. Thrown from a horse, or overturned in a carriage; pray, coachee, don't spill us.

SPINDLE SHANKS. Slender legs.

TO SPIRIT AWAY. To kidnap, or inveigle away. [Earlier simply *to spirit*, which comes from the noun: as early as 1654 the agents arranging for the illicit supply of men for the American plantations were called *spirits*, and in 1674 there was a special Proclamation against them.W:MWAM.]

SPIRITUAL FLESH BROKER. A parson.

SPIT. He is as like his father, as if he was spit out of his mouth; said of a child much resembling his father.

SPIT. A sword.

SPIT FIRE. A violent, pettish, or passionate person.

SPLICED. Married: an allusion to joining two ropes ends by splicing. *Sea term.* ['Authorised' by Smollett.F.]

SPLIT CROW. The sign of the spread eagle, which being represented with two heads on one neck, gives it somewhat the appearance of being split.

SPLIT CAUSE. A lawyer.

SPLIT FIG. A grocer. [Dialect has also *split-currant* and *nip-raisin;* in dialect too, *split-fig* and *-currant* denote a very stingy or miserly person.EDD.]

SPOIL IRON. The nick name for a smith. [Cf. the modern colloquial *spoil-bread*, a baker, and *spoil-paper*, an author (F) and the dialectal *spoil-wood*, a carpenter (EDD).]

SPOIL PUDDING. A parson who preaches long sermons, keeping his congregation in church till the puddings are over done.

SPOON HAND. The right hand.

TO SPORT. To exhibit: as Jack Jehu sported a new gig yesterday: I shall sport a new suit next week. To sport or flash one's ivory; to shew one's teeth. To sport timber: to keep one's outside door shut: this term is used in the inns of court to signify denying one's self. N.B. The word *sport* was in a great vogue ann. 1783 and 1784. [Still common.]

TO SPOUT. To rehearse theatrically.

SPOUTING. Theatrical declamation.

SPOUTING CLUB. A meeting of apprentices and mechanics to rehearse different characters in plays: thus forming recruits for the strolling companies.

SPREAD EAGLE. A soldier tied to the halberts in order to be whipped: his attitude bearing some likeness to that figure, as painted on signs. [Cf. the lashing to the wheel in the rigorously-applied form of Army Field Punishment No. 1 in C20. B & P.]

SPRING-ANKLE WAREHOUSE. Newgate, or any other gaol. *Irish.*

SPUNGE. A thirsty fellow, a great drinker. To spunge; to eat and drink at another's cost. Spunging-house; a bailiff's lock-up-house, or repository, to which persons arrested are taken, till they find bail, or have spent all their money; a house where every species of fraud and extortion is practised, under the protection of the law. [The first in Shakespeare, the second in Head in 1673 and therefore presumably cant, the third ca. 1700.OD.]

SPUNK. Rotten touchwood, or a kind of fungus prepared for tinder; figuratively, spirit, courage. [The last in Goldsmith, 1773.OD.—Probably from Gaelic *spong*, tinder.W.—In C19-20 slang, the former of the senses given for *mettle*.]

SQUAB. A fat man or woman: from their likeness to a well-stuffed couch, called also a squab. A new-hatched chicken. [All senses established by 1700.F.]

SQUARE TOES. An old man: square-toed shoes were anciently worn in common, and long retained by old men.

SQUEAK. A narrow escape, a chance: he had a squeak for his life. To squeak; to confess, peach, or turn stag. They squeak beef upon us: they cry out thieves after us. *Cant.* [With *to squeak* cf. the American cant *squeal*, both verb and noun.I.]

SQUEAKER. A bar boy; also a bastard or any other child. To stifle the squeaker; to murder a bastard, or throw it into the necessary house. Organ pipes are likewise called squeakers. The squeakers are meltable; the small pipes are silver. *Cant.*

SQUEEZE CRAB. A sour-looking, shrivelled, diminutive fellow.

SQUEEZE WAX. A good-natured foolish fellow, ready to become security for another, under hand and seal. [? Cant.]

SQUELCH. A fall. Formerly a bailiff caught in a barrackyard in Ireland, was liable by custom to have three tosses in a blanket, and a squelch; the squelch was given by letting go the corners of the blanket, and suffering him to fall to the ground. Squelch-gutted; fat, having a prominent belly. [Echoic.—Recorded 1620.OD.—Cf. dialectal *squelch*, to fall heavily, not mentioned before Johnson, and *go a squelch*, the same, and later adverbially *come down*, or *fall, squelch*.EDD.]

SQUIB. A small satirical or political temporary jeu d'esprit, which, like the firework of that denomination, sparkles, bounces, stinks, and vanishes. [Early C16.W.]

SQUINT-A-PIPES. A squinting man or woman: said to be born in the middle of the week, and looking both ways for Sunday; or born in a hackney coach, and looking out of both windows; fit for a cook, one eye in the pot, and the other up the chimney; looking nine ways at once.

SQUIRE OF ALSATIA. A weak profligate spendthrift, the squire of the company; one who pays the whole reckoning, or treats the company, called standing squire. [See *Alsatia*.]

SQUIRISH. Foolish. [In B.E., and probably cant. There is, perhaps, a democratic implication that any man who so devotedly serves another as a squire did his knight must necessarily be a fool.]

SQUIRREL. A prostitute: because she, like that animal, covers her back with her tail. *Meretrix corpore corpus alit.* Menagiana, ii. 128.

SQUIRREL HUNTING. See HUNTING.

STAG. To turn stag; to impeach one's confederates: from a herd of deer, who are said to turn their horns against any of their number who is hunted.

TO STAG. To find, discover, or observe.

STAGGERING BOB, WITH HIS YELLOW PUMPS. A calf just dropped, and unable to stand, killed for veal in Scotland: the hoofs of a young calf are yellow. [Dialectal.EDD.]

STALL WHIMPER. A bastard. *Cant.*

STALLING. Making or ordaining. Stalling to the rogue; an ancient ceremony of instituting a candidate into the society of rogues, somewhat similar to the creation of a herald at arms. It is thus described by Harman: The upright man taking a gage of bowse, i.e. a pot of strong drink, pours it on the head of the rogue to be admitted; saying—I, A.B. do stall thee, B.C. to the rogue; and from henceforth it shall be lawful for thee to cant for thy living in all places.

STALLING KEN. A broker's shop, or that of a receiver of stolen goods. [Cant.F.]

STALLION. A man kept by an old lady for secret services. [And, generally, a whoremonger as in Chapman, Rochester, Vanbrugh.F.]

STAM FLASH. To cant. *Cant.*

STAMMEL, or STRAMMEL. A coarse brawny wench. [*Stammel* in Deloney, 1597; probably cant. *Strammel* not recorded till 1706 and usually of an animal.OD.]

STAMP. A particular manner of throwing the dice out of the box, by striking it with violence against the table.

STAMPS. Legs. [This term and the next are interchangeable and cant.F.]

STAMPERS. Shoes.

STAND-STILL. He was run to a stand-still; i.e. till he could no longer move.

STAR GAZER. A horse who throws up his head; also a hedge whore. [Also in C16-18 an astrologer and in C17-18 *penis erectus*. F.—More poetical are the dialectal *star-craft*, astrology, astronomy, and *star-glint*, a shooting star, both obsolete, and the unfortunately obsolescent *star-sheen*, starlight.EDD.]

TO STAR THE GLAZE. To break and rob a jeweller's show glass. *Cant.*

STARCHED. Stiff, prim, formal, affected. [Good English.]

STARING QUARTER. An ox cheek. [In dialect, a laughing-stock.EDD.]

START, or THE OLD START. Newgate: he is gone to the start, or the old start. *Cant.* [Whence, in vagabond's cant, London.F.]

STARTER. One who leaves a jolly company, a milksop: he is no starter, he will sit longer than a hen. [In ordinary English a fickle, a restless, a cowardly person.OD.]

STARVE'EM, ROB'EM, AND CHEAT'EM. Stroud, Rochester, and Chatham: so called by soldiers and sailors, and not without good reason.

STATE. To lie in state; to be in bed with three harlots.

STAYTAPE. A taylor: from that article, and its coadjutor buckram, which make no small figure in the bills of those knights of the needle.

STEEL BAR. A needle. A steel bar flinger; a taylor, staymaker, or any other person using a needle.

STEENKIRK. A muslin neckcloth carelessly put on, from the manner in which the French officers wore their cravats when they returned from the battle of Steenkirk. [1692. Afterwards a fashion for both sexes. Later still, merely a cravat.F,W.]

STEEPLE HOUSE. A name given to the church by Dissenters. [In W. Yorkshire, Quakers thus of any church.EDD.]

STEPNEY. A decoction of raisins of the sun and lemons in conduit water, sweetened with sugar and bottled up.

STEWED QUAKER. Burnt rum with a piece of butter: an American remedy for a cold.

STICKS. Pops or pistols. Stow your sticks; hide your pistols. *Cant.* See POPS.

STICK FLAMS. A pair of gloves. [Cant.F.]

STIFF-RUMPED. Proud, stately. [In modern colloquialism, *stiff-arsed.*]

STINGBUM. A niggard. [Like the next, C17 cant.F.]

STINGO. Strong beer, or other liquor.

STIRRUP CUP. A parting cup or glass, drank on horseback by the person taking leave. [In dialect, also *s. dram* or *glass.* EDD.]

STITCH. A nick name for a taylor; also a term for lying with a woman. [The latter due to Dorset, the courtier poet.F.]

STITCHBACK. Strong ale.

STIVER-CRAMPED. Needy, wanting money. A stiver is a Dutch coin, worth somewhat more than a penny sterling.

STOCK. A good stock; i.e. of impudence. Stock and block; the whole: he has lost stock and block.

STOCK DRAWERS. Stockings. *Cant.*

STOCK JOBBERS. Persons who gamble in Exchange Alley, by pretending to buy and sell the public funds, but in reality only betting that they will be at a certain price, at a particular time; possessing neither the stock pretended to be sold, nor money sufficient to make good the payments for which they contract; these gentlemen are known under the different appellations of bulls, bears, and lame ducks.

STOMACH WORM. The stomach worm gnaws; I am hungry.

STONE. Two stone under weight, or wanting; an eunuch. Stone doublet; a prison. Stone dead; dead as a stone. [As testicle, *stone* is in Florio and Cotgrave and is good modern English as applied to animals.(F).]

STONE JUG. Newgate, or any other prison.

STONE TAVERN. Ditto. [To G's terms add *stone pitcher; s. jug* is probably the earliest.F.—Dialect has *stone-house*.EDD. —In nautical slang, *stone frigate*.B.]

STOOP-NAPPERS, or OVERSEERS OF THE NEW PAVEMENT. Persons set in the pillory. *Cant.*

STOP HOLE ABBEY. The nick name of the chief rendezvous of the canting crew of beggars, gypsies, cheats, thieves, &c. &c.

STOTER. A great blow. Tip him a stoter in the haltering place; give him a blow under the left ear. [Cant. F.]

STOUP. A vessel to hold liquor: a vessel containing a size, or half a pint, is so called at Cambridge. [In Shakespeare a two-quart measure for liquor.O.—A deep, narrow vessel usually of wood.Cf. *crust and stoup*, meat and drink.EDD.]

STOW. Stow you; be silent, or hold your peace. Stow your whidds and plant 'em, for the cove of the ken can cant 'em: you have said enough, the man of the house understands you. [Cant.F.]

STRAIT-LACED. Precise, over nice, puritanical. [Good English.]

STRAIT WAISTCOAT. A tight waistcoat, with long sleeves

coming over the hands, having strings for binding them behind the back of the wearer: these waistcoats are used in mad houses for the management of lunatics when outrageous.

STRAMMEL. See STAMMEL.

STRANGER. A guinea.

STRANGLE GOOSE. A poulterer.

STRAPPER. A large man or woman.

STRAPPING. Lying with a woman. *Cant.*

STRAW. The good woman in the straw; a lying-in-woman. His eyes draw straw; his eyes are almost shut, or he is almost asleep: one eye draws straw, and t'other serves the thatcher. [Dialect has *in (the) straw*, in childbed, and *down in the straw*, in parturition (of an animal); *to bring to the straw*, to bear, to bring forth a child; *out of the straw*, recovered from childbed. EDD.]

STRETCHING. Hanging. He'll stretch for it; he will be hanged for it. Also telling a great lie; he stretched stoutly. [In dialect *stretch the hemp* or *the neck*. EDD.—The American cant preserves the sense of hanging. I.]

STRIKE. Twenty shillings. *Cant.*

STRIP ME NAKED. Gin.

STROKE. To take a stroke; to take a bout with a woman.

STROLLERS. Itinerants of different kinds. Strolling morts; beggars or pedlars pretending to be widows.

STROMMEL. Straw. *Cant.*

STRONG MAN. To play the part of the strong man, i.e. to push the cart and horses too; to be whipt at the cart's tail.

STROUD GREEN. The aldermen and corporation formerly met at the Castle in Fleet-lane.

STRUM. A perriwig. Rum strum; a fine large wig. *Cant.*

TO STRUM. To have carnal knowledge of a woman; also to play badly on the harpsichord, or any other stringed instrument. A strummer of wire; a player on any instrument strung with wire.

STRUMPET. A harlot. [Origin unknown. W.—Good English from C14. OD.]

STUB-FACED. Pitted with the small-pox: the devil run over his face with horse stubs (horse nails) in his shoes.

STUBBLE IT. Hold your tongue. *Cant*. [Variant *stubble one's whid(d)s*.F.]

STULING KEN. See STALLING KEN. *Cant*.

STUM. The flower of fermenting wine, used by vintners to adulterate their wines.

STUMPS. Legs. To stir one's stumps; to walk fast.

STURDY BEGGARS. The fifth and last of the most ancient order of canters, beggars that rather demand than ask. *Cant*. [In Elizabethan times, *sturdy*=incorrigible and was used of rogues and vagabonds, who were often described as "sturdy and valiant beggars." *Sturdy beggars* was cant; the solus adjective has long been good English.W:A.]

SUCCESSFULLY. Used by the vulgar for *successively*: as, Three or four landlords of this house have been ruined successfully by the number of soldiers quartered on them. *Irish*. [In several dialects for *excessively*.EDD.]

SUCH A REASON PIST MY GOOSE, or MY GOOSE PIST. Said when any one offers an absurd reason.

SUCK. Strong liquor of any sort. To suck the monkey; see MONKEY. Sucky; drunk. [The first is cant.F.—Contrast dialectal *suck*, any watery drink, especially small beer.EDD.]

SUCKING CHICKEN. A young chicken.

SUDS. In the suds; in trouble, in a disagreeable situation, or involved in some difficulty. [Dialect has further meaning: in the sulks; while *drop into the suds* is to be punished.EDD.]

SUGAR SOPS. Toasted bread soaked in ale, sweetened with sugar, and grated nutmeg: it is eaten with cheese.

SUGAR STICK. The virile member. [Cf. 'opposite-number' *sugar-basin*.F.]

SUIT AND CLOAK. Good store of brandy, or other strong liquor, let down gutter lane. [Cant.F.]

SULKY. A one horse chaise, or carriage, capable of holding but one person: called by the French *désobligeant*. [1756. Now chiefly U.S.A., Australia and New Zealand.(OD).]

SUN. To have been in the sun; said of one that is drunk.

SUNBURNT. Clapped; also having male children. [In C16-

17 good English, superficial or hackneyed.F.—In dialect, palpable (lie).EDD.]

SUNDAY MAN. One who goes abroad on that day only, for fear of arrests.

SUNNY BANK. A good fire in winter.

SUNSHINE. Prosperity.

SUPERNACULUM. Good liquor, of which there is not even a drop left sufficient to wet one's nail. ['Garden' or mock Latin from C16 (e.g. Nashe, Jonson) for the practice by which, if the solitary drop from a well-drained glass reversed should, when set on the thumb-nail, run off, the drinker must drink again. In C18-19, also absolutely (as in Byron) for exceptionally good liquor.F.—From Ger. *auf den nagel trinken*, and analogous to Fr. *boire rubis sur l'ongle*.W.]

SUPOUCH. A landlady of an inn, or hostess.

SURVEYOR OF THE HIGHWAYS. One reeling drunk.

SURVEYOR OF THE PAVEMENT. One standing in the pillory.

SUS. PER COLL. Hanged: persons who have been hanged are thus entered in the jailor's books. [*Suspensus per collum*.Thackeray coined *suspercollate*, to hang,F.]

SUSPENCE. One in a deadly suspence; a man just turned off at the gallows.

SUTLER. A camp publican; also one that pilfers gloves, tobacco boxes, and such small moveables. [Former in Shakespeare(O), and good English.]

SWABBERS. The ace of hearts, knave of clubs, ace and duce of trumps, at whist; also the lubberly seamen, put to swab and clean the ship. [The latter twice in Shakespeare.O.]

SWAD, or SWADKIN. A soldier. *Cant*. [In C18 *swad, swadkin, swad-gill*. Originally rather dialect than slang: a country lout, a clumsy fellow. Whence, in early C19, *swaddy*, applied chiefly by sailors to soldiers. By 1900, *swaddy* was well established in the Regular Army for a (private) soldier and, as in 1914-1918, served occasionally as a vocative.OD, EDD, B & P.]

331

TO SWADDLE. To beat with a stick. [Usually *swaddle a person's sides*.EDD.]

SWADDLERS. The tenth order of the canting tribe, who not only rob, but beat, and often murder passengers. *Cant.*— Swaddlers is also the Irish name for methodists. [For origin of latter, see Southey's *Wesley*, 1820, at II, 109.EDD.]

SWAG. A shop. Rum swag; a shop full of rich goods. *Cant.*

SWAGGER. To bully, brag, or boast; also to strut. [Rather under a cloud *ca.* 1700-1900, but now good English. (F).]

SWANNERY. He keeps a swannery; i.e. all his geese are swans.

SWEATING. A mode of diminishing the gold coin, practised chiefly by Jews, who corrode it with aqua regia. Sweating was also a diversion practised by the bloods of the last century, who styled themselves Mohocks: these gentlemen lay in wait to surprise some person late in the night, when surrounding him, they with their swords pricked him in the posteriors, which obliged him to be constantly turning round; this they continued till they thought him sufficiently sweated.

SWEET. Easy to be imposed on, or taken in; also expert, dexterous, clever. Sweet's your hand; said of one dexterous at stealing. [Cf. *sweeten a victim*, in C18 to allay his suspicions, and in C17-18 to decoy and pluck him.EDD.]

SWEET HEART. A term applicable to either the masculine or feminine gender, signifying a girl's lover, or a man's mistress; derived from a sweet cake in the shape of a heart. [Thrice in Shakespeare.O.—Huloet in his *Abecedarium*, 1552: "*Darlynge*, a wanton term used in veneriall speach, as be these: honycombe, pyggisnye, swetehert, true love." F.—Cf. the dialectal *sweetheart-high*, high, i.e. old, enough for a sweetheart, and *sweethearting-day*, courting time.EDD.]

SWEETNERS. Guinea droppers, cheats, sharpers. To sweeten; to decoy, or draw in. To be sweet upon; to coax, wheedle, court, or allure. He seemed sweet upon that wench; he seemed to court that girl. [This last, C17.W.]

SWELLED HEAD. A disorder to which horses are extremely liable, particularly those of the subalterns of the army. This disorder is generally occasioned by remaining too long in one livery-stable or inn, and often arises to that height that it prevents their coming out of the stable door. The most certain cure is the *unguentum aureum*—not applied to the horse, but to the palm of the master of the inn or stable. N.B. Neither this disorder, nor its remedy is mentioned by either Bracken, Bartlet, or any of the modern writers on farriery.

SWIG. A hearty draught of liquor. [Noun and verb established in C17.OD.—Cf. *swig and pull*, a pleasantly long drink.EDD.]

SWIGMEN. Thieves who travel the country under colour of buying old shoes, old clothes, &c. or selling brooms, mops, &c. *Cant.* [C16.OD.]

TO SWILL. To drink greedily.

SWILL TUB. A drunkard, a sot. [Earlier *s.-bowl*, later *s.-pot*. F.—In dialect *swilling-tub, swill-belly, swill-kite*.EDD.]

SWIMMER. A counterfeit old coin.

SWINDLER. One who obtains goods on credit by false pretences, and sells them for ready money at any price, in order to make up a purse. This name is derived from the German word *schwindlin*, to totter, to be ready to fall; these arts being generally practised by persons on the totter, or just ready to break. The term *swindler* has since been used to signify cheats of every kind. ["Picked up (1762) from German Jews in London." The verb should be spelt *schwindeln*.W.]

TO SWING. To be hanged. He will swing for it; he will be hanged for it. [From *ca.* 1540.OD.]

SWING TAIL. A hog.

TO SWINGE. To beat stoutly. [Thrice in Shakespeare.O.]

SWINGING. A great swinging fellow; a great stout fellow. A swinging lie; a lusty lie. [The latter sometimes *a swinger*.F.]

SWIPES. Purser's swipes; small beer: so termed on board the king's ships, where it is furnished by the purser. ["Bad small beer." P.—Cf. dialectal *swipe*, to drink hastily and greedily, and *swiper*, a hard drinker.EDD.—"The name given by the seamen to the beer that (in the Navy) was formerly issued as a ration. The quantity was generous—four quarts a day while it lasted —but the quality and condition were appalling." B. —Extant in C20 at Marlborough College for a light beer served out to the older boys; and still heard occasionally as a colloquialism for any bad beer.]

SWISH TAIL. A pheasant; so called by the persons who sell game for the poachers.

TO SWIVE. To copulate. [Transitive in Chaucer, intransitive since *ca.* 1440. Good English till *ca.* 1700; became obsolete *ca.* 1800, except in 'literary' resuscitations. (OD).]

SWIVEL-EYED. Squinting.

SWIZZLE. Drink, or any brisk or windy liquor. In North America, a mixture of spruce beer, rum and sugar, was so called. The 17th regiment had a society called the Swizzle Club, at Ticonderoga, A.D. 1760. [Perhaps a play on *swig*.W.—In Yorkshire, *swizzlement*, and cf. *swizzler*, drunkard.EDD.]

SWOP. An exchange. [Or *swap;* in *Sir Gawayne*, C14, *swap*, used absolutely, signifies to 'strike hands' by way of confirming a bargain or an agreement; but as to exchange, not till late C16.OD.—"Low," says Johnson, who disliked native monosyllables.W:A.]

SYEBUCK. Sixpence. [Cf. *sice.*]

SYNTAX. A schoolmaster.

TABBY. An old maid: either from Tabitha, a formal antiquated name; or else from a tabby cat, old maids being often compared to cats. To drive Tab; to go out on a party of pleasure with a wife and family. [The latter derivation is correct. *Tabby*, old Fr. *atabis*, comes from the name of a Bagdad suburb; formerly applied to a kind of watered silk, but now, and for at least two centuries, to a cat marked like this silk.W: ROW.]

TACE. Silence, hold your tongue. *Tace* is Latin for a candle; a jocular admonition to be silent on any subject.

TACKLE. A mistress; also good clothes. The cull has tipt his tackle rum rigging; the fellow has given his mistress good clothes. A man's tackle; the genitals. [*The cull....* :cant.—Dialect has the word also for food or drink, food for cattle.EDD.]

TAFFY, i.e. Davy. A general name for a Welchman, St David

being the tutelar saint of Wales. Taffy's day; the first of March, St David's day. [*David* in Harrison's *England*, C16.F.]

TAG-RAG and BOBTAIL. An expression meaning an assemblage of low people, the mobility of all sorts. To tag after one like a tantony pig; to follow one wherever one goes, just as St Anthony is followed by his pig. [Shakespeare has *tag*, rabble, and *tag-rag*, people.O.—Early *tag and rag, tagrag; t.r. and b.* occurs in Pepys; another variant was *tag, rag, and cut-tail*.W.—In dialect, *tag-rag*=a vagabond, hence a low rabble, with *tag-ragly*, worthless; *tag and mag*, by the way, is the whole, every part, of something.EDD.]

TAIL. A sword. [Cant.F.]

TAIL DRAWERS. Thieves who snatch gentlemen's swords from their sides. He drew the cull's tail rumly; he snatched away the gentleman's sword cleverly. [Cant.]

TAILOR. Nine tailors make a man; an ancient and common saying originating from the effeminacy of their employment; or, as some have it, from nine tailors having been robbed by one man; according to others, from the speech of a woollen-draper, meaning that the custom of nine tailors would make or enrich one man.—A London tailor rated to furnish half a man to the trained bands, asking how that could possibly be done? was answered, By sending four journeymen and an apprentice. Put a tailor, a weaver, and a miller, into a sack, shake them well, and the first that puts out his head is certainly a thief.— A tailor is frequently styled pricklouse, from their assaults on those vermin with their needles.

TAILOR'S GOOSE. An iron with which, when heated, they press down the seams of clothes.

TAKEN IN. Imposed on, cheated.

TALE TELLERS. Persons said to have been formerly hired to tell wonderful stories of giants and fairies, to lull their hearers to sleep. Talesman; the author of a story or report: I'll tell you my tale, and my talesman. Tale bearers; mischief makers, incendiaries in families. [With *talesman* cf. dialectal *tale-master*. EDD.—Swift's *Tale of a Tub* is equivalent to Arnold Bennett's *Old Wives' Tale*, the latter a late C16, the former an early C16

335

phrase; cf. too the C16 *tale of Robin Hood, of a roasted horse,* and *Canterbury tale.*OD.]

TALL BOY. A bottle, or two-quart pot. [Also a tall, narrow glass (properly for ale) standing on a stem.EDD.]

TALLY MEN. Brokers that let out clothes to the women of the town. See RABBIT SUCKERS.

TALLYWAGS, or TARRYWAGS. A man's testicles. [In the singular, the member.F.—Thus too in dialect.EDD.]

TAME. To run tame about a house; to live familiarly in a family with which one is upon a visit. Tame army; the city trained bands.

TANDEM. A two-wheeled chaise, buggy, or noddy, drawn by two horses, one before the other; that is, *at length.* [A university joke, from the undergraduates' amusement at the frequent occurrence of *tandem* in their Latin text-books.W.—Good English from *ca.* 1830.F.]

TANGIER. A room in Newgate, where debtors were confined, hence called Tangerines.

TANTADLIN TART. A sirreverence, human excrement. [This derivative sense is approximated in dialect, which uses the word to designate cow-dung. A *t. tart* was originally a small light tart, later any dainty or fancy food.EDD.]

TANTRUMS. Pet, or passion: madam was in her tantrums. [Dialectally the singular=a whim, a foolish fancy.EDD.— Origin unknown.W.]

TANTWIVY. Away they went tantwivy; away they went full speed. Tantwivy was the sound of the hunting horn in full cry, or that of a post horn. [Usually *tantivy.* Originally an adverb: at full gallop. Perhaps imitative of a huntsman's horn.W.]

TAP. A gentle blow. A tap on the shoulder; an arrest. To tap a girl; to be the first seducer: in allusion to a beer barrel. To tap a guinea; to get it changed. [The two verb-senses are not in the OD.]

TAPE. Red, white, or blue tape; gin, or any other spirituous liquor.

TAPLASH. Thick and bad beer. ["The last and weakest running of small beer;" cf. *swipes.*P.—Occasionally and contemptuously, a publican.F.—Both senses, C17.OD.— Dialectal variants; *tap-blash, tap-lap.*]

TAPPERS. Shoulder tappers; bailiffs.

TAR. Don't lose a sheep for a halfpennyworth of tar; tar is used to mark sheep. A jack tar; a sailor. [The transition to the mistaken *lose* or *spoil a ship* is provided by dialectal *ship*, sheep. *Tar*, a sailor, *ca.* 1760, is perhaps from *tarpaulin*, though earlier we have *tar-breech*.OD,W.—"*Tarpaulin*. A practical seaman, particularly applied when appointments went by favour rather than by merit." B.]

TARADIDDLE. A fib, or falsity. [Elaboration on *diddle*.W.— Cf. dialectal *taradiddled* (almost obsolete), puzzled, bewildered. EDD.]

TARPAWLIN. A coarse cloth tarred over; also, figuratively, a sailor.

TARRING AND FEATHERING. A punishment lately inflicted by the good people of Boston on any person convicted, or suspected of loyalty: such delinquents being stripped naked, were daubed all over with tar, and afterwards put into a hogshead of feathers.

TART. Sour, sharp, quick, pert. [The first two senses have always been good English. The fourth sense may be connected with modern slang *tart*, defined by F as "primarily a girl, chaste or not; now [1903], unless loosely used, a wanton, mistress," though more probably the modern *tart* is a transference of the sweetness of the dish to one expected to be 'sweet.' (OD).]

TARTAR. To catch a Tartar; to attack one of superior strength or abilities. This saying originated from a story of an Irish soldier in the Imperial service, who, in a battle against the Turks, called out to his comrade that he had caught a Tartar. 'Bring him along then,' said he. 'He won't come,' answered Paddy. 'Then come along yourself,' replied his comrade. 'Arrah,' cried he, 'but he won't let me.'—A Tartar is also an adept at any feat, or game: he is quite a Tartar at cricket, or billiards. [*To catch a Tartar, ca.* 1660.OD.]

TAT. Tit for tat; an equivalent.

TATS. False dice. [Cant; cf. *tats-man*, a dicing gambler.F.]

TATLER. A watch. To flash a tatler; to wear a watch. [Cant. F.]

TATMONGER. One that uses false dice.

TATTERDEMALLION. A ragged fellow, whose clothes hang all in tatters. [Ca. 1600; a fantastic elaboration of *tatter*.W.]

TATTOO. A beat of the drum, or signal for soldiers to go to their quarters, and a direction to the sutlers to close the tap, and draw no more liquor for them: it is generally beat at nine in summer and eight in winter. The devil's tattoo; beating the foot against the ground, as done by persons in low spirits. [Originally (1644) *tap-to(o)*, the signal for closing the *taps* or taverns. From Dutch.W:ROW.]

TAW. A schoolboy's game, played with small round balls made of stone dust, called marbles. I'll be one upon your taw presently: a species of threat. [Cf. Northern *taw*, a whip.G.— With the phrase, cf. *bring to taw*, to compel a person to do something.EDD.]

TAWDRY. Garish, gawdy with lace or staring and discordant colours: a term said to be derived from the shrine and altar of St Audrey (an Isle of Ely saintess), which for finery exceeded all others thereabouts, so as to become proverbial; whence any fine dressed man or woman was said to be all St Audrey, and by contraction all tawdry. [Originally *St Audrey's lace* and connected with *St Audrey's fair*.W.—In dialect, *tawdry*=cheap finery, sham jewelry.EDD.]

TAWED. Beaten.

TAYLE. See TAIL.

TEA VOIDER. A chamber pot.

TEAGUELAND. Ireland. Teaguelanders; Irishmen. [*Teague*, contemptuous for an Irishman.F.]

TEARS OF THE TANKARD. The drippings of liquor on a man's waistcoat.

TEDDY MY GODSON. An address to a supposed simple fellow, or nysey.

TEIZE. To nap the teize; to receive a private whipping. *Cant.*

TEMPLE PICKLING. Pumping a bailiff: a punishment formerly administered to any of that fraternity caught exercising

their functions within the limits of the Temple. [C17 phrase.—
For a short and pithy account of the Temple, see Beresford
Chancellor's *Annals of Fleet Street.*]

TEN TOES. See BAYARD OF TEN TOES.

TEN IN THE HUNDRED. An usurer; more than five in
the hundred being deemed usurious interest. [5 per cent was
the statutory interest in C18.F.]

TENANT AT WILL. One whose wife usually fetches him
from the alehouse.

TENDER PARNELL. A tender creature, fearful of the least
puff of wind or drop of rain. As tender as Parnell, who broke
her finger in a posset drink. [Like *parnel* (*pernel*) alone from C14
onwards, *tender parnel* had long meant a priest's mistress, a harlot, a wanton young woman. From (*Saint*) *Petronilla.*OD.]

TERCEL GENTLE. A rich man. [So, 1690, in B.E., who says
that it also meant "a Knight or Gentleman of a good estate."
F.—Probably from hawking as a rich man's pastime, the *tercel*
being the male of the falcon gentle: one has but to relate *tassel
gentle*, Juliet's descriptive name for Romeo, with *tiercel*, the
male peregrine, called *tiercel* because he is a third smaller than
the female (Cotgrave).O;W:ROW.]

TERMAGANT. An outrageous scold; from Termagantes, a
cruel Pagan, formerly represented in divers shows and enter-
tainments, where being dressed *à la Turque*, in long clothes, he
was mistaken for a furious woman. ["Imaginary deity supposed in mediaeval Christendom to be worshipped by Moham-
medans, represented in mystery plays as a violent overbearing
personage." O.]

TERRA FIRMA. An estate in land.

TESTER. A sixpence: from *teston*, a coin with a head on it.

TETBURY PORTION. A **** and a clap. [Cf. *Rochester
portion.*]

THAMES. He will not find out a way to set the Thames on
fire; he will not make any wonderful discoveries, he is no conjuror. [Earliest example, 1778, but probably much earlier; an
equivalent use of the Rhine dates from *ca.* 1638.W.]

THATCH-GALLOWS. A rogue, or man of bad character.

THICK. Intimate. They are as thick as two inkle-weavers. [Synonymous dialectal phrases are *as thick as bees, blackberries, crowdy, Darby and Joan, Dick and Leddy, Harry and Mary, herrings in a barrel, inkle-makers, thack (thatch), thick, thieves, three in a bed, two dogs' heads, two in a bed.* EDD.]

THIEF. You are a thief and a murderer, you have killed a baboon and stole his face; vulgar abuse. ["A general term of reproach, not confined to stealing." P.]

THIEF IN A CANDLE. Part of the wick or snuff, which falling on the tallow, burns and melts it, and causing it to gutter, thus steals it away.

THIEF TAKERS. Fellows who associate with all kinds of villains, in order to betray them, when they have committed any of those crimes which entitle the persons taking them to a handsome reward, called blood money. It is the business of these thief takers to furnish subjects for a handsome execution, at the end of every sessions.

THINGSTABLE. Mr Thingstable; Mr Constable: a ludicrous affectation of delicacy in avoiding the pronunciation of the first syllable in the title of that officer, which in sound has some similarity to an indecent monosyllable.

THINGUMBOB. Mr Thingumbob; a vulgar address or nomination to any person whose name is unknown, the same as Mr What-d'ye-call'em. Thingumbobs; testicles. [Or one whose name is not to be mentioned. In C17 *thingum*, in C19-20 usually *thingummy*. W.]

THIRDING. A custom practised at the universities, where two-thirds of the original price is allowed by the upholsterers to the students for household goods returned to them within the year. [See the *Gradus ad Cantabrigiam*, a glossary of terms used at Cambridge, 1803.F,H.]

THIRTEENER. A shilling in Ireland, which there passes for thirteen-pence. [Or simply *thirteen*, as in Lover 1842.EDD.]

THOMAS. Man Thomas; a man's penis. [Fletcher, 1619.F.— In C19-20 often *John Thomas*.]

THOMOND. Like Lord Thomond's cocks,,all on one side. Lord Thomond's cock feeder, an Irishman, being entrusted with some cocks which were matched for a considerable sum, the night before the battle, shut them all together in one room, concluding, that as they were all on the same side, they would not disagree: the consequence was, they were most of them either killed or lamed before the morning.

THORNS. To be or sit upon thorns; to be uneasy, impatient, anxious for an event.

THORNBACK. An old maid. [From the fish. F.]

THOROUGH CHURCHMAN. A person who goes in at one door of a church, and out at the other, without stopping.

THOROUGH GOOD-NATURED WENCH. One who being asked to sit down, will lie down.

THOROUGH GO NIMBLE. A looseness, a violent purging.

THOROUGH COUGH. Coughing and breaking wind backwards at the same time.

THOROUGH STITCH. To go thorough stitch; to stick at nothing, over shoes, over boots. [Or just: thoroughly. EDD.]

THOUGHT. What did thought do? lay in bed and besh-t himself, and thought he was up; reproof to any one who excuses himself for any breach of positive orders, by pleading that he thought to the contrary.

THREE TO ONE. He is playing three to one, though sure to lose; said of one engaged in the amorous congress.

THREE-LEGGED MARE, or STOOL. The gallows, formerly consisting of three posts, over which were laid three transverse beams. This clumsy machine has lately given place to an elegant contrivance, called the *new drop*, by which the use of that vulgar vehicle a cart, or mechanical instrument a ladder, is also avoided; the patients being left suspended by the dropping down of that part of the floor on which they stand. This invention was first made use of for a peer. See DROP.

THREE-PENNY UPRIGHT. A retailer of love, who for the sum mentioned, dispenses her favours standing against a wall.

THREE THREADS. Half common ale, mixed with stale and double beer. [In B.E.; probably cant. (F).]

THREPS. Threepence.

THROTTLE. The throat, or gullet. [Frequent in dialect, which has also *throttle-deep*, up to the throat; *t.-poke*, an avaricious and selfish person; *t.-wet*, drink of any kind; *to moisten, slake, wet one's throttle*, to drink; *throttle the teapot*, have a drink of tea.EDD.]

TO THRUM. To play on any instrument stringed with wire. A thrummer of wire; a player on the spinnet, harpsichord, or guitar.

THRUMS. Threepence.

THUMB. By rule of thumb: to do any thing by dint of practice. To kiss one's thumb instead of the book; a vulgar expedient to avoid perjury in taking a false oath.

THUMMIKINS. An instrument formerly used in Scotland, like a vice, to pinch the thumbs of persons accused of different crimes, in order to extort confession.

THUMP. A blow. This is better than a thump on the back with a stone; said on giving any one a drink of good liquor on a cold morning. Thatch, thistle, thunder, and thump; words to the Irish, like the Shibboleth of the Hebrews.

THUMPING. Great: a thumping boy.

THWACK. A great blow with a stick across the shoulders.

TIB. A young lass. [Also, in C16-17, a wanton. Perhaps from *Isabel*.OD.]

TIBBY. A cat.

TIB OF THE BUTTERY. A goose. *Cant.*—Saint Tibb's evening; the evening of the last day, or day of judgment: he will pay you on St Tibb's eve. *Irish.*

TICK. To run o'tick: take up goods upon trust, to run in debt. Tick: a watch. See *Sessions Papers*. [Also *run a-tick*, to go abroad, especially with a view to robbery and larceny.D.—"A C17 clipped form of *ticket*. ... Perhaps from seamen's practice of getting goods on their pay-tickets." W.—With *tick*, a watch, cf. C19 slang, *ticker*; in American cant, *ticker*=the heart.I.]

TICKLE PITCHER. A thirsty fellow, a sot.

TICKLE TAIL. A rod, or schoolmaster. [Also, in colloquialism and dialect, a loose woman (EDD), and, in colloquialism, the member (F).]

TICKLE TEXT. A parson.

TICKRUM. A licence.

TIDY. Neat. [This sense is now good English. In G's day the word, thus used, had a provincial 'taint' (P). Originally, seasonable, timely, opportune. OD.]

TIFFING. Eating or drinking out of meal time, disputing or falling out; also lying with a wench. A tiff of punch; a small bowl of punch.

TILBURY. Sixpence: so called from its formerly being the fare for crossing over from Gravesend to Tilbury fort.

TILT. To tilt; to fight with a sword. To run full tilt against one; allusion to the ancient tilting with the lance.

TILTER. A sword. [Cant.]

TIMBER TOE. A man with a wooden leg.

TIM WHISKY. A light one-horse chaise without a head.

TINY. Little. [In Shakespeare thrice, always with *little*. O.]

TO TIP. To give or lend. Tip me your daddle; give me your hand. Tip me a hog; give me a shilling. To tip the lion; to flatten a man's nose with the thumb, and at the same time to extend his mouth with the fingers, thereby giving him a sort of lion-like countenance. To tip the velvet; tonguing a woman. To tip all nine; to knock down all the nine pins at once, at the game of bowls or skittles: tipping, at these games, is slightly touching the tops of the pins with the bowl. Tip; a draught: don't spoil his tip. [The first four examples are either cant or near-cant.—With the noun cf. obsolete Scottish *tip* for *two-penny* ale, but more probably short for *tipple*, liquor, or from *tip*, to drink off. OD.]

TIP-TOP. The best; perhaps from fruit, that growing at the top of the tree being generally the best, as partaking most of the sun. A tip-top workman; the best, or most excellent workman. [Reduplication on either *tip* or *top*. W.—From *ca.* 1700. OD.]

TIPPERARY FORTUNE. Two town lands, stream's town, and ballinocack; said of Irish women without fortune. [The terms are now obsolete. Breasts, pudend, fundament. F.]

TIPPLE. Liquor. [Both noun and verb are very old; *tippler* originally meant an alehouse-keeper. W.]

343

TIPPLERS. Sots who are continually sipping.

TIPSEY. Almost drunk. [From *tip*, to upset, tilt up.W.—From *ca.* 1570.OD.]

TIRING. Dressing: perhaps abbreviation of *attiring.* Tiring women, or tire women; women that used to cut ladies' hair, and dress them. [*Tire*, to dress, C14; to dress the hair, C16.OD.]

TIT. A horse. A pretty little tit; a smart little girl. A tit, or tid bit; a delicate morsel. Tommy tit; a smart lively little fellow.

TIT FOR TAT. An equivalent. [Earlier *tip for tap.* W.—Probably a blow for a blow.F.]

TO TITTER. To suppress a laugh. [Onomatopoeic.W.]

TITTER-TATTER. One reeling, and ready to fall at the least touch; also the childish amusement of riding upon the two ends of a plank, poised upon a prop underneath its centre, called also see-saw. Perhaps tatter is a rustic pronunciation of totter.

TITTLE-TATTLE. Idle discourse, scandal, women's talk, or small talk. [Alliterative reduplication on *tittle*, to prate.W: ROW.]

TITTUP. A gentle hand gallop, or canter. [From *ca.* 1700, with corresponding verb from *ca.* 1780.OD.—Frequent in dialect, where, in C19, *tittup* meant also a dance, festivity, or other large social gathering.EDD.]

TIZZY. Sixpence. [Perhaps an 'argotic perversion' of *tilbury*, q.v.W.]

TOAD. Toad in a hole; meat baked or boiled in pye crust. He or she sits like a toad on a chopping-block; a saying of any one who sits ill on horseback. As much need of it as a toad of a side-pocket; said of a person who desires any thing for which he has no real occasion. As full of money as a toad is of feathers.

TOAD EATER. A poor female relation, an humble companion or reduced gentlewoman, in a great family, the standing butt, on whom all kinds of practical jokes are played off, and all ill humours vented. This appellation is derived from a mountebank's servant, on whom all experiments used to be made in public by the doctor, his master; among which was the the eating of toads, formerly supposed poisonous. Swallowing toads

344

is here figuratively meant for swallowing or putting up with insults, as disagreeable to a person of feeling, as toads to the stomach. [Cf. Fr. *avaleur de couleuvres* and *toady*, which is later.W.]

TOAST. A health: also a beautiful woman whose health is often drank by men. The origin of this term (as it is said) was this: A beautiful lady bathing in a cold bath, one of her admirers out of gallantry drank some of the water; whereupon another of her lovers observed, he never drank in the morning, but he would kiss the toast, and immediately saluted the lady. [In M.E., a piece of bread, toasted and spiced, put into drinks to give them a flavour; the lady 'healthed in wine' dates from *ca.* 1700.W.]

TOASTING IRON, or CHEESE TOASTER. A sword. [The former thus in Shakespeare.O.]

TOBACCO. A plant, once in great estimation as a medicine.

> *Tobacco hic*
> *Will make you well if you be sick.*
> *Tobacco hic*
> *If you be well will make you sick.*

[Usual C16-17 form *tabaco*, though *tobacco* is recorded for 1597. *Tobacco-box* occurs in Ben Jonson in 1599, at which date he also has *tobacconist*, a smoker, this sense prevailing till *ca.* 1660 and lasting till *ca.* 1800.OD.—In dialect, though now obsolescent, *tobacco-flour,-meal*, is snuff: in France, tobacco was first used only as snuff. *Tobacco-night* is a lyke-wake, a watch over the dead, much tobacco being smoked on such occasions.EDD.]

TODDY. Originally the juice of the cocoa tree, and afterwards rum, water, sugar, and nutmeg. [I.e. the coco-nut tree.]

TODGE. Beat all to a todge; said of any thing beat to mash. [Properly spoon-meat, very thick soup.EDD.]

TOGE. A coat. *Cant.* [Shakespeare's form of *toga* is *toge*.O.]

TOGEMANS. A cloak. *Cant.*

TOKEN. The plague; also the venereal disease. She tipped him the token; she gave him a clap or pox. [The latter perhaps from an older sense of *token* (as in Skelton): the *pudendum muliebre*. F.—Both senses are cant, the former being usually in the plural. Shakespeare has *the Lord's tokens*, plague-spots.O.]

345

TOL, or TOLEDO. A sword; from Spanish swords made at Toledo, which place was famous for sword blades, of an extraordinary temper. [Is in Ben Jonson.W.—*Tol* became a cant form, especially in *rum tol*, a silver-hilted sword (see *rum*), and in *queer tol*, a very ordinary sword indeed.F.]

TOL TAWDRUM. To talk tol tawdrum; a term used by ladies to signify talking a little loosely, making use of double entendres. [Usually *toldrum* and occasionally meaning bombastic talk; connected with *tawdry*.EDD.]

TOLIBAN RIG. A species of cheat carried on by a woman, assuming the character of a dumb and deaf conjurer.

TOMBOY. A romping girl, who prefers the amusements used by boys, to those of her own sex. [At first a boisterous boy, then a boisterous girl, then (as in Shakespeare) a wanton; after *ca.* 1700, the second sense prevails in good English (F), but dialect favours the third; in dialect, too, a romping girl is *tom-lad*.EDD. Cf. the Lancashire synonym *Meg-Harry* and the Yorkshire *Rigsby*.P].

TOM CONY. A simple fellow.

TOM LONG. A tiresome story teller. It is coming by Tom Long, the carrier; said of any thing that has been long expected.

TOM OF BEDLAM. The same as abram man.

TOM THUMB. A dwarf, a little hop-o'-my-thumb.

TOMMY. Soft Tommy, or white tommy; bread is so called by sailors, to distinguish it from biscuit. [In 1914-1918 *tommy*, among soldiers, meant food in general; it had long been in use in the Regular Army. In C17 and later, *brown George* (cf. the Fr. *gros Guillaume*) designated a coarse brown loaf, and there may be a pun suggested by *brown musket* (C17) and *brown Bess* (C18), assisted perhaps by the Navy application of *brown George* to bread supplied by a contractor and officially known as *munition bread*, which soon, in both Navy and Army, came to be called *ammunition loaf* or *bread*. In the late C18 *brown George* generated *brown Tommy*, which became alternatively *Tommy Brown;* and *Tommy Brown* was speedily abbreviated to *Tommy*, whence *tommy*. As early as 1783, as Cobbett tells us, *tommy* signified brown bread and, at Chatham, white bread was just *bread*. It may be added that in C19 colloquialism *brown* (*T*)(*t*)*ommy* was the name given to bread supplied to convicts; also that, in dialect, *tommy*=a loaf of bread, here perhaps from *tom*, any food requiring mastication, especially bread, though, of course, *tommy* may have branched off in dialect with form *tom:* the latter is the more likely, for *tommy* is widespread in dialect, *tom* is not, and whereas *tommy* in dialect is recorded for 1828, no date is given for *tom*.OD,EDD,B; also W,F.]

TO-MORROW COME NEVER. When two Sundays come together; never. [Popularised by Swift.F.]

TOM T—DMAN. A night man, one who empties necessary houses.

TONGUE. Tongue enough for two sets of teeth; saying of a talkative person. As old as my tongue, and a little older than my teeth; a dovetail in answer to the question, How old are you? Tongue pad; a scold, or nimble-tongued person.

TONY. A silly fellow, or ninny. A mere tony; a simpleton. [C17, from *Antony*.OD.]

TOOL. The instrument of any person or faction, a cat's paw. See CAT'S PAW.

TOOTH MUSIC. Chewing.

TO TOP. To cheat, or trick; also to insult: he thought to have topped upon me. Top; the signal among taylors for snuffing the candles; he who last pronounces that word, is obliged to get up and perform the operation. [Note the old nautical phrase *top the glim*, snuff the candle.B.]

TOP DIVER. A lover of women. An old top diver; one who has loved old hat in his time.

TOP HEAVY. Drunk.

TOP LIGHTS. The eyes. Blast your top lights. See CURSE.

TOP SAIL. He paid his debts at Portsmouth with the top-sail; i.e. he went to sea and left them unpaid. So soldiers are said to pay off their scores with the drum; that is, by marching away.

TOPER. One that loves his bottle, a soaker. See TO HOAX. [Always good English; now, in fact, 'literary' (OD).]

TOPPING CHEAT. The gallows. *Cant.*

TOPPING COVE. The hangman. *Cant.* [In contemporary accounts of Dick Turpin's execution, the hangman is called the *topsman.*W.]

TOPPING FELLOW. One at the top or head of his profession. [Originally cant.F.—This literal use of *top* appears also in the American cant *toppings*, pastry or cake, that which, in short, tops off the meal.I.—In *Moll Flanders* one hears that, when some very capable highwaymen arrived at Newgate, the prisoners "were all desirous enough to see these brave, topping gentlemen." D.]

TOPPING MAN. A rich man. [Cant.F. The *topping* of this phrase and that of *topping fellow* have engendered the modern sense.]

TOPSY-TURVY. The top side the other way; i.e. the wrong side upwards: some explain it the top side turf ways, turf being always laid the wrong side upwards. [From *top+terve*, an obsolete verb meaning to turn. G has elaborated on Bailey.W: MWAM.]

TORCHECUL. Bumfodder. [Cant from the French.F.]

TORMENTOR OF CATGUT. A fiddler.

TORY. An advocate for absolute monarchy and church power; also an Irish vagabond, robber, or rapparee. ["*Tory*, outlaw, bandit, is the only purely Irish word in general English use." W:MWAM.]

TOSS OFF. Manual pollution. [Vile! Yet one has heard vulgar comedians use the phrase in obvious innuendo before large crowds.]

TOSS POT. A drunkard. [In Shakespeare.O.]

TOTTY-HEADED. Giddy, hair-brained.

TOUCH. To touch; to get money from any one; also to arrest. Touched in the wind; broken-winded. Touched in the head; insane, crazy. To touch up a woman; to have carnal knowledge of her. Touch bone and whistle; any one having broken wind backwards, according to the vulgar law, may be pinched by any of the company till he has touched bone (i.e. his teeth) and whistled.

TOUCH BUN FOR LUCK. See BUN.

TOUT. A look-out house, or eminence.

TOUTING. (From *tueri*, to look about.) Publicans forestalling guests, or meeting them on the road, and begging their custom: also thieves or smugglers looking out to see that the coast is clear. Touting ken; the bar of a public house. [Whence the modern *tout*, verb and noun. Derives from A.S. *totian*.W.]

TOW ROW. A grenadier. The tow row club; a club or society of the grenadier officers of the line. [Whence perhaps *tow-row*, hubbub, disturbance, first recorded (OD) *ca*. 1840.]

TOWEL. An oaken towel, a cudgel. To rub one down with an oaken towel; to beat or cudgel him.

TO TOWER. To overlook, to rise aloft as in a high tower. [Also, in old cant, to watch closely.F.]

TOWER. Clipped money: they have been round the tower with it. *Cant*.

TOWER HILL PLAY. A slap on the face, and a kick on the breech. [Perhaps cant.]

TOWN. A woman of the town; a prostitute. To be on the town; to live by prostitution.

TOWN BULL. A common whoremaster. To roar like a town bull; to cry or bellow aloud. [Cf. Swift's *town-rake*.F.]

TO TRACK. To go. Track up the dancers; go up stairs. *Cant*. [Cf. C20 slang, "Well, I must be tracking," i.e. going.]

TRADING JUSTICES. Broken mechanics, discharged footmen, and other low fellows, smuggled into the commission of the peace, who subsist by fomenting disputes, granting warrants and otherwise retailing justice: to the honour of the present times, these nuisances are by no means so common as formerly.

TRANSLATORS. Sellers of old mended shoes and boots, between coblers and shoemakers. [In dialect, cobblers.EDD.]

TO TRANSMOGRAPHY, or TRANSMIGRIFY. To patch up, vamp, or alter. [Usually *transmogrify*. From *ca*. 1650.OD.]

TO TRANSNEAR. To come up with any body. [Almost certainly cant.]

TRANTER. See CROCKER. [In Wessex, still a carrier. From M.L. *travetarius*, from L. *transvehere*, to transport. See

349

especially Hardy's *Under the Greenwood Tree*. W: RON.]

TRAP. To understand trap; to know one's own interest.

TO TRAPAN. To inveigle, or ensnare. [Cant.F.—Now *trepan*; from *trap*. The surgical *trepan* is of different origin.W:ROW.]

TRAPES. A slatternly woman, a careless sluttish woman. [Cf. the modern colloquialism *to trapes, trapse, traipse about,* to gad (about). The sense-development I take to be this:—*trape(s)*, to go on foot; to trudge; to walk heavily or wearily; to walk in a slovenly way; to walk about with dirty boots or with a garment (especially a dress) trailing; with both soiled boots and trailing dress; a woman who often or habitually so walks; a slovenly woman; a slattern.(W,EDD).]

TRAPS.Constables and thief-takers. *Cant.*

TRAPSTICKS. Thin legs, gambs: from the sticks with which boys play at trap-ball.

TRAVELLER. To tip the traveller; to tell wonderful stories, to romance.

TRAVELLING PIQUET. A mode of amusing themselves, practised by two persons riding in a carriage, each reckoning towards his game the persons or animals that pass by on the side next them, according to the following estimation.

A parson riding a grey horse, with blue furniture; game.

An old woman under a hedge; ditto.

A cat looking out of a window; 60.

A man, woman, and child, in a buggy; 40.

A man with a woman behind him;30.

A flock of sheep; 20.

A ditto of geese; 10.

A postchaise; 5.

A horseman; 2.

A man or woman walking; 1.

TRAY TRIP. An ancient game like Scotch hop, played on a pavement marked out with chalk into different compartments. [In Shakespeare a game at dice, in which success depended on throwing a three; also *trey*, three on a die.O.—Cf. modern slang *trey bit*, a 3d. piece.]

TRENCHER CAP. The square cap worn by the collegians, at the universities of Oxford and Cambridge.

TRENCHER MAN. A stout trencher man; one who has a good appetite, or, as the term is, plays a good knife and fork. [Coined by Shakespeare.O.]

TRESWINS. Threepence.

TRIB. A prison: perhaps from tribulation. [Almost certainly. Shakespeare's *the tribulation of Tower Hill* supplies the key if we compare it with G's entry at *Tower Hill Play;* Sir James Murray's explanation of Shakespeare's phrase (1613) by *tribulation* as a gang of roughs (this the context demands) is made very much more pointed by G's definition of *Tower Hill Play*, which the OD misses. *Trib* is a C17 cant word and Sir James supposed *the t. of T. Hill* to be a cant name. *Sed quid argumentor?....*]

TRICKUM LEGIS. A quirk or quibble in the law. [Cf. the obsolete Oxfordshire *trickumtrully*, to play false, to act unfairly (Blackmore, *Cripps*, 1876).EDD.]

TRIG. The point at which schoolboys stand to shoot their marbles at taw; also the spot whence bowlers deliver the bowl.

TO TRIG IT. To play truant. To lay a man trigging; to knock him down.

TRIGRYMATE. An idle female companion. [The word survives in dialect, but the companion is intimate and not necessarily female nor idle.EDD.]

TRIM. State, dress. In a sad trim; dirty.—Also spruce or fine: a trim fellow. [Shakespeare has *trim*=fine attire, and figuratively *our hearts are in the trim;* his adjective *trim*=pretty, his adverb=neatly.O.]

TRIMMING. Cheating, changing side, or beating. I'll trim his jacket; I'll thresh him. To be trimmed; to be shaved: I'll just step and get trimmed. [In old cant, *trim*=to cheat.F.]

TRIM TRAM. Like master, like man. [In C16 comes the first of the many rhyming jingles; it also in C16-17 meant a trifle, a gew-gaw, or a silly device, an absurdity.OD.]

TRINE. To hang; also Tyburn. [Cant, Harman onwards.F.]

TRINGUM TRANGUM. A whim, or maggot.

TRINING. Hanging.

TRINKETS. Toys, bawbles, or nicknacks. [Good English.]

TRIP. A short voyage or journey, a false step or stumble, an error in the tongue, a bastard. She has made a trip; she has had a bastard. [The first from late C17.OD.]

TRIPE. The belly, or guts. Mr Double Tripe; a fat man. Tripes &trullibubs; the entrails: also a jeering appellation for a fat man.

TO TROLL. To loiter or saunter about.

TROLLY LOLLY. Coarse lace once much in fashion.

TROLLOP. A lusty coarse sluttish woman. [Perhaps *troll-up*, a nickname like *gad-about*.W.]

TROOPER. Half-a-crown. You will die the death of a trooper's horse, that is, with your shoes on; a jocular method of telling any one he will be hanged.

TROT. An old trot; a decrepit old woman. A dog trot; a gentle pace. [The former is in Palsgrave, 1530; two centuries earlier, *trat(t)e*.OD.]

TROTTERS. Feet. To shake one's trotters at Bilby's ball, where the sheriff pays the fidlers; perhaps the Bilboes ball, i.e. the ball of fetters: fetters and stocks were anciently called the bilboes.

TO TROUNCE. To punish by course of law. [Recorded from C16. Littleton, 1678, has "*trounce:* male mulctare," to fine heavily, and the C16-17 uses of the verb mean or imply: to discomfit, to terrify, both obsolete by *ca.* 1700. As to beat soundly, *trounce* established itself *ca.* 1660. G's sense of the word is extant only in dialect.W:WAM.]

TRUCK. To exchange, swop, or barter; also a wheel such as ships' guns are placed upon. [The verb keeps a colloquial taint, but *truck* as noun has always been good English.]

TRUE BRITONS. This honourable corporation held their annual feast at the Three Kings, in the Minories, Oct.29, 1743, being lord mayor's day.

TRUG. A dirty puzzle, an ordinary sorry woman. [Cf. *trugging-house*, a brothel.F.—*Trug* may still be heard in Hampshire for a harlot, a low female companion, especially in *a soldier's trug*.EDD.]

TRULL. A soldier or a tinker's trull; a soldier or tinker's female companion.—*Guteli*, or *trulli*, are spirits like women, which shew great kindness to men, and hereof it is that we call light women Trulls. *Randle Holms's Academy of Armory.* [From a Teutonic group of words of similar form and meaning. In English since early C16. OD.—Now 'literary.' Holme's book appeared in 1688.]

TRUMPERY. An old whore, or goods of no value: rubbish.

TRUMPET. To sound one's own trumpet; to praise one's self.

TRUMPETER. The King of Spain's trumpeter; a braying ass. His trumpeter is dead, he is therefore forced to sound his own trumpet. He would make an excellent trumpeter, for he has a strong breath: said of one having a foetid breath.

TRUMPS. To be put to one's trumps; to be in difficulties, or put to one's shifts. Something may turn up trumps: something lucky may happen. All his cards are trumps; he is extremely fortunate. [The first sense is obsolete.]

TRUNDLERS. Peas. [In B.E., and probably cant. (F.)]

TRUNK. A nose. How fares your old trunk? does your nose still stand fast? an allusion to the proboscis or trunk of an elephant. To shove a trunk; to introduce one's self unasked into any place or company. Trunk-maker like; more noise than work.

TRUSTY TROJAN, or TRUSTY TROUT. A true friend.

TRYNING. See TRINING.

TUB THUMPER. A presbyterian parson. [Earlier *tub-preacher, pulpit-thumper.* The practice (*in* not on a tub) is referred to as early as 1538. W.—In C19 of any ranting parson, and in C20 of any violent and declamatory orator. OD.]

TUCKED UP. Hanged. A tucker up to an old bachelor or widower; a supposed mistress.

TUFT HUNTER. An university parasite, one who courts the acquaintance of nobility, whose caps are adorned with a gold tuft. [*Tuft*, Fr. *touffe*, has become the slang *toff.* W:A.]

TUMBLER. A cart; also a sharper employed to draw in pigeons to game; likewise a posture master, or rope-dancer. To shove the tumbler, or perhaps tumbril; to be whipt at the cart's tail.

TO TUNE. To beat: his father tuned him delightfully: perhaps from fetching a tune out of the person beaten, or from a comparison with the disagreeable sounds of instruments when tuning.

TUP. A ram; figuratively, a cuckold. [In venery, to copulate (transitive and intrans.).F.—Dialect has a picturesque phrase that it applies to persons: *to tup and lamb*, to live in complete conjugal agreement and concord.EDD.]

TUP RUNNING. A rural sport practised at wakes and fairs in Derbyshire: a ram, whose tail is well soaped and greased, is turned out to the multitude; any one that can take him by the tail, and hold him fast, is to have him for his own.

TU QUOQUE. The mother of all saints.

T—D. There were four t—ds for dinner; stir t—d, hold t—d, tread t—d, and mus-t—d; to wit, a hog's face, feet, and chitterlings, with mustard. He will never sh—e a seaman's t—d; i.e. he will never make a good seaman. [In OD, which records it at *ca.* 1000 and as a term of abuse as early as *ca.*1450. Not slang nor colloquialism, but a true vulgarism.]

TURF. On the turf; persons who keep running horses, or attend and bet at horse races, are said to be on the turf.

TURK. A cruel, hard-hearted man. Turkish treatment; barbarous usage. Turkish shore; Lambeth, Southwark, and Rotherhithe side of the Thames. [Cf. *to turn Turk*, to become a renegade, Shakespeare using *Turk* as generic for an infidel.O.—Cf. also *Turkise*, to play the Turk. The word has lost much of its sting, as in C19-20 *you young Turk!* F.—*Turk* has a strong following among the dialects.EDD.]

TURKEY MERCHANT. A poulterer.

TURNCOAT. One who has changed his party from interested motives. [Shakespearean.F.]

TURNIP-PATED. White or fair haired.

TURNPIKE MAN. A parson; because the clergy collect their tolls at our entrance into and exit from the world.

TUSKIN. A country carter or ploughman.

TUZZY-MUZZY. The monosyllable. [In Bailey. F.—Survives in dialect.EDD.]

TWADDLE. Perplexity, confusion, or any thing else: a fashionable term that for a while succeeded that of *bore*. See BORE.

TWANGEY, or STANGEY. A north country name for a taylor.

TWEAGUE. In a great tweague; in a great passion. Tweaguey; peevish, passionate. [Obsolete for *tweak*. OD.]

TO TWEAK. To pull: to tweak any one's nose.

TWELVER. A shilling. [Probably cant.]

TWIDDLE-DIDDLES. Testicles.

TWIDDLE-POOP. An effeminate looking fellow.

TO TWIG. To observe. Twig the cull, he is peery; observe the fellow, he is watching us. Also to disengage, snap asunder, or break off. To twig the darbies; to knock off the irons. [The former colloquial, the latter cant, though both examples are cant. F.]

TWIST. A mixture of half tea and half coffee; likewise brandy, beer, and eggs. A good twist; a good appetite. To twist it down apace; to eat heartily. [As appetite, very general in colloquial use in C19. EDD.]

TWISTED. Executed, hanged.

TO TWIT. To reproach a person, or remind him of favours conferred. [Good English.]

TWITTER. All in a twitter; in a fright. Twittering is also the note of some small birds, such as the robin, &c. [Imitative. W. —G is good on this word in his *P. Glos.*]

TWITTOC. Two. *Cant.*

TWO-HANDED. Great. A two-handed fellow or wench; a great strapping man or woman.

TWO HANDED PUT. The amorous congress. [In G, by an oversight, this entry, verbatim, occurs also at the end of the preceding entry.]

TWO THIEVES BEATING A ROGUE. A man beating his hands against his sides to warm himself in cold weather; called also Beating the Booby, and Cuffing Jonas.

TWO TO ONE SHOP. A pawn-broker's; alluding to the three blue balls, the sign of that trade; or perhaps to its being two to one that the goods pledged are never redeemed.

TYBURN BLOSSOM. A young thief or pickpocket, who in time will ripen into fruit borne by the deadly never green. [The great gallows known as Tyburn Tree stood almost exactly where the Marble Arch now stands. E. Beresford Chancellor, *The West End of Yesterday and To-Day*, 1926.—Here men were hanged till 1783, and as early as the C15 the district, owing to the grim associations of *Tyburn* (then *Tyborne*), began to be called *Maryborne*, corrupted to *Marylebone*. In C17, the journey of the condemned from Newgate to Tyburn was described as *going west* (a phrase whose further implications are treated in my article, 'Soldiers' Slang,' in *The Quarterly Review*, April 1931). W:A.]

TYBURN TIPPET. A halter: see Latimer's sermon before Edward VI. A.D. 1549. [This phrase, says Egan, was "rather obsolete in 1822." *Tyburn* had, however, been prominent for centuries: it is mentioned in a Latin chronicle of *ca.* 1200 and first in English in Langland, 1377.OD, where see an imposing list of compounds and phrases: note especially *to preach at Tyburn Cross*, to be hanged, Gascoigne, 1576.]

TYBURN TOP, or FORETOP. A wig with the foretop combed over the eyes in a knowing style: such being much worn by the gentlemen pads, scamps, divers, and other knowing hands.

TYE. A neckcloth. [The usual C18 spelling; first recorded in 1761, Churchill.OD.—Good English.]

TYKE. A dog, also a Clown: a Yorkshire tyke. [Old Norse *tik*, bitch, hence contemptuous Northern for a dog.W.—Then for a person, as in Shakespeare.O.—Of Yorkshiremen, "perhaps originally opprobrious, but now accepted and owned."OD.]

TYNEY. See TINY.

UNCLE. Mine uncle's; a necessary house. He is gone to visit his uncle; saying of one who leaves his wife soon after marriage. It likewise means a pawnbroker's: goods pawned are frequently said to be at mine uncle's, or laid up in lavender. [With the first, cf. the French *chez ma tante*.]

UNDERSTRAPPER. An inferior in any office, or department.

UNFORTUNATE GENTLEMEN. The horse guards, who thus named themselves in Germany, where a general officer seeing them very awkward in bundling up their forage, asked what the devil they were; to which some of them answered, unfortunate gentlemen.

UNFORTUNATE WOMEN. Prostitutes; so termed by the virtuous and compassionate of their own sex. [First mention. *Unfortunate* by itself not till 1844: in Hood's *Bridge of Sighs*.OD.]

UNGRATEFUL MAN. A parson, who at least once a week abuses his best benefactor, i.e. the devil.

UNGUENTUM AUREUM. A bribe.

UNICORN. A coach drawn by three horses.

UNLICKED CUB. A rude uncouth young fellow.

UNRIGGED. Undressed, or stripped. Unrig the drab; strip the wench. [The example is cant.F.]

UNTRUSS. To untruss a point; to let down one's breeches in order to ease one's self. Breeches were formerly tied with points, which till lately were distributed to the boys every Whit Monday by the churchwardens of most of the parishes in London, under the denomination of tags: these tags were worsteds of different colours twisted up to a size somewhat thicker than packthread, and tagged at both ends with tin. Laces were at the same time given to the girls.

UNTWISTED. Undone, ruined, done up.

UNWASHED BAWDRY. Rank bawdry. [Used notably by Ben Jonson in the dedication to *Volpone*.F.]

UP TO THEIR GOSSIP. To be a match for one who attempts to cheat or deceive; to be on a footing, or in the secret. I'll be up with him; I will repay him in kind.

UPHILLS. False dice that run high. [Cant, first in B.E. OD.]

UPPER BENJAMIN. A great coat. *Cant.* [The term displaced *Joseph:* "because of the preponderance of tailors named Benjamin, altered in deference to them." H.]

UPPER STORY or GARRET. Figuratively used to signify the head. His upper story or garrets are unfurnished; i.e. he is an empty or foolish fellow. [In Smollett, who uses the variant *upper works*.F.—The latter, like the obsolete *upper end*, was frequent in C19 dialect.EDD.]

UPPING BLOCK. (Called in some counties a leaping stock, in others a jossing block.) Steps for mounting a horse. He sits like a toad on a jossing block; said of one who sits ungracefully on horseback. [Dialect has the variants *upping chock*, *steps*, *stock*, *stone*.EDD.]

UPPISH. Testy, apt to take offence. [In *The Tatler*, 1710, and condemned by Swift several years later.F.—In dialect, ambitious, audacious.EDD.]

UPRIGHT. Go upright; a word used by shoemakers, taylors, and their servants, when any money is given to make them drink, and signifies, Bring it all out in liquor, though the donor intended less, and expects change, or some of his money, to be returned. Three-penny upright. See THREE-PENNY UPRIGHT.

UPRIGHT MAN. An upright man signifies the chief or principal of a crew. The vilest, stoutest rogue in the pack is generally chosen to this post, and has the sole right to the first night's lodging with the dells, who afterwards are used in common among the whole fraternity. He carries a short truncheon in his hand, which he calls his filchman, and has a larger share than ordinary in whatsoever is gotten in the society. He often travels in company with thirty or forty males and females, abram men, and others, over whom he presides arbitrarily. Sometimes the women and children who are unable to travel, or fatigued, are by turns carried in panniers, by an ass or two, or by some poor jades procured for that purpose. [In Awdelay, 1561.F.—With his privilege of passing the first night with every *dell* ("a young wench, able for generation, and not yet knowen or broken," Harman, 1567), cf. the French *droit du seigneur*, on which an unusual 'angle' is afforded by the poem so entitled in Laurence Hope's *Stars of the Desert*, 1903, and to which several luminously pertinent references are made in Conal O'Riordan's romantic historical comedy, *His Majesty's Pleasure*, 1925.]

UPSTARTS. Persons lately raised to honours and riches from

358

mean stations. [Originating *ca.* 1550, firmly established *ca.* 1600.OD.]

URCHIN. A child, a little fellow; also a hedgehog.

URINAL OF THE PLANETS. Ireland; so called from the frequent rains in that island. [In B.E., who adds: "As Heidelberg and Cologn, in Germany, have the same Name upon the same Account." F.]

USED UP. Killed: a military saying, originating from a message sent by the late General Guise, on the expedition at Carthagena, where he desired the commander in chief to order him some more grenadiers, for those he had were all used up.

V AGARIES. Frolics, wild rambles. [In C18 the word retained much of its original meaning, wandering; cf. Wolcot's "his eyes are oft vagarish." F.]

VAIN-GLORIOUS, or OSTENTATIOUS MAN. One who boasts without reason, or, as the canters say, pisses more than he drinks.

VALENTINE. The first woman seen by a man, or man seen by a woman on St Valentine's day, the 14th of February, when it is said every bird chuses his mate for the ensuing year.

TO VAMP. To pawn any thing. I'll vamp it, and tip you the cole; I'll pawn it, and give you the money. Also to refit, new dress, or rub up old hats, shoes, or other wearing apparel; likewise to put new feet to old boots. [First sense is cant, which in C19 has *vamp*, a robbery.F. As part of a shoe, M.E. *vampey*, from Old Fr. *avant-pie* (modern *pied*). W:ROW.—In 1914-1918 the soldiers used it as to eat. F & G.]

VAMPERS. Stockings. [Cant. B.E., 1690.F.]

VAN. Madam Van; see MADAM.

VAN-NECK. Miss or Mrs Van-neck; a woman with large breasts; a bushel bubby.

VARDY. To give one's vardy; i.e. verdict or opinion.

VARLETS. Now rogues and rascals, formerly yeomen's servants. [Derivative as early as C16.F.—The correct historic sense is that of a gentleman's son in the service of a knight.O.]

359

VAULTING SCHOOL. A bawdy-house; also an academy where vaulting and other manly exercises are taught. [In former sense, frequent in late C16 and in C17.F.]

VELVET. To tip the velvet; to put one's tongue into a woman's mouth. To be upon velvet; to have the best of a bet or match. To the little gentleman in velvet, i.e. the mole that threw up the hill that caused Crop (King William's horse) to stumble; a toast frequently drank by the tories and catholics in Ireland. [In the first example, *velvet*=tongue; probably a cant word.F.]

VENERABLE MONOSYLLABLE. *Pudendum muliebre.*

VERNONIANS. The gentlemen belonging to this honourable society held their meeting at the Rose Tavern, in Cheapside.

VESSEL OF PAPER. Half a quarter of a sheet.

VICAR OF BRAY. See BRAY.

VICE ADMIRAL OF THE NARROW SEAS. A drunken man that pisses under the table into his companions' shoes.

VICTUALLING OFFICE. The stomach. [Boxing slang from 1751 (Smollett). From the Government office concerned with the victualling of the ships of the Royal Navy.OD.]

VINCENT'S LAW. The art of cheating at cards, composed of the following associates: bankers, those who play booty; the gripe, he that betteth; and the person cheated, who is styled the vincent; the gains acquired, termage.

VINEGAR. A name given to the person who with a whip in his hand, and a hat held before his eyes, keeps the ring clear, at boxing-matches and cudgel-playing; also, in cant terms, a cloak.

VIXEN. A termagant; also a she fox, who, when she has cubs, is remarkably fierce. [Figuratively in Shakespeare.W.]

TO VOWEL. A gamester who does not immediately pay his losings, is said to vowel the winner, by repeating the vowels I.O.U. or perhaps from giving his note for the money according to the Irish form, where the acknowledgment of the debt is expressed by the letters I.O.U. which, the sum and name of the debtor being added, is deemed a sufficient security among gentlemen. [Steele, 1709, in *The Tatler*.OD.]

WABLER. Foot wabler; a contemptuous term for a foot soldier, frequently used by those of the cavalry.[I.e. *Wobbler*. In 1914-1918 one heard rarely *gravel-grinder* (cf. the Fr. *pousse-caillou*, pebble-pusher), seldom *worm-crusher*, occasionally *mud-crusher*, frequently *beetle-crusher*, and most frequently *foot-slogger*. B & P; and for a much fuller account, *The Quarterly Review, l.c.*]

WACUT. The brethren of this society held their meetings at the Bell, in Mincing-lane.

TO WADDLE. To go like a duck. To waddle out of Change Alley as a lame duck; a term for one who has not been able to pay his gaming debts, called his differences, on the Stock Exchange, and therefore absents himself from it. [This frequentative of *wade* is good English.]

WAG. An arch frolicsome fellow. [From *wag-halter*, a crack-rope, one fit to be hanged. The word has been ennobled.W: ROW.]

WAGGISH. Arch, gamesome, frolicsome.

WAGGON LAY. Waiting in the street to rob waggons going out or coming into town, both commonly happening in the dark. [Cant.]

WAGTAIL. A lewd woman. [From *ca.* 1590.OD.—In Shakespeare merely an obsequious person.O.—With G's sense, cf. the C17 *wag the tail*, to play the wanton.F.—From the bird's name; *Wagtail* occurs as a surname as early as 1189.W:A.— A late survival of *tail* in venery is the American cant employment of the word to denote sexual intercourse.I.]

WAITS. Musicians of the lower order, who in most towns play under the windows of the chief inhabitants at midnight, a short time before Christmas, for which they collect a christmas-box from house to house. They are said to derive their name of waits, from being always in waiting to celebrate weddings and other joyous events happening within their district. [Originally watchmen, Old Northern Fr. *waitier*, to stand on guard:"the waits of the City of London, which are a great preservation of men's houses in the night," Burton's *Diary*, Dec. 5, 1656.W.— "A band of music belonging to a town," in dialect.P.]

WAKE. A country feast, commonly on the anniversary of the tutelar saint of the village, that is, the saint to whom the parish church is dedicated. Also a custom of watching the dead, called Late Wake, in use both in Ireland and Wales, where the corpse being deposited under a table, with a plate of salt on its breast, the table is covered with liquor of all sorts; and the guests, particularly the younger part of them, amuse themselves with all kinds of pastimes and recreations: the consequence is generally more than replacing the departed friend. ["A.S. *wacu*, *wæcce*, watching (in *nightwacu*), survives as *wake* in dialectal sense of jollification and with special Irish sense." W.—For some very interesting customs, see EDD, which quotes the Yorkshire and Lancashire phrase, *make (a) wakes of anything*, to finish or demolish it, to make a disturbance.]

WALKING CORNET. An ensign of foot.

WALKING POULTERER. One who steals fowls, and hawks them from door to door.

WALKING STATIONER. A hawker of pamphlets, &c.

WALKING THE PLANK. A mode of destroying devoted persons or officers in a mutiny on ship-board, by blindfolding them, and obliging them to walk on a plank laid over the ship's side; by this means, as the mutineers suppose, avoiding the penalty of murder. [Also a piratical practice.]

WALKING UP AGAINST THE WALL. To run up a score, which in alehouses is commonly recorded with chalk on the walls of the bar.

WALL. To walk or crawl up the wall: to be scored up at a public house. Wall-eyed; having an eye with little or no sight, all white like a plaistered wall.

WALLOWISH. Maukish, ill-tasted. [In dialect, insipid, tasteless. EDD.]

TO WAP. To copulate. If she won't wap for a winne, let her trine for a make; if she won't lie with a man for a penny, let her hang for a halfpenny. Mort wap-a-pace; a woman of experience, or very expert at the sport. [This sense of *wap* (in normal English signifying to throw quickly or violently, but obsolete except in dialect) is not in OD.—It is listed in *The Scoundrel's*

Dictionary, 1754, as a gipsy word. *Wappened*, deflowered, wanton, occurs in Shakespeare. By *ca.* 1610 *wapping mort* and *dell* are the cant words for a whore. G's words and phrases, taken from B.E.,are all cant.F.—We may here note that of the words listed by F for a wanton, the following writers are responsible for these respective numbers of operative origins: Langland 2, Chaucer 6, Dunbar 3, Skelton 2, Shakespeare 24, Florio 4, Dekker 7, Marston 3, Jonson 2, Fletcher 4, Durfey 2, Smollett 2. The terms vary from the brutalities of the early writers to such euphemisms as *anonyma* and *incognita*; such Classical reminiscences (often corrupted) as *Aspasia, Cyprian, Laïs, Messalina, Phryne, Thaïs,* and *Vestal*; other literary allusions like *Columbine, Dalilah, Dulcibel, Dulcinea, Magdalen, Maid Marian*; the abusive *bitch, carrion, filth, pole-cat*; inadequacies like *abandoned woman* and *woman;* conventionalisms such as *houri, lady of easy virtue, woman of the town;* ironies like *prim* and *pure;* picturesqueries such as *bed-thrall* (W. Morris), *dart* (Skelton), *dragon* (Fletcher), *light o' love* (Nashe), *night-shade* (Fletcher), *placket* (Shakespeare), *ramp* (Chaucer), *short heels* (Chapman); and the simple dignity of *whore* and *harlot*.]

WAPPER-EYED. Sore-eyed. [Also, in dialect, restless-eyed. EDD.]

WARE. A woman's ware; her commodity.

WARM. Rich, in good circumstances. To warm, or give a man a warming; to beat him. See CHAFED. [The former since *ca.* 1560 and good English for two hundred years; degeneration set in *ca.* 1770; now and long definitely colloquial.(OD).]

WARMING-PAN. A large old-fashioned watch. A Scotch warming-pan; a female bedfellow.

WARREN. One that is security for goods taken up on credit by extravagant young gentlemen. Cunny warren; a girl's boarding-school, also a bawdy-house.

WASH. Paint for the face, or cosmetic water. Hog wash; thick and bad beer. [Dialectally, *wash*=weak beer.EDD.]

WASP. An infected prostitute, who like a wasp carries a sting in her tail.

WASPISH. Peevish, spiteful.

WASTE. House of waste; a tavern or alehouse where idle people waste both their time and money.

WATER. His chops watered at it; he longed earnestly for it. To watch his waters; to keep a strict watch on any one's actions. In hot water; in trouble, engaged in disputes.

WATER BEWITCHED. Very weak punch or beer. [In Ray's proverbs. In C19 very diluted tea. F.—In nautical language, "over-diluted liquor. Nowadays it is generally applied to tea." B.]

WATERPAD. One that robs ships in the river Thames.

WATER SCRIGER. A doctor who prescribes from inspecting the water of his patients. See PISS PROPHET. [In good English though now obsolete, *water-caster*, which, originating *ca*. 1600, came to connote a quack.OD.]

WATERY-HEADED. Apt to shed tears.

WATTLES. Ears. *Cant*. [From the wattles of cock or turkey. *Wattle* means literally a little bag. W.—In C19 *wattle*, ear, was elevated to the rank of slang.EDD.]

WEAR A—E. A one-horse chaise.

WEASEL-FACED. Thin, meagre-faced. Weasel-gutted; thin-bodied: a weasel is a thin long slender animal, with a sharp face. [Shakespeare has *weasel*=mean, greedy or sneaking.F.—Cf. dialectal *weasel body*, a Paul Pry.EDD.]

WEDDING. The emptying of a necessary house, particularly in London. You have been at an Irish wedding, where black eyes are given instead of favours; saying to one who has a black eye.

WEDGE. Silver plate, because melted by the receivers of stolen goods into wedges. *Cant*.

WEEPING CROSS. To come home by weeping-cross; to repent.

WELCH COMB. The thumb and four fingers. [Dialect has the further pejoratives, *Welsh*=a foreign language, *Welshman's hug*=the itch.EDD.—The *rabbit* is not from *rare bit*: cf. *Bombay duck*, fish.W.]

WELCH FIDDLE. The itch. See SCOTCH FIDDLE.

WELCH MILE. Like a Welch mile, long and narrow. His story is like a Welch mile, long and tedious.

WELCH RABBIT. (i.e. a Welch rare bit.) Bread and cheese toasted. See RABBIT.—The Welch are said to be so remarkably fond of cheese, that in cases of difficulty their midwives apply a piece of toasted cheese to the *janua vitæ*, to attract and entice the young Taffy, who on smelling it makes most vigorous efforts to come forth.

WESTMINSTER WEDDING. A match between a whore and a rogue.

WET PARSON. One who moistens his clay freely, in order to make it stick together.

WET QUAKER. One of that sect who has no objection to the spirit derived from wine.

WHACK. A share of a booty obtained by fraud. A paddy whack; a stout brawny Irishman. [Later, *whack* became neutral, as in Thackeray, 1840, and cf. dialectal *whack*, to divide, to share.F,EDD.]

WHAPPER. A large man or woman. [Later especially a great lie.]

WHEEDLE. A sharper. To cut a wheedle; to decoy by fawning or insinuation. *Cant.* [The verb also was cant; of German origin.W.]

WHEELBAND IN THE NICK. Regular drinking over the left thumb. [Almost certainly cant.(F).]

WHELP. An impudent whelp; a saucy boy. [Cf. modern *insolent puppy*.]

WHEREAS. To follow a whereas; to become a bankrupt, to figure among princes and potentates: the notice given in the Gazette that a commission of bankruptcy is issued out against any trader, always beginning with the word whereas. He will soon march in the rear of a whereas.

WHET. A morning's draught, commonly white wine, supposed to whet or sharpen the appetite. [The late C19-20 slang *wet*, a drink of liquor, may have been suggested by this, for although in A.S. and M.E. *wet* bore this sense, there is a gap from *ca.* 1200 to 1894, and even the specific *heavy wet*, malt liquor, is recorded first for 1821.(OD).]

WHETSTONE'S PARK. A lane between Holborn and Lincoln's-inn Fields,formerly famed for being the resort of women of the town. [B.E., *ca.* 1690: "famed for a nest of wenches, now de-park'd." Cf. *Whetstone-Park deer* or *mutton*, a whore.F.—The apostrophe *s* was generally omitted.—This group of houses had been erected by a vestryman of St Giles's, and the district was notorious at least as early as 1668. Alluded to by such writers as Pepys and Butler and prominent in many occasional poems and pamphlets. Beresford Chancellor, *Pleasure Haunts*.]

WHIDS. Words. *Cant*. [The cant *Whid*, a word, is found usually in the plural; Harman, 1567, has "to cut bene whydds," to speak pleasantly, and *cut whids*, to speak, was revived by Scott in 1821 and Charles Reade forty years later. In Scottish, a *whid* is, of course, not cant and there it means a fib, lie, an exaggerated story: thus Burns and Crockett. In East Anglian dialect, as Halliwell observes in 1847, it signifies a dispute, a quarrel. Scottish has also *whid* (less offensive and less condemnatory than *lie*): to equivocate, deceive, exaggerate, fib, lie. Probably from A.S. *cwide*, a statement, saying, proverb.OD, EDD.]

TO WHIDDLE. To tell or discover. He whiddles: he peaches. He whiddles the whole scrap; he discovers all he knows. The cull whiddled because they would not tip him a snack; the fellow peached because they would not give him a share. They whiddle beef, and we must brush; they cry out thieves, and we must make off. *Cant*. [Probably from the preceding: the first mention, *ca.* 1661, can hardly be cant, but all OD post-1690 examples are undoubtedly cant. In C19 slang it meant, either to enter into a parley or to hesitate verbosely.H.]

WHIDDLER. An informer, or one that betrays the secrets of the gang. [C17 cant.F.]

WHIFFLES. A relaxation of the scrotum.

WHIFFLERS. Ancient name for fifers; also persons at the universities who examine candidates for degrees. A whiffling cur; a small yelping cur. ["Men who make way for the corporation of Norwich, by flourishing their swords."G.—Also triflers and fickle persons.F.]

WHIGLAND. Scotland. [Originally, *ca.* 1667, *whig* meant a Covenanter, a Scottish rebel. In current sense, it dates, like *Tory*, from the Revolution of 1689.W.]

WHIMPER, or WHINDLE. A low cry. [Like *whine*, both as noun and as verb, have always been good English. Occasionally G fails to distinguish between good English of a familiar cast and colloquialism. *Whindle* passed from good English *ca.* 1720, and from colloquialism it has drifted to dialect.(OD).]

TO WHINE. To complain.

WHINYARD. A sword. [A short-sword, a hanger. From C15. *Ca.* 1660 it became jocular. Literarily revived by Scott and Robert Buchanan.OD.]

TO WHIP THE COCK. A piece of sport practised at wakes, horse-races, and fairs in Leicestershire: a cock being tied or fastened into a hat or basket, half a dozen carters blindfolded, and armed with their cart whips, are placed round it, who, after being turned thrice about, begin to whip the cock, which if any one strikes so as to make it cry out, it becomes his property; the joke is, that instead of whipping the cock they flog each other heartily.

WHIP JACKS. The tenth order of the canting crew, rogues, who having learned a few sea terms, beg with counterfeit passes, pretending to be sailors shipwrecked on the neighbouring coast, and on their way to the port from whence they sailed. [Also called *turnpike-sailors*.H.]

TO WHIP OFF. To run away, to drink off greedily, to snatch. He whipped away from home, went to the ale-house, where he whipped off a full tankard, and coming back whipped off a fellow's hat from his head.

WHIP-BELLY VENGEANCE, or pinch-gut vengeance, of which he that gets the most has the worst share. Weak or sour beer. [Or, in dialect, simple *whip-belly*; cf. the Lancashire *whistle-belly vengeance*.EDD.]

WHIPPER-SNAPPER. A diminutive fellow. [Usually contemptuous and of a boy.]

367

WHIPSHIRE. Yorkshire.

WHIPSTER. A sharp or subtle fellow. [Dialectally, either a tomboy or a doubtful character of either sex.EDD.—In Shakespeare, a contemptible fellow.O.]

WHIPT SYLLABUB. A flimsy, frothy discourse or treatise, without solidity.

WHIRLYGIGS. Testicles. [Originally and properly: a teetotum.EDD.]

WHISK. A little inconsiderable impertinent fellow.

WHISKER. A great lie.

WHISKER SPLITTER. A man of intrigue.

WHISKIN. A shallow brown drinking bowl. [A Northern word obsolete by 1900.EDD.]

WHISKY. A malt spirit much drank in Ireland; also a one-horse chaise. See TIM WHISKY. [*Whisky* represents the first two syllables of *usquebaugh*, Gaelic *uisge-beatha*, water of life; cf. Fr. *eau de vie*, brandy. Before 1700 *usquebaugh* was the usual form and in 1634 Howell praises the quality of Irish whisky and the hardy prowess of Irish whisky-drinkers.W:ROW.]

WHISTLE. The throat. To wet one's whistle; to drink. [The phrase has been current since Chaucer's day.OD.]

WHISTLING SHOP. Rooms in the King's Bench prison where drams are privately sold.

WHIT. (i.e. Whittington's.) Newgate. *Cant.*—Five rum-padders are rubbed in the darkmans out of the whit, and are piked into the deuseaville; five highwaymen broke out of Newgate in the night, and are gone into the country.

WHITE FEATHER. He has a white feather; he is a coward: an allusion to a game cock, where having a white feather is a proof he is not of the true game breed.

WHITE-LIVERED. Cowardly, malicious. [From the old superstition that cowards have bloodless livers.F.]

WHITE LIE. A harmless lie, one not told with a malicious intent, a lie told to reconcile people at variance.

WHITE SERJEANT. A man fetched from the tavern or alehouse by his wife, is said to be arrested by the white serjeant.

WHITE SWELLING. A woman big with child is said to have

a white swelling. [Medically, in G's day, the watery tumour of a joint.OD.]

WHITE TAPE. Geneva. [Like the next, probably cant.]

WHITE WOOL. Geneva: [i.e., gin.]

WHITECHAPEL. Whitechapel portion; two smocks, and what nature gave. Whitechapel breed; fat, ragged, and saucy: see ST GILES'S BREED. Whitechapel beau; one who dresses with a needle and thread, and undresses with a knife. To play at whist Whitechapel fashion; i.e. aces and kings first. [The first term became less brutal: *ca.* 1860, *Whitechapel fortune* =a clean gown and a pair of pattens.H.]

WHITECHAPEL PROVINCE. A club or brotherhood under the government of a praetor.

WHITEWASHED. One who has taken the benefit of an act of insolvency, to defraud his creditors, is said to have been whitewashed.

WHITFIELITE. A follower of George Whitfield, a Methodist. [The omission of the *d* is presumably intentional, to represent colloquial slipshoddery. The usual form was *Whit(e)fieldian*, the surname being spelt both ways.OD.]

WHITHER-GO-YE. A wife; wives being sometimes apt to question their husbands whither they are going.

WHITTINGTON'S COLLEGE. Newgate: built or repaired by the famous Lord Mayor of that name.

WHORE'S BIRD. A debauched fellow, the largest of all birds. He sings more like a whore's bird than a canary bird, said of one who has a strong manly voice. [Also a bastard.F.]

WHORE'S CURSE. A piece of gold coin, value five shillings and threepence, frequently given to women of the town by such as professed always to give gold, and who before the introduction of those pieces always gave half a guinea.

WHORE'S KITLING, or WHORE'S SON. A bastard.

WHORE-MONGER. A man that keeps more than one mistress. A country gentleman who kept a female friend, being reproved by the parson of the parish, and styled a whore-monger, asked the parson whether he had a cheese in his house; and being answered in the affirmative, 'Pray,' says he, 'does 'that one cheese make you a cheese-monger?' [In Tyndale, 1526, and a well-known word at least as early as C13: it occurs as a surname in the *Close Rolls* for 1296-1302.W:A.]

WHORE-PIPE. The penis.

WHOW-BALL. A milk-maid: from their frequent use of the word *whow*, to make the cow stand still in milking. Ball is the supposed name of the cow.

WIBBLE. Bad drink.

WIBLING'S WITCH. The four of clubs: from one James Wibling, who in the reign of King James I. grew rich by private gaming, and was commonly observed to have that card, and never to lose a game but when he had it not.

WICKET. A casement; also a little door.

WIDOW'S WEEDS. Mourning clothes of a peculiar fashion, denoting her state. A grass widow; a discarded mistress. A widow bewitched; a woman whose husband is abroad, and said, but not certainly known, to be dead. [The first from *ca.* 1715; the second from C16, the modern sense dating only from *ca.* 1850.OD,W.]

WIFE IN WATER COLOURS. A mistress, or concubine: water colours being, like their engagements, easily effaced, or dissolved. [Also a morganatic wife.F.]

WIGANNOWNS. A man wearing a large wig.

WIGSBY. Mr Wigsby; a man wearing a wig.

WILD ROGUES. Rogues trained up to stealing from their cradles. [Probably cant.]

WILD SQUIRT. A looseness. [Usually *w. squirts* and of cattle.EDD.]

WILD-GOOSE CHASE. A tedious uncertain pursuit, like the following a flock of wild geese, who are remarkably shy. [Originally (*ca.* 1590) a race that involved impetuous riding through all kinds of vegetation; a follow-my-leader race or riding, like the flight of geese.W:A.]

WILLING TIT. A free horse, or a coming girl. [Cf. Scottish *willin'-sweert*, half-willing, coy.EDD.]

WILLOW. Poor, and of no reputation. To wear the willow;

to be abandoned by a lover or mistress. [Latter in Shakespeare. F.]

WIN. A penny. [Cant. From C16. Perhaps from *Winchester*. OD.]

TO WIN. To steal. The cull has won a couple of rum glimsticks; the fellow has stolen a pair of fine candlesticks. [Cant. In B.E.—A favourite Army word in 1914-1918.]

WIND. To raise the wind; to procure money.

WINDFALL. A legacy, or any accidental accession of property. [In dialect as adjective, e.g. *windfall apples*, and as noun =a bastard.EDD.]

WINDMILLS IN THE HEAD. Foolish projects.

WINDOW PEEPER. A collector of the window tax. [Obsolete dialectal variants: *w. keeper* and *w. looker*.EDD.]

WINDWARD PASSAGE. One who uses or navigates the windward passage; a sodomite.

WINDY. Foolish. A windy fellow; a simple fellow. [In post-1914 soldiers' slang, afraid. B & P.]

WINK. To tip one the wink; to give a signal by winking the eye.

WINNINGS. Plunder, goods, or money acquired by theft. [Cant.]

WINTER CRICKET. A taylor..

WINTER'S DAY. He is like a winter's day, short and dirty. [Cf. dialectal *Winter Friday*, a cold, wretched-looking person. EDD.]

WIPE. A blow, or reproach. I'll give you a wipe on the chops. That story gave him a fine wipe. Also a handkerchief. [Probably cant. *Ca.* 1790 it superseded *wiper* as handkerchief.OD.]

WIPER. A handkerchief. *Cant.* [In C19 dialect, a severe blow, a stinging taunt or rejoinder.EDD.]

WIPER DRAWER. A pickpocket, one who steals handkerchiefs. He drew a broad, narrow, cam, or specked wiper; he picked a pocket of a broad, narrow, cambrick, or coloured handkerchief. [Both term and example are cant.]

TO WIREDRAW. To lengthen out or extend any book, letter, or discourse. [Contrast dialectal *wiredrawn*, restricted, impeded, and *wire-drawer*, a covetous or stingy person.EDD.]

WISE. As wise as Waltham's calf, that ran nine miles to suck a bull.

WISE MEN OF GOTHAM. Gotham is a village in Nottinghamshire; its magistrates are said to have attempted to hedge in a cuckow: a bush, called the cuckow's bush, is still shewn in support of the tradition. A thousand other ridiculous stories are told of the men of Gotham.

WISEACRE. A foolish conceited fellow. [From Ger. *Weissager*, Old High Ger. *wizago*, a prophet. As Blount in his *Glossographia*, 1674 edition, has it, a *wiseacre* is "one that knows or tells truth; we commonly use it *in malam partem* of a fool." W:ROW, and esp. W:MWAM.—Dialectal variant: *wisemore*. Note that in obsolete dialect *wise man* is a wizard, a dealer in astrology or magic, a fortune-teller, the female counterpart being *wise wife*, later *wise woman*.EDD.]

WISEACRE'S HALL. Gresham college.

WIT. He has as much wit as three folks, two fools and a madman.

WITCHER. Silver. Witcher bubber; a silver bowl. Witcher tilter; a silver-hilted sword. Witcher cully; a silversmith. [Word and examples are all cant.]

TO WOBBLE. To boil. Pot wobbler; one who boils a pot.

WOLF IN THE BREAST. An extraordinary mode of imposition, sometimes practised in the country by strolling women, who have the knack of counterfeiting extreme pain, pretending to have a small animal called a wolf in their breasts, which is continually gnawing them.

WOLF IN THE STOMACH. A monstrous or canine appetite.

WOMAN OF THE TOWN, or WOMAN OF PLEASURE. A prostitute.

WOMAN AND HER HUSBAND. A married couple, where the woman is bigger than her husband.

WOMAN'S CONSCIENCE. Never satisfied.

WOMAN OF ALL WORK. Sometimes applied to a female servant, who refuses none of her master's commands.

WOMBLETY CROPT. The indisposition of a drunkard after a debauch. See CROPSICK.

WOOD. In a wood; bewildered, in a maze, in a peck of troubles, puzzled, or at a loss what course to take in any business. To look over the wood; to ascend the pulpit, to preach: I shall look over the wood at St James's on Sunday next. To look through the wood; to stand in the pillory.

WOODCOCK. A taylor with a long bill. [Also in C16-17 a simpleton. F.]

WOOD PECKER. A bystander, who bets whilst another plays.

WOODEN HABEAS. A coffin. A man who dies in prison is said to go out with a wooden habeas. He went out with a wooden habeas, i.e. his coffin. [Thus also dialectal *wooden breeks, w. cloak, w. dress, w. jump, w. sark, w. shute, w. singlet.* EDD.]

WOODEN HORSE. To ride the wooden horse, was a military punishment formerly in use. This horse consisted of two or more planks, about eight feet long, fixed together so as to form a sharp ridge or angle, which answered to the body of the horse. It was supported by four posts, about six feet long, for legs. A head, neck, and tail, rudely cut in wood, were added, which completed the appearance of a horse. On this sharp ridge delinquents were mounted, with their hands tied behind them; and to steady them (as it was said), and lest the horse should kick them off, one or more firelocks were tied to each leg. In this situation they were sometimes condemned to sit an hour or two; but at length it having been found to injure the soldiers materially, and sometimes to rupture them, it was left off about the time of the accession of King George I. A wooden horse was standing in the parade at Portsmouth as late as the year 1750.

WOODEN RUFF. The pillory. See NORWAY NECK-CLOTH.

WOODEN SURTOUT. A coffin.

WOOLBIRD. A sheep. *Cant.* [Of the same order of wit as the modern slang *cow-juice, sky-juice,* milk, rain.]

WOOL GATHERING. Your wits are gone a wool gathering,

saying to an absent man, one in a reverie, or absorbed in thought. [Cf. dialectal *wool-gather*, to collect the tufts of wool left by sheep on hedges, bushes, etc., a task that the thrifty farmer entrusted to the unskilled and the weak; *to go wool-gathering*, figurative, is in Florio.EDD,W.]

WOOLLEY CROWN. A soft-headed fellow.

WORD GRUBBERS. Verbal critics, and also persons who use hard words in common discourse. [Cf. C19 *verb-grinder*, a pedantic critic or teacher.F.]

WORD PECKER. A punster, one who plays upon words.

WORD OF MOUTH. To drink by word of mouth; i.e. out of the bowl or bottle instead of a glass.

WORLD. All the world and his wife; every body, a great company. [With this phrase of Swift, cf. Fr. *tout le monde et son père*.W.]

WORM. To worm out; to obtain the knowledge of a secret by craft, also to undermine or supplant. He is gone to the diet of worms; he is dead and buried, or gone to Rot-his-bone. [The former in Addison, 1715.OD.]

WRAP RASCAL. A red cloak, called also a roquelaire. [Earlier a loose overcoat.OD.]

WRAPT UP IN WARM FLANNEL. Drunk with spirituous liquors. He was wrapt up in the tail of his mother's smock; saying of any one remarkable for his success with the ladies. To be wrapt up in any one; to have a good opinion of him, or to be under his influence.

WRINKLE. A wrinkle-bellied whore; one who has had a number of bastards: child bearing leaves wrinkles in a woman's belly. To take the wrinkles out of any one's belly; to fill it out by a hearty meal. You have one wrinkle more in your a-se; i.e. you have one piece of knowledge more than you had, every fresh piece of knowledge being supposed by the vulgar naturalists to add a wrinkle to that part. [Concerning the third example, we note that *wrinkle*, trick or wile, dates from *ca.* 1400; as a clever trick, from *ca.* 1730; as a 'tip,' from *ca.* 1818.OD.]

WRY MOUTH AND A PISSEN PAIR OF BREECHES. Hanging.

WRY NECK DAY. Hanging day.
WYN. See WIN.

XANTIPPE. The name of Socrates' wife; now used to signify a shrew or scolding wife. [So in Shakespeare, the first
mention.O.]

YAFFLING. Eating. *Cant.* [Old; cited by Halliwell.F.—
The C19 dialectal *yaffle*, to eat, especially to eat and/or to
drink both greedily and noisily, may be a derivative from the
cant verb, the earliest dialectal record being *ca.* 1820. F gives
the cant, EDD the dialect, but, in the absence of comment by
W or OD, I merely offer a conjecture.]
TO YAM. To eat or stuff heartily. [In C19 nautical slang,
food. F.—*Ca.* 1860, "used by the lowest class all over the world."
H.—A native West African word.W.]
YANKEY, or YANKEY DOODLE. A booby, or country
lout: a name given to the New England men in North America.
[Afterwards to U.S. Americans in general.—Perhaps from
Dutch *Jan Kees*, supposed to have been a nickname for early
Dutch colonists in U.S.A., but more probably from the Dutch
diminutive *Janke*, i.e. Johnny.W:ROW.—As a new Eng-
lander, 1765; as a Northern-State American, 1796; as anyone
born in U.S.A., 1798.OD.]
YARMOUTH CAPON. A red herring: Yarmouth is a fam-
ous place for curing herrings. [From *ca.* 1660.OD.]
YARMOUTH COACH. A kind of low two-wheeled cart
drawn by one horse, not much unlike an Irish car. [Jocular.
A MS. record of 1732 states: ".... something of the nature of
a sledge." OD.]
YARMOUTH PYE. A pye made of herrings highly spiced,
which the city of Norwich is by charter bound to present annually to the king. [From *ca.* 1700.OD.]
YARUM. Milk. *Cant.* [Also *yarrum, yaram* (Harman, 1567).OD.
—One of the *pan(n)a)(um* group of cant words.]

YEA AND NAY MAN. A quaker, a simple fellow, one who can only answer yes or no. [Contrast dialectal *yea-nay*, wavering, irresolute, and compare *by fair yea and nay*, by a solemn affirmation.EDD.]

YELLOW. To look yellow; to be jealous. I happened to call on Mr Green, who was out: on coming home, and finding me with his wife, he began to look confounded blue, and was, I thought, a little yellow. [From *ca.* 1580 *yellow* was symbolic of jealousy: as in Shakespeare, Dekker, Burton, Massinger, Butler.F.]

YELLOW BELLY. A native of the Fens of Lincolnshire: an allusion to the eels caught there.

YELLOW BOYS. Guineas. [Dryden has the term; in Shirley and Middleton as *yellow-hammers*.F.—In C19 slang, any gold coin.EDD.]

YELLOW CAT. The golden lion, a noted brothel in the Strand, so named by the ladies who frequented it.

TO YELP. To cry out. Yelper; a town cryer, also one apt to make great complaints on trifling occasions. [From A.S. *gielpan*, to boast, and cognate with *yell*. Echoic.W.]

YEST. A contraction of yesterday. [Or of *yester*. Scottish and North-Country dialect preserved *yester* (nor is it quite obsolete) long after it became archaic or at best 'literary' in good English: *yester-e'en*, often contracted to *yestreen; yester morn; that's nae yester tale*, that's a very old story.EDD.]

YOKED. Married. A yoke; the quantum of labour performed at one spell by husbandmen, the day's work being divided in summer into three yokes. *Kentish term.* [The former, earliest in Shakespeare.OD.]

YORKSHIRE TYKE. A Yorkshire clown. To come Yorkshire over any one: to cheat him. [With the former, cf. *tyke*, q.v. Of the phrase, the more modern form is *to come* or *put Yorkshire on*, to which the antidote is *to be Yorkshire too;* note also *go Yorkshire*, each to pay his share.EDD.]

TO YOWL. To cry aloud, or howl. [Cf. the Yorkshire *yowler*, a malcontent, and the obsolete Edinburgh *yowlie*, a policeman. EDD.]

ZAD. Crooked like the letter Z. He is a mere zad, or perhaps zed; a description of a very crooked or deformed person. [*Go zedding* (Hampshire), to zig-zag.EDD.—For another old sense, cf. Shakespeare's "Thou whoreson zed, thou unnecessary letter."F.]

ZANY. The jester, jack pudding, or merry Andrew, to a mountebank. [Originally a professional clown's buffoon (as in Shakespeare) or a charlatan's buffoon, a conjuror's assistant, but from *ca.* 1700 a jester and from *ca.* 1800 a fool. From *Zanni*, diminutive of the Italian *Giovanni*, John. Blount in 1674 mentions "a famous Italian Zani, or mimick, who acted here in England, 1673."W:ROW.—In dialect, with variant *zinny*, the word means a fool, a simpleton, a sawney.EDD.]

ZEDLAND. Great part of the west country, where the letter Z is substituted for S ; as zee for see, zun for sun, &c. &c. This prevails through the counties of Devonshire, Dorsetshire, and Somersetshire.

ZNEES. Frost or frozen. Zneesy weather; frosty weather. [Like the next, this entry has the true ring of dialect, perhaps for *sneeze, sneezy*.]

ZNUZ. The same as znees.

ZOC, or SOC. A blow. I gid him a zoc; I gave him a blow. *West Country*. [Normally *sock*: "I gave him a sock on the jaw" is a C19 and current colloquialism. In C18-19, *give one sock*, and from *ca.* 1890 *give one socks*, means to give a thorough beating or thrashing. Likewise, *to sock* has, from *ca.* 1700, meant the same —a little less severely. Both noun and verb were originally cant.OD.]

ZOUCH, or SLOUCH. A slovenly ungenteel man, one who has a stoop in his gait. A slouched hat; a hat with its brims let down, or uncocked. [The former is a West Country form. *Slouch* originally, as in Barclay in 1515 (and as still in U.S.A.), signified a lout.W.—*Slouch hat* not till 1837.OD.]

ZOUNDS. An exclamation, an abbreviation of *God's wounds*.

ZUCKE. A withered stump of a tree. [Usually *Zuche*. In W:S we find this pertinent passage:—"*Chuck*. A tree-stump, Old Fr.

chouq, apparently related to *souche*, a stump (Henry de Chokes, *Close Rolls*, 1205-1337, Roger de la Zuche *or* de la Suche *or* de la Chuche, *ib*). Hence [the surnames] *Choak, Chugg, Chucks*. Also a nickname (Robert Choc, *Pipe Rolls*, 1158-1192, William Choc, *Hundred Rolls*, 1273). Cf. *Block*."]

FRANCIS GROSE

SKETCH FOR A PORTRAIT

> A merrier man
> Within the limits of becoming mirth,
> I never spent an hour's talk withall;
> His eyes beget occasion for his wit;
> And every hazard that the one doth catch
> The other turns to a mirth moving jest.

I

CAPTAIN Francis Grose, F.S.A., born at Greenford, Middlesex, either late in 1730 or early in 1731, was the eldest son of Francis Grosse or Grose, d. 1769, and his wife Ann, daughter of Thomas Bennett of Kingston, Oxfordshire.

The elder Grose, whose pedigree is in the College of Arms, was a native of Berne in Switzerland. He came to England early in the 18th Century and, a well-to-do jeweller resident at Richmond, Surrey (of which county he was made a J.P.), he fitted up the coronation crown of George II according to the Rev. Mark Noble and *The Gentleman's Magazine;* of George III according to *The Dictionary of National Biography.* His fine collection of prints and shells was sold in 1770, and the auction catalogue of his prints, books of prints, and drawings is preserved in the library of the British Museum.

Francis Grose the younger received a classical education, but he did not proceed to a university. He studied art in Shipley's drawing school and in 1766 he was elected a member of the Incorporated Society of Artists. From June 12, 1755, to 1763 he was Richmond Herald. In 1757 he became a member of the Society of Antiquaries. From 1763 to the end of 1769 he acted as Adjutant and Paymaster in the Hampshire Militia. His only account books, he said, were his hip-pockets: into that on the right hand he put what he received; from the left-hand pocket he disbursed. Despite the largeness of his pockets, he did not find this a very satisfactory method, for the unscrupulous imposed on him. One may presume that, soon after succeeding to the fortune bequeathed to him by his father in December 1769, Grose left the Hampshire Militia, and it is known that he did not take long to spend that fortune; in 1778 he became Captain and Adjutant of the Surrey Militia, a post that he retained until his death. In 1778, probably at the summer camp, he was at Cocksheath near Maidstone, and it was at about this date that he was court-martialled: precisely why, we do not know, but almost certainly for some boyish prank. In April 1778, however, he had been at Kingston, Surrey, "tied by the leg at this place with the Surrey Regiment of

Militia," as, on the 18th of that month, he wrote to William Hutchinson, the solicitor-antiquary. That his post was no sinecure appears in his letter of February 10, 1779, written also from Kingston, Surrey: "I am, and indeed have been for near a year, tied fast by the leg, to the drudgery of the Drill, endeavouring to teach a parcel of awkward and vicious boobies their right hands from their left, without being able to steal one hour for the pencil." Six weeks later, and again to Hutchinson, he mentions that his regiment consists of 800 men, "all raised in the purlieus of London," and that "my military business is not over agreeable, though it is what I have been accustomed to from fifteen years of age." In October 1780 he was with his men at Rochester. From 1781 or 1782, if one may judge by his 'output,' his duties became much less onerous.

In 1773 he had issued the first part of his *Antiquities of England and Wales*, completed in 1787: part of the letterpress was furnished by others, while most of the drawings were his own work. In 1784 he sold an important part of his library, which was bought by that very discriminating bookseller Thomas Payne; Payne, by the way, provides the material for one of Austin Dobson's *Eighteenth Century Vignettes*. The following year saw him launch *A Classical Dictionary of the Vulgar Tongue*, and in 1785-1789 he published two works on military antiquities, in which he was an expert.

After touring Scotland, where he was entertained by Robert Riddell the antiquary and where he met Burns, he issued *The Antiquities of Scotland* in 1789-1791. Late in the former year he lost his friend and favourite companion, William Rawle the antiquary and one of the King's accoutrement-makers. In 1790 he 'reconnoitred' Ireland and decided to write its Antiquities. In the spring of the next year he went to that country, but on May 12 he died from an apoplectic fit that seized him as he dined in Dublin with Horace Hone, the miniature-painter and the son of Grose's old friend Nathaniel Hone the portrait-painter. He was buried at Drumcondra Church (Drumcondra Castle), near Dublin. The *St James's Evening Chronicle* proposed this epitaph:

Here lies Francis Grose.
On Thursday, May 12, 1791,
Death put an end to his
VIEWS AND PROSPECTS.

Grose had married Catherine, the beautiful daughter of Mr. Jordan of Canterbury, where he resided for some years, probably during his Hampshire Militia days. By her he had five daughters and two sons. Both his sons became soldiers, the one dying in India, the other rising to the Deputy-Governorship of New South Wales, where, primarily, he was Major Commandant of the New South Wales Corps. Grose himself was the gayest of an interesting and capable family. Of his four brothers, one wrote a very tolerable book on ethics; another, *A Voyage to the East Indies* (1757), which was successful as well as much esteemed; the third was knighted for his services to the Law, while the fourth did well for himself in Threadneedle Street, London.

II

Grose not only met but made great friends with Robert Burns. Soon after he reached Scotland he "found his way," says Allan Cunningham, "to Friars-Carse, where some of the ablest antiquaries of Scotland occasionally met: and at the 'board of Glenriddell' he saw Burns for the first time. It is a tradition in the vale [of Glenriddell] that the Englishman heard with wonder the sarcastic sallies, epigrammatic remarks, and eloquent bursts of the Scot." Burns too was impressed—and amused. Grose, not with unalloyed pleasure, found himself preceded all over Scotland by Burns' *On Captain Grose's Peregrinations through Scotland*. The first two stanzas and the last two are the most significant in this delightful poem:

Hear, Land o' Cakes, and brither Scots,
Frae Maidenkirk to Johnny Groat's;
If there's a hole in a' your coats,
      I rede ye tent it:
A chiel's among ye, takin notes,
      And, faith, he'll prent it.

383

If in your bounds ye chance to light
Upon a fine, fat, fodgel wight,
O' stature short, but genius bright,
           That's he, mark weel;
And wow! he has an unco slight
              O'cauk and keel.

But wad ye see him in his glee,
For meikle glee and fun has he,
Then set him down, and twa or three
           Guid fellows wi' him;
And port, O port! shine thou a wee,
           And then ye'll see him!

Now, by the powers o' verse and prose!
Thou art a dainty chiel, O Grose!
Whae'er o' thee shall ill suppose,
           They sair misca' thee;
I'd take the rascal by the nose,
           Wad say, Shame fa' thee!

Burns asked Grose to call on Dugald Stewart, "a man after your own heart" with a "sterling independence of mind." Writing later to Cardonnel, a well-known antiquary, Burns penned a further poem, with the result that in Edinburgh many condolingly inquired after the Captain:
        Is he slain by Highlan' bodies,
        And eaten like a wether-haggis?
two verses from *Ken Ye ought o' Captain Grose*, composed to a famous Scottish air. In a festive moment, the poet dashed off this epigram:
        The Devil got notice that Grose was a-dying,
        So whip! at the summons, old Satan came flying:
        But when he approach'd where poor Francis lay moaning,
        And saw each bed-post with its burden a-groaning,
        Astonish'd, confounded, cry'd Satan: "By God,
        I'll want 'im, cre I take such a damnable load!"

So far, friendly banter and jovial ridicule. But it was for Grose that Burns wrote his masterpiece, *Tam o' Shanter*, for he was delighted with the Captain's "extensive powers of story-telling and grog-imbibing" (Hotten).

III

Grose, indeed, was nothing if not sociable. John Camden Hotten described him as "the greatest antiquary, joker, and porter-drinker of his day," and Pierce Egan relates that he "was extremely fond of taking his porter of an evening at the King's Arms, in Holborn, nearly opposite Newton Street, a house distinguished for the company of wits, men of talent, and the most respectable tradesmen in the neighbourhood of Bloomsbury Square.... Here the Captain was the hero of the tale." He was also one of those who frequented the Feathers Tavern, on the East side of what is now Leicester Square. In the back-parlour assembled such well-known men as 'Athenian' Stuart; Samuel Scott the marine painter; William ('old') Oram, the Surveyor to the Board of Works; Luke Sullivan the miniature-painter; Thomas Hearne, the artist whose tinted topographical drawings, like those of Grose himself, helped to initiate water-colour; Henderson the actor; John Ireland, literary watch-maker; George Baker the amateur collector of prints and, on one occasion, bibliographer. And Grose met such men as Dr Griffiths, Arthur Murphy, and Quick the comedian at Hooper his bookseller-publisher's in High Holborn, where a room was set apart for literary chit-chat.

Grose often, in fact generally, had a companion. One of his favourites was his man Batch, "who," as Egan tells us, "was a sort of companion and servant united.... Batch and his master used frequently to start at midnight from the King's Arms, in search of adventures. The Back Slums of St Giles's were explored again and again; and the Captain and Batch made themselves as affable and jolly as the rest of the motley crew among the beggars, cadgers, thieves, etc., who at that time infested the 'Holy Land' [St Giles's district]. The 'Scout-Kens' [watch-houses], too, were often visited by them, on the 'look-out' for a bit of fun; and the dirty 'smoke-pipes' in Turnmill

Street did not spoil the Captain's taste in his search after character. Neither were the rough squad at St. Kitts, and 'the sailor-boys cap'ring a-shore' at Saltpetre Bank, forgotten in their nightly strolls....In short, wherever a 'bit of life' could be seen to advantage, or the 'knowledge-box' of the Captain obtain anything like a 'new light' respecting mankind, he felt himself happy, and did not think his time misapplied. It was from these nocturnal sallies, and the slang expressions which continually assailed his ears, that Captain Grose was first induced to compile A Classical Dictionary of the Vulgar Tongue."

In his last years, "the Captain had a funny fellow....Tom Cocking....as an amanuensis, and who was also a draughtsman of considerable merit" (Egan); this Cocking caught the Captain's manner of drawing and a humorous nickname.

IV

There are some pleasant contemporary descriptions and characterisations of Grose, and none that is unfavourable. The Rev. Mark Noble, who knew him well, in 1804 wrote that "Grose, to a stranger, might have been supposed not a surname, but one selected as significant of his figure: which was more of the form of Sancho Pança than Falstaff; he partook greatly of the properties of both. He was as low, squat and rotund as the former, and not less a sloven [as early as 1773 a friend had noted that he was "rather negligent in dress"]; equalled him too in his love of sleep, and nearly so in his proverbs. In his wit he was a Falstaff. He was a butt for other men to shoot at, but it always rebounded with a double force. He could eat with Sancho, and drink with the Knight. In simplicity, probity, and a compassionate heart, he was wholly of the Pança breed; his jocularity could have pleased a prince. His learning, sense, science, and honour, might have secured him the favour, not the rejection, of the all-accomplished conqueror of France." He was also, declared Noble, "an inimitable boon companion."

The love of sleep was remarked on by an amateur artist of

386

the Antiquarian Society, who, under a likeness that he made of Grose, penned these verses:

Now *****, like bright Phoebus, is sunk into rest,
Society droops for the loss of his jest;
Antiquarian debates, unoccasion'd with mirth,
To genius and learning will never give birth.
Then wake, brother member, our friend from his sleep,
Lest Apollo should frown, and Bacchus should weep.

Grose once confided to a correspondent: "I am, and ever have been, the idlest fellow living, even before I had acquired the load of adventitious matter which at present stuffs my doublet," on which Hone of the *Every-Day Book* comments: "In truth, Grose was far from an idle man; he had great mental activity, and his antiquarian knowledge and abilities were great."

Great, too, his bulk. On his first visit to Dublin, he wandered everywhere in his eager curiosity and one evening he strolled into the chief meat-market. The butchers, as usual, cried "What do you buy? What do you buy, Master?" Grose said that he needed nothing. At last one of the vendors started up, eyed the Captain all over, and exclaimed "Well, Sir, though you don't want anything at present, only say you buy your meat of me; and by God you'll make my fortune." And Grose's later companion, Cocking or 'The Guinea Pig,' relates that at night he used to strap his master to the bed so that the bed-clothes did not slide from his rotundity. While the facetious Captain "delighted much in punning upon his own figure," he preferred that others should not do so, although he would probably have enjoyed the D.N.B.'s description, "a sort of antiquarian Falstaff."

About a fortnight after Grose's death, Joseph Walker wrote a brief memoir in *The Dublin Chronicle*. Having praised his pencil and his pen, Walker adds: "Nor was he less admirable for his companionable qualities. Few men shone more in conversation....Naturally cheerful himself, he flashed merriment around him; nor did his sallies of pleasantry or poignant humour ever give pain, for they were not excited either by the mental or physical defects of his auditors. Associating with the ornaments of literature, he abounded in literary anecdote; and having read extensively and observed narrowly, he edified while he exhilarated."

Another aspect of his character was that his carelessness about the future linked up with his eccentricity, easy manners, gaiety and active pleasantries. In the words of the obituary in *The Gentleman's Magazine*, June 1791,—"Living much abroad, and in the best company at home, he had the easiest habits of adapting himself to all tempers; and, being a man of general knowledge, perpetually drew out some conversation that was either useful to himself or agreeable to the party. He could observe upon most things with precision and judgement; but his natural tendency was to humour, in which he excelled, both by the selection of anecdotes and his manner of telling them... His figure rather assisted him....He had neither the pride nor malignity of authorship....His friendships were of the same cast, constant and sincere, overlooking little faults and seeking out greater virtues. He had a good heart, and, abating those little indiscretions common to most men, could do no wrong.. His humour was of that nature which exhilarates and enlivens without leaving behind it a sting; and though, perhaps, none possessed more than himself the faculty of 'setting the table in a roar,' it was never at the expence of virtue or good manners. Of the most careless, open, and artless disposition....A tale of distress never failed to draw commiseration from his heart."

In the same periodical, July 1791, there is a poem entitled *A Sketch of Francis Grose*, written on November 30, 1773, in which the anonymous author, who claims to have known him intimately, speaks of Grose's "dimpled chin, his rosy cheek, his skin from inward lining sleek;" despite his corpulence, Grose, "with light and laughter in his eyes," was notably easy in movement and of a good deportment; "humble—and modest to excess....he's yet too proud to worship State and haunt with courtly bend the Great;" "on comic themes, in grave disputes, his sense the nicest palate suits;" "a social, gen'rous soul" and "with good-nature blest."

V

Of Grose there are seven portraits:—

1. An original miniature portrait by Dr Bruce (and reproduced by W. Hone): aged 25, dressed in military uniform, and sitting in a chair.

2. Of Grose in 1770 as a monk, along with his friends Nathaniel Hone and Theodore Forrest the barrister; drawn and engraved by Hone himself. Nathaniel Hone, d. 1784, was a foundation member of the Royal Academy; his picture of "the two friends as friars was considered too irreverent, and had to be modified before [it] was allowed to be exhibited, but the mezzotint shows the original state" (Whitten).

3. The full-length by Dance and engraved by Bartolozzi; it appeared in vol. I of the Supplement to the English Antiquities. This is considered to be the best.

4. The one given to the Antiquarian Society with the verses "Now *****, like bright Phoebus..." Attributed, says W. Hone, to the Rev James Douglas, who had originally been a soldier and whose chief work was the *Naenia Britannica*, 1786. "An excellent"portrait, says Hone again; but Grose disliked this picture of himself asleep in a chair as much as he did the verses.

5. As "The English Antiquary" in Ray's caricature portraits.

6. The supposed likeness in *The Lounger's Miscellany;* not originally meant for Grose, but not far 'out.'

7. Another, very imperfect.

VI

Grose, it is said, will always be remembered as an artist. In 1768, at the Incorporated Society of Artists, he hung a stained drawing, 'High Life below Stairs.' In the next and following years he exhibited, at the Royal Academy, tinted drawings chiefly of architectural remains. The British Museum possesses some of the originals of the numerous illustrations that he did for his own works. In Redgrave's *Dictionary of Artists of the English School*, Grose is mentioned thus: "He had a good taste, drew well, and the figure very creditably."

From the already cited poem of 1773 we learn that

389

He's judg'd, as artist, to inherit
No small degree of Hogarth's spirit;
Whether he draws, from London air,
The Cit, swift driving in his chair,
O'erturn'd with precious surloin's load,
And frighted Madam in the road,
While to their darling ville they haste,
So fine in asiatic taste;
Or bastard sworn to simple Loon,
Or sects that dance to Satan's tune.

In 1788 (second edition, 1791) Grose published his *Rules for drawing Caricaturas, with an Essay on Comic Painting*. The Rules, short and efficient, are illustrated with four plates; these "mathematical diagrams," as he calls them, are extremely clever and very simple. The Essay, which is little more than a Note, is desultory, but sane and good-humoured.

Always generous and open-handed, he gave away many of his drawings; "nor was his portefeuille ever closed to those engaged in any literary undertaking which his elegant pencil could illustrate" (Walker).

VII

The following list of Grose's publications does not pretend to be bibliographer-proof, but it is believed to be essentially adequate:—

The Antiquities of England and Wales, 6 vols., 1773-1787; 4 vols. to England and Wales, and a Supplement in 2 vols. on Jersey and Guernsey. New edition, 8 vols., 1783-1797.

Antiquarian Repertory, 1775, etc. Reprinted in 4 vols., 1807-09.

Advice to the Officers of the British Army. A Satire. 1782. Six or seven later editions, which include one in U.S.A. in 1867, this being a facsimile reprint of 'the sixth London edition.'

A Guide to Health, 1783. Another edition, 1796.

A Classical Dictionary of the Vulgar Tongue, 1785. See separate note.

A Treatise on Ancient Armour and Weapons, 2 vols., 1786-89, that of 1789 being a supplement.

The History of Dover Castle, 1786. (Editing.)

Military Antiquities of the English Army, 2vols., 1786-88. A revised and enlarged edition, 1801. New augmented edition, 1812.
A Provincial Glossary, 1787; 2nd edition, revised and augmented, 1790; 'a new edition, corrected,' 1811. Samuel Pegge's posthumous supplement, 1814.
Rules for Drawing Caricaturas, with an Essay on Comic Painting, 1778; 2nd edition, 1791. Reprinted in W. West's *Fifty Years' Recollections of an old Bookseller*, 1837. A French translation, 1802.
The Antiquities of Scotland, 2 vols., 1789-1791; another edition, 1797.
The Grumbler. (Essays.) 1791.
The Antiquities of Ireland, 2vols., 1791-95. Edited by E. Ledwich.
The Olio....Essays, Dialogues, Letters, 1792; another impression, 1793. A 'second' edition, 1796.

Essays on Gothic Architecture, by Thomas Warton, the Rev J. Bentham, Captain Grose, and the Rev J. Milner, 1800: 2nd edition, enlarged, 1802; 3rd edition, 1808.
Two articles in *Archaeologia*.
"Parodies of Milton and Homer, often attributed to Grose, were probably by Thomas Bridges." D.N.B.

A Dictionary of the Vulgar Tongue.
First edition, 1785; 2nd, 1788; 3rd, 1796. The first contains about 3,000 entries, the third nearly 4,000. There is little difference between the second and third editions, the third being slightly fuller.
The *Lexicon Balatronicum*, 1811, is virtually the same as the third edition, despite the claims of the title-page:—"*Lexicon Balatronicum*. A Dictionary of Buckish Slang, University Wit, and Pickpocket Eloquence. Compiled originally by Captain Grose. And now considerably altered and enlarged, with the modern changes and improvements, by a Member of the Whip Club." This is printed for C. Chappel, the earlier editions for Hooper.
Pierce Egan's edition, 1823, which he has the effrontery to

describe as the third, is actually the fifth. It is true that Egan increases the number of entries by roughly one-sixth, but his additions are typically Regency slang and he inserted a good deal of self-advertisement. I have not used Egan, for I wished to reprint *Grose*, and the third edition, 1796, may fairly be taken as Grose's final revision: there is very little doubt that between the second edition (1788) and his death (1791) he gathered a few additional notes to amplify certain of the entries in the second edition. Egan talks loudly of his refining of Grose, but while he omits two words that Grose had spelt with the initial and terminal letter and intermediate asterisks and had treated sensibly, he retains several others that, had his aim been to refine, he should have excluded. Egan erects a pretty façade of pretence, but the edifice is the same. Perhaps Egan, writing only thirty-one years after Grose's death, felt that a moral excuse was necessary or, at the least, advisable. The present editor, writing one hundred and forty years after Grose's death, need only point to the historical value of this dictionary.

VIII

Ignored by Professor Elton in his *Survey of English Literature, 1730-1880*, and by Garnett and Gosse in their *English Literature: An Illustrated Record*, Grose is described as "excellent draughtsman and accomplished scholar" by Sir John Edwin Sandys in *The Cambridge History of English Literature*.

While Grose occasionally furnished notes to the editors of Shakespeare, he was in turn assisted by others in his three main works on topographical antiquities, "but never without the most grateful acknowledgments" (Noble). Thomas Pennant, for instance, helped him in the *Antiquities of England* by giving him several drawings made by Moses Griffith; Pennant, by the way, accompanied Grose to the Isle of Man in 1774. These three works on antiquities were very heavily illustrated and are now rather valuable; even in 1773 the Captain had a very considerable reputation as an antiquarian; *Ireland*, however, was mainly due to the labours of Dr Ledwich. To Samuel Hooper (the publisher of *The Antiquities of England and Wales*), to whom he was a good and constant friend despite his opinion that

Hooper "never did any one thing I desired him," Grose gave all the drawings: after his death, Hooper, out of the profits from this work, presented to his widow "a bank note for 800*l*." (West.)

In his kindly way, Grose allowed the *Advice to Officers* to pass as the work of a needy young captain named Williamson. That very different publication, *Ancient Armour and Weapons*, formed, as it were, the prelude to his *Military Antiquities* and was not superseded until the appearance of Meyrick's *Ancient Armour* in 1824; the *Military Antiquities* was an even better book. The plates in both were etched by John Hamilton, vice-president of the Society of Artists of Great Britain.

The posthumous *Olio* was little more than a hotch-potch of *disjecta membra* that Grose would never have thought of publishing; but it happened that his executor was also his publisher. "Probably only partially by Grose" (D.N.B.).

In the poem of late 1773 we find this summary:

> Restless besides, he loves to roam,
> And when he seems most fix'd at home,
> Grows quickly tir'd, and breaks his tether,
> And scours away in spite of weather;
> Perhaps by sudden start to France,
> Or else to Ireland takes a dance,
> Or schemes for Italy pursues,
> Or seeks in England other Views.
>
> So oft to various parts has been,
> So much of towns and manners seen,
> He yet with Learning keeps alliance,
> Far travel'd in the field of Science;
> Knows more, I can't tell how, than those
> Who pore whole years on verse and prose.
>
> Deep in Antiquity he's read;
> And, tho' at College never bred,
> As much of things appears to know,
> As erst knew Leland, Hearne, or Stowe.

IX

W. Hone, Nichols of the Anecdotes and Illustrations, and
Mark Noble say that the *Dictionary of The Vulgar Tongue* "by no
means added to his reputation." Luckily, Grose had taken the
long, the historical view. He probably realised that many
would speak ill of him, yet he had the courage to persist in
what, with his clarity of vision and antiquarian background,
he could hardly have failed to see was a work of great importance.

Of the two best nineteenth-century authorities on English
slang and cant, colloquialism and vulgarism, John S. Farmer
and John Camden Hotten, the latter has passed judgment on
Grose. To his encomia of the value of the *Dictionary* we may
subscribe, with his moral charges we may agree, with the re-
servation that Hotten tends to give a false impression of the
proportion of offensive words and indelicate phrases to the
total number of entries; that proportion was small. "It was
Grose...who, in...1785, collected the scattered Glossaries of
cant and secret words, and formed one large work, adding to
it all the vulgar words and slang terms used in his own day.
The indelicacy and extreme vulgarity of the work renders
it unfit for ordinary use, still it must be admitted that it
is by far the most important work which has ever appeared
on street or popular language; indeed, from its pages every
succeeding work has....drawn its contents. The great fault
of Grose's book consists in the author not contenting himself
with slang and cant terms, but inserting every 'smutty' and
offensive word that could be discovered. However, Harman
and Grose are, after all, the only authors who have as yet treated the subject in an original manner, or who have written on
it from personal inquiry." My own opinion is that Grose took
any vulgarism that came his way without going out of his way
to take any and every vulgarism. In his excellent bibliography
of slang and cant, Hotten notes that the British Museum copy
of the first edition probably belonged to Grose, "as it contains
numerous manuscript additions which afterwards went to
form the second edition," and he returns to the charge with

severe reprimand and enthusiastic praise:—"I find all the editions equally disgraceful.... Excepting the obscenities, it is really an extraordinary book, and displays great industry, if we cannot speak much of its morality. It is the well from which all the other authors—Duncombe, Caulfield, Clarke, Egan, &c. &c.—drew their vulgar outpourings, without in the least purifying what they had stolen." Hotten might have added that they lacked Grose's scholarship, his industry, his sense of humour, his wit, his penetrating insight into human nature and human motives, and the rare gift of investing with lively interest well nigh everything that he touched: qualities pre-eminently present in the *Dictionary of the Vulgar Tongue*.

The value of the *Dictionary* is further attested by the frequency with which it is mentioned by Hotten (in the course of his *Slang Dictionary*), by Farmer and Henley, by Weekley, and by the editors of *The Oxford Dictionary*.

x

The sources used in this brief sketch are few: but perhaps they are adequate.

A. Life and Character:—

The Gentleman's Magazine, 1791, I, 492-4, 581; II, 660.

The Literary Life of Thomas Pennant, by Himself, 1793, at pp. 17, 22.

A History of the College of Arms, by the Rev. Mark Noble, 1804.

Portraits and Lives of Remarkable and Eccentric Characters, 2 vols., 1811, at II, 163-5. A very rare book.

J. B. Nichols: *Literary Anecdotes*, 9 vols., 1812-15, at II, 656-9.

J. B. Nichols: *Literary Illustrations*, 6 vols., 1817-31; supplement in 1848 and 1858. At I, 447 ff. (four letters to Hutchinson, 1778-80) and VIII, 277-8 (two letters of 1790 to Dr Percy).

Pierce Egan's edition of Grose's *Dictionary*, 1823. Also for criticism.

J. T. Smith: *Nollekens and his Times*, 1828, in Whitten's admirable edition, 1920.

John Taylor: *Records of my Life*, 2 vols., 1832, at I, 318.

William West: *Fifty Years' Recollections*, enlarged edition, 1837.

William Hone: *Every-Day Book*, 3 vols., 1838, at I, 655-8.

S. Redgrave: *Dictionary of Artists of the English School*, 1874; in enlarged edition, 1878.

H. Austin Dobson: *Eighteenth Century Vignettes*, 2nd series, 1894. Cursory.

Dictionary of National Biography. Also for criticism.

Notes and Queries, I, ix, 350; III, i, 64 and xi, 280-1; V, xii, 148.

Everyman, Jan. 15, 1931, article by the present editor of Grose.

B. Literary Criticism:—

J. T. Smith: *A Book for a Rainy Day*, 1845, as revived by Whitten in 1905—another admirable edition.

John Camden Hotten: *The Slang Dictionary*, 1859.

T. Seccombe: *The Age of Johnson*, 1899.

The Cambridge History of Literature, XII, 275, 349, 510; XIV, 224, 540.

Everyman, Jan. 22, 1931, article on the *Dictionary* by the present writer.